The Politics of
Global Governance

The Politics of Global Governance

International Organizations in an Interdependent World

edited by
Paul F. Diehl

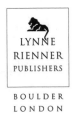

LYNNE
RIENNER
PUBLISHERS

BOULDER
LONDON

Published in the United States of America in 1997 by
Lynne Rienner Publishers, Inc.
1800 30th Street, Boulder, Colorado 80301

and in the United Kingdom by
Lynne Rienner Publishers, Inc.
3 Henrietta Street, Covent Garden, London WC2E 8LU

Library of Congress Cataloging-in-Publication Data
The Politics of global governance : international organizations in an
    interdependent world / edited by Paul F. Diehl.
    Includes bibliographical references and index.
    ISBN 1-55587-654-4 (hc : alk. paper)
    ISBN 1-55587-638-2 (pbk. : alk. paper)
    1. International organization. 2. International agencies. 3. Non-
governmental organizations. I. Diehl, Paul F. (Paul Francis)
JX1954.P582   1996
341.2—dc20   96-9719
                                                                  CIP

British Cataloguing in Publication Data
A Cataloguing in Publication record for this book
is available from the British Library.

Printed and bound in the United States of America

The paper used in this publication meets the requirements
⊗ of the American National Standard for Permanence of
Paper for Printed Library Materials Z39.48-1984.

5 4

Contents

Part 1

INTRODUCTION

THERE are two predominant views of international organizations among the general public. The first is a cynical view that emphasizes the dramatic rhetoric and seeming inability to deal with vital problems that are said to characterize international organizations and the United Nations in particular. According to this view, international organizations should be treated as insignificant actors on the international stage. The other view is an idealistic one. Those who hold this view envisage global solutions to the major problems facing the world today, without recognition of the constraints imposed by state sovereignty. Most of the naive calls for world government are products of this view. An understanding of international organizations and global governance probably requires that neither view be accepted in its entirety, nor be wholly rejected. International organizations are neither irrelevant nor omnipotent in global politics. They play important roles in international relations, but their influence varies according to the issue area and situation confronted.

This book is designed to provide a balanced and realistic view of international organizations. Toward this end, the selections in this collection dispel a number of myths. Narrow views about how international organizations make decisions or respond to conflict are called into question. An understanding of international organizations requires knowledge of how, where, and why they operate. Only then can we learn to recognize their limitations as well as their possibilities. We begin the study of international organizations by briefly tracing the origins of the present United Nations system.

The League of Nations was formed following World War I, and it represented an attempt at international cooperative efforts to prevent war. The breakdown of the League system in the 1930s was the product of many factors, although the failure of will by the major powers of the era and the unwieldy requirements for concerted action certainly were the primary causes. As with most experiments, the initial results were far from ideal,

1

but the total effort gives some basis for optimism. In the case of the League of Nations, it was not able to prevent World War II, but it did provide a means for cooperation and consultation among states on a variety of issues not confined to security matters, although this was the major purpose for which it was created.

It is, therefore, perhaps not surprising that world leaders sought to form another general international organization at the conclusion of World War II. The occurrence of war has generally had a stimulating effect on the development of international organizations in the modern era.[1] What may be surprising to some is the similarity between the League of Nations and its successor, the United Nations.[2] The Security Council and the General Assembly of the United Nations had comparable antecedents under the League system. Furthermore, the United Nations was also predicated on the assumption that continued cooperation among the victorious coalition in the previous war would insure global stability. One might think that given the League experience, the United Nations would suffer similar setbacks. Although the United Nations and its affiliated agencies have not achieved most of the goals set out in its charter, neither have they been insignificant in dealing with many of the most pressing problems in the world. This can be attributed to the radically differing environments faced by the League and the United Nations.

After 1945, the international system was structured in a bipolar fashion, with each superpower retaining an interest in maintaining its status. Consequently, there was little pressure from the rapid systemic upheaval that characterized the periods prior to the world wars. This does not imply that conflict has abated; rather, such conflict has been more limited and less threatening to the international system or the existence of the United Nations. Second, there seemed to be a greater recognition of a need for cooperation among states. The ideas behind the United Nations are not new ones, but the prospects of global devastation from nuclear war or environmental disaster were sufficient to prompt a greater commitment to international organizations. It has become clear that various problems, such as pollution, hunger, and nuclear proliferation, are not amenable to action by only one or several states.

Finally, the United Nations acquired a symbolic importance that the League of Nations lacked. States feel obligated to justify their actions before the main bodies of the United Nations, even when they may appear contrary to the charter principles. As the United States did during the Cuban missile crisis, states may use the United Nations as a means to legitimize their actions or policy positions.[3] Most important, however, states are exceedingly hesitant to withdraw from membership in the United Nations, even when that organization's actions appear contrary to their national interests. Such reluctance prevents the debilitating loss of significant actors that plagued the League during most of its existence.

The end of the Cold War (now conventionally designated as 1989) signaled a new era for the United Nations and international organizations in general. On the one hand, the end of the superpower rivalry removed many of the barriers that had heretofore prevented the United Nations from taking action, especially in the security realm. The United Nations supported global military action against Iraq in the Persian Gulf War, the first such global collective enforcement effort since the Korean War. The United Nations also authorized more peacekeeping operations in the five years that followed the end of the Cold War than in the forty-five years that preceded it; many of these new operations took on functions such as humanitarian assistance, nation-building, and election supervision that previously were not within the province of U.N. peacekeeping. On another front, the European Union took further notable steps toward complete economic integration, and other nascent regional economic blocs, such as the Asian-Pacific Economic Cooperation (APEC) entity and that formed under the North American Free Trade Agreement (NAFTA), began to take shape.

The prospects for expanding the roles, functions, and powers of international organizations in global governance seemed bright at the beginning of the 1990s. Yet a series of events underscored the problems and limitations of international organizations as they approached the twenty-first century. The enhanced ability of the UN Security Council to authorize new peacekeeping missions did not necessarily translate into greater effectiveness in halting armed conflict or promoting conflict resolution. The United Nations was largely ineffective in stopping the fighting in Bosnia, could not produce a political settlement in Somalia, and was too slow to prevent genocide in Rwanda. Despite its successes, the European Union stumbled badly in its peace efforts toward Bosnia, and attempts to create a common currency as well as other integration efforts promise significant domestic and foreign political controversy. Other organizations, such as the North Atlantic Treaty Organization (NATO), now struggle with the new environment and the redefinition of their roles as their original purposes have been significantly altered or rendered obsolete. As we approach the twenty-first century, international organizations play a greater role than they ever have in history. Yet we are still reminded that state sovereignty and lack of political will by members inhibit the long-term prospects of those organizations for creating effective structures of global governance.

The United Nations and its affiliates are the most significant international organizations, but they are hardly the only ones. In this century the number of international organizations has grown substantially. Although definitions and estimates may vary, the total number of all types of international organizations may exceed ten or twenty thousand. The list includes a wide range of memberships and purposes, and they vary in significance from the Inter-American Tropical Tuna Commission to the World Bank.

One method of classifying international organizations is according to their membership potential and scope of purpose.[4] International organizations can either be designed for universal membership, potentially including all states in the world, or the membership may be limited, as are many regional organizations. We may also classify international organizations according to the breadth of their concerns. Specific purpose organizations may be confined to one problem, such as the South East Asia Treaty Organization (SEATO) Medical Research Laboratory, or one issue area, such as the Food and Agriculture Organization (FAO), whereas general purpose organizations are concerned with a variety of problems in several issue areas. Most international organizations are nongovernmental entities in the limited membership, specific purpose category.

The only universal, general purpose organization (and its affiliated agencies)—the United Nations—receives a disproportionate amount of attention in this volume. The United Nations and its agencies remain the centerpiece among international organizations in the security realm and play prominent roles in most other issue areas. Although the United Nations is centrally important, any treatment of international organizations and global governance would be incomplete without a consideration of the thousands of other international organizations throughout the world. Over the past decade, two other types of international organizations have played increasingly important roles in global governance: nongovernmental organizations (NGOs), such as the International Red Cross, and regional organizations, such as the European Union. Accordingly, included here are articles that demonstrate how NGOs and regional organizations form webs or networks that intersect, replace, or supplement those IO webs composed primarily of global intergovernmental organizations such as the United Nations.

Part 1 offers an overview of the creation and the termination of international governmental organizations. Richard Cupitt, Rodney Whitlock, and Lynn Williams Whitlock reveal that international organizations have enormous staying power in international relations. Their adaptability has apparently not slowed the creation of new, more specialized organizations, and trends for NGOs show a similar, almost exponential increase.[5]

Part 2 focuses on the various theoretical approaches to the study of international organizations. It is evident that the ways analysts have studied international organizations have changed dramatically over the last fifty or more years. The reader is especially advised to note the description and critique of regime analysis. This approach is currently the most prominent in the field, and accordingly, some of the subsequent articles in this book adopt that framework.

Part 3 details the decisionmaking processes of international organizations. The range of activities and the bureaucratic actors and processes that are often hidden from public view are revealed in these selections. Furthermore, proposals to change the most visible aspect of decisionmaking—voting—are assessed. After the first three parts, the reader will have a broad view of the place of international organizations in the world system and the patterns of their activities. Armed with this understanding, the reader is directed to the actions of international organizations in three major issue areas: peace and security, economic, and social and humanitarian. In Parts 4 through 6, one can appreciate the number of organizations involved, the scope of activities undertaken, and the variation in effectiveness across organizations and issue areas. While the first three parts highlight common patterns in international organizations, the next three parts provide more details and reveal the diversity of these bodies.

Part 4 explores the effectiveness of traditional peacekeeping operations, but also considers the changes that the end of the Cold War has wrought. That series of events has led peacekeeping strategy to evolve into its "second generation" and has also called into question the existence and purposes of NATO, the bedrock of deterrence and security in Europe over the past fifty years; one article addresses each of these concerns. The economic issue area, addressed in Part 5, is one of great importance especially to many underdeveloped countries. An article on the New International Economic Order (NIEO) shows how those Third World countries would like to change the current method of global governance with respect to economic issues. Articles on the World Bank, International Monetary Fund, and Inter-American Bank for Development illustrate how those institutions have played a role in creating the structure of international finance and development, how they have adapted (or not) to changing demands, and how they paradoxically may both enhance and mitigate the dependence of poorer countries on their wealthier counterparts. Part 6, on humanitarian activities, shows the interface of many organizations in a variety of important concerns, including hunger, human rights, the status of women, environmental protection, and humanitarian relief.

Part 7 returns to the more general concerns addressed at the outset of the book: What roles can international organizations play in global governance? We conclude this collection with two differing perspectives, mirroring somewhat the idealist and cynical viewpoints noted above, on the promise and inherent limitations of international organizations in global society.

Notes

1. See J. David Singer and Michael Wallace, "International Government Organizations and the Preservation of Peace, 1816–1964" *International Organization*, 24 (1970): 520–547.

2. For a definitive comparison. see Leland Goodrich, "From League of Nations to United Nations" *International Organization*, 1 (1947): 3–21.

3. Ernst Haas, "Collective Legitimization as a Political Function of the United Nations" *International Organization*, 20 (1966): 367–379.

4. Harold Jacobson, *Networks of Interdependence,* 2nd edition (New York: Random House, 1984), pp. 11–13.

5. John Boli and George Thomas, "Organizing the World Polity: INGOs Since 1875." Paper presented at the annual meeting of the International Studies Association, Chicago, 1995.

1

The (Im)mortality of International Governmental Organizations

Richard Cupitt, Rodney Whitlock & Lynn Williams Whitlock

Introduction

[Over] twenty-five years ago, Wallace and Singer (1970a) made the first systematic effort to describe change in the population of international governmental organizations (IGOs) in the modern state system. They found, after controlling for an increase in the number of countries in the system between 1815 and 1964, "the familiar linear relationship between the passage of time and the amount of intergovernmental organization in the system" (Wallace and Singer, 1970a, p. 282). In a concurrent study, they also found that the number of IGOs increased markedly after the world wars (Wallace and Singer, 1970b). More recently, Jacobson, et al. (1986) revealed that the growth in the number of conventional IGOs continued into the 1980s, though at a progressively slower pace.[1]

International cooperation through multilateral institutions, such as IGOs, is not expected to be either extensive or durable from a realist or neo-realist viewpoint (Carr, 1964; Grieco, 1990; Morgenthau, 1978; Walt, 1987; and Waltz, 1979). Essentially, there is one argument: the constant pursuit of gains relative to other states diminishes their chances for lasting cooperation. Indeed, the mere existence of a large and growing population of IGOs implies an unexpected degree of cooperation in the international system from a neorealist perspective. This helps justify the realist view that IGOs are rarely more than "bit players" in international politics (Dougherty and Pfaltzgraff, 1990, p. 25).

In contrast, neoliberals, both institutionalists and Grotians, claim that international cooperation is widespread (Adler and Haas, 1993; Keohane, 1984; Kratochwil and Ruggie, 1986; Murphy, 1994; Stein, 1990; and Young

Reprinted by permission of Gordon and Breach Publishers from *International Interactions*, Vol. 21, No. 4, 1996, Richard Cupitt, Rodney Whitlock, and Lynn Williams Whitlock, "The (Im)mortality of International Governmental Organizations."

1989). From these perspectives, multilateral institutions, especially IGOs, not only indicate and facilitate cooperation but also influence state behavior by agenda setting, compliance monitoring and other functions (Diehl, 1989; Jacobson, 1984; Murphy, 1994; and Keohane, 1988). Neoliberals also argue that the institutional basis for international cooperation will be very durable.

Studies of the number of IGOs in the international system, however, provide limited evidence about the more important theoretical issue—the *durability* of IGOs. Besides research on the League of Nations, few works examine the demise of IGOs. In one exception, Murphy (1994) concludes that "world organizations" have played crucial roles in economic development and the search for security since the Crimean War and that survival crises among those organizations are related to fundamental changes in world order.[2] Despite the lack of attention, evidence about the durability of IGOs would address a core problem in the study of international relations. Grieco (1988 and 1990), for example, asserts that the durability of institutional cooperation among nations is a central question in the debate between realists and neoliberals. Similarly, Powell (1994, p. 341) argues that whether multilateral institutional cooperation continues "in the face of a change in the underlying distribution of power" is one of the pure and unsettled research issues in the neorealist-neoliberal debate. In an effort to formalize the realist-liberal debate, Niou and Ordeshook (1991) raise the importance of durable international institutions to an even higher role, suggesting that such institutions are critical to international stability both for the realist vision of balance of power and the liberal vision of a collective security system.

In this article, the authors use standard population statistics to assess the durability of conventional IGOs in the international system for the years 1865–1989. Following a brief discussion of IGOs and institutional persistence (with examples from the literature on international relations, the U.S. bureaucracy, and international business), the authors examine the infant mortality, average age at death, median age, crude birth rates, and crude death rates for conventional IGOs. The authors then make a basic assessment of the durability of IGOs in the international system.

The Durability of
International Cooperative Institutions

From a realist perspective, modern IGOs arose as a means for the status quo powers to preserve order and seek peace after the Napoleonic Wars, which so forcefully exposed the failure of both 18th century diplomacy and nationalism as paths to peace (Morgenthau, 1978, p. 392). IGOs reflected the common interests of the great powers, usually defined in terms of balancing military threats. Idealists or utopians were merely "clothing own interest in the guise of a universal interest," so that international morality was really a function of power (Carr, 1964, p. 75).

The League of Nations was the first attempt to standardize universal security concerns, similar to what public international unions had done for the postal services, health services, telecommunications, and other government interests (Carr, 1964, p. 28). Established at a time of political and economic discord, realists argue that the League failed because its creators did not understand that security interests were not often held in common, leaving little room for cooperation. Realists claim to recognize:

> . . . the undeniable fact that . . . what the national government does or does not do is much more important for the satisfaction of individual wants than what an international functional agency does or does not do. . . . The neglect with which the public treats international functional agencies is but the exaggerated reflection of the minor role these agencies play for the solution of important international issues (Morgenthau, 1978, p. 518).

This neglect stems from the realist belief that states are always more sensitive to relative than absolute gains (Grieco, 1990, pp. 46–47). In addition, the degree to which the importance of relative gains exceeds absolute gains increases when states face the prospect of great shifts in the balance of power, such as when a common challenger has been defeated. At those times, even former friends become suspect because of the "danger that relative gains from joint action may advantage partners and may thus foster the emergence of what at best might be a potentially more domineering friend and at worst could be a potentially more powerful future adversary" (Grieco, 1990, p. 45). The neorealist shift in focus to the system level of analysis does not greatly modify this view. Waltz (1979, p. 198), for example, asserts that states weigh relative gains more heavily than absolute gains and that states become more sensitive to relative gains when they confront a substantial change in the existing world order. Consequently, "institutions are unable to mitigate anarchy's constraining effects on inter-state cooperation," so IGOs become rudimentary facilitators of power politics (Grieco 1988, p. 485).

Clearly, the fluidity of the balance of power ensures that the fortunes of specific IGOs or other international institutions rise and fall in tune with the ephemeral interests of the powers of the time (Carr, 1964; Gilpin, 1981; Grieco, 1990). Neither realist nor neorealist theory allows much room for predictions about the rise or fall of specific coalitions of great military powers. While realists explain the demise of the League of Nations in terms of its failure to reflect the balance of power, it's hard to predict exactly when the League would cease to function from their analyses. Waltz (1979, p. 124), for example, does not indicate when military coalitions will change in relationship to changes in the distribution of power, other than to assert that such changes will occur periodically.

In part, earlier findings are so challenging because conventional IGOs seem likely to be among the most durable forms of international cooperation.

In fact, though Wallace and Singer (1970a) emphasize their effort was only one of description, Jacobson, et al. (1986) explicitly challenge realist theory. Taking a neoliberal view, they suggest that the "complexity of modern life creates many pressures for states to establish additional IGOs," probably at a very rapid rate (Jacobson, et al. 1986, p. 157). According to Jacobson (1984), where technological and economic progress sparked the growth in the number of IGOs in the 19th century, two global wars and decolonization spawned an explosion of IGOs in the 20th century.

Generally, neoliberal scholars argue that cooperation should be very durable, even if the basic structural variables that lead to cooperation change substantially (Stein, 1990; Young, 1989). Young (1989, pp. 64–65), for example, concludes that even immoral and inefficient international institutions are likely to endure. Neoliberals argue that international institutions do more than merely reflect the distribution of power and serve as an alternative means for states to pursue power politics. From a neoliberal perspective, IGOs help coordinate state behavior, shape judgements about the interests and commitments of others, and influence state preferences (Keohane, 1989, pp. 5 and 161; Niou and Ordeshook, 1991, p. 510). Neoliberals contend that IGOs have some autonomy and as autonomous actors IGOs influence states through the use of oversight, majority rules, weighted voting, monitoring compliance, support for allies, support for specific international services (Murphy, 1994, pp. 219–221). While neorealists and neoliberals both see power in the international system as decentralized, neoliberals deny that anarchy is the key to understanding international relations. Instead, the extent of mutual interests and the degree of institutionalization are the most significant variables.

Neoliberals disagree among themselves, however, on the central role of the state and rationality in the behavior of IGOs (Kratochwil and Ruggie, 1986). Neoliberal rational institutionalists, such as Robert Keohane, Vinod Aggarwal, and Arthur Stein, retain states as the central focus of their work, but they argue that even under conditions of anarchy states will frequently engage in cooperative behavior, facilitated by international institutions that reduce uncertainty (especially about the behavior of others) and reduce transaction costs (Keohane, 1989; Niou and Ordeshook, 1991). To rational institutionalists, IGOs should persist only as long as their constituent states have an incentive to maintain them (Keohane, 1989, p. 167). Most rational institutionalists focus their research on the start or maintenance of cooperation, and only peripherally on the mortality of specific institutions (Keohane, 1989; Murphy, 1994). From a rational institutionalist perspective, however, there are many reasons to expect that IGOs should survive long after fundamental changes in the distribution of international power would lead one to expect from a realist or neorealist view. Among other reasons, Stein (1990, pp. 50–53) suggests that IGOs will prove persistent in the face of changes in the distribution of power and other fundamental determinants of international relations because national governments only review their policies, including support for IGOs, periodically, while officials may wish to build a reputation for preserving tradition (and not breaking commitments). Kratochwil and Ruggie (1986) indicate that institutional cooperation may prove durable if it acquires an orthodoxy among policy-makers and the public. They also claim that states may attempt to preserve the policy transparency associated with complying with IGO rules and procedures, even when other IGO functions and activities become less valuable (Kratochwil and Ruggie, 1986). Most importantly, rational institutionalists contend that states may have positive preferences, both instrumental and empathetic, for gains by other states. In those situations, international institutions can facilitate the spirit of "generalized reciprocity" among states (Keohane, 1989, pp. 231–232). As Keohane (1989, p. 167) admits, however, the predictions of institutionalists "about the demise of specific institutions are less clear" than their predictions about institutional origins and persistence.

Neoliberals in the Grotian tradition, in contrast, forgo the analysis of preferences and pay-off structures so prevalent in the institutionalist approach. Instead, they argue that the rise and fall of international institutions corresponds to critical internal contradictions or the grossest alterations in the fundamental world order, not mere shifts in either the distribution of military or economic power alone (Cox, 1977; Keohane, 1989; Kratochwil and Ruggie, 1986; Murphy, 1994; Young, 1982). To Grotian neoliberals, for example, the values of a "deeply embedded liberalism" in many levels of the international community seems a more robust explanation of international cooperation in the post–World War II era than calculated bargaining by various states (Ruggie, 1982). If IGOs correspond to the deeply embedded values of a world order, then they should survive at least as long as that order. Grotian neoliberals, especially those with a Gramscian view, also see world orders in an evolutionary context, so that an IGO that serves a value critical to succeeding world orders might very well survive in perpetuity. Robert Cox, for example, indicates that the International Labour Organization managed that feat (Cox, 1977). From this perspective, more and more IGOs emerge to construct and reinforce international rules and values in an incremental fashion, even when opposed by the dominant power of the age (Murphy, 1994, pp. 78–79).

When world orders have changed remains unsettled from this viewpoint. Murphy (1994), for example, argues that key transitions in global governance occur with the rise of public international unions in the late 1800s, with the League and UN systems in the mid-1900s, and with a new generation of IGOs in the1970s. Treating the League and UN systems as a single strand of global governance conflicts with the view of Ruggie (1983, p. 208) that embedded liberalism did not emerge until after World War II.

Murphy (1994, p. 82) finds that most of the public international unions formed in the 19th century "faced moments of crisis when they could no longer rely on their early sponsors and benefactors." Eleven of those organizations did not mobilize support among powerful constituencies, including nonstate, substate, and transnational actors, and were abolished before 1920 (Murphy, 1994, p. 83). This accounts for only one third of the world organizations of the time, suggesting that the majority proved very durable even with the pressures of global military conflict. Evidence from other fields, however, gives mixed portents for the likely durability of IGOs.

Historically, military alliances do not appear to be very durable, with defense pacts surviving an average of only ninety-four months for the period 1815–1965 (Bueno de Mesquita and Singer, 1973). A number of post–World War II alliances, however, have proven much more durable, such as the North Atlantic Treaty Organization (NATO). Military alliances, moreover, represent only a tiny fraction of the total forms of international cooperation, and rarely have the institutional basis of typical IGOs.

The evidence on international joint ventures (IJVs) also raises some questions regarding the durability of IGOs. In the private sector, IJVs are a common form of international commercial cooperation. Though no comprehensive study of the population of IJVs exists, research indicates that IJVs fail somewhere between 30 and 50% of the time (Berg and Friedman, 1978; Franko, 1971, pp. 3–4; Killing, 1983; Kogut, 1988; and Morris and Hergert, 1987).

The study of U.S. government agencies, in contrast, offers solace for neoliberals. In a seminal work, Kaufman (1976) discovers, from a population of 175 organizations in the U.S. government in existence in 1923, that only twenty-seven (15.4%) "died" by 1973.[3] While not strictly comparable, many of the arguments Kaufman (1976) uses to explain the persistence of domestic government agencies are applicable to IGOs. National administrative agencies created by statute or with statutory recognition, for example, might endure because of the arduous process involved in changing legislation. As treaty obligations usually require national implementing legislation, this should hold true for IGOs. Other reasons Kaufman (1976) notes for the longevity of U.S. agencies that appear applicable in an international setting include complicated budget processes, personal or career motivations, organizational loyalties, defenders of the agency in the legislative or other branches of government, and interest group support (Jacobson, 1984; or Diehl, 1989). Finally, as Milner (1992), Powell (1994), and others have argued, international cooperation may be akin to a two-level game, one between states and one within each state. This implies that the durability of domestic bureaucracies could have a direct impact on the durability of associated multilateral institutions, following the "second image reversed" argument.

While relatively few U.S. agencies appeared to die between 1923 and 1973, births and deaths appear to take place in spurts. Most importantly, the overall number of agencies increases by 283 over the same time span (Kaufman, 1976).[4] Because the increase in the number of new agencies outweighs the increased age of persistent agencies, the median age of government organizations is twenty-seven years in both 1923 and 1973 (Kaufman, 1976, p. 34). Kaufman (1976, p. 34) concludes that the "government organizations examined do indeed display impressive powers of endurance."

Methods

Wallace and Singer (1970a, pp. 245–246) defined IGOs as having two or more states as members, holding regular plenary sessions, and having some sort of permanent secretariat and headquarters. Using the criteria adopted by the United Nations Economic and Social Council (ECOSOC) to distinguish IGOs from international nongovernmental organizations (INGOs), IGOs must also have been created by a formal agreement between governments. These criteria are roughly similar to those used in more recent studies (Feld, Jordan, and Hurwitz, 1988; Jacobson, et al., 1986; Jacobson, 1984). Two differences between Wallace and Singer (1970a) and other studies should be noted. Wallace and Singer (1970a, p. 246) do not use the more standard membership criteria of three governments for an IGO, but do this largely to prevent some key organizations from being deleted when their membership temporarily fell to two states. Unlike the Jacobson studies (Jacobson, et al., 1986; Jacobson, 1984), they also excluded IGOs that were federations of other IGOs, whose membership is not in any part selected by another IGO, and does not have a distinct secretariat (Wallace and Singer, 1970a, p. 248).

For our study, we use the standard definition of IGOs as organizations created by three or more governments, based on a formal agreement, and having some permanent secretariat or headquarters. This definition fits with data on international organizations (IOs) from the Union of International Associations (UIA), which produces the most definitive dataset on IOs. We rely heavily on the data from the Union of International Associations presented in various issues of the *Yearbook of International Organizations*.[5] The UIA relies first on self-reported characteristics of various bodies, but couples this information with editorial checks for accuracy against periodicals, official documents, and press sources (UIA, 1994/95, volume 1, pp. 1616–1634). The UN ECOSOC and other bodies officially recognize the UIA and its publications as an authoritative source for information on IOs. Wallace and Singer (1970a), Jacobson, et al. (1986), and Jacobson (1984) relied on the UIA *Yearbook* for their information.

We examine IGOs in five categories identified by the UIA. The first four groups, Class A through Class D, are conventional IOs, whose definition has remained standard throughout UIA publications. Class A, federations of international organizations, has dozens of INGOs but only one IGO, the United Nations. Class B, universal membership organizations, includes all IGOs with membership, administration, and policies that have a balanced and widespread geographic quality, such as the International Atomic Energy Agency or the Universal Postal Union. Inter-continental membership organizations, Class C, includes IGOs with membership and activities that are not bound by a particular continent, but not so widespread to be a Class B organization, such as the North Atlantic Treaty Organization and the Asian-Pacific Postal Union. Finally, Class D, regionally defined membership organizations, includes all IGOs with membership and activities confined to a particular continent or sub-continent, such as the African Postal Union. In contrast to Wallace and Singer (1970a), we chose to include federations of international organizations (Class A), because the UIA now distinguishes them from less autonomous bodies emanating from other international organizations (Class E).

Unlike Jacobson, et al. (1986) and Jacobson (1984), we excluded Class E bodies, defined by the UIA as emanating from another international organization, person, or place. Examples of Class E bodies include the UNESCO Scientific Cooperation Bureau for the European and North American Region, the Commonwealth Tertiary Education Commission, and the Intergovernmental Council for Coordination of Cooperation of Non-Aligned Countries in the Field of Information and Communication. The authors chose to exclude these and other Class E bodies because it seems likely that the durability of any one of these organizations would depend directly on the durability of the IGO from which it derives. In contrast, federations of IGOs (Class A bodies) are not dependent on the durability of a single IGO, so would make better subjects for analysis. We also exclude conference series (even if they have governments as members) and treaties because neither have all the other characteristics of IGOs.

The authors also chose to include Class F bodies, organizations having a special form, including foundations and funds. It includes some important IGOs, such as the International Monetary Fund and other financial organizations. The UIA treats this Class as somewhat transitional, but it clearly differs from recently reported or proposed organizations (Class J), untraceable bodies (Class U), or inactive or dissolved bodies (Class H). In addition, the remaining classifications, conference series (Class S), multilateral treaties and agreements (Class T), religious orders, fraternities or secular institutes (Class R), or bodies in one country that have an international orientation (Class G), would not be appropriate.

Though the UIA classifies both IGOs and INGOs by this method, we chose to exclude INGOs from the analysis. As Jacobson (1984, p. 7) notes, generally IGOs are more important because authoritative policies are more often a result of the actions of IGOs rather than INGOs. This is not to say that some INGOs, such as those involved with the Olympic movement, can have a much greater impact on a city or country than some IGOs, but that IGOs tend to have greater authority in international affairs. From a theoretical view, since IGOs limit membership to states unlike INGOs, then the analysis of IGOs should speak more directly to the issues raised by both realists and neoliberals (especially the rational institutionalists). In addition, the operations of INGOs are often more opaque than IGOs, while the size of the INGO population is much greater, so a much greater element of error is likely to be introduced into the study by including INGOs. Finally, despite the many differences between IGOs and INGOs in composition and authority, there appears to be a strong correlation between the population of IGOs and INGOs, so findings on IGOs should provide a basis for subsequent studies on the entire population of IOs (Jacobson, et al., 1986; Jacobson, 1984; and Wallace and Singer, 1970a).

As Wallace and Singer (1970a) detailed, determining the date of establishment for an IGO is quite difficult. In this study, we relied on the date found in the 1994/95 issue of the UIA *Yearbook*. This was supplemented by examining earlier editions and related publications by the UIA.[6] As difficult as it is to establish the year an IGO begins to function, identifying the date of dormancy is even more problematic. There are very few "death certificates" issued when IOs become dormant, and unlike the death certificate a coroner produces, we will offer no evidence on the "cause" of a specific IGO death. Each instance would require a case autopsy (without assurance that there would be much agreement), which is beyond the scope of this study. Establishing benchmark mortality figures, however, may reveal patterns of mortality that may unveil potential causal relationships.

We used the date noted by the UIA whenever possible. In cases where the date of dormancy was unclear, we extracted the last date of communication by the IGO with the UIA by tracing updates in the *Yearbook* series. This information was supplemented first by data on the last reported contact or date an IGO ceased to function ascribed by the UIA for the Class H organizations. The UIA defines Class H organizations as those IOs which are dissolved, currently inactive, or are otherwise dormant. Generally, these dates do not appear in the *Yearbook,* but are available from the electronic dataset maintained by the UIA. Again, this was supplemented by examining previous issues of the UIA *Yearbook* and other sources, including searching the Lexis/Nexis databases. Given the difficulty in getting an accurate assessment of the year of establishment or cessation, the data only reflect years.

The time frame of the analysis covers the years 1865–1989. Often, a focus on more contemporary organizations is made analytically, largely because IGOs do not appear in large numbers until relatively recently. Claude (1964, p. 18), for example, argues that the conditions that necessitated IGOs were not in sufficient combination until the 19th century. This was also why Wallace and Singer (1970a) defined IGOs in terms of cooperation between two rather than three states

We, as did Jacobson, et al. (1986) and Wallace and Singer (1970a), follow a demographic convention of working with multi-year cohorts.

Following these studies, the authors blocked the dates of IGO establishment and dormancy or death into five-year cohorts. The last cohort in the analysis is 1985–1989.

The dearth of IGOs in the 19th century poses a problem for this study. Most conventional demographic analyses assume a large population (Newell, 1988; Saunders, 1988). Statistics are reported, for example, in terms of an amount per 1,000 population, where the population is often in the millions. Though the UIA identifies one IGO forming as early as 1397, it was not until 1856 that there were more than five IGOs in existence simultaneously. Given the relatively small number of IGOs functioning in the first half of the 19th century, we compressed information on the seven IGOs created prior to 1859 into a single cohort representing 1855–1859. We used their actual age at their time of death in the calculations. Even so, the small number of IGOs in the first few cohorts makes the indicators very sensitive to relatively minor changes in the population.

There are multiple demographic measures that address the issue of durability in a population. Using the date of establishment as the date of birth and the date of dormancy or official termination as the date of death, we will first apply infant mortality (defined as a percentage of those born in a given year dying within one year of their birth) and five-year infant mortality (defined as a percentage of those born in a given year dying within five years of their birth) to the population. Clearly, the higher either infant mortality rate (IMR), the easier it is to argue that IGOs are ephemeral creations.

Life expectancy, a common demographic measure, was ill-suited to the analysis.[7] Instead, we examine the average age at the time of death and the median age of the population to assess durability. The lower the average age at time of death or the median age, obviously, the more ephemeral the nature of IGOs. We also know, however, that the vast majority of IGOs are of relatively recent origin (Jacobson, et al., 1986; Wallace and Singer, 1970a). We anticipate this will bias the calculations of median age against durability in the later cohorts.

Calculating the median age of the population also creates some analytical concerns. Birth and death rates of IGOs will have a critical impact on the stability of the calculations of median age. We calculate birth and death rates by the number of each per 1,000 IGOs in the previous cohort, so this measure does not start until 1860. From previous studies, however, we also know that birth rates correlate positively with the number of states in the international system (Jacobson, et al., 1986; Wallace and Singer, 1970a). Upon examination, however, both the raw and standardized (divided by the number of states) IMRs, and the birth rate and death rate appear almost perfectly correlated, so we limited the analysis to the raw rates. Though not direct measures of durability, we expect that the higher the death rate, relative to the birth rate, the more likely IGOs are ephemeral by nature.

Findings

The five classes yielded 1,209 IGOs formed before 1990. Of those 1,209 IGOs, we were able to gather the data we sought for 989 IGOs. Fully 105 of the 1,209 IGOs identified by the UIA had no date of establishment, and 7 IGOs had no date of termination. Finally, we found no data on either establishment or termination for 63 IGOs, making 989 IGOs available for inclusion in the analysis.[8]

The number of IGOs in our study increases rapidly over time, which parallels the findings of previous studies. Only 283 of those 989 IGOs die during the time span of the study. In other words, over 71% of the IGOs were alive in 1989. Of the IGOs formed since 1865, 15 survived for over a century, all surviving through the final year of the study.[9] Though about twice the ratio for deaths among U.S. agencies, it is for a time span more than twice as long. It is also at the low end of the estimates of IJV failure rates. At the same time, it's worth noting that the phenomenal increase in the number of new IGOs is greater than the increase in the number of U.S. agencies and perhaps as great as the dramatic expansion in IJVs (Culpan, 1993; Kaufman, 1976, pp. 48–49).

The infant mortality rates vary substantially, in some cases by more than four standard deviations from the mean, obscuring any long-term trend (see Figure 1.1). For the majority of cohorts, the IMRs are quite low. In 18 of the 27 cohorts, the one-year IMR is 0, for example, while the five-year IMR is 0 in 12 cohorts. In other words, most IGOs survive their earliest years in the international arena, which conforms most with the neoliberal view.

Sharp increases in both IMRs, however, emerge in 1900, 1910, and 1940, years of crisis in the underlying balance of power in Europe and Asia. In addition, there is a gradual increase in the five-year IMR after 1970, when many claim that U.S. hegemony began to decline. This level of variation in the IMRs implies that attempts to create durable IGOs are much more successful at some times than others. These eras are associated with times of fundamental changes in the world order and balance of power, as one expects from realist, neorealist, and neoliberal views.

The average age at the time of death also varies considerably, with five cohorts experiencing no deaths (producing an average of 0 years of age at death), to about 30 years at the time of death for the 1885, 1915, and 1935 cohorts (see Figure 1.2). After World War II, the variation decreases sharply as the population rises, stabilizing between 15–20 years of age at the time of death.

Of the 283 IGOs that die prior to 1990, 197 (70%) die before reaching 20 years of age, which parallels the findings on public international unions and a post-infancy survival crisis.[10] Compared to U.S. domestic agencies, where 18 of 23 were over 30 years old at the time of death, this suggests that

Figure 1.1 Infant Mortality Rates

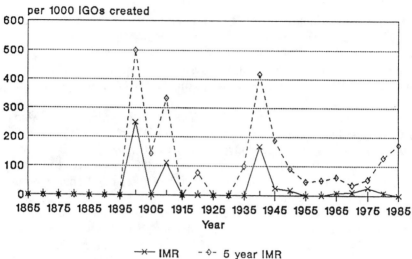

per 1000 IGOs created

Year

—✕— IMR   - ◇- 5 year IMR

a critical passage exists somewhat later than the years covered in the IMRs (Kaufman, 1976, p. 61). Older organizations do appear to die in larger numbers before or in the early years of both world wars, especially in the 1915 and 1935 cohorts, as well as the 1885 cohort, however, as one expects from a realist or neorealist perspective.

The median age of IGOs also varies substantially, from zero in the 1945 cohort to about twenty-two years in the 1915 cohort. Starting with the 1955 cohort, however, the median age is stable at ten years of age until the 1985 cohort (see Figure 1.2). Overall, these numbers indicate that IGOs maintain a relatively young population.

The drop in median age after World War II stems from the sharp increase in the birth rate in 1945, despite the 1945 cohort also having the highest death rate (see Figure 1.3). Relative to the death rate, and relative to all but the birth rate for the initial cohorts (which is high because of the small size of the population), there is a striking increase in the number of new IGOs for the 1945 cohort.

The number of IGOs in the system directly increases because the birth rate exceeds the death rate for all but three cohorts (1910, 1935, and 1985). Certainly, the increase in the number of states can create more opportunities for multilateral cooperation, but this does not explain why birth rates so consistently exceed death rates. This is not an isolated phenomenon as the increase in the number of IGOs closely parallels a swell in the number of U.S. domestic agencies after World War II, and the dramatic expansion in the number of IJVs during this era (Culpan, 1993; Kaufman, 1976, pp. 48–49). Though suffering twice the death rate for U.S. government agencies,

Figure 1.2 Age of IGOs (All IGOs and those dying)

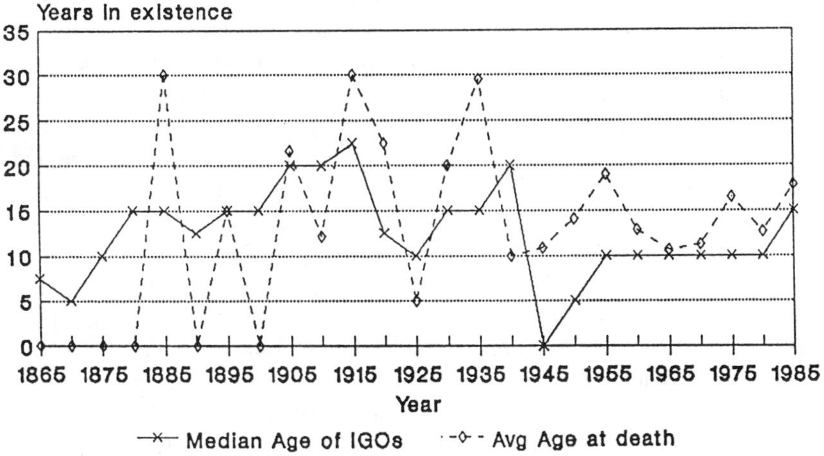

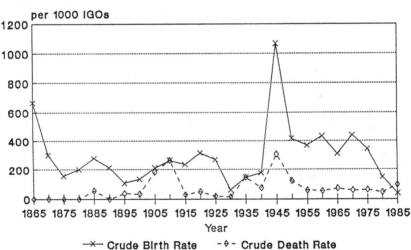

Years in existence

—✕— Median Age of IGOs   ··◇·· Avg Age at death

Figure 1.3 Birth Rate and Death Rate

per 1000 IGOs

—✕— Crude Birth Rate   ·◇· Crude Death Rate

however, IGOs die at a rate substantially lower than the failure rate for IJVs. This certainly conforms more closely with a neoliberal view.

Two of the cohorts where the death rate exceeds the birth rate, 1910 and 1935, mark the years immediately preceding the two world war cohorts. The third convergence precedes the end of the Cold War. This suggests that the convergence of these two variables may be a *leading* indicator of change, either violent or peaceful, in the underlying structure of global conflicts.

Along with the death rate during 1945, this would help explain the finding that IGOs grow in number (and stature) in the aftermath of major power wars (Wallace and Singer, 1970b). As IGOs are more prone to termination before or during eras of global conflict, including World War II, the great increase in the number of new IGOs in the aftermath of World War II (and somewhat less so after World War I) may reflect a pent-up demand or need for institutional forms of international cooperation. Suppressed before and during eras of global war, the demand for IGOs may not be able to be met until new post-conflict political relationships emerged.

Alternatively, declining birth rates and rising IMRs and death rates may well be associated with the level of resources available to states to participate in IGOs. At the end of World War II, states (compared to their societies) may have had surplus of resources to devote to multilateral cooperation, and IGOs may have appeared to be an efficient way to use state resources, which could explain the high birth rate. Since the global recessions of the 1970s, a relative decline in resources available for states to use for IGOs, and dissatisfaction with IGOs that did not quickly prove their worth, may explain the diminishing birth rate for IGOs, as well as the increase in the five-year IMR.

Finally, if mainly older, Cold War institutions are dying now, it may be that instead of starting new institutions, states associated with the former Soviet Union are abandoning their IGOs by transferring allegiance to Western IGOs. Shortly after the years in this study, for example, the Warsaw Treaty Organization (WTO), the Council of Mutual Economic Assistance (CMEA), and its nearly stillborn successor, the Organization for International Economic Cooperation (OIEC), all ceased to function. While new IGOs have emerged to replace Cold War institutions (such as the Partnership for Peace), post-communist states appear to have a preference for joining established Western IGOs, such as the International Monetary Fund. This might imply a greater degree of satisfaction with the prevailing world order and its associated IGOs compared to levels of satisfaction by powerful states that emerged after previous world wars.[11] If so, fewer wholly new IGOs might be desired, even though some IGOs passed away.

Conclusions and Implications

In *Theory of International Politics,* Waltz (1979, p. 137) claims that "the death rate for states is remarkably low." The results of this study indicate that the death rate for IGOs is also remarkably low, at least from a neorealist perspective, as the demise of IGOs only reflects the grossest of viscidities in the distribution of power since 1855. Some IGOs are especially persistent. Of the 34 IGOs functioning in 1914, for example, 18 were still operating in 1989. Surely, many IGOs have survived global wars, decolonization, and the creation, dissolution, or integration of many states.

At the same time, from a neoliberal viewpoint, most of the IGOs that die, do so during times of international political turmoil when the balance of power seems most in flux. While neoliberals allow that changes in the fundamental balance of power should influence the durability of international institutions, it appears that sharp increases in the death rate occur only during those times.

From the variability in the IMRs, average age at death, median age, birth rate, and death rate for IGOs, it appears that the realist, neorealist, and neoliberal arguments have merit. In most eras, most attempts to forge IGOs prove durable. In some periods, however, efforts to build IGOs are short-lived. The lack of a consistent pattern intimates that the debate between neo-realists and neoliberals is misspecified (or at least underspecified), an inference that echoes the arguments of others (Powell, 1994).

The most difficult transition for IGOs appears in their relative adolescence, when the majority of IGOs that ever die do so. This provides the most support for the views of Grotian neoliberals. At the same time, it may follow the liability-of-newness argument found in the organization ecology literature, but with a delayed impact (Stinchcombe, 1965). Once through this dangerous passage, IGOs may survive for decades, comparing favorably with the longevity of domestic agencies and international joint ventures, and long out-living most military alliances.

Notes

1. Though the number of IGOs created by other IGOs substantially increased instead (Jacobson, et al., 1986: 145).

2. Murphy (1994: 82–83) provides some data on eleven world organizations abolished before 1920 and the disposition of their functions.

3. These included agencies of federal executive departments and the Executive Office of the President, excluding defense agencies.

4. Kaufman (1976) did not look at the years between 1923 and 1973, and so did not attempt to determine how many organizations were born after 1923 but died before 1973.

5. We used the 1991 volume most often, but also the volumes for 1992, 1988, 1984 (the *Intergovernmental Organizations Handbook*), 1951, and 1908 (the *Annuaire de la Vie Internationale*) extensively.

6. See endnote 4.

7. Life expectancy calculations assume the birth rate is stable and progressive and that births outnumber the individuals in any age cohort, neither of which can be assumed here (Saunders, 1988; Newell, 1988).

8. Of the original 1,209 IGOs, the distribution by IGO type is 2 (0.2%) in Class A, 45 (3.7%) in Class B, 51 (4.2%) in Class C, 305 (25.2%) in Class D, 659 (54.5%) in Class F, and 147 (12.2%) in Class H. After excluding IGOs with missing data, 2 (0.2%) are in Class A, 45 (4.6%) in Class B, 50 (5.8%) in Class C, 275 (27.8%) in Class D, 490 (49.5%) in Class F, and 127 (12.8%) in Class H. As these two distributions are very nearly identical, excluding the cases with missing data should not greatly bias the results.

9. The West African International Bank, founded in 1863, however, ceased to function in 1990.

10. If one excludes the 116 IGOs functioning in 1989 but yet to reach twenty years of age, the percentage of IGOs that die before reaching twenty only increases slightly (from around 20% to nearly 23%).

11. See Stoll and Champion (1985) for a discussion of the relationship between satisfaction with the structure of the international system and global conflict.

References

Adler, Emanuel and Peter M. Haas (1992) "Conclusion: Epistemic Communities, World Order, and the Creation of a Reflective Research Program." *International Organization*, Vol. 46, pp. 367–390.

Berg, Sanford V. and Phillip Friedman (1978) "Joint Ventures in American Industry." *Mergers and Acquisitions*, Vol. 13, pp. 28–41.

Bueno de Mesquita, Bruce and J. David Singer (1973) "Alliance, Capabilities and War: A Review and Synthesis." *Political Science Annual*, Vol. 4, pp. 237–280.

Carr, Edward H. (1964) *The Twenty Years' Crisis 1919–1939*. New York: Harper & Row.

Claude, Inis L. Jr. (1964) *Swords into Plowshares: The Problems and Progress of International Organization*, 3rd edition. New York: Random House.

Cox, Robert W. (1977) "Labor and Hegemony." *International Organization*, Vol. 31, pp. 385–424.

Culpan, Refik, ed. (1993) *Multilateral Strategic Alliances*. New York: International Business Press.

Diehl, Paul F. (1989) *The Politics of International Organizations: Patterns and Insights*. Chicago: Dorsey Press.

Dougherty, James E. and Robert L. Pfaltzgraff, Jr. (1990) *Contending Theories of International Relations*. New York: Harper & Row.

Feld, Werner J. and Robert S. Jordan with Leon Hurwitz (1988) *International Organizations: A Comparative Approach*. New York: Praeger.

Franko, Lawrence G. (1971) *Joint Venture Survival in Multinational Corporations*. New York: Praeger.

Grieco, John M. (1990) *Cooperation among Nations: Europe, America, and Non-Tariff Barriers to Trade*. Ithaca: Cornell University.

Jacobson, Harold K., William M. Reisinger and Todd Mathers (1986) "National Entanglements in International Governmental Organizations." *American Political Science Review*, Vol. 80, pp. 141–159.

Jacobson, Harold K. (1984) *Networks of Interdependence: International Organizations and the Global Political System*. New York: Alfred A. Knopf.

Kaufman, Herbert (1976) *Are Government Organizations Immortal?* Washington, D.C.: The Brookings Institution.

Keohane, Robert (1989) *International Institutions and State Power: Essays in International Relations Theory*. Boulder: Westview Press.

Keohane, Robert (1988) "International Institutions: Two Approaches." *International Studies Quarterly*, Vol. 32, pp. 379–396.

Keohane, Robert (1984) *After Hegemony: Cooperation and Discord in the World Political Economy*. Princeton: Princeton University.

Killing, J. Peter (1983) *Strategies for Joint Venture Success*. New York: Praeger.

Kogut, Bruce (1988) "Joint Ventures: Theoretical and Empirical Perspectives." *Strategic Management Journal*, Vol. 9, pp. 319–332.

Kratochwil, Friedrich and John Gerard Ruggie (1986) "International Organization: A State of the Art on an Art of the State." *International Organization,* Vol. 40, pp. 753–775.

Newell, Colin (1988) *Methods and Models in Demography.* New York: Guilford.

Morgenthau, Hans J. (1978) *Politics Among Nations.* New York: Alfred A. Knopf.

Morris, Deigan and Michael Hergert (1987) "Trends in International Cooperative Agreements." *Columbia Journal of World Business,* Vol. 22, pp. 15–21.

Murphy, Craig N. (1994) *International Organization and Industrial Change: Global Governance since 1850.* New York: Oxford University Press.

Niou, Emerson M.S. and Peter C. Ordeshook (1991) "Realism versus Neoliberalism: A Formulation." *American Journal of Political Science,* Vol. 35, pp. 481–511.

Powell, Robert (1994) "Anarchy in International Relations Theory: The Neorealist-Neoliberal Debate." *International Organization,* Vol. 48, pp. 313–344.

Ruggie, John Gerard (1983) "International Regimes, Transactions, and Change: Embedded Liberalism in the Postwar Economic Order." In Stephen D. Krasner (ed.), *International Regimes.* Ithaca: Cornell University Press.

Saunders, John (1988) *Basic Demographic Measures: A Practical Guide for Users.* Lanham, Md.: University Press of America.

Stein, Arthur A. (1990) *Why Nations Cooperate: Circumstance and Choice in International Relations.* Ithaca: Cornell University Press.

Stinchcombe, Arthur L. (1965) "Organizations and Social Structures." In James G. March (ed.), *Handbook of Organizations.* Chicago: Rand McNally.

Stoll, Richard J. and Michael Champion (1985) "Capability Concentration, Alliance Bonding, and Conflict Among the Major Powers." In Alan N. Sabrosky (ed.), *Polarity and War: The Changing Structure of International Conflict.* Boulder: Westview.

Union of International Associations (various editions) *Yearbook of International Organizations.* New Providence: K.G. Sauer.

Wallace, Michael and J. David Singer (1970a) "Intergovernmental Organization in the Global System, 1815–1964: A Quantitative Description." *International Organization,* Vol. 24, pp. 239–287.

Wallace, Michael and J. David Singer (1970b) "Inter-Governmental Organization and the Preservation of Peace, 1816–1965: Some Bivariate Relationships." *International Organization,* Vol. 24, pp. 520–547.

Walt, Stephen M. (1987) *The Origins of Alliances.* Ithaca: Cornell University Press.

Waltz, Kenneth (1979) *Theory of International Politics.* Reading, Mass.: Addison-Wesley.

Young, Oran R. (1989) *International Cooperation: Building Regimes for Natural Resources and the Environment.* Ithaca: Cornell University Press.

Young, Oran R. (1983) "Regime Dynamics: The Rise and Fall of International Regimes." In Stephen D. Krasner (ed.), *International Regimes.* Ithaca: Cornell University Press.

Part 2

THE STUDY OF INTERNATIONAL ORGANIZATIONS

INTERNATIONAL organizations are a relatively new phenomenon, with the League of Nations being the first universal, general purpose example. The study of international organizations is even more recent. It was not until the 1930s that David Mitrany published his classic book on functionalism, *A Working Peace System.* It was not until 1947 that an academic journal, entitled *International Organization,* devoted to the subject, first appeared. Yet, over this brief period, scholars have changed dramatically the way they study international organizations. The articles in Part 2 trace the evolution of those changes and offer evaluations of two of the most influential theoretical approaches: regime analysis and functionalism.

Friedrich Kratochwil and John Gerard Ruggie trace the development of international organizations as a field of study. Not surprisingly, early studies focused on the institutional characteristics of these new international actors; scholars of U.S. and foreign governments were pursuing a similar focus during this time. Gradually, as Kratochwil and Ruggie argue, the focus shifted to the processes and roles of international organizations. In the last two decades, however, regime analysis has become a preeminent method of analysis. What is an international regime and how did regime analysis come about?

An international regime is composed of sets of explicit or implicit principles, norms, rules, and decisionmaking procedures around which actor expectations converge in a given area of international relations and which may also help to coordinate their behavior. There are numerous examples of international regimes. The international trade regime, based largely on the General Agreement on Tariffs and Trade (GATT), and the ocean regime, based on the Law of the Sea Treaty, are two examples. Regimes are not necessarily based on formal agreements; an international energy regime, for example, may emerge from custom rather than treaties between states. International organizations enter the picture to the extent that they can perform a variety of roles in the context of an international regime. They may be instrumental in the creation of a regime, by providing the forum in which the regime is defined or negotiated or as a coordinating body by which regular patterns of behavior are created. International organizations may be the culmination of a process of regime definition. In other cases, international organizations may be the mechanism by which regime procedures are regulated (as in the Non-Proliferation regime) or adapted (as has been attempted in the United Nations Conference on Trade and Development).

International organizations are increasingly involved in global affairs, but not all efforts at international cooperation are taking place within an international organization framework. Therefore, focusing only on international organizations leads analysts to miss many important patterns of interstate interaction within a given issue area. Regime analysis can capture the behavior of states and other actors in that issue area as well as the role of international organizations.

Since the development of the regime framework, the use of regime analysis has expanded to become a common framework for the study of international organizations and international political economy. Yet, the scheme is still a controversial one. Susan Strange provides a spirited critique of regime analysis, focusing on the vagueness of the regime concept and its bias toward the status quo, among other points. The reader should not be too hasty in drawing judgments about regime analysis from this article, however. Many of the criticisms put forth are best understood as reflections of the underdevelopment of this method of analysis. Strange implicitly offers a valid set of challenges to scholars using international regime analysis that they must consider as they further refine this framework. If regime analysis is more than a passing fad, as is now evidently the case, this method of analysis will improve and mature as it permeates the discipline.

The most prominent theoretical approach to our understanding of the creation and growth of international organizations is functionalism. Functionalism posits that the growth of technology and mass political participation in states will create pressures for those states to cooperate in international organizations. Increasing interdependence leads states to cooperate in order to solve common problems and to take advantage of the greater efficiency (similar to economies of scale) from such cooperation. Functionalism envisions that states begin cooperation in technical, relatively noncontroversial (in a political sense) areas; these are often referred to as *low politics* issues. The organizations formed in these contexts are very specialized and generally have limited membership. Later, cooperation in these limited areas may expand and spill over into more controversial issues, such as security or other *high politics* areas.

Harold Jacobson, William Reisinger, and Todd Mathers explore the growth of international organizations and state membership in those

organizations. In particular, they consider whether the patterns they uncover are consistent with the expectations of functionalist theory. They
demonstrate that a state's propensity to join an international organization
is related to its economic and political development, as well as to the number of years it has been a part of the international system. Such findings
are consistent with the functionalist notions that technological growth and
increased political participation, which are coterminus with development,
are associated with growth in the number and scope of membership of international organizations. The extent of the growth that has occurred in
limited membership, international nongovernmental organizations (INGOs)
is also consistent with functionalist expectations. The authors conclude
their essay with some predictions on the future growth of international organizations and a warning that new ways must be discovered to deal with
a world containing a more densely woven web of increasing numbers of
international organizations.

2

International Organization:
The State of the Art

Friedrich Kratochwil & John Gerard Ruggie

International organization as a field of study has had its ups and downs throughout the post–World War II era and throughout this century for that matter. In the interwar period, the fate of the field reflected the fate of the world it studied: a creative burst of work on "international government" after 1919, followed by a period of more cautious reassessment approaching the 1930s, and a gradual decline into irrelevance if not obscurity thereafter. Although they sometimes intersected, the fate of theory and the fate of practice were never all that closely linked after World War II. Indeed, it is possible to argue, with only slight exaggeration, that in recent years they have become inversely related: the academic study of international organization is more interesting, vibrant, and even compelling than ever before, whereas the world of actual international organizations has deteriorated in efficacy and performance. Today, international organization as a field of study is an area where the action is; few would so characterize international organizations as a field of practice.

Our purpose in this article is to try to figure out how and why the doctors can be thriving when the patient is moribund. To anticipate the answer without, we hope, unduly straining the metaphor, the reason is that the leading doctors have become biochemists and have stopped treating and in most cases even seeing patients. In the process, however, new discoveries have been made, new diagnostic techniques have been developed, and our understanding has deepened, raising the possibility of more effective treatment in the long run.

What we are suggesting, to pose the issue more directly, is that students of international organization have shifted their focus systematically

Reprinted from *International Organization,* Vol. 40, No. 4, 1986, Friedrich Kratochwil and John Gerard Ruggie, "International Organization: A State of the Art on an Art of the State," by permission of The MIT Press, Cambridge, Massachusetts. © 1986 by the World Peace Foundation and the Massachusetts Institute of Technology.

away from international institutions, toward broader forms of international institutionalized behavior. . . . This evolution has brought the field to its current focus on the concept of international regimes. To fully realize its potential, the research program must now seek to resolve some serious anomalies in the regime approach and to link up the informal ordering devices of international regimes with the formal institutional mechanisms of international organizations.

In the first section of this article, we present a review of the literature in order to trace its evolution. This review draws heavily on articles published in *International Organization*, the leading journal in the field since its first appearance in 1947, and a source that not only reflects but in considerable measure is also responsible for the evolution of the field. The second section critiques the currently prevalent epistemological practices in regime analysis and points toward lines of inquiry which might enhance the productive potential of the concept as an analytical tool. Finally, we briefly suggest a means of systematically linking up regimes and formal organizations in a manner that is already implicit in the literature.

Progressive Analytical Shifts

As a field of study, international organization has always concerned itself with the same phenomenon: in the words of a 1931 text, it is an attempt to describe and explain "how the modern Society of Nations governs itself."[1] In that text, the essence of government was assumed to comprise the coordination of group activities so as to conduct the public business, and the particular feature distinguishing international government was taken to lie in the necessity that it be consistent with national sovereignty. Few contemporary students of international organization would want to alter this definition substantially.[2]

However, there have been identifiable shifts in how the phenomenon of international governance has been conceived, especially since World War II—so much so that the field is often described as being in permanent search of its own "dependent variable." Our reading of the literature reveals four major analytical foci, which we would place in roughly the following logical—and more or less chronological—order.

Formal Institutions

The first is a formal institutional focus. Within it, the assumption was made or the premise was implicit that (1) international governance is whatever international organizations do; and (2) the formal attributes of international organizations, such as their charters, voting procedures, committee structures, and the like, account for what they do. To the extent that the actual operation of institutions was explored, the frame of reference was their constitutional mandate, and the purpose of the exercise was to discover how closely it was approximated.[3]

Institutional Processes

The second analytical focus concerns the actual decision-making processes within international organizations. The assumption was gradually abandoned that the formal arrangements of international organizations explain what they do. This perspective originally emerged in the attempt to come to grips with the increasingly obvious discrepancies between constitutional designs and organizational practices. Some writers argued that the formal arrangements and objectives remained relevant and appropriate but were undermined or obstructed by such political considerations as cold war rivalry and such institutional factors as the veto in the UN Security Council, bloc voting in the UN General Assembly, and the like.[4] Others contended that the original designs themselves were unrealistic and needed to be changed.[5]

Over time, this perspective became more generalized, to explore overall patterns of influence shaping organizational outcomes.[6] The sources of influence which have been investigated include the power and prestige of individual states, the formation and functioning of the group system, organizational leadership positions, and bureaucratic politics. The outcomes that analysts have sought to explain have ranged from specific resolutions, programs, and budgets, to broader voting alignment and the general orientation of one or more international institutions.

Organizational Role

In this third perspective, another assumption of the formal institutionalist approach was abandoned, namely, that international governance *is* whatever international organizations *do*. Instead, the focus shifted to the actual and potential roles of international organizations in a more broadly conceived process of international governance.[7] This perspective in turn subsumes three distinct clusters.

In the first cluster, the emphasis was on the roles of international organizations in the resolution of substantive international problems. Preventive diplomacy and peacekeeping were two such roles in the area of peace and security,[8] nuclear safeguarding by the International Atomic Energy Agency (IAEA) was another.[9] Facilitating decolonization received a good deal of attention in the political realm,[10] providing multilateral development assistance in the economic realm.[11] The potential role of international organizations in restructuring North-South relations preoccupied a substantial number of scholars throughout the 1970s,[12] as did the possible contributions of international organizations to managing the so-called global commons.[13] Most recently, analysts have challenged the presumption that the roles of international organizations in this regard are invariably positive; indeed, they have accused international organizations of occasionally exacerbating the problems they are designed to help resolve.[14]

The second cluster of the organizational-role perspective shifted the focus away from the solution of substantive problems per se, toward certain long-term institutional consequences of the failure to solve substantive problems through the available institutional means. This, of course, was the integrationist focus, particularly the neofunctionalist variety.[15] It was fueled by the fact that the jurisdictional scope of both the state and existing international organizations was increasingly outstripped by the functional scope of international problems. And it sought to explore the extent to which institutional adaptations to this fact might be conducive to the emergence of political forms "beyond the nation state."[16] Neofunctionalists assigned a major role in this process to international organizations, not simply as passive recipients of new tasks and authority but as active agents of "task expansion" and "spillover."[17] Other approaches concerned themselves less with institutional changes than with attitudinal changes, whether among national elites, international delegates, or mass publics.[18]

The third cluster within the organizational-role perspective began with a critique of the transformational expectations of integration theory and then shifted the focus onto a more general concern with how international institutions "reflect and to some extent magnify or modify" the characteristic features of the international system.[19] Here, international organizations have been viewed as potential dispensers of collective legitimacy,[20] vehicles in the international politics of agenda formation,[21] forums for the creation of transgovernmental coalitions as well as instruments of transgovernmental policy coordination,[22] and as means through which the global dominance structure is enhanced or can possibly come to be undermined.[23]

The theme that unifies all works of this genre is that the process of global governance is not coterminous with the activities of international organizations but that these organizations do play some role in that broader process. The objective was to identify their role.

International Regimes

The current preoccupation in the field is with the phenomenon of international regimes. Regimes are broadly defined as governing arrangements constructed by states to coordinate their expectations and organize aspects of international behavior in various issue-areas. They thus comprise a normative element, state practice, and organizational roles.[24] Examples include the trade regime, the monetary regime, the oceans regime, and others.

The focus on regimes was a direct response both to the intellectual odyssey that we have just traced as well as to certain developments in the world of international relations from the 1970s on.

When the presumed identity between international organizations and international governance was explicitly rejected, the precise roles of organizations *in* international governance became a central concern. But, apart from the focus on integration, no overarching conception was developed *of* international governance itself. And the integrationists themselves soon abandoned their early notions, ending up with a formulation of integration that did little more than recapitulate the condition of interdependence which was assumed to trigger integration in the first place.[25] Thus, for a time the field of international organization lacked any systematic conception of its traditional analytical core: international governance. The introduction of the concept of regimes reflected an attempt to fill this void. International regimes were thought to express both the parameters and the perimeters of international governance.[26]

The impact of international affairs during the 1970s and beyond came in the form of an anomaly for which no ready-made explanation was at hand. Important changes occurred in the international system, associated with the relative decline of U.S. hegemony: the achievement of nuclear parity by the Soviet Union; the economic resurgence of Europe and Japan; the success of OPEC together with the severe international economic dislocations that followed it. Specific agreements that had been negotiated after World War II were violated, and institutional arrangements, in money and trade above all, came under enormous strain. Yet—and here is the anomaly—governments on the whole did not respond to the difficulties confronting them in beggar-thy-neighbor terms. Neither systemic factors nor formal institutions alone apparently could account for this outcome. One way to resolve the anomaly was to question the extent to which U.S. hegemony in point of fact had eroded.[27] Another, and by no means entirely incompatible route, was via the concept of international regimes. The argument was advanced that regimes continued in some measure to constrain and condition the behavior of states toward one another, despite systemic change and institutional erosion. In this light, international regimes were seen to enjoy a degree of relative autonomy, though of an unknown duration.[28] In sum, in order to resolve both disciplinary and real-world puzzles, the process of international governance has come to be associated with the concept of international regimes, occupying an ontological space somewhere between the level of formal institutions on the one hand and systemic factors on the other. . . .

These shifts in analytical foci of course have never been complete; not everyone in the field at any one time works within the same perspective, and once introduced into the field no perspective ever disappears altogether.

Problems in the Practice of Regime Analysis

One of the major criticisms made of the regimes concept is its "wooliness" and "imprecision."[29] The point is well taken. There is no agreement in the literature even on such basic issues as boundary conditions: Where does one regime end and another begin? What is the threshold between non-regime and regime? Embedding regimes in "meta-regimes," or "nesting" one within another, typifies the problem; it does not resolve it.[30] The same is true of the proposal that any set of patterned or conventionalized behavior be considered as prima facie evidence for the existence of a regime.[31]

The only cure for wooliness and imprecision is, of course, to make the concept of regimes less so. Definitions can still be refined, but only up to a point. . . . Ultimately, there exists no external Archimedian point from which regimes can be viewed as they "truly" are. This is so because regimes are conceptual creations, not concrete entities. As with any analytical construction in the human sciences, the concept of regimes will reflect commonsense understandings, actor preferences, and the particular purposes for which analyses are undertaken. Ultimately, therefore, the concept of regimes, like the concept of "power," or "state," or "revolution," will remain a "contestable concept. . . . "[32]

Regimes and Organizations

The progressive shift in the literature toward the study of international regimes has been guided by an abiding concern with the structures and processes of international governance. Despite remaining problems with this framework of analysis, . . . a great deal has been accomplished in a relatively short span of time. Along the way, however, . . . international institutions of a formal kind have been left behind. This fact is of academic interest because of the ever-present danger of theory getting out of touch with practice. But it is also of more than academic interest. The secretary general of the United Nations, to cite but one serious practical instance, has lamented that the malfunctioning of that institution seriously inhibits interstate collaboration in the peace and security field.[33] This is not the place to take up detailed institutional shortcomings in the world of international organizations. Nor would we be the ones to propose a return to the institutionalist approaches of yesteryear. Nevertheless, in order for the research program of international regimes *both* to contribute to ongoing policy concerns *and* better reflect the complex and sometimes ambiguous policy realm, it is necessary to link up regimes in some fashion with the formal mechanisms through which real-world actors operate. In point of fact, the outlines of such linkages are already implicit in the regime approach.

There has been a great deal of interest in the regimes literature recently in what can be described as the "organizational-design" approach. The key issue underlying this approach is to discern what range of international policy problems can best be handled by different kinds of institutional arrangements, such as simple norms of coordination, the reallocation of international property rights, or authoritative control through formal organizations. For example, an international fishing authority would probably be less appropriate and less able to avoid the early exhaustion of fisheries' stock than would the ascription of exclusive property rights to states. Where problems of liability enter the picture, however, as in ship-based pollution, authoritative procedures for settling disputes would become necessary. The work of Oliver Williamson and William Ouchi is very suggestive here, demonstrating the relative efficacy of the institutionalization of behavior through "hierarchies" versus through transaction-based informal means.[34] Robert Keohane has pioneered this territory in his "functional" theory of international regimes, from which organizational designs can be similarly derived.[35]

Three additional dimensions of the organizational-design issue would be emphasized. The intersubjective basis of international regimes suggests that *transparency* of actor behavior and expectations within regimes is one of their core requirements. And, as has been shown in such diverse issue-areas as international trade, investment, nuclear nonproliferation, and human rights, international organizations can be particularly effective instruments by which to create such transparency.[36] The appropriate design of the mechanisms by which international organizations do so, therefore, should be given every bit as much consideration as the design of the mechanisms of substantive problem solving.

The second is *legitimation*. A regime can be perfectly rationally designed but erode because its legitimacy is undermined.[37] Or a regime that is a logical nonstarter can be the object of endless negotiations because a significant constituency views its aims to be legitimate.[38] If a regime enjoys both it is described as being "stable" or "hegemonic." The important point to note is that international organizations, because of their trappings of universality, are the major venue within which the global legitimation struggle over international regimes is carried out today. Work in this genre goes back at least to Inis Claude and includes important recent contributions by Robert Cox and Stephen Krasner.[39]

The third dimension we would describe as *epistemic*. Stephen Toulmin has posed the issue well: "The problem of human understanding is a twofold one. Man knows, and he is also conscious that he knows. We acquire, possess, and make use of our knowledge; but at the same time, we are aware of our own activities as knowers."[40] In the international arena, neither the processes whereby knowledge becomes more extensive nor the means whereby reflection on knowledge deepens are passive or automatic.

They are intensely political. And for better or for worse, international organizations have maneuvered themselves into the position of being the vehicle through which both types of knowledge enter onto the international agenda.[41] As Ernst Haas has sought to show in his seminal work, in these processes of global epistemic politics lie the seeds of the future demand for international regimes.[42]

In short, the institutional-design approach, complemented by a concern with transparency creation, the legitimation struggle, and epistemic politics, can push the heuristic fruitfulness of the regime research program "forward" yet another step, linking it "back" to the study of international organizations.

Notes

1. Edmund C. Mower, *International Government* (Boston: Heath, 1931).

2. The basic terms of the definition are entirely compatible with the most recent theoretical work in the field, Robert O. Keohane, *After Hegemony* (Princeton: Princeton University Press, 1984). The precise meaning of the terms of course has changed significantly, as we shall see presently.

3. A distinguished contribution to this literature is Leland M. Goodrich and Anne P. Simons, *The United Nations and the Maintenance of International Peace and Security* (Washington, D.C.: Brookings, 1955). See also Klaus Knorr, "The Bretton Woods Institutions in Transition," *International Organization* [hereafter cited as *IO*] 2 (February 1948); Walter R. Sharp, "The Institutional Framework for Technical Assistance," *IO* 7 (August 1953); and Henri Rolin, "The International Court of Justice and Domestic Jurisdiction," *IO* 8 (February 1954).

4. Norman J. Padelford, "The Use of the Veto," *IO* 2 (June 1948); Raymond Dennett, "Politics in the Security Council," *IO* 3 (August 1949); M. Margaret Ball, "Bloc Voting in the Ceneral Assembly," *IO* 5 (February 1951); Allan Hovey, Jr., "Obstructionism and the Rules of the General Assembly," *IO* 5 (August 1951); and Arlette Moldaver, "Repertoire of the Veto in the Security Council, 1946–1956." *IO* 11 (Spring 1957).

5. See, among others, Sir Gladwyn Jebb, "The Role of the United Nations," *IO* 6 (November 1952); A. Loveday, "Suggestions for the Reform of UN Economic and Social Machinery," *IO* 7 (August 1953); Wytze Corter, "GATT after Six Years: An Appraisal," *IO* 8 (February 1954); Lawrence S. Finkelstein, "Reviewing the UN Charter," *IO* 9 (May 1955); Robert E. Riggs, "Overselling the UN Charter— Fact or Myth," *IO* 14 (Spring 1960); and Inis L. Claude, Jr., "The Management of Power in the Changing United Nations," *IO* 15 (Spring 1961).

6. The most comprehensive work in this genre remains Robert W. Cox and Harold K. Jacobson, eds., *The Anatomy of Influence: Decision Making in International Organization* (New Haven: Yale University Press, 1973).

7. Inis L. Claude's landmark text, *Swords into Plowshares* (New York: Random House, 1959), both signaled and contributed to this shift.

8. Lincoln P. Bloomfield, ed., *International Force—A Symposium, IO* 17 (Spring 1973); James M. Boyd, "Cyprus: Episode in Peacekeeping," *IO* 20 (Winter 1966); Robert O. Matthews, "The Suez Canal Dispute: A Case Study in Peaceful Settlement," *IO* 21 (Winter 1967); Yashpal Tandon, "Consensus and Authority

behind UN Peacekeeping Operations," *IO* 21 (Spring 1967); David P. Forsythe, "United Nations Intervention in Conflict Situations Revisited: A Framework for Analysis," *IO* 23 (Winter 1969); John Gerard Ruggie, "Contingencies, Constraints, and Collective Security: Perspectives on UN Involvement in International Disputes," *IO* 28 (Summer 1974); and Ernst B. Haas, "Regime Decay: Conflict Management and International Organization, 1945–1981," *IO* 37 (Spring 1983).

9. Robert E. Pendley and Lawrence Scheinman, "International Safeguarding as Institutionalized Collective Behavior," in John Gerard Ruggie and Ernst B. Haas, eds., special issue on international responses to technology, *IO* 29 (Summer 1975); and Joseph S. Nye, "Maintaining a Non-Proliferation Regime," in George H. Quester, ed., special issue on nuclear nonproliferation, *IO* 35 (Winter 1981).

10. Ernst B. Haas, "The Attempt to Terminate Colonization: Acceptance of the UN Trusteeship System," *IO* 7 (February 1953); John Fletcher-Cooke, "Some Reflections on the International Trusteeship System," *IO* 13 (Summer 1959); Harold K. Jacobson, "The United Nations and Colonialism: A Tentative Appraisal," *IO* 16 (Winter 1962); and David A. Kay, "The Politics of Decolonization: The New Nations and the United Nations Political Process," *IO* 21 (Autumn 1967).

11. Richard N. Gardner and Max E Millikan, eds., special issue on international agencies and economic development, *IO* 22 (Winter 1968).

12. Among many other sources, see Branislav Gosovic and John Gerard Ruggie, "On the Creation of a New International Economic Order: Issue Linkage and the Seventh Special Session of the UN General Assembly," *IO* 30 (Spring 1976).

13. David A. Kay and Eugene B. Skolnikoff, eds., special issue on international institutions and the environmental crisis, *IO* 26 (Spring 1972); Ruggie and Haas, eds., special issue, *IO* 29 (Summer 1975); and Per Magnus Wijkman, "Managing the Global Commons," *IO* 36 (Summer 1982).

14. The most extreme form of this criticism recently has come from the political right in the United States; cf. Burton Yale Pines, ed., *A World without the U.N.: What Would Happen If the United Nations Shut Down* (Washington, D.C.: Heritage Foundation, 1984). But the same position has long been an article of faith on the political left as well; cf. Cheryl Payer, "The Perpetuation of Dependence: The IMF and the Third World," *Monthly Review* 23 (September 1971), and Payer, "The World Bank and the Small Farmers," *Journal of Peace Research* 16, no. 2 (1979); and the special issue of *Development Dialogue*, no. 2 (1980).

15. Various approaches to the study of integration were summarized and assessed in Leon N. Lindberg and Stuart A. Scheingold, eds., special issue on regional integration, *IO* 24 (Autumn 1970).

16. Ernst B. Haas, *Beyond the Nation State: Functionalism and International Organization* (Stanford: Stanford University Press, 1964).

17. In addition to Haas, ibid., see Philippe C. Schmitter, "Three Neo-Functionalist Hypotheses about International Integration," *IO* 23 (Winter 1969); Leon N. Lindberg and Stuart A. Scheingold, *Europe's Would-Be Polity: Patterns of Change in the European Community* (Englewood Cliffs, N.J.: Prentice-Hall, 1970); Joseph S. Nye, *Peace in Parts: Integration and Conflict in Regional Organization* (Boston: Little, Brown, 1971). For a critique of the neofunctionalist model, see Roger D. Hansen, "Regional Integration: Reflection on a Decade of Theoretical Efforts," *World Politics* 21 (January 1969).

18. Henry H. Kerr, Jr., "Changing Attitudes through International Participation: European Parliamentarians and Integration," *IO* 27 (Winter 1973); Peter Wolf, "International Organizations and Attitude Change: A Re-examination of the Functionalist Approach," *IO* 27 (Summer 1973); David A. Karns, "The Effect of Interparliamentary Meetings on the Foreign Policy Attitudes of the United States Congressmen,"

IO 31 (Summer 1977); and Ronald Inglehart, "Public Opinion and Regional Integration," *IO* 24 (Autumn 1970).

19. The phrase is Stanley Hoffmann's in "International Organization and the International System," *IO* 24 (Summer 1970). A similar position was advanced earlier by Oran R. Young, "The United Nations and the International System," *IO* 22 (Autumn 1968).

20. Inis L. Claude, Jr., "Collective Legitimization as a Political Function of the United Nations," *IO* 20 (Summer 1966); cf. Jerome Slater, "The Limits of Legitimization in International Organizations: The Organization of American States and the Dominican Crisis," *IO* 23 (Winter 1969).

21. A representative sampling would include Kay and Skolnikoff, eds., special issue, *IO* 26 (Spring 1972); Robert Russell, "Transgovernmental Interaction in the International Monetary System, 1960–1972," *IO* 27 (Autumn 1973); Thomas Weiss and Robert Jordan, "Bureaucratic Politics and the World Food Conference," *World Politics* 28 (April 1976); Raymond E Hopkins, "The International Role of 'Domestic' Bureaucracy," *IO* 30 (Summer 1976); and John Gerard Ruggie, "On the Problem of 'The Global Problematique': What Roles for International Organizations?" *Alternatives* 5 (January 1980).

22. The major analytical piece initiating this genre was Robert O. Keohane and Joseph S. Nye, "Transgovernmental Relations and International Organizations," *World Politics* 27 (October 1974); cf. their earlier edited work on transnational relations and world politics, *IO* 25 (Summer 1971).

23. Robert Cox's recent work has been at the forefront of exploring this aspect of international organization: "Labor and Hegemony," *IO* 31 (Summer 1977); "The Crisis of World Order and the Problem of International Organization in the 1980's," *International Journal* 35 (Spring 1980); and "Gramsci, Hegemony and International Relations: An Essay in Method," *Millennium: Journal of International Studies* 12 (Summer 1983).

24. The most extensive analytical exploration of the concept may be found in Stephen D. Krasner, ed., *International Regimes* (Ithaca, N.Y.: Cornell University Press, 1983), most of which was first published as a special issue of *IO* in Spring 1982. Page references will be to the book.

25. Robert O. Keohane and Joseph S. Nye, "International Interdependence and Integration," in Fred I. Greenstein and Nelson W. Polsby, eds., *Handbook of Political Science,* vol. 8 (Reading, Mass.: Addison-Wesley, 1975). The point is also implicit in Ernst Haas's self-criticism, "Turbulent Fields and the Theory of Regional Integration," *IO* 30 (Spring 1976).

26. John Gerard Ruggie, "International Responses to Technology: Concepts and Trends," *IO* 29 (Summer 1975).

27. This is the tack taken by Susan Strange, "Still an Extraordinary Power: America's Role in a Global Monetary System," in Raymond E. Lombra and William E. Witte, eds., *Political Economy of International and Domestic Monetary Relations* (Ames: Iowa State University Press, 1982); and Bruce Russett, "The Mysterious Case of Vanishing Hegemony: Or, Is Mark Twain Really Dead?" *IO* 39 (Spring 1985).

28. See Krasner, "Introduction," *International Regimes,* and Keohane, *After Hegemony,* for discussions of this thesis.

29. See Susan Strange, in this collection.

30. This route is taken by Vinod K. Aggarwal, *Liberal Protectionism: The International Politics of Organized Textile Trade* (Berkeley: University of California Press, 1985).

31. Oran R. Young, "Regime Dynamics: The Rise and Fall of International Regimes," in Krasner, ed., *International Regimes.*

32. On "contestable concepts," see William Connally, *The Terms of Political Discourse,* 2d ed. (Princeton: Princeton University Press, 1983).

33. United Nations, *Report of the Secretary-General on the Work of the Organization,* 1982 (A/37/1).

34. Oliver Williamson, *Markers and Hierarchies* (New York: Free, 1975), and William Ouchi and Oliver Williamson, "The Markets and Hierarchies Program of Research: Origins, Implications, Prospects," in William Joyce and Andrew van de Ven, eds., *Organization Design* (New York: Wiley, 1981). From the legal literature, see Guido Calabresi and Douglas Melamed, "Property Rules, Liability Rules, and Inalienability: One View of the Cathedral," *Harvard Law Review* 85 (April 1972); Philip Heyemann, "The Problem of Coordination: Bargaining with Rules," *Harvard Law Review* 86 (March 1973); and Susan Rose-Ackerman, "Inalienability and the Theory of Property Rights," *Columbia Law Review* 85 (June 1985).

35. Keohane, *After Hegemony.* Some policy recommendations that flow from the approach are spelled out by Robert O. Keohane and Joseph S. Nye, "Two Cheers for Multilateralism," *Foreign Policy* 60 (Fall 1985).

36. The GATT multilateral surveillance mechanisms are, of course, its chief institutional means of establishing intersubjectively acceptable interpretations of what actors are up to. For a treatment of investment which highlights this dimension, see Charles Lipson, *Standing Guard: Protecting Foreign Capital in the Nineteenth and Twentieth Centuries* (Berkeley: University of California Press, 1985); for nonproliferation, see Nye, "Maintaining a Nonproliferation Regime," and for human rights, John Gerard Ruggie, "Human Rights and the Future International Community," *Daedalus* 112 (Fall 1983). The impact of intergovernmental information systems is analyzed by Ernst B. Haas and John Gerard Ruggie, "What Message in the Medium of Information Systems?" *International Studies Quarterly* 26 (June 1982).

37. Puchala and Hopkins, "International Regimes," in Krasner, ed., *International Regimes,* discuss the decline of colonialism in terms that include this dimension.

38. The New International Economics Order is a prime example.

39. See Claude, "Collective Legitimization"; Cox, "Labor and Hegemony," "The Crisis of World Order," and "Gramsci, Hegemony, and International Relations"; and Krasner, *Structural Conflict.*

40. Toulmin, *Human Understanding,* p. 1.

41. Ruggie analyzes this process in "On the Problem of 'The Global Problematique.'"

42. Haas, "Words Can Hurt You," and Haas, "Why Collaborate? Issue-Linkage and International Regimes," *World Politics* 32 (April 1980).

3

Cave! Hic Dragones:
A Critique of Regime Analysis

Susan Strange

I nstead of asking what makes regimes and how they affect behavior, [this article] seeks to raise more fundamental questions. In particular, it queries whether the concept of regime is really useful to students of international political economy or world politics; and whether it may not even be actually negative in its influence, obfuscating and confusing instead of clarifying and illuminating, and distorting by concealing bias instead of revealing and removing it.

It challenges the validity and usefulness of the regime concept on five separate counts. These lead to two further and secondary (in the sense of indirect), but no less important grounds for expressing the doubt whether further work of this kind ought to be encouraged. The five counts (or "dragons" to watch out for) are first, that the study of regimes is, for the most part, a fad, one of those shifts of fashion not too difficult to explain as a temporary reaction to events in the real world but in itself making little in the way of a long-term contribution to knowledge. Second, it is imprecise and woolly. Third, it is value-biased, as dangerous as loaded dice. Fourth, it distorts by overemphasizing the static and underemphasizing the dynamic element of change in world politics. And fifth, it is narrow-minded, rooted in a state-centric paradigm that limits vision of a wider reality.

Two indirect criticisms—not so much of the concept itself as of the tendency to give it exaggerated attention—follow from these five points. One is that it leads to a study of world politics that deals predominantly

The title translates as "Beware! here be dragons!"—an inscription often found on pre-Columbian maps of the world beyond Europe.

Reprinted from *International Organization,* Vol. 36, No. 2, 1982, Susan Strange, "*Cave! hic dragones:* A Critique of Regime Analysis," by permission of The MIT Press, Cambridge, Massachusetts. © 1982 by the Massachusetts Institute of Technology.

with the status quo, and tends to exclude hidden agendas and to leave unheard or unheeded complaints, whether they come from the underprivileged, the disenfranchised or the unborn, about the way the system works. In short, it ignores the vast area of nonregimes that lies beyond the ken of international bureaucracies and diplomatic bargaining. The other is that it persists in looking for an all-pervasive pattern of political behavior in world politics, a "general theory" that will provide a nice, neat, and above all simple explanation of the past and an easy means to predict the future. Despite all the accumulated evidence of decades of work in international relations and international history (economic as well as political) that no such pattern exists, it encourages yet another generation of impressionable young hopefuls to set off with high hopes and firm resolve in the vain search for an El Dorado. . . .

Five Criticisms of the Concept of Regimes

A Passing Fad?

The first of my dragons, or pitfalls for the unwary, is that concern with regimes may be a passing fad. A European cannot help making the point that concern with regime formation and breakdown is very much an American academic fashion. . . . Europeans concerned with matters of strategy and security are usually not the same as those who write about structures affecting economic development, trade, and money, or with the prospects for particular regimes or sectors. Even the future of Europe itself never dominated the interests of so large a group of scholars in Europe as it did, for a time, the American academic community. Perhaps Europeans are not generalist enough; perhaps having picked a field to work in, they are inclined to stick to it too rigidly. And conversely, perhaps Americans are more subject to fads and fashions in academic inquiry than Europeans, more apt to conform and to join in behind the trendsetters of the times. Many Europeans, I think, believe so, though most are too polite to say it. They have watched American enthusiasm wax and wane for systems analysis, for behavioralism, for integration theory, and even for quantitative methods indiscriminately applied. The fashion for integration theory started with the perceived U.S. need for a reliable junior partner in Europe, and how to nurture the European Communities to this end was important. The quantitative fashion is easily explained by a combination of the availability of computer time and the finance to support it and of the ambition of political scientists to gain as much kudos and influence with policy makers as the economists and others who had led the way down the quantitative path. Further back we can see how international relations as a field of study separate from politics and history itself developed in direct response to the horrors of two world wars and the threat of a third. And, later, collective goods theories responded to the debates about burden-sharing in NATO, just as monetarism and supply-side economics gained a hearing only when the conditions of the 1970s cast doubts on Keynesian remedies for recession, unemployment, and inflation.

The current fashion for regimes arises, I would suggest, from certain, somewhat subjective perceptions in many American minds. One such perception was that a number of external "shocks," on top of internal troubles like Watergate and Jimmy Carter, had accelerated a serious decline in American power. In contrast to the nationalist, reactionary response of many Reaganites, liberal, internationalist academics asked how the damage could be minimized by restoring or repairing or reforming the mechanisms of multilateral management—"regimes." A second subjective perception was that there was some sort of mystery about the uneven performance and predicament of international organizations. This was a connecting theme in Keohane and Nye's influential *Power and Interdependence*, which struck responsive chords far and wide.

But the objective reality behind both perceptions was surely far less dramatic. In European eyes, the "decline" arises partly from an original overestimation of America's capacity to remake the whole world in the image of the U.S.A. In this vision, Washington was the center of the system, a kind of keep in the baronial castle of capitalism, from which radiated military, monetary, commercial, and technological as well as purely political channels carrying the values of American polity, economy, and society down through the hierarchy of allies and friends, classes and cultural cousins, out to the ends of the earth. The new kind of global empire, under the protection of American nuclear power, did not need territorial expansion. It could be achieved by a combination of military alliances and a world economy opened up to trade, investment, and information.

This special form of nonterritorial imperialism is something that many American academics, brought up as liberals and internationalists, find hard to recognize. U.S. hegemony, while it is as nonterritorial as Britain's India in the days of John Company or Britain's Egypt after 1886, is still a form of imperialism. The fact that this nonterritorial empire extends more widely and is even more tolerant of the pretensions of petty principalities than Britain was of those of the maharajahs merely means that it is larger and more secure. It is not much affected by temporary shocks or setbacks. Yet Americans are inhibited about acknowledging their imperialism. It was a Frenchman who titled his book about American foreign policy *The Imperial Republic*.[1]

Moreover, Americans have often seemed to exaggerate the "shocks" of the 1970s and the extent of change in U.S.-Soviet or U.S.-OPEC relations. Nobody else saw the pre-1971 world as being quite so stable and ordered as Americans did. Certainly for Third-Worlders, who had by then lived through two or three recent cycles of boom and slump in the price of their country's major exports—whether coffee, cocoa, tin, copper, sugar, or bananas—plus perhaps a civil war and a revolution or two, the "oil-price shock" was hardly the epoch-making break with the stable, comfortable, predictable past that it seemed to many Americans. If one has been accustomed for as long as one can remember to national plans and purposes being frustrated and brought to nothing by exogenous changes in the market, in technology or in the international political situation between the superpowers—over none of which your own government has had the slightest control—then a bit more disorder in a disorderly world comes as no great surprise.

To non-American eyes therefore, there is something quite exaggerated in the weeping and wailing and wringing of American hands over the fall of the imperial republic. This is not how it looks to us in Europe, in Japan, in Latin America, or even in the Middle East. True, there is the nuclear parity of the Soviet Union. And there is the depreciated value of the dollar in terms of gold, of goods, and of other currencies. But the first is not the only factor in the continuing dominant importance to the security structure of the balance of power between the two superpowers, and the second is far more a sign of the abuse of power than it is of the loss of power. The dollar, good or bad, still dominates the world of international finance. Money markets and other markets in the United States still lead and others still follow; European bankrupts blame American interest rates. If the authority of the United States appears to have weakened, it is largely because the markets and their operators have been given freedom and license by the same state to profit from an integrated world economy. If Frankenstein's monster is feared to be out of control, that looks to non-Americans more like a proof of Frankenstein's power to create such a monster in the first place. The change in the balance of public and private power still leaves the United States as the undisputed hegemon of the system.[2]

To sum up, the fashion for regime analysis may not simply be, as Stein suggests,[3] rehash of old academic debates under a new and jazzier name—a sort of intellectual mutton dressed up as lamb—so that the pushy new professors of the 1980s can have the same old arguments as their elders but can flatter themselves that they are breaking new ground by using a new jargon. It is also an intellectual reaction to the objective reality.

In a broad, structuralist view (and using the broader definition of the term) of the structures of global security, of a global credit system, of the global welfare system (i.e., aid and other resource transfers) and the global knowledge and communications system, there seems far less sign of a falling-off in American power. Where decline exists, it is a falling-off in the country's power and will to intervene with world market mechanisms (from Eurodollar lending to the grain trade) rather than significant change in the distribution of military or economic power to the favor of other states. Such change as there is, has been more internal than international.

The second subjective perception on the part of Americans that I wish to address is that there is some mystery about the rather uneven performance in recent times of many international arrangements and organizations. While some lie becalmed and inactive, like sailing ships in the doldrums, others hum with activity, are given new tasks, and are recognized as playing a vital role in the functioning of the system. I would personally count the GATT, FAO, and UNESCO in the first group, the World Bank and the regional banks, the BIS, and IMCO in the second. The IMF holds a middle position: it has largely lost its universal role but has found an important but more specialized usefulness in relation to indebted developing countries.

The mixed record of international organizations really does need explaining. But Americans have been curiously reluctant, to my mind at least, to distinguish between the three somewhat different purposes served by international organizations. These can broadly be identified as *strategic* (i.e., serving as instruments of the structural strategy and foreign policy of the dominant state or states); as *adaptive* (i.e., providing the necessary multilateral agreement on whatever arrangements are necessary to allow states to enjoy the political luxury of national autonomy without sacrificing the economic dividends of world markets and production structures); and as *symbolic* (i.e., allowing everybody to declare themselves in favor of truth, beauty, goodness, and world community, while leaving governments free to pursue national self-interests and to do exactly as they wish).

In the early postwar period, most international organizations served all three purposes at once. They were strategic in the sense that they served as instruments of the structural strategies of the United States. Also, they were often adaptive in that they allowed the United States and the other industrialized countries like Britain, Germany, France, and Japan to enjoy both economic growth and political autonomy. Finally, many organizations were at the same time symbolic in that they expressed and partially satisfied the universal yearning for a "better world" without doing anything substantial to bring it about.

In recent years the political purposes served by institutions for their members have tended to be less well balanced; some have become predominantly strategic, some predominantly adaptive, and others predominantly symbolic. This has happened because, where once the United States was able to dominate organizations like the United Nations, it can no longer do so because of the inflation of membership and the increasing divergence between rich and poor over fundamentals. Only a few organizations still serve U.S. strategic purposes better than bilateral diplomacy can serve them; they are either top-level political meetings or they deal with military or monetary matters in which the United States still disposes of predominant power. In other organizations the tendency toward symbolism, expressed in a proliferation of Declarations, Charters, Codes of Conduct, and other rather empty texts, has strengthened as the ability to reach agreement on positive action to solve real global problems has weakened. This applies especially to the United Nations and many of its subsidiary bodies, to UNCTAD, IDA, and many of the specialized agencies. The one growth area is the adaptive function. The integration of the world economy and the advance of technology have created new problems, but they also have often enlarged the possibility of reaching agreement as well as the perceived need to find a solution. Such predominantly adaptive institutions are often monetary (IBRD, IFC, BIS) or technical (ITU, IMCO, WMO).

Imprecision

The second dragon is imprecision of terminology. "Regime" is yet one more woolly concept that is a fertile source of discussion simply because people mean different things when they use it. At its worst, woolliness leads to the same sort of euphemistic Newspeak that George Orwell warned us would be in general use by 1984. The Soviet Union calls the main medium for the suppression of information *Pravda* (Truth), and refers to the "sovereign independence of socialist states" as the principle governing its relations with its East European "partners." In the United States scholars have brought "interdependence" into general use when what they were describing was actually highly asymmetrical and uneven dependence or vulnerability. In the same way, though more deliberately, IBM public relations advisers invented and brought into general and unthinking use the term "multinational corporation" to describe an enterprise doing worldwide business from a strong national base.

Experience with the use of these and other, equally woolly words warns us that where they do not actually mislead and misrepresent, they often serve to confuse and disorient us. "Integration" is one example of an overused word loosely taken to imply all sorts of other developments such as convergence as well as the susceptibility of "integrated" economies to common trends and pressures—a mistake that had to be painstakingly remedied by careful, pragmatic research.[4]

"Regime" is used to mean many different things. In the Keohane and Nye formulation ("networks of rules, norms and procedures that regularize behavior and control its effects")[5] it is taken to mean something quite narrow—explicit or implicit internationally agreed arrangements, usually executed with the help of an international organization—even though Keohane himself distinguishes between regimes and specific agreements. Whereas other formulations emphasize "decision-making procedures around which actors' expectations converge," the concept of regime can be so broadened as to mean almost any fairly stable distribution of the power to influence outcomes. In Keohane and Nye's formulation, the subsequent questions amount to little more than the old chestnut, "Can international institutions change state behavior?" The second definition reformulates all the old questions about power and the exercise of power in the international system. So, if—despite a rather significant effort by realist and pluralist authors to reach agreement—there is no fundamental consensus about the answer to the question, "What is a regime?", obviously there is not going to be much useful or substantial convergence of conclusions about the answers to the other questions concerning their making and unmaking.

Why, one might ask, has there been such concerted effort to stretch the elasticity of meaning to such extremes? I can only suppose that scholars, who by calling, interest, and experience are themselves "internationalist" in aspiration, are (perhaps unconsciously) performing a kind of symbolic ritual against the disruption of the international order, and do so just because they are also, by virtue of their profession, more aware than most of the order's tenuousness.

Value Bias

The third point to be wary of is that the term regime is value-loaded; it implies certain things that ought not to be taken for granted. As has often happened before in the study of international relations, this comes of trying to apply a term derived from the observation of national politics to international or to world politics.

Let us begin with semantics. The word "regime" is French, and it has two common meanings. In everyday language it means a diet, an ordered, purposive plan of eating, exercising, and living. A regime is usually imposed on the patient by some medical or other authority with the aim of achieving better health. A regime must be recognizably the same when undertaken by different individuals, at different times, and in different places. It must also be practiced over an extended period of time; to eat no pastry one day but to gorge the next is not to follow a regime. Nor does one follow a regime if one eats pastry when in Paris but not in Marseilles. Those who keep to a diet for a day or two and abandon it are hardly judged to be under the discipline of a regime.

Based on the same broad principles of regularity, discipline, authority, and purpose, the second meaning is political: the government of a society by an individual, a dynasty, party or group that wields effective power over the rest of society. Regime in this sense is more often used pejoratively than with approval—the "ancien regime," the "Franco regime," the "Stalin regime," but seldom the "Truman" or "Kennedy" regime, or the "Attlee" or "Macmillan," the "Mackenzie King" or the "Menzies" regime. The word is more often used of forms of government that are inherently authoritarian, capricious, and even unjust. Regimes need be neither benign nor consistent. It may be (as in the case of Idi Amin, "Papa Doc" Duvallier, or Jean-Bedel Bokassa) that the power of the regime is neither benign nor just. But at least in a given regime, everyone knows and understands where power resides and whose interest is served by it; and thus, whence to expect either preferment or punishment, imprisonment or other kinds of trouble. In short, government, rulership, and authority are the essence of the word, not consensus, nor justice, nor efficiency in administration.

What could be more different from the unstable, kaleidoscopic pattern of international arrangements between states? The title (if not all of the content) of Hedley Bull's book, *The Anarchical Society,* well describes the general state of the international system. Within that system, as Bull and others have observed, it is true that there is more order, regularity of behavior, and general observance of custom and convention than the pure realist expecting the unremitting violence of the jungle might suppose. But by and large the world Bull and other writers describe is characterized in all its main outlines not by discipline and authority, but by the absence of government, by the precariousness of peace and order, by the dispersion not the concentration of authority, by the weakness of law, and by the large number of unsolved problems and unresolved conflicts over what should be done, how it should be done, and who should do it.

Above all, a single recognized locus of power over time is the one attribute that the international system so conspicuously lacks.

All those international arrangements dignified by the label regime are only too easily upset when either the balance of bargaining power or the perception of national interest (or both together) change among those states who negotiate them. In general, moreover, all the areas in which regimes in a national context exercise the central attributes of political discipline are precisely those in which corresponding international arrangements that might conceivably be dignified with the title are conspicuous by their absence. There is no world army to maintain order. There is no authority to decide how much economic production shall be public and how much shall be privately owned and managed. We have no world central bank to regulate the creation of credit and access to it, nor a world court to act as the ultimate arbiter of legal disputes that also have political consequences. There is nothing resembling a world tax system to decide who should pay for public goods—whenever the slightest hint of any of these is breathed in diplomatic circles, state governments have all their defenses at the ready to reject even the most modest encroachment on what they regard as their national prerogatives.

The analogy with national governments implied by the use of the word regime, therefore, is inherently false. It consequently holds a highly distorting mirror to reality.

Not only does using this word regime distort reality by implying an exaggerated measure of predictability and order in the system as it is, it is also value-loaded in that it takes for granted that what everyone wants is more and better regimes, that greater order and managed interdependence should be the collective goal. . . . There is a whole literature that denies that order is "the most fundamental concern" and that says that the objectives of Third World policy should be to achieve freedom from dependency and to enhance national identity and freer choice by practicing "uncoupling" or delinking or (yet another woolly buzz-word) by "collective self-reliance."

Now, these ideas may be unclear and half-formed. But in view of the Islamic revival and the newfound self-confidence of several newly industrialized countries (NICs), it would be patently unwise for any scholar to follow a line of inquiry that overlooks them. Let us never forget the folly of League of Nations reformers, busily drafting new blueprints while Hitler and Mussolini lit fires under the whole system. Should we not ask whether this too does not indicate an essentially conservative attitude biased toward the status quo? Is it not just another unthinking response to fear of the consequences of change? Yet is not political activity as often directed by the desire to achieve change, to get more justice and more freedom from a system, as it is by the desire to get more wealth or to assure security for the haves by reinforcing order?

Too Static a View

The fourth dragon to beware is that the notion of a regime—for the semantic reasons indicated earlier—tends to exaggerate the static quality of arrangements for managing the international system and introducing some confidence in the future of anarchy, some order out of uncertainty. In sum, it produces stills, not movies. And the reality, surely, is highly dynamic, as can fairly easily be demonstrated by reference to each of the three main areas for regimes considered in this collection: security, trade, and money.

The international security regime (if it can be so called) has not been derived from Chapter VII of the U.N. Charter, which remains as unchanged as it is irrelevant. It has rested on the balance of power between the superpowers. In order to maintain that balance, each has engaged in a continuing and escalating accumulation of weapons and has found it necessary periodically to assert its dominance in particular frontier areas—Hungary, Czechoslovakia, and Afghanistan for the one and South Korea, Guatemala, Vietnam, and El Salvador for the other. Each has also had to be prepared when necessary (but, fortunately, less frequently) to engage in direct confrontation with the other. And no one was ever able to predict with any certainty when such escalation in armaments, such interventions or confrontations were going to be thought necessary to preserve the balance, nor what the outcome would be. Attempts to "quick-freeze" even parts of an essentially fluid relationship have been singularly unsuccessful and unconvincing, as witness the fate of the SALT agreements, the European Security Conference, and the Non-Proliferation Treaty.

In monetary matters, facile generalizations about "the Bretton Woods regime" abound—but they bear little resemblance to the reality. It is easily forgotten that the original Articles of Agreement were never fully implemented, that there was a long "transition period" in which most of the proposed arrangements were put on ice, and that hardly a year went by in the entire postwar period when some substantial change was not made (tacitly or explicitly) in the way the rules were applied and in the way the system functioned. Consider the major changes: barring the West European countries from access to the Fund; providing them with a multilateral payments system through the European Payments Union; arranging a concerted launch into currency convertibility; reopening the major international commodity and capital markets; finding ways to support the pound sterling. All these and subsequent decisions were taken by national governments, and especially by the U.S. government, in response to their changing perceptions of national interest or else in deference to volatile market forces that they either could not or would not control.

Arrangements governing international trade have been just as changeable and rather less uniform. Different principles and rules governed trade between market economies and the socialist or centrally planned economies, while various forms of preferential market access were practiced between European countries and their former colonies and much the same results were achieved between the United States and Canada or Latin America through direct investment. Among the European countries, first in the OEEC and then in EFTA and the EC, preferential systems within the system were not only tolerated but encouraged. The tariff reductions negotiated through the GATT were only one part of a complex governing structure of arrangements, international and national, and even these (as all the historians of commercial diplomacy have shown) were subject to constant revision, reinterpretation, and renegotiation.

The trade "regime" was thus neither constant nor continuous over time, either between partners or between sectors. The weakness of the arrangements as a system for maintaining order and defining norms seems to me strikingly illustrated by the total absence of continuity or order in the important matter of the competitive use of export credit—often government guaranteed and subsidized—in order to increase market shares. No one system of rules has governed how much finance on what terms and for how long can be obtained for an international exchange, and attempts to make collective agreements to standardize terms (notably through the Berne Union) have repeatedly broken down.

The changeable nature of all these international arrangements behind the blank institutional facade often results from the impact of the two very important factors that regime analysis seems to me ill-suited to cope with: technology and markets. Both are apt to bring important changes in the distribution of costs and benefits, risks and opportunities to national economies and other groups, and therefore to cause national governments to change their minds about which rules or norms of behavior should be reinforced and observed and which should be disregarded and changed.

Some of the consequences of technological change on international arrangements are very easily perceived, others less so. It is clear that many longstanding arrangements regarding fishing rights were based on assumptions that became invalid when freezing, sonar, and improved ship design altered the basic factors governing supply and demand. It is also clear that satellites, computers, and video technology have created a host of new problems in the field of information and communication, problems for which no adequate multilateral arrangements have been devised. New technology in chemicals, liquid natural gas, nuclear power, and oil production from under the sea—to mention only a few well-known areas—is dramatically increasing the risks involved in production, trade, and use. These risks become (more or less) acceptable thanks to the possibility of insuring against them. But though this has political consequences—imposing the cost of insurance as a kind of entrance tax on participation in the world market economy—the fact that no structure or process exists for resolving the conflicts of interest that ensue is an inadequately appreciated new aspect of the international system.

Technology also contributes to the process of economic concentration, reflected in the daily dose of company takeovers, through the mounting cost of replacing old technology with new and the extended leadtime between investment decisions and production results. Inevitably, the economic concentration so encouraged affects freedom of access to world markets and thus to the distributive consequences in world society. The nationalist, protectionist, defensive attitudes of states today are as much a response to technical changes and their perceived consequences as they are to stagnation and instability in world markets.

Since the chain of cause and effect so often originates in technology and markets, passing through national policy decisions to emerge as negotiating postures in multilateral discussions, it follows that attention to the end result—an international arrangement of some sort—is apt to overlook most of the determining factors on which agreement may, in brief, rest.

The search for common factors and for general rules (or even axioms), which is of the essence of regime analysis, is therefore bound to be long, exhausting, and probably disappointing. Many articles abound in general conclusions about regimes, their nature, the conditions favoring their creation, maintenance, and change, and many of the generalizations seem at first reading logically plausible—but only if one does not examine their assumptions too closely. My objection is that these assumptions are frequently unwarranted.

State-centeredness

The final but by no means least important warning is that attention to these regime questions leaves the study of international political economy far too constrained by the self-imposed limits of the state-centered paradigm. It asks, what are the prevailing arrangements discussed and observed among governments, thus implying that the important and significant political issues are those with which governments are concerned. Nationally, this is fairly near the truth. Democratic governments have to respond to whatever issues voters feel are important if they wish to survive, and even the most authoritarian governments cannot in the long run remain indifferent to deep discontents or divisions of opinion in the societies they rule. But internationally, this is not so. The matters on which governments, through international organizations, negotiate and make arrangements are not necessarily the issues that even they regard as most important, still less the issues that the mass of individuals regards as crucial. Attention to regimes therefore accords to governments far too much of the right to define the agenda of academic study and directs the attention of scholars mainly to those issues that government officials find significant and important. If academics submit too much to this sort of imperceptible pressure, they abdicate responsibility for the one task for which the independent scholar has every comparative advantage, the development of a philosophy of international relations or international political economy that will not only explain and illuminate but will point a road ahead and inspire action to follow it.

Thus regime analysis risks overvaluing the positive and undervaluing the negative aspects of international cooperation. It encourages academics to practice a kind of analytical *chiaroscuro* that leaves in shadow all the aspects of the international economy where no regimes exist and where each state elects to go its own way, while highlighting the areas of agreement where some norms and customs are generally acknowledged. It consequently gives the false impression (always argued by the neofunctionalists) that international regimes are indeed slowly advancing against the forces of disorder and anarchy. Now it is only too easy, as we all know, to be misled by the proliferation of international associations and organizations, by the multiplication of declarations and documents, into concluding that there is indeed increasing positive action. The reality is that there are more areas and issues of nonagreement and controversy than there are areas of agreement. On most of the basic social issues that have to do with the rights and responsibilities of individuals to each other and to the state—on whether abortion, bribery, drink or drug pushing or passing information, for example, is a crime or not—there is no kind of international regime. Nor is there a regime on many of the corresponding questions of the rights and responsibilities of states toward individuals and toward other states.

In reality, furthermore, the highlighted issues are sometimes less important than those in shadow. In the summer of 1980, for example, INMARSAT announced with pride an agreement on the terms on which U.S.-built satellites and expensive receiving equipment on board ship can be combined to usher in a new Future Global Maritime Distress and Safety System, whereby a ship's distress call is automatically received all over a given area by simply pressing a button. For the large tankers and others who can afford the equipment, this will certainly be a significant advance; not so for small coasters and fishing boats. In the same year, though, millions died prematurely through lack of any effective regime for the relief of disaster or famine. Meanwhile, the Executive Directors of the International Monetary Fund can reach agreement on a further increase in quotas, but not on the general principles governing the rescheduling of national foreign debts.

Moreover, many of the so-called regimes over which the international organizations preside turn out under closer examination to be agreements to disagree. The IMF amendments to the Articles of Agreement, for example, which legitimized the resort to managed floating exchange rates, are no more than a recognition of states' determination to decide for themselves what strategy and tactics to follow in the light of market conditions. To call this a "regime" is to pervert the language. So it is to call the various "voluntary" export restrictive arrangements bilaterally negotiated with Japan by other parties to the GATT "a multilateral regime." Since 1978 the Multi-Fibre "Agreement," too, has been little more, in effect, than an agreement to disagree. Similarly, UNESCO's debate on freedom and control of information through the press and the media resulted not in an international regime but in a bitter agreement to disagree.

One good and rather obvious reason why there is a rather large number of issues in which international organizations preside over a dialogue of the deaf is simply that the political trend within states is toward greater and greater intervention in markets and greater state responsibility for social and economic conditions, while the major postwar agreements for liberal regimes tended the other way and bound states to negative, noninterventionist policies that would increase the openness of the world economy.

In a closely integrated world economic system, this same trend leads to the other aspect of reality that attention to regimes obscures, and especially so when regimes are closely defined as being based on a group of actors standing in a characteristic relationship to each other. This is the trend to the transnational regulation of activities in one state by authorities in another, authorities that may be, and often are, state agencies such as the U.S. Civil Aeronautics Authority, the Department of Justice or the Food and Drug Administration. There is seldom any predictable pattern of "interaction" or awareness of contextual limitations to be found in such regulation.

Other neglected types of transnational authority include private bodies like industrial cartels and professional associations or special "private" and semiautonomous bodies like Lloyds of London, which exercises an authority delegated to it by the British government. This club of rich "names," underwriters, and brokers presides over the world's largest insurance and reinsurance market, and consequently earns three-quarters of its income from worldwide operations. By converting all sorts of outlandish risks into costs (the premiums on which its income depends), Lloyds plays a uniquely important part in the smooth functioning of a world market economy.

By now the limits on vision that may be encouraged as a secondary consequence of attention to regimes analysis have been implied. The aspects of political economy that it tends to overlook constitute the errors of omission that it risks incurring. I do not say that, therefore, *all* regime analyses commit these errors of omission; I can think of a number that have labored hard to avoid them. But the inherent hazard remains. They should not have to labor so hard to avoid the traps, and if there is a path to bypass them altogether it should be investigated.

The second indirect reason for skepticism about the value of regime analysis is that it persists in the assumption that somewhere there exists that El Dorado of social science, a general theory capable of universal application to all times and places and all issues, which is waiting to be discovered by an inspired. intrepid treasure-hunter. I confess I have never been convinced of this; and the more I know of political economy, the more skeptical I become. If (as so many books in international relations have concluded) we need better "tools of analysis," it is not because we will be able to dig up golden nuggets with them. Those nuggets—the great truths about human society and human endeavor—were all discovered long ago. What we need are constant reminders so that we do not forget them.

Notes

1. Raymond Aron, *The Imperial Republic: The U.S. and the World, 1945–1973* (Englewood Cliffs, N.J.: Prentice-Hall, 1974).

2. For a more extended discussion of this rather basic question, see my "Still an Extraordinary Power," in Ray Lombra and Bill Witte, eds., *The Political Economy of International and Domestic Monetary Relations* (Ames: Iowa State University Press, 1982); James Petras and Morris Morley, "The U.S. Imperial State," mimeo

(March 1980); and David Calleo, "Inflation and Defense," *Foreign Affairs* (Winter 1980).

3. See Arthur Stein, "Coordination and Collaboration: Regimes in an Anarchic World," in Stephen Krasner (ed.), *International Regimes* (Ithaca, N.Y.: Cornell University Press, 1983), p. 116.

4. Yao-so Hu, *Europe under Stress* (forthcoming).

5. Robert Keohane and Joseph Nye, *Power and Interdependence* (Boston: Little, Brown, 1977).

4

National Entanglements in International Governmental Organizations

Harold K. Jacobson, William M. Reisinger
& Todd Mathers

The global political system now contains more than 1,000 international governmental organizations (IGOs) of one type or another, and states are deeply entangled in this expanding web. Denmark heads the list by belonging to 164 IGOs; 19 states are members of 100 or more, and the mean number of memberships held by member states of the Group of 77, the Third World Caucus, is over 61. The entanglement of states and international governmental organizations has rapidly increased. The United Nations and its related agencies, the European communities, the Organization of American States, and the North Atlantic Treaty Organization are well known, but states have joined together and created a great many more formal institutional structures than those prominent examples. This study describes the growing web of IGOs, analyzes the propensity of states to join them, and assesses the broad consequences of a state's total IGO memberships for its economic performance and conflict behavior. It then raises questions about the implications for international relations of a continuation of the multiplying entanglement between states and IGOs, particularly in light of the apparent resistance to this trend evidenced by the U.S. and British withdrawal from the United Nations Educational, Scientific and Cultural Organization (UNESCO).

Functionalism as an Explanation

The theory of "functionalism," developed by David Mitrany (1933, 1966) and his followers, remains virtually the only corpus of scholarship about IGOs that offers general explanations of why states create and join such organizations, and what the consequences of this would be. Mitrany and

Reprinted from *American Political Science Review,* Vol. 80, No. 1, March 1986 by permission of the American Political Science Association. © 1986.

others also saw their version of functionalism as a prescription to guide the development of the global political system. Because their version of functionalism is the only theoretical persuasion available to guide this analysis, it will be the point of departure.

Functionalism maintains that states create and join international governmental organizations because of two broad historical tendencies that date from the nineteenth century: the extension and deepening of political participation within states, and the continual advance of technology. Functionalism argues that mass participation in political life will inexorably increase, that general populations everywhere are primarily interested in increasing their own standard of living, and that mass participation will make economic welfare the dominant concern of governments. Functionalism also argues that technology offers immense possibilities for improving living standards, but that international cooperation is essential to take full advantage of the opportunities provided by technology; states are simply too small. In the perspective of functionalism, IGOs are the consequence of political pressures and technological opportunities.

Functionalism would expect and prefer that the membership and mandates of an IGO be determined by the problem at issue; the overwhelming majority of IGOs would and should have limited memberships and specific mandates. The point of establishing an IGO, according to functionalism, is to facilitate international cooperation with respect to a specific technical issue, not to establish a general political authority with broad scope and domain.

Functionalism postulates that entanglement in a web of IGOs will make states less bellicose. Given the pressures to join IGOs, and the economic benefits presumably gained from membership and participation in them, states would be loathe to jeopardize these benefits by escalating interstate disagreements to violent conflicts that would inevitably destroy IGOs. Moreover, the increased opportunities for communication that IGOs provide should make it easier for states to avoid or settle disagreements before they reach the stage of violent conflict. States ought to have an incentive to reach agreement because, presumably, they have a common interest in economic expansion.

To what extent do the international governmental organizations in the contemporary global political system and the interaction between them and their member states conform to these functionalist tenets? How adequate is functionalism as an overall explanation for the pervasiveness of IGOs? This analysis examines the validity of functionalist tenets and assesses the extent to which functionalism must be supplemented for a full comprehension of the phenomenon of IGOs. It also raises questions about the adequacy of functionalism as a prescriptive guide to the future development of the global political system.

The Universe of IGOs

As a first stage in the analysis, it is necessary to describe the web of international governmental organizations as it currently exists. The basic source for information about the number and characteristics of IGOs is the *Yearbook of International Organizations*, which is published periodically by the Union of International Associations (UIA) in Brussels.[1] The data used in this analysis are derived from the nineteenth edition, which was published in 1981 (UIA, 1981).

Starting with the nineteenth edition, the *Yearbook* divides the organizations that are included into two major categories and four subcategories. The number of IGOs included in each subcategory in the 1981 *Yearbook* are:[2]

I. Conventional International Bodies	
A. Federations of International Organizations	1
B. Universal Membership Organizations	31
C. Inter-Continental Organizations	48
D. Regionally Delimited Organizations	264
II. Other International Bodies	
E. Emanations and Semi-Autonomous Bodies	405
F. Organizations of Special Form	287
G. Internationally Oriented National Bodies	39
H. Inactive or Dissolved Bodies	26
Total	1,101

In addition, seven organizations listed in the *Yearbook* had been proposed, but were not yet in existence in 1981. Including these, 1,108 IGOs are listed in the *Yearbook*, 1,075 of which were active in 1981.

The only IGO included in subcategory A is the United Nations. The United Nations' specialized agencies and other similar agencies comprise subcategory B. The International Exhibition Bureau and the International Olive Oil Council are examples of the type of organization included in subcategory C. The European communities are the most prominent of the organizations included in subcategory D.

The 344 organizations included in subcategories A through D are indisputably IGOs. The 731 organizations included in subcategories E through G have a more ambiguous status. Subcategory E includes such organizations as the United Nations Conference on Trade and Development, which, though it is a creation of the United Nations, has a larger budget, staff, and program than most of the organizations listed in subcategories C and D. It also includes some bodies, such as the U.N.'s Joint Inspection

Unit, that because of their small size or apparent lack of autonomy are more questionable cases. Organizations such as the Integrated Global Services System and the Joint Nordic Organization for Lappish Culture and Reindeer Husbandry are included in subcategory F. The first is an offshoot of UNESCO and the second of the Nordic Council, but both are more than suborgans, and in their characteristics resemble many of the organizations included in subcategories C and D. Subcategory G includes many of the joint ventures set up by the member states of the Council for Mutual Economic Assistance (CMEA), as well as such bodies as the Nigeria-Niger Joint Commission for Cooperation. . . .

True to the prediction and preference of functionalism, the overwhelming majority of the IGOs that are included in the data set and could be classified according to their function and membership have specific mandates and limited memberships: 96.8% have functionally defined specific mandates, and 80.6% limit their membership according to one or another criteria. Of the total, 54.1% have mandates related to economic matters, and 56.4% limit their membership according to geographic criteria.

The Dynamic Evolution of the Web of IGOs

The preceding description provides an initial guide to the nature of the web of IGOs, but it is necessary to go beyond this. A sense of the dynamic processes involved in the creation of the web of IGOs can be gained from an analysis of the past, and trends from the past can be projected to foreshow likely developments if these trends continued unabated.

The analysis can be structured conveniently according to four periods. The first period starts in 1815, the year the Napoleonic Wars ended and the first IGO, the Central Commission for the Navigation of the Rhine, was created. It ends in 1914 with the outbreak of World War I. The second period starts in 1915 and ends in 1939, with the outbreak of World War II. The third period begins in 1940 and ends in 1959. This is the period of World War II and the construction of the postwar international order. The final period starts in 1960 and ends in 1981, the last year for which data were available for inclusion in this analysis.

The rationale for breaking the post–World War II period in 1960 is that 17 states, the largest number ever, gained independence in 1960. By 1960, it was clear that colonialism was doomed and the nation-state system would be extended to the entire globe. As of 1959 there were 90 independent states in the global political system, 69 of which had been in existence in 1945 when the postwar period began. Between 1960 and 1981, 70 more would be added. Starting in 1960, decolonization fundamentally altered the global political system, at least in terms of the number of independent states included within it. The emergence of the new states led to an explosion in the membership of those IGOs that had come into existence before 1960 and—as will be seen—in the number of IGOs.

With the use of this periodization, several trends become apparent. Before examining these trends, however, it is important to emphasize that most IGOs are relatively recent creations. Of the 880 IGOs for which the date of founding is available, 94.1% were established after 1939, and 70.3% were established from 1960 through 1981. This pace of multiplication is astounding, and showed no sign of slowing. Indeed, more than 40% additional organizations were created in the decade of the 1970s ($n = 354$) than were created in the 1960s ($n = 250$).

The first notable trend is that progressively relatively fewer IGOs met the Union of International Associations criteria for being "conventional international bodies"; that is, for inclusion in the first four subcategories in the *Yearbook*. Sixty-five percent ($n = 13$) met these criteria in the period 1815–1914, 59.4% ($n = 19$) in the period 1915–1939, 47.1% ($n = 98$) in the period 1940–1959, and 31.8% ($n = 199$) in the period 1960–1981. By far the largest share of the increase in other international bodies was accounted for by IGOs in subcategories E and F, which tend to be organizations that owe their existence to decisions of organizations already existing.

Stating the trend in another way, with the passage of time IGOs created more and more offshoots. The obvious advantage of this practice is that often all that is required to create a new IGO is a majority vote, not a new treaty that would require signature and ratification to take effect. Governments of states may also believe that it will be easier for them to keep track of IGOs that are offshoots of other IGOs than those that are totally disconnected from any existing structure. Whatever the reason, a large portion of the increase of IGOs since 1960 has been in the UIA category "other international bodies." The pace of creation of IGOs in the UIA category "conventional international bodies" reached a peak in the 1960s when 110 were established; only 86 were created in the period 1970–1981.

A second notable trend is the significant difference between the distribution of types of membership criteria for the international governmental organizations that were founded prior to 1940 and for those that were founded starting that year. The proportion of IGOs founded before 1940 that have no criteria in their constitutions limiting membership to particular political, geographic, economic, or cultural groups of states is much higher than it is for IGOs founded later.

This does not mean that in the years since World War II began states have not formed a large number of IGOs with potentially universal membership. Twenty-five such organizations were founded prior to 1940, and 143 starting that year. The absolute number for the post–World War II era is impressively high. What it does mean is that after World War II began, limited-membership IGOs multiplied much more rapidly than those with potentially universal memberships. Starting in 1940, more than 80% of the

IGOs that have been founded and were still in existence in 1981 limited their membership according to some criterion. In total, 682 limited-membership organizations were established during this period, and the real number is undoubtedly higher, since the UIA does not have founding dates for all IGOs. Geography has always been the criterion most frequently used for limiting membership, and this continues to be the case.

This trend should be interpreted in light of the fact that the sovereign states of the nineteenth and early twentieth centuries were much more homogeneous than they are in the late twentieth century. A universal-membership organization formed in the earlier years had a much less diverse membership then than it does now or would have if it were formed in the present period.

That the relative proportion of IGOs that could have universal membership should fall off is logical. It would not be surprising if there were some upper limit on the number of universal-membership IGOs that could be included in a global political system, even though this limit might be flexible over time.

Another factor is that as decolonization proceeded in the post–World War II period, and the number of sovereign states grew at an explosive rate, the opportunities for creating limited-membership IGOs also expanded rapidly. Organizations could be created both among new states and among new and old states. International bodies could make possible the continuation and extension of activities that were organized within the framework of a single sovereignty in the colonial era.

A consequence of the trend favoring limited-membership IGOs in the post–World War II period is that organizations established from 1940 on tend to have significantly smaller numbers of members than those established prior to this date. The mean number of member states of IGOs in the latter category is 42.9, while that of those in the former category is 20.4.

To explore further the trend of an increasing proportion of limited-membership IGOs, it is useful to categorize states in order to see the extent to which different types of states have formed exclusive IGOs. A threefold categorization based on broad political and economic alignments divides states among those that are members of the Organization for Economic Cooperation and Development (OECD),[3] those that are members of the Warsaw Treaty Organization (WTO),[4] and those that do not belong to either of these organizations, a group that for this reason is called "Other."

These three categories are mutually exclusive and roughly place states into the groupings that are used in conventional political analyses. The members of OECD are those that are customarily referred to as the "West," and the members of WTO are those that are usually referred to as the "Soviet bloc" or group. The residual category of "Other" includes those states that are referred to as the Third World.[5]

Of the 563 IGOs for which membership information is available, 103 were comprised exclusively of states that were members of OECD; 28 exclusively of states that were members of WTO; and 178 exclusively of other states. Most of the Western IGOs were the basic agencies and offshoots of: the OECD, the North Atlantic Treaty Organization, the European communities, and the Nordic Council. Beyond the Warsaw Treaty Organization itself, the 28 Soviet-group IGOs were primarily derivatives of the Council for Mutual Economic Assistance (CMEA).[6] CMEA includes three non-European states, Cuba, Mongolia, and Vietnam, that for most purposes of this analysis are included in the "Other" category. In 1981 there were 38 IGOs comprised exclusively of CMEA members; these included the 28 comprised exclusively of WTO members.

The IGOs that were comprised exclusively of states in the category "Other" were less likely to be derivatives of other organizations than those comprised exclusively of OECD and WTO states. Of the IGOs comprised only of states in the category "Other," 58.6% were in the UIA category of "conventional international bodies," while only 47.1% of the OECD-only IGOs and 42.9% of the WTO-only IGOs were in this category. The economically more advanced Western and Soviet-group states have been refining their existing relationships through establishing additional organizations, albeit often subsidiary ones, while Third World states have been establishing relatively more new relationships and consequently more new primary organizations.

Since 1960, more IGOs comprised exclusively of states in the category "Other" have been established than IGOs of any other type. In the 1960s and 1970s, they accounted for about 40% of the IGOs formed in each decade. During the 1970s, these states began to create substantial numbers of IGOs in the UIA category "other international bodies"; they created 39 of these and 35 "conventional international bodies." By the 1970s, Western states were creating more than three UIA secondary-category IGOs for every one primary-category IGO that they established.

IGOs comprised solely of states in the category "Other" offer the greatest potential for growth in the near future. In 1981, only slightly more than one such organization existed for each state in this category, while there were more than three WTO-only IGOs and more than four OECD-only IGOs for each state in those categories. States in the category "Other" could expand considerably the number of "conventional international bodies" among themselves, and they could increase the ratio between IGOs of this type and "other international bodies," moving toward the level established by the Western states. The evidence of the 1960s and the 1970s is that states in the "Other" category are moving in these directions.

There were also 104 IGOs in existence in 1981 that were comprised of states from both the OECD and "Other" groupings; they did not include any members from the WTO group. Thirty-one of these organizations were established in the 1960s, in the immediate aftermath of decolonization, and 22 in the 1970s. Many of these organizations could be regarded as providing elements of the framework of the world market economy.

The third notable trend is a tendency toward greater differentiation and variety in the mandates of the IGOs that have been established since 1939. While this trend is not as pronounced as the other two, it nevertheless is important. In the 1940s and 1950s, an unprecedentedly large number of organizations that were established—28, or 13.5% of the total—had mandates dealing with security. Starting in the 1960s, progressively larger numbers of newly formed IGOs had mandates in the social field. This expansion of the numbers of IGOs with mandates to deal with social issues was most marked among OECD-only IGOs, although the "Other" group also moved to establish relatively more IGOs with social mandates. The record of the Soviet group is somewhat different. Only one of the 28 WTO-only IGOs has a mandate to deal with social issues; it was established in the 1970s. The Warsaw Treaty Organization's mandate is security; the remaining 26 (92.9%) of the WTO-only IGOs have economic mandates. Table 4.1 shows the distribution by function of the IGOs that were established starting in 1960 and were comprised exclusively of members of one or another group.

The growing differentiation of IGOs reflects a widely observed tendency toward specialization in political institutions. Security organizations were so relatively prominent in the 1940s and 1950s because the post–World War II political order was being created. This order has been relatively stable since those years, as is reflected in the fact that only 3.1%

Table 4.1 Distribution by Function of IGOs Comprised Exclusively of Members of Particular Political-Economic Groups Established from 1960 through 1981 (in percentages)

Function	Group[a]		
	OECD	WTO	Other
General	4.5	0	3.8
Economic	47.0	96.0	73.7
Social	47.0	4.0	18.8
Security	1.5	0	3.8
	100.0	100.0	100.1
No. of cases	66	25	133

Chi Square = 29.28
Cramer's Phi = .26
Sig. = .00

Note: a. OECD = Organization for Economic Cooperation; WTO = Warsaw Treaty Organization.

($n = 19$) of the IGOs established in the period starting in 1960 have security mandates. The increasing focus on social issues mirrors the focus on such issues that developed within states, particularly the advanced industrial Western countries, in the 1960s.

With their overwhelming concentration on economic issues, WTO-only IGOs stand apart from the general trend. Beyond the basic security commitment of the Warsaw Treaty, the Soviet-group states appear to have been almost inexorably drawn into economic cooperation, but they either have little desire or little necessity for institutionalized inter-governmental cooperation in other areas. The CMEA-only organizations are also heavily concentrated in the economic area (92.1%, $n = 35$).

In sum, the web of IGOs in existence in 1981 was dense and complex. Although functionalist tenets accurately describe the broad characteristics of the web and its dynamic evolution, one must go beyond functionalism for a more detailed description and for a fuller understanding of the growth of the web. The basic dynamic forces in the global political system—the urge to create a new order in the aftermath of a destructive war and decolonization—had a strong impact on the processes and course of institution building, as one would expect. IGOs are, after all, instruments of states, and states are likely to follow policies in this sphere that are similar and related to those that they follow in other spheres. The evolution of the web of IGOs also reflects an internal development within states: the greater attention paid by governments to social issues. An important exception to this trend, however, is the paucity of WTO-only IGOs directed toward social issues.

The Propensity of States to Join IGOs

The analysis so far has indicated that states belong to varying numbers of international governmental organizations. Now that the web of IGOs has been described, this varying propensity of states to join these organizations can be analyzed in detail. Functionalist tenets again provide the point of departure.

To give an indication of the varying propensity of states to be members of IGOs, Table 4.2 lists the 26 states that held the highest number of IGO memberships in 1981. For each state, it gives both the total number of full and associate memberships in all categories of IGOs, and the number of full memberships in "conventional international bodies." Denmark's leading the list is explained by the fact that its unique position as a member of both the European communities and the Nordic Council gives it an unusual opportunity to belong to a large number of "other international bodies."

Fourteen of the 26 states, including all of those in the top 10, are from Western Europe; 3 are from Eastern Europe and 3 from Asia and the Middle

Table 4.2   States with the Highest Number of IGO Memberships

Rank Order	State	Full and Associate Memberships in All Categories of IGOs	Full Memberships in UIA[a] Principal Category IGOs
1	Denmark	164	91
2	France	155	95
3	Norway	154	86
4	Sweden	IS3	87
5	United Kingdom	140	83
6	Finland	139	78
7	Federal Republic of Germany	135	83
8	The Netherlands	131	82
9	Belgium	127	77
10	Italy	124	72
11	United States	122	67
12	Spain	113	76
13	Canada	110	69
14	Japan	106	63
15	Iceland	105	54
16.5	Australia	104	67
16.5	Soviet Union	104	67
18	India	102	61
19	Brazil	100	60
20	Poland	99	69
21	Algeria	96	57
22.5	Austria	95	62
22.5	Yugoslavia	95	58
25	Egypt	94	60
25	Mexico	94	56
25	Switzerland	94	65

a. UIA = Union of International Associations.

East; 2 are from North America and 2 from Latin America; and 1 is from Africa and 1 from Oceania. These membership data reflect the fact that the IGO web is most dense and complex in Western Europe, where it began with the creation of the Central Commission for the Navigation of the Rhine in 1815. What is most impressive about this list of 26 states and the participation of states in IGOs more generally, however, is the extent to which the web has become global. Even Vanuatu, which just gained independence in 1981, held 11 IGO memberships that year, 4 of which were in "conventional international bodies." Joining IGOs has become among the first actions that governments take as soon as sovereignty is gained.

Functionalism argues that states will be propelled to join IGOs because popular pressures to increase living standards will lead their governments to engage in international collaboration to take advantage of the opportunities that technology offers to respond constructively to these pressures. Following this argument, one would expect that states with more opportunities for popular pressures to be expressed and at higher levels of technological development would belong to a relatively greater number of IGOs. The extent of party competition is an appropriate indicator for the first variable, and per capita gross national product (GNP) is an appropriate indicator for the second. For this analysis, Freedom House's fourfold classification of states in 1980 as (1) multiparty, (2) dominant-party, (3) one-party, and (4) no-party (Gastil, 1981) is used to indicate the extent of party competition. The per capita GNP figures used are those for 1980 published by the World Bank in its *World Bank Atlas 1982* (IBRD, 1982a).

True to the functionalist argument, party competition and per capita GNP do predict IGO memberships.[7] An ordinary least squares regression with these two independent variables produces an equation with $R^2 = .29$ ($n = 160$, sig. $= .00$). The functionalist argument is supported, but less than 30% of the variance is explained, which leads to a quest for further factors that might influence the propensity of states to belong to IGOs.

Since the phenomenon of decolonization proved so important in the growth of the web of IGOs, it could also be an important factor in explaining the propensity of states to belong to IGOs. At the most basic level, the longer a state has had sovereignty the more opportunities it would have had to join IGOs. Since more than 90% of the IGOs in the global political system were established after World War II, it seems appropriate to assume that the exact order of states coming to independence in the nineteenth century or early twentieth century, or even earlier, would have little bearing on their propensity to belong to IGOs in the late twentieth century. Thus years of sovereignty—or of membership in the global political system—are measured starting in 1945. Since the data used in the analysis are for 1981, this independent variable has values from 0 to 37, 0 being for territories that did not have sovereignty in 1981, and 37 being for states that gained sovereignty in 1945 or earlier.

Traditional thought about world politics has always accorded special status to great powers. Given their presumed propensity to be extensively involved in world politics, one would expect greater powers to have more IGO memberships than lesser powers. GNP is the most convenient single indicator of power. The GNP figures used here are also taken from the *World Bank Atlas, 1982*.

Adding date of entry into the global political system and power to the two independent variables used previously sharply improves the explanatory power of the ordinary least squares equation. With the four variables included, the equation is:

IGO Memberships =
$$36.29 + 1.43 \text{ System Years}$$
$$(5.33) \quad (.14)$$
$$+ .002 \text{ Per Capita GNP}$$
$$(.00)$$
$$- 4.43 \text{ Party Competition} + .00002 \text{ GNP}$$
$$(1.34) \qquad\qquad\qquad (.00)$$

$R^2 = .61$; standard error of estimate = 1961; and level of significance = .00. (The partial coefficients are unstandardized; numbers in parentheses are standard errors.)

This equation explains more than 60% of the variance.[8] . . . Years in the global political system is the most powerful predictor. An ordinary least squares regression equation with it as the sole independent variable yields $R^2 = .46$, larger than the R^2 of the equation utilizing the two independent variables suggested by functionalist tenets.

The effects of the four independent variables in the regression equation can be understood more clearly by interpreting the coefficients in terms of the measurement of the independent variables. According to the equation, each additional year a state has been in the global political system increases its total number of IGO memberships by 1.4; each additional 100 dollars in per capita GNP increases the total by 1.8; each step toward a multiparty system increases the total by 4.4; and, each additional 10 billion dollars in GNP increases the total by 1.6. . . .

Functionalism and the
Future Evolution of the Web of IGOs

Functionalism provided a good point of departure for an examination of the multiplying entanglement between states and IGOs in the latter half of the twentieth century. It gave reliable initial guidance about the type of IGOs that would be established, the factors that would propel states toward IGO membership, and the consequences of IGO membership for the economic performance and conflict behavior of states. Yet functionalism fell short of providing a comprehensive explanation. It had to be supplemented by traditional explanations of international politics.

The evolving web of international governmental organizations has modified the global political system, as functionalism argued that it would, but it has not yet radically transformed this system, as functionalism hoped would happen. The radical transformation may yet come. In the meantime, however, international governmental organizations, in addition to modifying the political system, institutionalize aspects of traditional international politics.

The evolution of the web of IGOs has been affected by the broad historical currents of world politics, as well as by the dynamics foreseen by functionalism. Decolonization explains much of what has happened, and surely the exclusive organizations established by both Western states and members of the Soviet group owe their origins in part to the deep rift between these two groupings stemming from the Cold War.

Probably the multiplying entanglement between states and IGOs will continue in the immediate future, and perhaps even at the same dizzying pace. The complexity of modern life creates many pressures for states to establish additional IGOs. What has happened so far demonstrates the overwhelming sense of governments throughout the world that states no longer provide large enough frameworks for tackling pressing problems. As for modalities, there are not many barriers to the continuing generation of IGO offshoots. Finally, simply on the basis of mathematical possibilities, there are enormous opportunities for creating IGOs among Third World states. The regression equation developed here would predict that as the GNP and per capita GNP of Third World states rises, and if the competition of political parties within them increases, the number of IGOs to which each Third World state belongs will increase substantially. If the IGO web were to become as dense in the Third World as it already is in the West, the total number of IGOs would have to be multiplied several times.

The mere statement of these possibilities raises an issue that will have to be faced. The functionalist persuasion was enunciated and became popular before a dense web of IGOs existed; it provided an important impulse toward creating this web. The evolution of the web, however, cannot continue indefinitely on the basis of early basic ideas. States in the contemporary global political system on the average already belong to one IGO for every 356,490 of their inhabitants. The ratio is considerably more extreme for countries with numerically limited populations. For New Zealand it is one IGO for every 42,466; for Cape Verde, one for every 11,571; for Jordan, one for every 43,108; and for Costa Rica, one for every 28,013. Even for as populous a country as the United States, that belongs to fewer than the predicted number of organizations, the ratio is one for every 1,865,900. If the United States finds it administratively trying to formulate constructive policies for the organizations to which it belongs, as it does, what must the situation be like for countries that belong to proportionately more IGOs and have much smaller bureaucracies?

In most countries a relatively small number of bureaucrats along with a few delegates are charged with the responsibility of overseeing the work of and formulating policies for some 60 international governmental organizations. The impossibility of doing these tasks well in such circumstances is obvious. When the majority of states in an IGO are in such a position, the control of the direction of the organization can easily drift to the secretariat or to a minority of activist delegates who can muster majority support. States, and particularly those that provide the greatest financial support, can easily lose control. The United States and other Western countries allege that this has happened in UNESCO, and the U.S. and British withdrawal from UNESCO is a result of deep disagreement with the policies of the organization. Whatever the wisdom of the U.S. and U.K. decisions in this particular instance, there is a general problem. Somehow the multiplying entanglement of states and IGOs will have to take account of administrative realities and possibilities.

Functionalist theory expresses a preference for international governmental organizations becoming relatively autonomous from the states that comprise them. Functionalist theory sees such relatively autonomous IGOs gradually guiding states. UNESCO, which became relatively autonomous, could demonstrate the unreality of this vision. Given the fact of national control over resources, IGOs are at some risk when they ignore the preferences of the most powerful states. To do so may make them irrelevant to contemporary affairs, or, more seriously, could jeopardize their existence.

It is clear that creative ideas that go beyond functionalism are needed to guide the future evolution of the web of international governmental organizations. Such ideas will have to take into account and build on the empirical evidence presented here. Ways need to be discovered for effectively, constructively, and reliably engaging states in the web of IGOs that is continually being woven even more densely.

Notes

1. The *Yearbook* contains information about both international governmental and international nongovernmental organizations. The first edition of the Yearbook was published in 1909, and the most recent in 1983. The information contained in the *Yearbook* comes from responses to a questionnaire sent to the secretariats of international organizations by the Union of International Associations. The amount of information contained in the *Yearbook* about each IGO thus varies. There is a headquarters address for virtually all the IGOs that are listed, the date of founding for almost 80%, the member states for some 50%, the size of the staff for 12%, and the size of the budget for less than 3%.

2. Curiously, the numbers in the summary statistics included in the nineteenth edition do not correspond with the number of organizations that are actually listed. There are more IGOs listed in subcategories D through F of the *Yearbook,* and fewer in categories C and G, than the summary statistics indicate. In addition, some organizations that have been inactive or are dissolved are included in categories B through G of the listing, and as mentioned in the text, these categories also include some IGOs that had been proposed but were not yet in existence in 1981. These latter organizations have been placed in a separate category, I, in the data set.

3. The members of the OECD are Austria, Australia, Belgium, Canada, Denmark, Finland, France, Federal Republic of Germany, Greece, Iceland, Ireland, Italy, Japan, Luxembourg, the Netherlands, New Zealand, Norway, Portugal, Spain, Sweden, Switzerland, Turkey, the United Kingdom, and the United States of America.

4. The members of the Warsaw Treaty Organization for the purposes of this analysis are Bulgaria, the Byelorussia Soviet Socialist Republic, Czechoslovakia, the German Democratic Republic, Hungary, Poland, Romania, the Ukrainian Soviet Socialist Republic, and the Union of Soviet Socialist Republics. Byelorussia and the Ukraine are not formally members of WTO, but they are members of several IGOs, and since they are part of the Soviet Union, which is a member of WTO, it seems appropriate to include them in this category.

5. It includes the 121 states that were members of the Group of 77 in 1981, and 50 other states and territories. Some of the 50 were not independent, but they nevertheless belonged to various IGOs, and thus should not be excluded from analyses. Were they independent, they probably would join the Group of 77, as indeed some of them have done after gaining independence in the years since 1981. The 50 also includes some small European sovereignties and other states such as

Israel, Taiwan, and South Africa that are difficult to classify. All of these states need to be included in some group, and the latter group of states that are difficult to classify resembles the states in the "Other" category with respect to economic characteristics more than it resembles those in the OECD or WTO categories. The categories are used in the descriptions that follow, so that the inclusion of any particular state is not necessary: when IGOs composed exclusively of "Other" states are described, these bodies in fact seldom include those states that are difficult to classify.

6. The members of CMEA are Bulgaria, Cuba, Czechoslovakia, the German Democratic Republic, Hungary, Mongolia, Poland, Romania, the Union of Soviet Socialist Republics, and Vietnam.

7. In this analysis, the term "IGO memberships" is defined as including both full and associate memberships in organizations in both of UIA's categories. States' IGO membership using this inclusive definition correlate almost perfectly the total arrived at using various narrower definitions. The generalizations derived from analyses using the most inclusive definition would also be valid if a more restrictive definition were preferred.

8. Using states' full memberships only in IGOs included in the UIA category of conventional international organizations as the dependent variable yields a very similar equation.

References

Gastil, Raymond D. 1981. The Comparative Survey of Freedom—The Ninth Year. *Freedom at Issue,* 59:3–18.

International Bank for Reconstruction and Development (IBRD). 1982a. *World Bank Atlas, 1982.* Washington, D.C.

Mitrany, David. 1933. *The Progress of International Government.* New Haven: Yale University Press.

Mitrany, David. 1966. *A Working Peace System.* Chicago: Quadrangle.

Union of International Associations (UIA). 1981. *Yearbook of International Organizations, 1981.* 19th ed. Brussels.

Part 3

DECISIONMAKING

THE common public perception of decisionmaking in international organizations is a narrow one. Many see the decision process confined to formal, roll-call votes on symbolic resolutions by member states in a large legislative sessions; the various United Nations General Assembly resolutions are familiar examples that seem to confirm this perception. In this section, we hope to dispel this stereotype and give the reader a more sophisticated view of the activities and processes of international organizations.

The first article in Part 3, by Robert Cox and Harold Jacobson, provides a framework in which to analyze the decisionmaking processes of international organizations. First, it is evident that the decisions and activities of international organizations are not confined to formal votes. Cox and Jacobson present a taxonomy of seven kinds of decisions, which include well-known symbolic actions such as equating Zionism with racism. Yet, they also include supervisory decisions, for example, the International Atomic Energy Agency (IAEA) inspections of nuclear facilities throughout the world.

Just as the decisions of international organizations involve more than symbolic actions, so too does the process of decisionmaking involve more than delegates from member states. Cox and Jacobson also identify a set of seven actors that play roles of varying significance in the decisionmaking process. These actors include the executive heads of international organizations and members of the mass media, in addition to the delegates appointed by their national governments. The actual influence of a particular actor depends on the organization and the situation at hand, but the authors correctly point out that personal attributes of the individual can have a great impact. The dynamic leadership of Dag Hammarskjold was a critical factor in the peacekeeping missions carried out by the United Nations during the late 1950s and early 1960s.

Among the most important actors in the decisionmaking processes of international organizations is the leader of the organization, or the executive head. Former UN Secretary-General Javier Pérez de Cuéllar outlines the various roles and functions played by the leader of the United Nations. Not surprisingly, the Secretary-General has specific duties and powers conferred upon him or her by the United Nations Charter. Yet the charter only briefly refers to these duties and powers. As Pérez de Cuéllar reveals, much of the power of the executive head of the United Nations derives from administrative control over the bureaucracy and from informal powers derived from the prestige attached to the office and the personality characteristics of the person occupying the position. In an international organization in which the members retain the bulk of the power to make and fund decisions, executive heads will be inherently limited in their influence; yet they still may exert an important influence over decisions through persuasion, agenda setting, and implementation.

Although formal voting is not the only aspect of decisionmaking in international organizations, it is often an important component. Many international organizations adhere to the "one state–one vote" standard. This results in a situation whereby micro-states such as Tuvalu have the same theoretical voting strength as the People's Republic of China. In other organizations, such as the International Monetary Fund (IMF) and World Bank, votes are weighted according to criteria such as economic wealth or level of budgetary contribution. At various times, the United States and other Western states have demanded a greater voice in the decisionmaking of the United Nations General Assembly based on the disproportionate amount of the organization's budget contributed by these states. The General Assembly bases its voting allocation on the concept of sovereign equality, the effect of which is that each state receives one vote.

Mirroring the Western demands for voting reform in the UN General Assembly has been the call from many states for changing the composition and voting rules of the UN Security Council. Germany and Japan have clamored for permanent seats on the Security Council based on their strong global economies and financial support of UN activities. Third World countries have sought to expand the number of seats on the Security Council to give themselves a greater say in a body no longer stalemated by the Cold War. Various other proposals would weaken or share the veto power held by the five permanent members. Peter Wallensteen reviews and assesses various proposals for altering the Security Council system. Although there may be several desirable changes among those proposals, any alteration would require an amendment of the UN Charter (only once before has the United Nations altered the composition of the Security Council, increasing the membership to fifteen), something that must be approved by the five permanent members (whose veto could kill any amendments), exactly the states whose power would be diminished by such a change.

5

The Framework for Inquiry

Robert Cox & Harold K. Jacobson

Decision making in international organizations occurs within a context comprising the functions, the institutional framework and basic procedures, and the historical development of the agency. Because both the decision-making processes and the distribution of influence are initially shaped by these factors, considering them is an essential first stage in any analysis.

Given the nature of the international system, the creation of an international organization requires concrete action by states. Usually, although not always, such actions are consecrated in a treaty. In any case, understanding must be achieved about what is to be done and how.

International organizations have been set up to perform a variety of tasks: keeping the peace, promoting economic development, allocating the radio frequency spectrum, reducing obstacles to trade, ensuring that technology is used only for peaceful purposes, and facilitating the maintenance of stable exchange rates—to name only a few. While a certain level of agreement about what it is to do is necessary when an international organization is created, all parties need not share the same conception of the agreement. On the contrary, there are often sharp differences, and these differences can provide essential clues to future dynamic developments in international organizations.

Nor does an agreement about what an organization is to do necessarily represent all the ambitions nursed by the parties to the agreement concerning the ultimate functions of the organization. Many states may look upon international organizations principally as instruments for preserving their hegemony or improving their status. Moreover, personal motives, for example the wish to occupy top jobs, can operate along with considerations of state interests in creating new international agencies. Such motivations as these, whether expressed or unexpressed, are also important in shaping later developments in international organizations.

Whatever their specific tasks and fields of activity, international organizations can be divided into two broad categories according to the way in which they perform these tasks. Some organizations are established to provide a forum or framework for negotiations and decisions, others to provide specific services. This dichotomy establishes two ideal types: the *forum organization* and the *service organization*. Organizations in the first category provide a framework for member states to carry on many different activities ranging from the exchange of views to the negotiation of binding legal instruments. States also often use such forums for the collective legitimation of their policies or for propaganda. Organizations in the second category conduct activities themselves; they provide common or individual services or both. Inclusion in this second group depends upon who conducts the services. If the services are carried out directly by individual states, even though they may have been agreed to within the framework of an international organization, that agency would not belong in the service category. The organization itself must carry out the services. An agency that collects, analyzes, and disseminates information would fit into this category unless the information were intended mainly to facilitate discussions within the framework of the organization, in which case it would be classified as a forum organization.

In reality, of course, many international organizations fall into both categories. ILO, for example, has an extensive technical assistance program, but it also provides a framework for the negotiation of International Labor Conventions. Similarly ITU, UNESCO, WHO, IAEA, and IMF execute services in their own right and at the same time provide frameworks for discussions and negotiations among their member states.

The distinction nevertheless has meaning, and the distribution of an agency's endeavors between the two types of activity may significantly affect patterns of decision making and influence. On the most elementary level, the more an organization leans toward service, the larger its international bureaucracy and the greater the bureaucracy's potential role in certain types of decision making. This classification scheme also provides helpful clues about how an organization can be studied—particularly what bodies of theory developed in other contexts might be most germane. Organizational theory can have great relevance for understanding decision making in service organizations, and the more strongly an agency tends in this direction, the more directly applicable this body of theory is. Conversely, theories about negotiation, such as game theory, can be extremely helpful in analyzing decision-making patterns in forum organizations.

This distinction between forum and service organizations relates to the way in which agencies perform their functions, not to the importance these functions have for member states and not to the authority possessed by the agencies. Whatever their mode of activity, the importance and authority of different organizations varies, and different states perceive them in different terms. An agency that is regarded as crucial by one state may be considered trivial by another, and there is similar variance in the responsiveness of states to the decisions of international organizations. These differences too are important.

They are immediately apparent when one examines the structure of international organizations. The formal powers of the organization and its organs, the extent of regionalism, the forms of representation, the voting procedures, and the organization of the international bureaucracy, all tend to be prescribed at the time an international agency is formed. The initial understanding about how an international organization is to perform its functions inevitably represents compromises among conflicting points of view; all parties must be given some incentives to participate. If an organization is to have functions that might affect significant values, those in control of these values will generally demand structural and procedural devices to ensure for themselves the means of exerting special influence. How far they will press their demands and how successful they will be will depend upon the configuration of forces they face at the time. They might be dissuaded from pressing their claims too far by actual and potential counterclaims in the same functional area or in another. In general, the broader the mandate of the organization, the more likely will be such counterclaims. Conscience or conceptions of long-run self-interest can also serve as moderating forces. Whatever the outcome, these initial understandings provide the basic rules for subsequent decision making.

In some instances the parties to an agreement establishing an international organization will not only prescribe the structures and procedures for decision making but also attempt to specify doctrines according to which decisions should be taken. Thus the constitutional documents of IMF and GATT contain detailed codes of conduct, and the charters of several other international agencies tend in this direction. The more they lean toward such specification, the more the organizations' activities are likely to be set in a particular mold and the harder it will be to shift their direction.

Regardless of the rigidity of their charters, though, once international organizations are established, in many instances they evolve in ways that could not have been foreseen by their founders. To some extent this is because the interests and intentions of the member states change over time, sometimes because of developments within states or in relations among states. Moreover, states may modify their interests and intentions with respect to international organizations as a consequence of participation in them. As in other contexts interaction among actors can result in changed views. In addition, international bureaucracies created to serve international organizations may add new ambitions to those of the states: from the pursuit of specific technical goals the aim might be extended to the desire to make international relations more peaceful or to redistribute the wealth between rich and poor countries. Thus, once established, organizations take on a life of their own and develop their own inner dynamics.

Many of the major changes that take place in international organizations can be identified and measured in terms of the organizations' activities and accomplishments. An organization may change in its functions, either with respect to subject matter—by adding new areas of action or abandoning old ones—or with respect to modes of action—by switching, for example, from forum to service activities. Changes in functions can be traced in the programs of international organizations. There may be changes in the scale of operations, significant increases or, though not so likely, decreases in programs, for which budgets may provide an indicator. There may also be changes in the authority of an organization, either because members become more responsive to its decisions or because the organization begins to make enactments of a new kind that place more demands upon members. There is no necessary correlation between growth in scale and growth in authority; an organization's budget might grow at the same time that its importance for member states or its authority declined. Finally, there may be changes in the relative importance of an international organization within the issue-area or areas with which it is concerned. The extent to which the organization performs essential functions within the issue-area is relevant here. The existence or creation of another rival organization with overlapping jurisdiction would be an indication of significant change in this respect. Changes of the kinds suggested here may be explained by changes in membership of the organization, in the top personnel of the organization's bureaucracy, in the matters preoccupying member states, or in the new currents of ideas that may emerge.

Changes may be gradual, but one must watch for sudden discontinuities in an organization's history, significant changes in direction that could be termed turning points. Such turning points might occur in relation to any of the features mentioned in the previous paragraph—functions, scale, authority, or importance in the issue-area. They may also arise from dramatic and important changes in input—for example, in the intentions of major participants or in the membership of the organization. What constitutes a turning point is the abruptness, the unpredictability of a significant change, "an impulse which breaks through, untrammelled by the past."[1] . . .

Decision Making: A Taxonomical Analysis

Once the context provided by the functions, structure, and historical evolution of an agency is known, one can begin to consider patterns of decision making and the distribution of influence. For this purpose it is useful to classify decisions. . . .

This taxonomy divides decisions of international organizations into seven categories: representational, symbolic, boundary, programmatic, rule-creating, rule-supervisory, and operational.

Representational decisions affect membership in the organization and representation on internal bodies. They include decisions concerning the admission and exclusion of members, validation of credentials, determination of representation on executive organs and committees, and the manner in which the secretariat is composed, especially at the higher level.

Symbolic decisions are primarily tests of how opinions are aligned; no practical consequences in the form of actions flow directly from these decisions. The intention in symbolic issues is to test the acceptability of goals or ideologies intensely espoused by one group of actors or the legitimacy of long accepted norms of dominant elites. In some cases these goals or ideologies may relate to broad issues of international politics, in others, to matters specific to the organization's field. In an organization with a mandate in the economic field, decolonization might be an example of a broad issue; improving the lot of developing countries would be an example of a goal specifically related to an organization. Some decisions that might fall within the definitions of other categories may be considered primarily symbolic; but as soon as the direct consequences of the decisions become appreciable, as for example in the controversies over the representation and participation of the communist states in ILO, these decisions fall into another category, in this instance, representational. The criteria for classification as symbolic are thus: the positive one of symbolic intention on the part of the decision makers; and the negative one of the absence of significant practical consequences flowing directly from the decision. The absence of direct consequences does not mean that symbolic decisions are unimportant. On the contrary, in the long run they may have profound consequences because of their effects on the milieu within which international relations are conducted.

This category of decisions can be singled out in order to test the hypothesis that symbolic issues tend to become acute during periods when the organization is adjusting to major changes in the environment that may entail shifts in the structure of influence and in the basic goals and policies of the organization. Such decisions may thus provide a particularly sensitive measure of changes in the internal distribution of influence.

Boundary decisions concern the organization's external relations with other international and regional structures on the matter of (1) their respective scopes, (2) cooperation among organizations, and (3) initiatives taken in one organization to provoke activity in another. . . . GATT and UNCTAD share overlapping jurisdictions, and to a lesser extent the same situation also exists among other organizations. When this occurs, boundary problems inevitably arise.

Programmatic decisions concern the strategic allocation of the organization's resources among different types of activity—the principal types are forum or service—and different fields of activity, which tend to be specific to each individual agency. Allocations usually result from negotiations among the actors concerning the main goals and division of emphasis among the programs of the organization. Budgets are often the framework within which the programmatic decisions are taken.

Rule-creating decisions define rules or norms bearing upon matters within the substantive scope of the organization. The outcome of the decisions may in some cases be formal instruments such as conventions, agreements, or resolutions. Illustrations of decisions covered in this category include GATT's activity in the negotiation of agreements for tariff reductions, the establishment of Special Drawing Rights by the IMF, as well as the preparing of labor and health conventions by ILO and WHO. Rules may also be created in less formal ways; for example, speeches by the executive head or others that may never explicitly be the subject of votes may nonetheless articulate widely shared norms or goals with which the organization may come to be identified in the minds of many of its constituents. Such actions may in significant cases be considered as rule-creating decisions.

Some rule-creating decisions may resemble programmatic decisions because they seem to imply that certain priorities should be followed in making allocations; but decisions are considered to be programmatic only when they include a definition of priorities specifically for purposes of allocation, or, as is more usual, when they make an actual allocation in terms of budget or personnel.

Rule-supervisory decisions concern the application of approved rules by those subject to them. These decisions may involve various procedures ranging from highly structured to extremely subtle ones. The process of rule supervision passes through several stages, and organizations may develop distinct procedures for each of these stages.[2] The first stage is detection or gathering information about the observance or ignoring of rules. For example, are states complying with the frequency allocations agreed to within ITU? the standards set in International Labor Conventions? the safeguard provisions of IAEA? or the nondiscriminatory trading rules of GATT? Detection may be performed by states acting unilaterally or jointly, by the international bureaucracy, by a private panel, or by some combination of these.

Verifying whether or not the rules are observed is the second stage. This function may also be performed in various ways. Decisions could be entrusted to experts, to the international bureaucracy, or to representatives of member states, to list the most obvious alternatives. Proceedings could be public or private.

The final stage in rule supervision is applying sanctions or punishments for the violation of rules or awarding privileges for compliance with them. As in the other stages decisions about penalties and rewards can be made in several ways.

Operational decisions relate to the providing of services by the organization or the use of its resources in accordance with approved rules, policies, or programs. Examples are decisions about projects for specific technical assistance undertaken by UNESCO or other agencies or the granting of loans by IMF. They are essentially tactical allocations of resources made within broad strategic (programmatic) allocations. Frequently, such tactical, operational decisions are made largely between representatives of individual states and the international bureaucracy. In such decisions criteria referring to the pursuit of general goals may be diluted as a consequence of pressures for services and the need to retain clients' support.

Operational decisions may lead cumulatively to programmatic decisions. The inclusion of a program in an agency budget may be the culmination of a process in which the initiative came originally from an operational decision by the executive head or a segment of the international bureaucracy.

The extent to which operational decisions are effectively subordinated to programmatic decisions may indicate the degree of control that the executive head exercises over the bureaucracy. Weak control may lead to a dispersal of activities, which strengthens the relations between particular clients and segments of the bureaucracy but weakens the overall directing of resources. Strong control may give the executive head greater initiative to enlarge the tasks and enhance the autonomy of the organization.

In order to describe how decisions are usually arrived at for each of these categories of decision in a particular international organization, it will be useful to classify the actors involved, to consider the ways in which they may exercise influence, and to list the modes of decision making that may be employed.

The actors in international organizations may be classified according to the following categories:

1. Representatives of national governments (who may be appointed by various ministries)
2. Representatives of national and international private associations (including interest groups and commercial enterprises)
3. The executive heads of organizations
4. High officials and other members of the bureaucracy of each organization
5. Individuals who serve in their own capacity formally or informally as advisers
6. Representatives of other international organizations
7. Employees of the mass media

Of course, not all of these classes of actors will be active in all organizations. For each category of decisions, however, the actors will fall into one or more of these classes, and it is important to know which of these categories of actors typically have the most influence on the outcome. . . .

Actors and Their Source of Influence

As conceived in this study, the actors are individuals who participate directly in the decisions of an international organization. The power of actors—that is, their capacity to exercise influence—is derived both from their position or office and from their personal characteristics. The representatives of some states or the occupants of some positions within international organizations will be important in certain decisions regardless of who they are. Even in these cases, though, the personal characteristics of individuals can enhance or diminish the power that would normally accrue to someone in their position. For example, Ambassador Goldberg had considerable power in the United Nations because he was the United States representative, but some of his power was also attributable to his personal qualities and skills as a negotiator and to his political connections.

Position includes as potentiality the resources of the collectivity represented by the individual and the priority given by the authorities of the collectivity to the use of these resources for influence in the organization. These resources can be of different orders: states may possess economic and military strength, which may be accorded deference in certain decisions; high international officials may command information and recognition, which allows them the initiative in proposing action or resolving conflict. Every position also carries with it its own history of previous attitudes and actions that predispose the behavior of the incumbent in certain directions; it includes also certain limitations in the form of binding instructions imposed by higher authorities in the collectivities represented.

Personal characteristics include skills necessary to carry out the duties and exploit the possibilities of a position: mobilizing the resources of the collectivity represented to achieve influence in the organization, shaping instructions for performing the duties of the position, and influencing the behavior of other actors.

An actor's power or his capacity to exercise influence is thus compounded of his position and his personal attributes. For the sake of clarity the relationship can be expressed in symbolic form:

$$P \pm A = C$$

Position or office (P) modified by (in this formula, plus or minus) personal attributes (A) equals the power or the capacity (C) of the individual actor. C is a function of P and also a function of A, but P and A vary independently.

Although the form in which this symbolic statement is written assumes that A will add to or detract from P, in some circumstances the relationship may be multiplicative or more complex. This equation is not intended to create an illusion of precise mathematical treatment. Some of the concepts have not been, and probably cannot be, represented in a numerical form that would lend itself to mathematical application.

Among the personal attributes that might enhance an individual's power in an international organization are his personal charisma, ideological legitimacy, administrative competence, expert knowledge, long association with an organization, negotiating ability, and ability to persist in intransigence. The personal status he has acquired outside the organization through such things as wealth, election to an important office, scientific achievements, and possession of significant influence in an important collectivity will also affect his power. The advantages of these personal attributes vary with organizations. For example, negotiating ability might be especially valuable in organizations like GATT where consensus must be achieved, while the ability to persist in intransigence might be a telling factor in UNCTAD if the outcome was to be a declaratory resolution.

An actor's power attributable to his position may be represented symbolically here as:

$$X_C (G \pm S) = P$$

That is, the capability of the position of an actor (P) is a function of the priority (X_C) that the authorities of the collectivity attach to converting their capabilities in international affairs generally (G), as modified by their capabilities in the specific field of the organization in question (S) into influence in the organization. This anticipates somewhat the discussion of the components of the general and the specific capabilities of states to be presented in the next section, dealing with the environment, but it should be noted here that other kinds of power besides material power are included. Thus this symbolic statement can be used for other collectivities as well as states.

Substituting the components of the actor's position for P, the symbolic statement for an actor's power is:

$$X_C (G + S) \pm A = C$$

Like the authorities of the collectivities they represent, actors also exercise judgment about the conversion of their capabilities into influence. Here, we are referring to active influence in the sense discussed in the previous section. For both the individual actor and the authorities of the collectivity, the decision whether or not they should seek to use available resources to gain influence will depend upon several factors, including the intensity of their feelings about the issues at stake and their estimates of the probability and the costs of obtaining their goals. In estimating such probabilities actors make assumptions about the influence of others as well as about the likely extent of opposition and support. If they seek to exercise influence, the degree of their success will depend on how all the other influences within the organization are distributed on the issue at stake. For example, when faced with a united opposition, the representative of a powerful state might find it impossible to achieve an objective, whereas in other circumstances he would succeed easily.

Obviously, the influence that an individual actor actually exercises in an international organization may differ considerably from his capacity or power. Putting it in abbreviated fashion, the influence of an individual actor (I) is the result of his power (C) as modified by his decision to attempt to convert his power into influence (X_a) and by the distribution of all other influences within the organization on a particular issue (D). Symbolically, this can be expressed as:

$$X_a \cdot C \cdot D = I$$

The distribution of all other influences includes the pattern of alignments on a particular issue, as well as how other actors feel about it, the weight of their opinions, and their power. Thus it includes those who would support, oppose, or be indifferent. It also includes the deference accorded to the actor in question by other actors.

As the focal point of analysis shifts from the capacities of actors to their influence, attention must be given to their attitudes and perceptions and more broadly to process. Attitudes and perceptions are crucially important factors affecting actors' behavior; they have an effect, among other things, on whether or not the actors will seek to convert their capacities into influence. Process, the working out of strategies to obtain goals, the building of alliances, coalitions, and consensus, determines the configuration of forces within an organization.

The fundamental questions concerning attitudes and perceptions are how actors see the organization in question and how they understand its purposes and potentialities, particularly in terms of their own interests and objectives. The distribution and interplay between personal goals and public goals must be investigated in this connection. Personal goals involve such things as jobs, prestige, and tourism. There is every reason to suspect that personal goals play as great a part in international as in national or local politics. Public goals include those relating to both the substantive concerns of the organization and the interests of the collectivities that the actors represent. Concern for survival and growth of the organization as a whole or of subunits might be derived either from public or personal goals. Actors may have different points of view formed by their experience and professional training, as lawyers, economists, scientists, or engineers, for example, which mold their attitudes in certain directions. Actors may be grouped according to common perceptions of the organization and according to the intensity of their commitment to the organization and its goals.

A particularly significant case of regularities in perceptions and attitudes takes the form of organizational ideology. As defined here, an organizational ideology would contain—

1. An interpretation of the environment as it relates to action by the organization
2. Specification of goals to be attained in the environment
3. A strategy of action for attaining these goals

Organization ideologies might be narrow or broad. Functionalism is an ideology that is applicable to international organizations representing a variety of objectives. (The precise nature of these objectives is largely irrelevant, but they must be specific.) Functionalism stresses developing collaboration among states with regard to specific objectives as a means of gradually eroding the authority of nation-states in favor of world institutions. Marxist and populist ideologies compete with functionalism as other broad interpretations of the aims and strategies of international organizations. International organizations are seen in the Marxist view as expressing power relations between socialist and capitalist blocs; to the populist, they appear as a means of exerting pressure by the numerous poor upon the few rich. Along with these broad organizational ideologies are narrower and more task-oriented ideologies. Thus "education for development" is an ideology of UNESCO and to some extent ILO, and nondiscrimination or the most favored nation are ideologies of GATT and IMF. It is of interest to ascertain whether such organizational ideologies exist, how they came into being, and how widely they are shared. Other important questions are whether they are especially linked with certain actors, whether they are publicized, and whether competing organizational ideologies exist.

Perceptions and attitudes are particularly important in identifying who pushes for what. No one assumes, however, that attitudes and perceptions impel actors in only one direction. On the contrary, actors may often be subject to conflicting pressures, and one of the reasons why special attention is given to organizational ideologies is to see the extent to which these pressures act counter to other motivational forces. A particularly interesting question is whether dual loyalties emerge with some actors, leading them not only to represent the views of their collectivity in the organization but also to exert influence on their collectivity in line with the consensus reached by the organization or in conformity with organizational ideology.

The formal structures and procedures of the organization are the institutional constraints within which the strategies of the actors are developed.

But when attitudes are translated into strategies within these formal constraints, the actors create additional and often informal structures.

These structures created in the political process itself may be studied in various ways. In the first place, we look for persistent groupings of actors.[3] These may be formal groupings such as caucuses or informal networks involving an in-group or establishment of actors who occupy key positions and who normally consult among each other about important decisions. Persistent groupings may enhance or decrease the possibility of an individual actor's exercising influence. An actor may find it easier to attain his objectives because of his membership in a coalition, or an opposing coalition may place obstructions in his path.

Such groupings determine, secondly, the configurations of influence within organizations, which may take forms approximating (1) unanimity; (2) one dominant coalition, possibly led by a dominant actor; (3) polarization between two rival coalitions; (4) a larger number of alliances, none of which dominates; or (5) crosscutting cleavages on different issues with no general pattern. The coalition policies of executive heads and members of international bureaucracies, as well as those of national representatives, are important factors determining these configurations.

Finally, there is the identification of elites made up of influential individual participants, elites that cut across groupings and configurations and thus show the stratification of influence in the organization. It is by knowing who is most influential that we can infer which resources are the most significant determinants of influence. . . .

The purpose of trying to measure influence goes beyond simply wishing to know which particular actors have the most influence at any particular time. Finding out more about the characteristics and sources of influence of each of the most influential actors is one step toward inferring more generally the relative importance of different sources of influence in different international organizations. What other sources of influence compete most effectively with a position as representative of a powerful state? In which organizations do administrative competency or expert ability carry most weight? Which give preeminence to ideological legitimacy, that is, the definition and articulation of an ideological position, whether in the form of an organizational ideology or of one of the major ideologies of world politics?

Analyzing the backgrounds of the most influential actors and the roads they have followed to gain influence should give some clues to the relative importance of various personal attributes and should help to single out the positions or offices that are most likely to be springboards to influence. In some organizations these may be membership on the executive board; in others, posts in the secretariat. Some study of persons without influence may also be revealing, particularly if they might have been expected to be influential because of their positions. . . .

Environmental Impacts

The next step is to isolate that influence which is attributable to environment. International organizations are aspects of international relations or more broadly of world politics. To understand international organizations we must devise a framework that will make the decisions and actions taken through them intelligible in the context of events where they originate and which they may affect. International organizations are thought of in this study as systems that are not fully autonomous, but rather are subject to environmental forces that become major constraints upon the determinants of decisions.

These decisions, it is assumed, will reflect a pattern of expectations and demands that can be perceived in the world situation, for example, the desire of states for greater security from external violence or for freedom from unilateral domination by one powerful country, or the desire for redistribution of the world's resources or for widespread acceptance of some particular principles of political organization or ideology. The pattern of expectations and demands—in particular, the relative strength of different demands—and the extent of compatibility or of conflict among different demands—is in turn assumed to be determined by certain objectively ascertainable conditions in the world, including the relative military and economic power of states, their level of economic development and social mobilization, governmental effectiveness, and the basic principles of organization of different polities.

Three major variables describe the general environment: the stratification of state power, the economic and political characteristics of states, and the patterns of alignment and conflict among states. . . . In the consideration of the first variable it is assumed that some relationship exists between the power of a state in international affairs generally and its power in international organizations. Since power is a primary factor in influence, there is likely to be a connection between a state's power in relation to other states and its influence in international organizations generally. The point of considering the stratification of power is to explore this relationship. We would expect the United States and the USSR, as powerful states, to have greater influence than Canada, Sweden, or India in any international organization, irrespective of its functional field; and we would expect Canada, Sweden, or India to have greater influence over decisions than Nicaragua, Gabon, or Cambodia.

The second major variable in the description of the general environment is the distribution of states according to their economic and political characteristics. Here it is assumed that the economic development of a state is important in determining the demands the state will place on an international organization, especially the type and priority of services demanded—for example, whether it would prefer an organization to be a clearinghouse for information or an agency for redistributing the world's wealth.

It has also frequently been assumed that the internal polity of a state affects such aspects of its behavior in international organizations as its style of participation, its degree of commitment to the organizations, and its responsiveness to their decisions. International organizations have sometimes been seen as the creations of democratic states in their own image. Their assemblies have been compared figuratively with the elected assemblies of democratic polities—as parliaments of mankind. The ideals of international organization have been seen as the logical extension of the ideals of democracy—universal respect for the rights of the individual and the need to provide opportunities for his social fulfillment. But in practice can we find any discernible differences in the way democratic and non-democratic states behave in and toward international organizations? . . .

Two dimensions of polities are particularly significant. In the first place, it is important to know whether the polity is democratic in the sense that there is a regularly accepted and reasonably orderly competition for political power. Second, when countries cannot be described as democratic in this sense, it is important to know whether the state is one that is in the hands of a revolutionary group seeking to mobilize the population with the aim of transforming society to fit its own ideology or whether it belongs in a third class, those where a more conservative group holds the reins and is preserving in broad outlines the existing structure of social power and wealth. These three types are called *competitive, mobilizing,* and *authoritarian.* It should be stressed that the criteria distinguishing them relate to internal politics, not to external alignments. The classification is designed to help uncover any meaningful relations between the internal character of the state's polity and its external behavior, particularly in international organizations.

Another set of questions arises in this connection. It has often been thought characteristic of revolutionary governments that they use foreign policy issues as a means of mobilizing domestic support. Will it, then, be found that the mobilizing regimes are most active in initiating and supporting symbolic decisions in international organizations? Will these regimes be more concerned than others that symbolic decisions and rule-creating or rule-supervisory decisions conform with their ideologies?

It may be assumed that authoritarian regimes care less whether the positions they take in international organizations reflect the characteristics of the regime. They can tolerate a hiatus between the principles they formally support in an international forum and their practices at home precisely because their populations are not mobilized and articulate on the issues involved, and the regimes are not seeking to mobilize them. Ideological consistency will thus be less important for authoritarian regimes than for polities concerned with mobilization. In regard to competitive polities, it is often assumed that such polities are more penetrable, "open" societies and thus more likely to acquiesce in the authority of international organizations. There is more likelihood that groups within these societies will protest failures to observe international obligations. . . .

Patterns of conflicts and alignments on major world political and ideological issues constitute the third variable used to describe the general environment. It is assumed that these patterns will have some effect on decision making in international organizations even when the subject matter of particular decisions may seem remote from the conflicts in which world political alignments originated. For example, many technical issues have acquired political overtones because of the East-West conflict. On the other hand, classical functionalist theory would have predicted that the more technical an issue is the more likely the chances are of avoiding the complications of politics. Thus the exact effect of these patterns on particular types of decisions at particular times and in particular organizations has to be considered.

Most international organizations also operate in the context of an environment that is specific to the organization. For example, decision making in GATT is undoubtedly affected by the position of states in the world economy—their share in world trade and the proportion of their GNP derived from trade. The specific environment is conceived in quite broad terms to include such things as technological developments affecting communications in the case of ITU, and articulated bodies of opinion like labor movements in that of ILO. Two concepts developed with regard to the general environment can be applied to the specific environment: the stratification of power (or capabilities) and the pattern of alignments and conflicts. . . .

The environment specific to an international organization may be either linked with or independent of the general environment. In most instances there is probably some relationship, but its strength will vary with different fields. The relation between decision making and the general specific environments can be examined empirically. One or the other could be more important, and the specific environment could act as an intervening variable. . . . Just as each organization has a specific environment, so it may be argued has each issue-area, or even—at the limit—each decision. The concept of specific environment can be applied with some flexibility.

Notes

1. The phrase is from Geoffrey Barraclough, *History in a Changing World* (Oxford: Basil Blackwell, 1955), pp. 183–84. Barraclough was referring to "three great turning points when European society swung upwards on to a new plane" (p. 79). The same concept can be applied in the microcosmic history of international organizations.

2. The stages outlined here were suggested by the work of Fred C. Iklé. See especially his *Alternative Approaches to the International Organization of Disarmament* (Santa Monica, Calif.: RAND Corporation, 1962).

3. Various attempts have already been made to identify groupings. See especially Chadwick F. Alger, "Interaction in a Committee of the United Nations General Assembly," in *Quantitative International Politics,* ed. J. David Singer (New York: Free Press, 1968), pp. 51–84; Arend Lijphart, "The Analysis of Bloc Voting in the General Assembly," *American Political Science Review* 57 (December 1963): 902–17; and Bruce M. Russett, "Discovering Voting Groups in the United Nations," *American Political Science Review* 60 (June 1966): 327–39. However, neither participants' observations of interactions in a committee room nor the analysis of roll call votes, the two techniques involved in these attempts, fully measures what is involved in the concept of persistent groupings of actors used here. Among other things neither gives adequate attention to actors who are not representatives of states.

6

The Role of the UN Secretary-General

Javier Pérez de Cuéllar

I shall try to discuss the role of the Secretary-General regardless of who may be Secretary-General at any point in time. Men come and go, but institutions remain. The Charter of the United Nations contains a chapter (Chapter XV) devoted to the Secretariat. It consists of Articles 97 to 101. It assigns two different functions to the Secretary-General: one political and the other administrative. The political function, though much studied and discussed, has never been very precisely defined. The way it is used depends on the state of international relations at the time and also on the political character of the Secretary-General—on his (or, one day, perhaps, her) courage, prudence, and fidelity to the aims of the Charter. This elasticity, if I may call it that, is not peculiar to this office: in varying degrees, it occurs in any institution which has to respond to the complexity of human affairs.

The Secretary-General's Political Functions

Anyone who has the honour to be cast as Secretary-General has to avoid two extremes in playing his, or her, role. On one side is the Scylla of trying to inflate the role through too liberal a reading of the text: of succumbing, that is, to vanity and wishful thinking. On the other is the Charybdis of trying to limit the role to only those responsibilities which are explicitly conferred by the Charter and are impossible to escape: that is, succumbing to modesty, to the instinct of self-effacement, and to the desire to avoid controversy. There are, thus, temptations on both sides.

Both are equally damaging to the vitality of the institution. I submit that no Secretary-General should give way to either of them.

The first, the temptation to aggrandizement, can discredit the institution of Secretary-General, and thus the organization as a whole, because it can lead the Secretary-General into courses of action which are not realistically sustainable. When, because of lack of support from the Security Council or the General Assembly, these courses of action have to be abandoned or reversed, the prestige of the organization is bound to suffer. The second, the temptation to extreme caution, can be equally discredited because situations can, and do, arise when the Secretary-General has to exercise his powers to the full, as the bearer of a sacred trust, and as the guardian of the principles of the Charter. Moreover, in choosing the safer course, he risks causing, through disuse, paralysis of the peacemaking and other functions which the Charter vests in him.

The political functions of the Secretary-General are defined in Articles 98 and 99.[1] These authorize him, respectively, to make an annual report to the General Assembly on the work of the organization, and to bring to the attention of the Security Council any matter which, in his opinion, may threaten the maintenance of international peace and security. These functions cannot be fully understood unless we first identify how the Secretary-General fits into the scheme envisaged in the Charter.

Article 7 designates the Secretariat as one of what the founding fathers chose to call the principal organs of the UN. The Secretariat, in turn, is described in Article 97 as comprising a Secretary-General *and* such staff as the organization might require. However, it is the Secretary-General who appoints the staff and it is he alone who is accountable to the member states for the work of the Secretariat. This means that he is co-responsible with the other organs (the General Assembly, the Security Council, and so on) for achieving the organization's aims and purposes. He has thus a dual capacity: in addition to acting as chief administrative officer in the meetings of the General Assembly, the Security Council, the Economic and Social Council, and the Trusteeship Council, he has the independent responsibilities of 'a principal organ'. This may seem a rather fine constitutional point, but failure to understand it can have an adverse effect on attitudes and policies towards the UN.

Misunderstanding can arise from the associations of the word 'secretary' as used in such expressions as the secretary of a committee. Many of the founders of the UN wanted to give a different designation to the occupant of this office. Franklin Roosevelt wished to call him the World's Moderator;[2] some others proposed having a President and a Director-General for the UN.[3] This gives rise to a question: in choosing the less high-sounding and more conventional term 'Secretary-General', and in entrusting to one person the leadership of the political, administrative, and constitutional functions of the Secretariat, did the framers of the Charter wish to limit the Secretary-General's rights and duties to those given to his predecessor in the League of Nations? I am sure that the answer is no. For they departed radically from the Covenant of the League by including Article 99 and part of Article 98, and thereby giving the Secretary-General the authority to take the initiative in apprising the Security Council of potential threats to international peace and security, and to make an annual report to the General Assembly.

This was not a fortuitous development. On the contrary, it was dictated by the experience of the League of Nations. The League's Covenant, and its practice, were based on a purely administrative conception of the post of Secretary-General. The calamitous events which led to the Second World War revealed that this had been a mistake. A dangerous void had existed: in a situation of dissent and disarray among the European powers, there was no one who could speak for the wider international interest, an interest greater than the sum of the interests of the member states. There was no one in a position to initiate timely intervention by the League to avert the collapse of the international system. The framers of the Charter were most anxious not to let such a void occur again. This explains the difference between Article 6 of the League Covenant and Articles 97 to 101 of the UN Charter. Sir Eric Drummond, the first Secretary-General of the League, is said to have remarked that if Article 99 of the Charter had been at his disposal, the position of his office—and, by implication, the influence of the League on events—would have developed differently.

Let me now return to Articles 98 and 99 of the Charter. Article 98 is the constitutional basis on which the Secretary-General makes an annual report to the General Assembly on the work of the organization. This is not meant to be, and should never become, a mere rapporteur's job: 'the work of the organization' is a broad term. It includes, but is not confined to, whatever the organization has done, or had failed to do, or is required to do. Its submission is one of the ways in which the Secretary-General can act as an initiator and can galvanize the efforts of the other parts of the UN. I myself have sought to give a thematic focus to the annual reports submitted during my mandate. . . . [4]

As for Article 99 of the Charter, this, as I have said, authorizes the Secretary-General to bring to the attention of the Security Council any matter which in his opinion may threaten the maintenance of international peace and security. This authority contains the three elements of right, responsibility, and discretion. The Secretary-General's right is apparent from the wording and has never been the subject of dispute. However, the other two elements—responsibility and discretion—are interrelated. In considering them, it is worth bearing in mind that, when the Charter was being drafted, a proposal to amend the Article so as to make its invocation a *duty* of the Secretary-General had to be withdrawn.[5]

Before invoking the Article, the Secretary-General has to consider carefully how his initiative will fare, given the agreement or lack thereof among the Permanent Members and also the positions of the Non-permanent Members. A situation may in certain cases be aggravated and not eased if the Secretary-General draws attention, under Article 99, and the Security Council then does nothing. Situations that threaten the peace are usually highly complicated and require a flexible and finely tuned response from the Secretary-General. Hence the discretion allowed him by Article 99. Two situations with equally dangerous potential may have to be dealt with in two different ways, depending on how far they can be insulated from great power rivalries, how far the parties are susceptible to moral suasion, and, in some cases, whether one or both of them is reluctant to face exposure in the Security Council. It is worth adding that the possibility that invocation of Article 99 might displease a member state, whether or not a party to the dispute, most certainly ought *not* to be a consideration inhibiting the Secretary-General.

I have said earlier that the chastening failure of the League of Nations was much in the mind of the drafters of the UN Charter. Article 99 makes it clear that they envisage the Secretary-General, in addition to his other functions, as someone with the power to anticipate and prevent crises. The words 'in his opinion' and 'may threaten' clearly signify, first, that the right vested in him can be exercised in relation not only to actual but also to potential causes of conflict; and, second, that he is expected to evaluate constantly and independently all matters which have a bearing on peace and security. It is also noteworthy that the Article uses the much broader term 'matter' and not 'situation or dispute'. The term covers all developments which (to quote the words of the Preparatory Commission of the United Nations) 'could have serious political implications remediable only by political action'.

The Secretary-General is thus given a reservoir of authority, a wide margin of discretion, which requires the most careful political judgement and is limited only by prudence. The ways in which this authority would be exercised and this discretion used could not have been anticipated at the time the Charter was framed. Nor did the drafters of the Charter foresee the circumstances in which Article 99 would be invoked. They had relied on a scheme of collective security predicated on agreement among the Permanent Members of the Security Council. When this basic assumption of great power unanimity broke down, indecision or inaction in the Council was often the result. Over the years, therefore, the practice grew for the Secretary-General himself to help to moderate conflicts or negotiate solutions, without, of course, detracting in any way from the Council's primary role. This kind of action by the Secretary-General does not necessarily require a formal invocation of Article 99. In my own experience, it has usually had to be discharged without such invocation. A topical instance is the reported use of chemical weapons in the Iran-Iraq war.[6]

Article 99 is concerned with action by the Secretary-General *vis-à-vis* the Security Council. He is given comparable powers *vis-à-vis* the General Assembly by the rule which accords him the right to place on the Assembly's provisional agenda all items which he deems necessary.[7] In both these cases, this function of the Secretary-General is not merely an attribute of his office but also one of the essential ways in which the UN can respond to the demands of the international situation. In the present state of international affairs, the Security Council is often unable to adopt a resolution because of division among its Permanent Members. Equally often, it makes a recommendation which is rejected by one of the parties, or it adopts a resolution which is not supported, or is perceived as not being supported, by some important states directly or indirectly involved. In all such cases, the Secretary-General has to act as the main intermediary between the parties, and to help pave the way, if he can, for an eventual accommodation or agreement between them. . . . In such efforts, the Secretary-General has to improvise, and may sometimes feel compelled to suggest means other than those which had been envisaged by the Security Council in its original discussions of the matter. The same is true with the General Assembly. Controversy often persists after the Assembly adopts a resolution. Here again, it becomes the duty of the Secretary-General to ensure, as far as he can, that the parties remain open to dialogue.

A caveat, however, must be entered here. It is of great importance that trust should be placed in the Secretary-General by the Security Council, by the General Assembly, and by governments, but delegation of responsibility to him should not be a way for member states to escape the responsibilities placed on them by the Charter. We must cling to the Charter concept of collective action for peace and security, and we must do nothing to weaken the chances of eventually putting it into practice. It cannot be repeated too often that it is the Security Council which bears the primary responsibility for such action. Disharmony between the different organs does not help the effective development of the UN. Moreover, it would gravely harm the interests of peace if the Secretary-General were ever to become a façade, behind which there was only deadlock and disagreement. He must not become an alibi for inaction. No authority delegated to the Secretary-General, and no exercise by him of this authority, can fill the existing vacuum in collective security. This vacuum is due to dissension among the Permanent Members of the Security Council, to the failure of member states to resort to the Charter's mechanisms for the settlement of disputes, and to their lack of respect for the decisions of the Security Council.

When the Secretary-General exercises his good offices, under the specific mandates given him, and within the general purview of Article 33 of the Charter, which requires the parties to a dispute to seek a solution by peaceful means, the UN is using quiet diplomacy, the diplomacy of reconciliation. There does not seem to be enough appreciation of the advantages of the UN in this respect. This is indicated by the many instances today where the UN is bypassed.

Multilateral diplomacy of the kind in which the Secretary-General is frequently engaged differs from traditional diplomacy in several ways. As it is conducted in accordance with the principles of the Charter, it does not place the weaker party in an unfavourable position. It seeks an objective and lasting settlement of a dispute and not merely one which responds to the expediencies of the day. In a multilateral approach, all the member states of the UN have a direct or indirect influence: this can assure, as much as anything can, that the vital interests of all parties are taken into account. Such an approach can spot points of potential agreement which may not be obvious at first sight or in the context of power-political interests. The aim of traditional diplomacy was often limited to a stable balance of power: whether the balance conformed to justice was a lesser concern. But peace as envisaged by the UN Charter is a just peace: take that moral dimension away and we are back to the disorder and the injustice of power politics.

If quiet diplomacy is to succeed, it needs the confidence of all parties. And that means that the Secretary-General must not only be impartial but must be perceived to be so. He must not allow his independence of judgement to be impaired or distorted by pressures from governments. He should have no part in any diplomatic deal or undertaking which ignores the principles of the Charter or the relevant pronouncements of the competent organs of the UN.

However, moral concern must not become moral hubris. The Secretary-General must not allow himself to be influenced by his own judgement of the moral worth of either party's position or, for that matter, by what the leaders or media of one country glibly say about the position of the other. Subjective attitudes must not be allowed to hinder progress towards mutual understanding between the parties.

This is perhaps the severest demand the job makes on the Secretary-General. It is hard to suppress one's sympathies and preferences and harder still to endure the frustrations and discouragements which quiet diplomacy entails. But the Secretary-General does not have the option of being partial or of being discouraged. In saying that, however, I do not claim that the Secretary-General has at his disposal moral resources greater than his fellow men. What I do assert is that he cannot shoulder the burden of his office without unlimited patience, and an unfailing sense of justice and humanity.

When states are in conflict, the Secretary-General has to try to understand the roots of insecurity, the fears and resentments and the legitimate aspirations which inspire a people or a state to take the positions they do. International conflicts often occur when one party and its supporters ignore the fears of the other. If a third party is to succeed in resolving the conflict, he has to address the fears of each with empathy and imagination.

This process is not equally helpful in all cases, and should not be endless in any case. Sometimes the leadership of a state takes a stubborn stand and seems immune to rational persuasion. In such a case, the Secretary-General should go on as far as the point at which further exercise of his good offices can only disguise the reality: he should then state the facts plainly, without denunciation but without hiding the facts.

Apart from the exercise of good offices, the Secretary-General is often entrusted with other functions by the main organs of the UN. Often a report is requested from him. I strongly believe that such requests should not be made as a matter of routine or to cover up the failure of the body concerned to agree on effective action. Another common occurrence is for the Secretary-General to be asked to secure compliance with a resolution. Difficulties can then arise if there is disagreement amongst the member states about how the resolution is to be interpreted. There are very few absolutes in international affairs. The principles of the Charter no doubt command everyone's assent. But, because of different perceptions and values, there is often controversy about how they should be applied in a complicated situation. In such a case, the powers delegated to the Secretary-General do not always provide the answer. All he can do is to interpret as faithfully as he can the directives of the competent bodies, and the rights and obligations of the UN under international law.

Impartiality is thus the heart and soul of the office of the Secretary-General. His impartiality must remain untainted by any feeling of indebtedness to governments which may have supported his appointment. I attach the greatest importance to th's point and I therefore suggest that we should re-establish the healthy convention that no person should ever be a candidate, declared or undeclared, for this office. It is a post that should come *unsought* to a qualified person. However impeccable a person's integrity may be, he cannot in fact retain the necessary independence if he proclaims his candidacy and conducts a kind of election campaign, overt or covert. Some promises are bound to be made during his canvassing. But the only promise a future Secretary-General can properly make is to fulfil his duties under the Charter. There is no reason to fear that the convention I propose would make it more difficult for the member states to select a Secretary-General. Governments will always have a list of persons whom they consider qualified for the office. If it was a firm rule that such persons and their governments should go no further than answering enquiries about their availability, this would, I am sure, reinforce the moral authority which any Secretary-General must have.

In today's world, neither the functions of the Secretary-General nor multilateral diplomacy should be limited to good offices or negotiation. One of the UN's duties in a crisis is to be alert to all the nuances, and to use its contacts with governments to try to allay the underlying fears and suspicions. If it is successful in this, it may elicit concessions which the adversaries, left to themselves, would never consider. However, this requires a conscious decision on the part of the member states to strengthen the role of the Secretary-General and to provide him with better means to keep a watch over actual and potential points of conflict. At present, the UN lacks independent sources of information: its means of obtaining up-to-date information are primitive by comparison with those of member states—and indeed of most transnational corporations. To judge whether a matter may threaten international peace and security, the Secretary-General needs more than news reports and analyses made by outside experts: he needs full and impartial data, and he needs to be able to monitor developments world-wide. To enable the Secretariat to do this would in no way alter the distribution of functions and powers between the principal organs of the UN. Strengthening the institutional basis of preventive diplomacy would not diminish the role of the Security Council: on the contrary, it would enhance its effectiveness. The Secretary-General is, after all, a collaborator of the Security Council and not its competitor.

The Secretary-General's Administrative Role

I have so far concentrated on the political role of the Secretary-General, as this is the part of his responsibilities which attracts the most interest. But equally important is his administrative function under Article 97 of the Charter which designates him as the chief administrative officer of the organization.

The responsibilities of the UN are now so widespread in the political, economic, social, and humanitarian fields that the Secretariat requires a staff highly qualified in most of the modern scientific and cultural disciplines. Articles 100 and 101 of the Charter saw the Secretariat as a genuinely international civil service, responsible only to the organization, and gave the Secretary-General the exclusive power of appointing the staff, bearing in mind the need for the highest standards of efficiency, competence, and integrity.

It is ironic and unfortunate that, while there has been a dramatic rise in the Secretary-General's political responsibilities, his powers in the administrative field have been steadily eroded over the years. First of all, governments profess their dedication to the principle of an independent international civil service, but few refrain from trying to bring pressure to bear in favour of their own particular interests, especially on the personnel side. Second, the distribution of functions between the legislature and the executive, so essential to sound management, tends to be blurred when increasingly detailed directives about management policy are issued by the General Assembly. All this raises serious questions of organizational responsibility. The member states cannot ignore these if they want an efficient apparatus at their disposal to fulfil the purposes of the Charter. The problem has been aggravated by the financial crisis caused by the withholding of part of their contributions by a number of member states. The morale of the staff, the efficient execution of programmes, and the orderly management of the organization—all are jeopardized by the member states' failure to agree on a budgetary process and a scale of contributions acceptable to all. . . .

The international civil service is facing perhaps its most serious challenge ever. It would best be strengthened if member states would accept that the Secretary-General should carry out his functions as chief administrative officer without undue interference or political pressure. It must be recognized that it is the responsibility of the Secretary-General to ensure that the organization has at its disposal the staff necessary to perform all the functions given to it by the legislative bodies. It would be a refreshing change if the General Assembly and individual member states were to exercise more forbearance and give the Secretary-General the flexibility he needs to ensure the smooth and efficient functioning of the Secretariat. . . .

The Special Position of the Secretary-General

The Secretary-General has a constituency unlike any other. It is a two-tier constituency. On the one hand, he is elected by the governments of sovereign states, and it is to them that he is answerable for the way he discharges his mandate. But every one of those governments is attached to its own perceptions of its national interests, which means that the Secretary-General could not perform his duties under the Charter if he did not sometimes act above and beyond national positions.

Of course the Secretary-General is supposed to represent the member states' common interest in implementation of the principles laid down in the Charter. But the problem is that common interest does not always exist—or, rather, is not always perceived to exist. As I said earlier, when there are conflicting interpretations of these principles in a particular situation, the Secretary-General can be pulled in opposite directions by the member states. When agreement does not exist among governments, the first-tier constituency—the governments which elected him—can offer the Secretary-General little strength and support. It is then that he sometimes has to think of his second-tier constituency, namely the peoples for whom those governments act—all the peoples of the world who together form a single constituency for peace.

It is, therefore, not only the right but also the duty of the Secretary-General to maintain contact as best he can with the adherents of the principles of the UN Charter who exist in every society in the world. Time and the meagre resources at his disposal limit him severely in this respect. He must, nevertheless, do all he can to expound the principles of the United Nations, and what he is doing to implement them, to the parliaments, the media, and the universities of different countries. In doing so, he does not seek to incite criticism of their governments' policies; his aim is to encourage a clearer and fairer view of matters affecting other countries, and sometimes the whole world. I have been assured by many governments that, far from creating difficulties for them, such action by the Secretary-General helps them to counteract the parochialism of their domestic opinion.

I should like to end on a personal note. The Secretary-General is constantly subjected to many and diverse pressures. But in the last analysis, his office is a lonely one. He cannot stand idle. Yet helplessness is often his lot. The idealism and hope of which the Charter is a luminous expression have to confront the narrow dictates of national policies. The Secretary-General's efforts must be based on reason but, behind many a government's allegedly logical position, there are myths and silent fears. The voice of the Charter is often drowned by clashes and conflicts between states. If the Secretary-General is to ride above these contradictions in international life, two qualities are essential.

One is faith that humanity can move—and indeed is moving—towards a less irrational, less violent, more compassionate, and more generous international order. However grim the past and present may seem, the Secretary-General has to remain firm in his belief that, although people are swayed by short-term interests and local preoccupations, the movement towards good has an enduring appeal, and that good will triumph in the end.

The other essential quality is to feel that he is a citizen of the world. This sounds a cliché, but the Secretary-General would not deserve his mandate if he did not develop a sense of belonging to every nation or culture, reaching out as best he can to the impulse for peace and good that exists in all of them. He is a world citizen because all world problems are *his* problems; the Charter is his home and his ideology, and its principles are his moral creed.

Notes

1. Art. 98 of the Charter provides: 'The Secretary-General shall act in that capacity in all meetings of the General Assembly, of the Security Council, of the

Economic and Social Council, and of the Trusteeship Council, and shall perform such other functions as are entrusted to him by these organs. The Secretary-General shall make an annual report to the General Assembly on the work of the Organization.' Art. 99 of the Charter provides: 'The Secretary-General may bring to the attention of the Security Council any matter which in his opinion may threaten the maintenance of international peace and security.'

2. As one history of the UN Charter puts it: 'The President [Roosevelt] . . . brought up a suggestion that he wanted to see worked into the plan of organization, namely, provision for a head of the entire institution. . . . [He] seems to have used the term "moderator" in describing his idea of this official.' Ruth B. Russell and Jeanette E. Muther, *A History of the United Nations Charter* (Washington, DC, 1958), p. 979. Secretary-General U Thant later said: 'President Roosevelt suggested that the chief officer of the United Nations should be called "moderator" and I know of no better single word to describe my own idea of the office.' U Thant, *The Role of the Sectretary-General*, address delivered at the Dag Hammarskjöld Memorial Scholarship Fund of the UN Correspondents' Association, 16 Sept. 1971.

3. Under one proposed 'Possible Plan for a General International Organization': 'There would be two permanent international officials, the President and the Director-General. The latter would confine himself to administrative functions. The President, "a person of widely recognized eminence", would preside over the executive council, and perform such other duties of a "general political character" as were entrusted to him by the general assembly or by the executive council.' S. M. Schwebel, 'The Origins and Development of Article 99 of the Charter', *British Year Book of International Law 1951*, pp. 373–4.

4. Annual Reports by the present Secretary-General have the following DPI reference numbers: DPI/721-40992 (Sept. 1982); DPI/785-41191 (Sept. 1983); DPI/829-41364 (Sept. 1984); DPI/862-41361 (Sept. 1985); DPI/897-41114 (Sept. 1986).

5. United Nations Conference on International Organization, San Francisco, 1945, *Documents*, vol. 7 (London, 1945), pp. 392 and 556.

6. See the following Reports of the Secretary-General: S/16433 (26 Mar. 1984); S/17127 (17 Apr. 1985); S/17911 (12 Mar. 1986).

7. Rule 13(G) of the General Assembly Rules of Procedure (UN publication sales no. E.85.I.13).

7

Representing the World:
A Security Council for the 21st Century

Peter Wallensteen

An Active Security Council

Since the end of the Cold War, the UN Security Council has become in-creasingly active in international conflicts and their solution. This is the conventional wisdom supported by the empirical evidence of late. We may note that the Security Council has

- taken action in more armed conflicts, in absolute numbers
- taken action in a higher share of all on-going armed conflicts
- made more decisions per month and week
- made more mandatory decisions according to Chapter VII
- sent out more peace-keeping operations.[1]

This means that by 1994 the Security Council had in areas of international peace and security become a permanently meeting body, where decisions were often made behind closed doors. It had also become a more important decision-making body than any other organ of the UN or any other inter-national body dealing with international security. NATO lacked universal rep-resentation; the CSCE had at its disposal a lesser range of possible actions; and the EU/WEU showed less consensus on important security issues.[2]

This impressive change did not, however, make the Security Council more important than major-power governments. The administrations in the USA, the UK and France remained central authorities. Security Council decisions also required the support of the Russian Federation and the Peo-ple's Republic of China.[3] The Security Council was probably involved in fewer conflicts than the USA, the UK and France individually. Its permanent

Reprinted from Peter Wallensteen, "Representing the World: A Security Council for the 21st Century," *Security Dialogue* © 1994, Vol. 25, No. 1, pp. 63–75, by per-mission of Sage Publications Ltd.

members also operated through extensive bilateral dealings and separate international organizations (e.g. OAS, the Commonwealth, the European Union, the CIS). All five powers continued to take unilateral actions without consulting with the others or the UN in all steps (e.g. the USA in Panama, Russia in Georgia and China in Tibet).[4]

Legitimacy and Representation

While the increased activity of the Security Council has been generally applauded, a debate has emerged on aspects of its work. One question centres on its *achievements:* have its actions led to the result anticipated by the decisionmakers, or have alternative courses of actions been available? Secretary-General Boutros-Ghali has raised these issues, with some proposals.[5] Another question is the issue of *legitimacy.* Has the authority of the UN generally been accepted, or has it been dependent on particular powers? Has the UN treated similar conflicts in a comparable way? For instance, Amer has shown how interventions were handled in very different ways during the 1980s. Gott concludes that the UN has been an 'intrinsically conservative institution'.[6]

In this article, the question of *legitimacy* is of central concern. Legitimacy can be seen as a lubricant of a system. It means that the members, the subjects of decisions, follow the decisions as they are made in accordance with established practices and by recognised authorities. Decisions made under legitimate authority, in other words, do not necessarily have to be forced upon the members or subjects. They are obeyed because they are legitimate, even though they may run counter to individual preferences. This is how democratic societies operate internally. In a member-controlled organization, this is also what would be expected. We might also postulate a connection between achievements and legitimacy. Legitimate decisions will probably be subject to less resistance, as there will be more global support for them as well as more local hesitation to oppose them.

Thus, we need to ask: are the Security Council decisions made in ways which have general support of the international community for whom the UN speaks? The near-unanimous nature of many of its decisions would imply this. . . . There are cases of abstentions and negative votes by non-permanent members. Still, the ability to make decisions shows that there has been a high degree of agreement over the course of action in the international community. The actions taken have been what the constituent members of the world community have been willing to accept. Although there has been disagreement it has not been so serious as to polarize or impede decision-making in the Security Council.

Nevertheless, concern has been expressed, for instance in the general debates in the General Assembly as well as in the special enquiry made by the Secretary-General to the member-states, over the powers given to the permanent members of the Security Council.[7] It is argued that countries from one part of the world have a stronger voice than the rest, and that moreover this is a minority of the world's population. In other words, UN authority may be challenged along a North-South dichotomy, a global geographical dimension. Behind this is an idea that legitimacy is dependent on a reasonable geographical or 'geo-demographic' distribution of influence. Although this is by no means clear from the record, this challenge assumes that Security Council members tend to act as representatives of particular regions. The argument could be bolstered by reference to the principle used in domestic affairs of states. Areas with the largest population also have sizeable representation. On the other hand, it is equally common for areas with less population to be, in fact, over-represented. Skewed distributions still can be legitimate.

All the same, this challenge makes the geographical distribution of seats in the Security Council a major issue. The present non-permanent seats are the only ones that are elected. They are distributed in a formula which gives 20% of the seats to Western Europe and Other States (apart from Western Europe also including North America, Australia, New Zealand, what is known as the WEOS group), 10% to Eastern Europe, 50% to Africa and Asia and 20% to South America. The distribution is somewhat favourable to Western and Eastern Europe, compared to a strict demographic representation, but still obviously within the confines of what is regarded as legitimate.[8]

The issue becomes more complicated with regard to the permanent seats. Only one of these belongs to a Third World country, China, with WEOS taking 60% and Eastern Europe 20% of the seats. This becomes a strong argument against the present composition of the permanent seats. The more powerful positions, it could be argued, should correspond more closely to 'equal' representation. According to what formula should such an 'equal' distribution be designed? Should one, for instance, use the present regional distribution for the full Security Council as the point of the departure (i.e. giving 33% of all seats to the WEOS group)? Probably the political debate will not be based on such formulas. Rather it will concentrate on the interests of particular countries. In the end, however, the resulting distribution will be important for general acceptance of constitutional changes.

This is evident when we note another angle in the debate: the costs of the UN operations, especially the expenditures for peace-keeping activity. Some countries are assessed more for peace-keeping than others, even more than certain permanent members. This applies in particular to Germany and Japan. Relatively few countries support UN peace-keeping by more than one tenth of 1% of their defence budgets. . . . For most countries UN peacekeeping was still a minor concern compared to national defence.

In absolute figures, however, Germany and Japan both contributed more than China, UK and France. China was also surpassed by countries such as Italy, Canada and Sweden. This raises the issue of 'financial' representation. There is a common understanding, dating back to the American Revolution, of 'no taxation without representation'. Germany and Japan have strong cases for seats as permanent members. They pay more than could be expected but have less formal influence. The argument could be made that also 'faithful' contributors could demand more influence. Countries giving a higher ratio of their 'security investments' to the UN could demand special treatment. Japan and Germany would again qualify, but so would other countries which in relative terms give the organization more financial support than the present permanent members (e.g. Canada and Nigeria).

It is obvious that Germany and Japan have stronger cases than others, not least due to their political stability, democratic constitutions, close cooperation with the USA and economic significance in general. The primary objection to such a criterion for representation derives from the concern with the geo-demographic distribution. Germany and Japan would both be seen to strengthen the position of the richer part of the world in the Security Council. On these grounds, there might be resistance. However, it could also be said that their permanent seats would make the Security Council reflect more closely economic power in the world. The Security Council would become parallel to the Group of Seven (G-7), or perhaps even make G-7 obsolete. In other words, the validity of a criterion such as financial representation can be debated. On the positive side, it introduces economic significance as an additional consideration to the customary emphasis on military might.

To arrive at the same time at an acceptable geographical distribution *and* a form of economic representation for the Security Council raises the issue of the total number of seats. Within the present framework of 15 members, the two principles would clash: seats for Germany and Japan could be made only at the expense of other seats, possibly threatening a reduction of seats available to Third World countries. The logical conclusion is to enlarge the Security Council. Also this option has some limits, however. It is commonly assumed that any institution will be more effective (i.e. swifter) in decision-making if it can remain small. A Security Council paralysed by lengthy debates and considerable and open in-fighting will make for slower action, with impact on its global standing. The size has to be limited.

Thus, there are *three criteria* for an effective and legitimate Security Council: It would have to be *small in size;* have a reasonable *geographical composition,* giving room for larger countries, without eliminating powerful ones; and have a degree of *economic representation.*

To solve this quandary we will have to consider the present setting of the Security Council. Ten seats are filled in two-year terms through elections by the General Assembly. An agreed regional distribution is used, as mentioned previously. Five seats, i.e. one third of the Security Council, are permanent, and with distinct advantages. This permanent membership involves two aspects. First, it means that some members of the most powerful organ are not elected by the members of the organization which they are set to lead. In terms of responsibility, the leadership of the permanent members are accountable to their own populations, not to the organization as such. For the permanent members this provides an independence of action and freedom from manoeuvring in the General Assembly. It runs counter, however, to normal democratic procedures for free associations. This has implications for legitimacy and effectiveness of the decisions of the organization. Secondly, there is the right of veto which is attached to the permanent membership: i.e. that only decisions which are not actively opposed by one of the permanent members can be made by the organization. Together these two aspects give the permanent members a strong influence over the decisions of the Security Council. The Secretary General, for instance, is elected for five years and participates in the deliberations of the Council, without voting rights. The post does not represent any particular grouping, although all holders have so far come from other than permanent members.[9]

The considerations behind these arrangements reflected the realities of the situation in 1945: the main victors of World War II constructed the new organization. It also rested on the experiences of the League of Nations. The possibility that decisions could be made against a strong member would have meant that the organization could be used in a conflict between major powers. In such a confrontation a big power might (threaten to) leave the organization. This experience is still relevant. The strength of the United Nations depends on the power that the permanent members are willing to give to the organization. The UN does not command forces or finances of its own. The compulsory and voluntary contributions of its member-states determine its military strategy and overall economy. Thus, there has to be consonance between the real distribution of power in the world and influence inside the United Nations in order for the organization to be operative. At the same time, however, its legitimacy rests on the ability of the weaker states to exert influence. This pressures the organization to become more representative, geographically as well as economically, without losing its ability to make decisions. This is the delicate balancing act that always has to be upheld when considering constitutional issues of the UN.

Senatorial Members and Qualified Majority

Are there other ways to handle the delicate balancing act than those developed and agreed in San Francisco in 1945? First, let us consider the *permanent membership*. There is a demand from states to become permanent members for varying reasons. Different schemes are possible for solving this problem. One which is gaining support has already been indicated: to increase the number of permanent members. Germany and Japan are candidates, but among public proposals also Italy and India have been mentioned. It is not far-fetched to assume that Nigeria and Brazil would aspire to such seats. A Security Council with another two to five permanent members would also have to consider adjusting the decision rules. It has been suggested that new permanent members would enter without veto powers. The Security Council would, thus, consist of three types of members: five permanent ones with veto, two to five permanent members without a veto and ten (or more? or less?) non-permanent members without individual veto.[10] In this way, economic and geographical representation could be maintained, the Council would still be reasonably small (ca 17–20 members), and the present permanent members would remain. Such a scheme has considerable political attraction.

For the sake of the argument, it is interesting to explore a move in the opposite direction. By making *all* members of the Security Council equal on the model of the present non-permanent members—i.e. all Council members would be elected for two years by the General Assembly—a complete and radical reform of representation would be achieved. This would meet the demands for geographical representation, if the formula for the present distribution of non-permanent members were retained. On the other hand, this reform would not address the needs of the delicate balancing act we just identified. This proposal does not consider the distribution of power, and might not become accepted. If somehow forced on the organization, it might lead to withdrawal by powerful states.

What would be a third reform alternative which could meet the need for the delicate balancing act? One possibility is to convert the permanent seats into six-year mandates, on the model of many domestic constitutions (e.g. the US Congress). This would mean the creation of a set of senatorial positions. Such a membership would outlast the normal reign of most governments (where electoral mandates constitutionally mostly last for three to five years). The principle of elections to the highest organ would at the same time be instituted and strengthened. It would give Japan and Germany a chance of becoming senatorial members, as could India, Brazil or Nigeria. If this were combined with a certain enlargement of the Security Council, the proposal might become politically more acceptable. If the Security Council were increased from the present 15 to 18, 21 or 24 members, while retaining one third of the seats for more privileged positions, the more powerful seats would increase from the present 5 (today's permanent seats) to 6, 7 or 8 seats. Potentially this would allow for the inclusion of present permanent members as well as present candidates, but now as 'senators'. The advantage in this reform would be to bring home the principle of accountability of the most important members to the main body of the organization. Furthermore, as the basic principle of this proposal is one of unrestrained elections, countries could be re-elected. Let us explore this possibility one step further.

As already indicated, the other aspect of the present permanent seats is the possibility to *veto* particular decisions. If the number of privileged seats is increased, as envisioned in the first reform proposal, this would also mean increasing the number of conflicts which might remain outside the reach of the organization. Seven to ten powerful states are likely to be involved in a great number of conflicts in the world, and would presumably prefer to direct the Security Council in accordance with their own interests. This could mean either to keep the UN out—or call it in, but on their terms. This would be a most unsatisfactory form of ensuring international peace and security. This is an important drawback with the first reform proposal, although it avoids giving veto rights to the new permanent members. Their significance could still have a restraining impact of the activity of the organization. Also in the third proposal this element is there: The enlargement of senatorial seats would threaten, paradoxically, to make the UN less capable of acting, by reducing the agenda of actions.[11]

The logical conclusion is that it is not appropriate to retain the veto, when extending the permanent membership or when creating senatorial seats. Instead, it would be preferable to institute a normal constitutional rule: serious decisions require a qualified majority. If a rule specifying that actions under Chapter VII of the Charter require the consent of three-quarters of the Security Council membership, the veto of an individual member would disappear, but it would be replaced with a collective veto. A minimum of one quarter of the Security Council membership would be able to block a decision. In a Security Council of 15 members, 4 could prevent actions; if the total is 18, 21 or 24 it would require 5, 6 and 6 respectively, with rounding off rules. If the blocking minority is defined as the share of the full membership, whether all members are present or not at a particular meeting, this rule becomes predictable and obvious.

What would be the effects of such reforms on the UN Security Council? Table 7.1 spells out some implications, primarily in geopolitical terms. It specifies the likely composition in terms of regional distribution with the introduction of senatorial seats replacing permanent seats. For comparison, the distribution of the present Security Council is included. It should be recalled that this proposal does not include a change in the voting rules. Thus election to a seat requires a 2/3 majority among all voting members of the General Assembly, as is currently the case for non-permanent membership.

The regional groups, the formulas as well as their application are likely to be a subject of discussion in case the proposed reforms are considered. The power of the stronger is assumed to be reflected in the present formulas, and consequently they constitute the point of departure. Even so,

Table 7.1 Geographical Composition of the Security Council (SC)

	Present SC	Derived formula	Present SC with formula	Reform proposals		
Total number	15	%	15	18	21	24
Permanent/Senatorial seats						
(33% of all seats)	5	99	5	6	7	8
W. Europe and Others (= P1, P2, P3)	3	33	2	2	2	3
Eastern Europe (= P4)	1	13	1	1	1	1
Africa-Asia (= P5)	1	40	2	2	3	3
S. America	0	13	0	1	1	1
Non-permanent/Non-senatorial seats						
(66% of all seats)	10	100	10	12	14	16
W. Europe and Others	2	20	2	3	3	3
E. Europe	1	10	1	1	1	2
Africa-Asia	5	50	5	6	7	8
S. America	2	20	2	2	3	3

Note: Formula for regional distribution of *senatorial* seats is derived from the composition of the present *full* Security Council, with minor adjustments. Permanent members are distributed according to regional memberships. P1 = USA, P2 = UK, P3 = France, P4 = Russia, P5 = China. Formula for regional distribution of *non-permanent/non-senatorial* seats is the one in use today: Western European and other states 20%, Eastern Europe 10%, Africa-Asia 50%, South America 20%.

the formulas cannot be applied strictly, as there will be difficulties in determining how to approximate numbers, etc. Table 7.1 is a way to begin a discussion.

The first column in Table 7.1 shows the present composition of the Security Council, when permanent members are distributed to relevant regional groupings. The strength of the WEOS group is quite obvious: It has three out of five permanent seats (i.e. 60%) and two of the non-permanent seats (i.e. 20%): this is five out of fifteen or 33% of all seats.

The second column shows the formulas that can be derived from the present composition of the Security Council. For the permanent (i.e. proposed senatorial) seats the composition of today's full Council is used, whereas present practice for non-permanent seats is retained. The third column shows the impact of introducing elected senatorial seats according to the derived formula for a Security Council of the present size, that is fifteen members. The Western European grouping would have one seat less, and that seat would go to Africa-Asia. This North-West vs South-East dimension comes clearly out in many reform proposals. It is interesting to compare this with the first scheme outlined above, assuming it would mean that ten permanent seats were created from a body of twenty seats. The WEOS group would then have four permanent members (USA, UK, France, Germany), i.e. 40%, proportionally less than today. If Japan, one additional Asian country and one African country were to be added to the permanent seats, the share of Africa-Asia would rise to 40%. Also in this scenario WEOS yields relative weight to Africa-Asia.

The following three columns of Table 7.1 show the possible composition of a differently enlarged Security Council. In all scenarios, the Africa-Asia group emerges as the most numerous one. This is, as we have just seen, also a likely outcome of other proposals under consideration. It should be noted that regional concerns impact on the election chances of present permanent members. Only in the case of a 24-member Security Council would all present permanent members have the possibility of being elected senatorial members. With the proposed reforms of Table 7.1, Germany would have to compete with major European countries to get a senatorial seat. Japan, on the other hand, would have a good chance of acquiring one of Africa-Asia's seats. For both, as well as other contenders, the reforms of Table 7.1 retain the possibility of acquiring a non-senatorial seat. If the reform proposal incorporates the abolition of the veto, such seats would not necessarily be unattractive. This would be even more true if the present rule against re-election were removed.

What would be the implication of the proposed reforms for the decision-making and in particular the individual or collective veto? As the present Security Council has in fact a collective veto, requiring nine consenting votes for a decision (in addition to the permanent member's individual veto, according to Article 27 in the Charter), the idea of collective veto is not new. It has rarely (if ever?) been used in a vote, but probably plays a role in the deliberations leading to decisions.[12] The proposed qualified majority rule is, thus, simply an extension of an existing regulation. Table 7.2 specifies some implications of such a rule.

From Table 7.2 we see that Africa-Asia together with South America already today has a veto as a combined group, as well as through one permanent member, China, if it were to act within the regional bloc. The only individual region without a veto is South America alone. The reforms would affect this pattern only partly. In a Security Council with 18 seats and where five go to the WEOS group, this group would retain its veto.[13] Eastern Europe would lose its veto, however. In a 21-seat Security Council WEOS would lose the collective veto, but regain it in a 24-seat Council. If the two 'European' groups combine, as shown at the bottom of Table 7.2, their veto would be restored. In a polarization between North-West and the South-East, both groups would be able to block each other, thus either paralysing the organization or providing incentives for consensus-building.[14]

The original argument for the veto—the danger that the organization could be used against a major power by a hostile majority—is partly alleviated with the qualified majority rule. It requires that a major power has allies or can muster enough abstentions to prevent a negative decision in the Council. If that power has been elected, such support is likely to exist.

Table 7.2 Who Has a Veto in the Security Council?

	Present SC	Possible Reforms		
Total number	15	18	21	24
Required for veto	7 (or 1 PM)	5	6	6
Separate Groups				
Western Europe and Others	5	5	5	6
	Veto due to PM	Veto	No veto	Veto
Eastern Europe	2	2	2	3
	Veto due to PM	No veto	No veto	No veto
Africa-Asia	6	8	10	11
	Veto due to PM	Veto	Veto	Veto
South America	2	3	4	4
	No veto	No veto	No veto	No veto
Combined groups				
Western + Eastern Europe	7	7	7	9
	Veto	Veto	Veto	Veto
Africa-Asia + S. America	8	11	14	15
	Veto	Veto	Veto	Veto

Note: Qualified majority rule for decisions over the application of Chapter VII. Assuming proposed reforms of Table 7.1 and assuming groups vote in united blocs. PM = permanent member.

Also, as new elections will always be coming up, there is a chance of influencing the majority in the Council. Instead of shifting conflicts to occur outside the organization, the chances might increase that they are channelled within the constitutional framework of the organization. The real danger would instead be that a major power might not be elected to the Council at all, and could thus choose to leave the organization. The probability of this happening is difficult to assess. It can be debated whether this is a more likely and less preferable outcome than the present use of the veto, which may serve to remove significant issues from the agenda.

The regional groups are not as cohesive as the figures in Table 7.2 imply on all issues all the time. In fact, the rich-poor dichotomy could cut through some of the groups. Africa-Asia includes Japan as well as Cambodia and Afghanistan, oil producers as well as nomadic societies. The diversity on many of the issues to arise after the Cold War makes bloc voting increasingly unlikely, particularly if issues such as apartheid in South Africa and the Israel-Arab conflict find solutions. The new issues emerging—such as containing and solving domestic ethnic issues, handling climate changes which impact on security, humanitarian and environmental consequences of the many Third World wars, human rights violations, etc.—are likely to give rise to new and varying constellations of states and powers. In this more volatile and mobile situation, also UN voting patterns would become more unpredictable, making regions less unified on issues of peace and security. Concluding this, it appears that enlarging the UN Security Council to 18 members and replacing the veto with a qualified majority on Chapter VII questions would seem a fitting way of responding to the changing times. The most practical gain is the one in accountability of all the members of the Security Council. At the same time, however, this proposal manages the problems of geographical and financial representation while retaining swiftness of action.

Is It Practical?

For such a reform proposal to be implemented, there would have to be some who would gain from the change, and some who lose but would not oppose it vehemently. The winners in the proposal are likely to be found in Asia: Japan and the new industrial states in Pacific Asia would increase their representation. These countries, largely bent on industrial and economic development, are likely to become important in the next century. They would probably support changes or even come to demand them. The losers are those members who are now permanent members and who in the future would have to stage election campaigns to retain a corresponding role. If these are countries who firmly believe in democratic principles for domestic affairs, they should have less hesitation in engaging in such a procedure. In fact, they would have a considerable advantage, knowing how to campaign. As no defeat would be permanent, such an outcome should be manageable. The importance of democratic principles would be strongly demonstrated to the world. In other cases, a reform of the permanent membership might, in the end, be a question of changes also in domestic politics.

In fact, domestic democratization of most societies might be a precondition for changes to become practical. Studies show that democratic states are less likely to fight wars among each other.[15] Domestic democratization may be a condition for a future of peace between countries. Today's democratic Germany and Japan appear as open societies without expansionist and militarist tendencies. The spread of democratic domestic politics around the world would probably reduce the fear of sharing control over the United Nations and the Security Council. In effect, domestic and international democratization may go hand in hand, reducing the risk of international conflict as well as laying the foundation for a functioning international system. The reform proposal might become more practical as democracy spreads around the world. Whether it should or could be implemented before or after such a development is for the debate to determine.

Notes

1 See A. Aust, 'The Procedure and Practice of the Security Council Today', in *The Development of the Role of the Security Council*. Workshop 1992, The

Hague Academy of International Law (Martinus Nijhoff: Dordrecht, 1993), pp. 365–374; Birger Heldt, ed., *States in Armed Conflict 1990–91* (Uppsala: Department of Peace and Conflict Research, 1992); Birger Heldt, Peter Wallensteen, Erik Melander and Kjell-Åke Nordquist, 'Major Armed Conflicts in 1992', *SIPRI Yearbook 1993* (Oxford University Press, 1993); Karin Lindgren, *States in Armed Conflict 1989* (Uppsala: Department of Peace and Conflict Research, 1993); J. David Singer, 'Peace in the Global System: Displacement, Interregnum, or Transformation?' in Charles W. Kegley, Jr., ed., *The Long Postwar Peace. Contending Explanations and Projections* (New York: HarperCollins, 1991), pp. 56–84; Peter Wallensteen, 'The Security Council in Armed Conflicts, 1986–1991', in Birger Heldt, *States in Armed Conflict, 1990–91,* pp. 11–27; and Peter Wallensteen, 'UN Peacekeeping Interventions in Conflict Situations', 43rd Pugwash Conference, Stockholm, 9–15 June 1993.

2. Another important group is G-7, which brings together the world's strongest economic states. It does not deal directly with military security although it has made statements on foreign policy issues. G-7 does not have a permanent secretariat of its own.

3. See A. Aust, 'The Procedure and Practice of the Security Council Today'.

4. This is not to say that the UN is always present where it might be expected to be. For instance, the UN played no role in the talks leading to the interim agreements between Israel and the PLO on 13 September 1993.

5. See Boutros Boutros-Ghali, *An Agenda for Peace* (New York: United Nations, 1992). For recent research on the conditions for durable peace see Kjell-Åke Nordquist, *Peace after War. On Conditions for Durable Inter-state Boundary Agreements* (Uppsala: Department of Peace and Conflict Research, 1992).

6. See Ramses Amer, *The United Nations and Foreign Military Intervention. A Comparative Study of the Application of the Charter* (Uppsala: Department of Peace and Conflict Research, 1992) and Richard Gott, 'The UN cannot be reformed', *Third World Resurgence,* 1992, no. 32, pp. 30–32.

7. The impression is that member-states implement the mandatory decisions. With respects to sanctions, however, there are reported loopholes, and defection might increase with the increasing number of mandatory resolutions, as surveillance becomes more demanding and is, in fact, left to the member-states themselves.

8. The number of non-permanent seats has been changed as the General Assembly grew in numbers. In 1966 the Security Council was enlarged to its present 15 seats; see Sydney D. Bailey, *The Procedure of the UN Security Council* (Oxford: Clarendon Press, Second edition, 1988).

9. Small countries may, as former UN Secretary-General Dag Hammarskjöld argued, have a greater need of the UN, as major powers will always be able to fend for themselves. Thus, the Secretary-General could be seen as a channel of influence for smaller countries. However, the Secretary-General is bound by the decisions of the Security Council. A hitherto unexplored idea is to make the Secretary-General an independent member of the Security Council with the right to vote, on an equal level with states. This would be parallel to the way Chief Executive Officers of major corporations are sometimes included on the boards of their companies.

10. Logically, we would expect also a category of non-permanent members with veto rights.

11. This conclusion builds on the record of UN inability to deal with central Cold War issues or matters close to particular permanent members.

12. See Sydney D. Bailey, *The Procedure . . . ,* pp. 201–209 for a discussion on the role of the veto, and on procedural issues as distinct from substantial ones. In 1945–1986, 203 proposals were vetoed.

13. A dispute may arise as to whether WEOS is entitled to a fifth seat or South America to a fourth one. Mathematically both regions would have 2.4 non-senatorial seats. The assumption here is that power prevails and that the seat is taken by WEOS.

14. Table 2 retains the formula for regional distribution from Table 1. Moving in a more 'geo-democratic' way by using the present non-permanent membership formula for the entire Security Council would in effect only give veto to the Africa-Asia group. In a rich-poor polarization, however, both sides would be able to exert a veto.

15. See Bruce M. Russett et al., *Grasping the Democratic Peace. Principles for a Post–Cold War World* (Princeton, N.J.: Princeton University Press, 1993).

Part 4

PEACE AND
SECURITY AFFAIRS

THE cynical view of international organizations has been most prevalent in the area of peace and security affairs. The incidence of war around the world over the past fifty years attests to the mostly failed efforts of international organizations to prevent the outbreak of war. With no international police force on the immediate horizon, there is little prospect for global governance mechanisms that can prevent large-scale violence. Furthermore, the collective security provisions in Chapter 7 of the UN Charter have never been fully implemented (the Korean and Kuwaiti efforts were not truly international operations, conducted under international command with broadly representative groups of contributing states).

Historically, there are several reasons for the relative ineffectiveness of the United Nations and other regional organizations in preventing war. First, and most obviously, was the stalemate among the permanent members of the Security Council, with the split largely along ideological lines. Cold War tensions and the great power veto in the Security Council often prevented the United Nations from launching concerted actions when faced with threats to international peace and security. The superpower rivalry was also manifested in proxy conflicts around the world, making the ability of regional bodies to form consensus on actions difficult. Second, international organizations have been hampered by a lack of political will on the part of the members to take strong action, even when consensus exists. The financial and human costs associated with security operations are considered too high by many key states who believe they have few direct national interests affected by conflicts far from their home base. Finally, international organizations usually become involved in disputes only after one or more of the disputants has threatened or actually used military force. At that stage, it becomes very difficult to resolve the dispute without further violence.

The end of the Cold War and the establishment of a so-called new world order gave many idealists great hope for the role of international organizations in the realm of peace and security affairs. The Security Council was no longer stalemated and greater consensus on taking strong action in conflicts such as the Persian Gulf War and Haiti emerged. Furthermore, many regional organizations, such as the European Union, sought to develop policies for dealing with conflicts in their own backyards. There was also increasing global attention to the concept of early warning, the notion that the international community should be able to detect nascent conflict before it reaches the militarized stage and thereby take action that actually prevents violence rather than just dealing with its aftermath.

Failures in Bosnia, Somalia, and Rwanda revealed that international organizations could not be expected to succeed in all the ventures they undertook, and the lack of political will and the presence of complex conflicts remained obstacles to the establishment of a true new world order. Even though the United Nations could reach decisions more easily on security matters than ever before (witness the explosion in the number of peacekeeping operations since 1989), the strategies adopted were not uniformly more successful than in the Cold War era. Currently, international organizations are still struggling with the new global environment and searching for the right mix of organizational structures, procedures, and strategies to deal with the variety of security challenges that they now face. The three selections in Part 4 consider these questions and seek to shed some light on how the international community might adapt to a world without a superpower rivalry, but one still threatened by international militarized conflict.

Perhaps the organization most affected by the end of the Cold War was the North Atlantic Treaty Organization (NATO). For over forty years, NATO stood as a deterrence and defense organization poised against possible aggression by the Soviet Union and its allies in the Warsaw Pact. With the breakup of the Soviet Union, the diminished military capacity of Russia, and the end of the Warsaw Pact (with some of its members even applying for NATO membership), NATO grapples with redefining its purposes. The article by Charles Glaser reviews the security interests still faced by the United States and its European allies and makes a case for the retention of NATO, as the most effective mechanism to insure those interests. He compares NATO to other potential arrangements, including a more traditional collective security arrangement as well as unilateral national initiatives, which some isolationists consider superior to any supranational arrangements. The evolution of NATO over the coming years may yield some insights into the persistence of international organizations noted in the Cupitt, Whitlock, and Whitlock article at the beginning of this volume as well as potentially serving as a model for future regional security arrangements.

In the early 1980s, international peacekeeping efforts were largely moribund, and it was thought that this strategy for dealing with international conflict might be abandoned. Yet the peacekeeping strategy was renewed with vigor starting in 1989, with more UN peacekeeping operations being deployed in the five years following than in the almost forty-five years of the Cold War period. The remaining two articles in Part 4 address two variants of the peacekeeping strategy, the traditional and the "second-generation" varieties.

Traditional peacekeeping operations are characterized by the deployment of a small number of neutral, lightly armed troops, with the consent of the host state, to act as an interposition or buffer force between protagonists, usually after a cease-fire, but prior to conflict resolution. The Paul Diehl article looks at the conditions under which traditional peacekeeping operations are successful. It is clear from his analysis that peacekeeping is not an appropriate strategy for all situations. Even when peacekeeping is successful in stopping the fighting, it provides little or no impetus for resolving the underlying sources of conflict between the disputants. The deployment of peacekeeping troops for more than a quarter of a century in Cyprus illustrates the inherent problem of what to do after the fighting stops. His findings also suggest that peacekeeping operations will encounter significant difficulties in civil conflicts and internationalized civil wars, exactly the kind of conflict likely to be more numerous in the post–Cold War era.

John Mackinlay and Jarat Chopra look at "second-generation" peacekeeping missions, which differ from traditional peacekeeping operations in several ways. Second-generation operations often involve a more coercive element and more permissive rules of military engagement, with host-state consent not necessarily being a prerequisite. These newer peacekeeping operations are often much larger than traditional operations and may perform a range of functions that go well beyond the interposition function of traditional forces; second-generation operations may participate in humanitarian assistance, state building, election supervision, and arms control verification to name a few new roles. Second-generation operations thus far have a mixed record of success, with positive outcomes in operations in Namibia and Cambodia matched by serious problems in Rwanda and Bosnia. The authors highlight what they think will be necessary for second-generation operations to be more effective, but they also recognize that not all those conditions are likely to be fulfilled, at least in the immediate future.

8

Why NATO Is Still Best:
Future Security Arrangements
for Europe

Charles L. Glaser

The end of the Cold War and the dissolution of the Soviet Union have generated extensive interest in redesigning Europe's security structures. Cold War dangers have dramatically receded, raising questions about the continuing necessity of the North Atlantic Treaty Organization (NATO). New dangers in Central Europe, already too apparent in the former Yugoslavia, have fueled doubts about the ability of Europe's institutions, including the Conference on Security and Cooperation in Europe (CSCE), the European Community (EC), the EC's defense component—the Western European Union (WEU)—as well as NATO, to manage the dangers of post-Soviet Europe.

Although discussion of various institutional arrangements is already extensive, little systematic analysis of their relative strengths and weaknesses is available. This article attempts to fill the gap: it first explores U.S. and Western European interests and potential threats to these interests; it then assesses the ability of specific proposed security arrangements to confront these threats.

The first section distinguishes three types of current or future war the West might face. The first danger is of deliberate attack from a major power in the East—a resurgent Russia. The second is war in the East, including wars that begin in Central Europe but could draw in the West. The third is war within Western Europe, possibly exacerbated by war in the East.

The dangers that these wars pose to the West depend on their probability and on the Western interests they would threaten. Based on the current state of debate, my assessments are that the probability of a resurgent

Reprinted from *International Security,* Vol. 18, No. 1 (Summer 1993), pp. 5–50, Charles Glaser, "Why NATO Is Still Best: Future Security Arrangements for Europe," by permission of MIT Press. © 1993 by the President and Fellows of Harvard College and the Massachusetts Institute of Technology.

Russia is small but is not necessarily decreasing; that the probability of more wars in the East is significantly higher than during the Cold War; and that the probability of war between the West's major powers in the near future is virtually nil, although uncertainty exists about whether this peace is guaranteed indefinitely. Even readers who disagree should nevertheless find my analysis useful: because I explicitly link my analysis of security structures to conclusions about specific threats, they should find it straightforward to revise my policy conclusions.

In designing policies for dealing with these dangers, particularly war in the East, the West must decide what types of interests are at stake—is Western policy intended to protect security, economic, or humanitarian interests? Clarifying the nature of Western interests informs decisions about the magnitude of the costs and risks the West should be willing to undertake.

The second section assesses the capability of five significantly different security structures to deal with the types of war discussed in the previous section. One option is to preserve NATO, while transforming it to deal with post-Soviet realities and possibly expanding its responsibilities. A second possibility is that an increasingly integrated Western Europe will take predominant responsibility for its security, with formal military links to the United States essentially eliminated. For example, under the direction of the EC, the military capabilities and political influence of the WEU could significantly increase, while the United States withdrew from Europe. Third, a leading candidate for replacing a Western alliance, whether NATO-based or EC-based, is a continent-wide collective security system in which all European countries agree to oppose any aggressor in the hope of posing an overwhelming deterrent. A fourth possibility is a concert in which the major powers coordinate their foreign policies to minimize potential conflicts among themselves. A fifth option, which I term defensive unilateral security, emphasizes defensive military capabilities in an effort to minimize the tensions that offensive capabilities can generate: instead of all countries committing to oppose any aggressor, all countries reduce their ability to attack one another, while maintaining their ability to defend themselves. Although some of these options are incompatible with each other, others—for example NATO and WEU—could be complementary.[1]

The final section draws together conclusions. The theme running throughout my analysis is that the West should be willing to invest in hedges against war with Russia and war within the West: even though these wars are unlikely, their extremely high costs justify buying insurance. I find that NATO is likely to provide a better hedge than any of the alternatives. NATO can meet Western requirements in all three types of war—hedging against a resurgent Russia, providing the means to extend security guarantees to Central European countries, and reducing the already low probability of future tensions within Western Europe—both by preserving

America's role in Europe as a defensive balancer and by maintaining institutions for concert-like coordination within the West. A Western European alliance could serve some of these functions but, by excluding the United States, would not provide the reassurance that NATO offers Western Europe. Beyond NATO, the West needs concert-like arrangements with Russia to ensure that Western policies do not generate Russian insecurity. Collective security and defensive unilateral security turn out to be useful primarily for attempting to preserve good political relations within the West. In solving this problem, however, they suffer a variety of military and political shortcomings.

The case for NATO is best viewed as an extended transition strategy—the preservation of NATO for a couple of decades into the post-Soviet era is prudent in the face of uncertainties surrounding both Russia and Western Europe. If thereafter the potential dangers appear even more unlikely than today, the West will then be better prepared to reevaluate different arrangements. Nevertheless, with the end of the Cold War having eliminated major divisions between East and West, the preservation of NATO will require increasingly effective political leadership on both sides of the Atlantic.

The hardest decision facing the West is whether to provide security guarantees to the countries of Central Europe and certain former republics of the Soviet Union. Calls for collective security neglect this issue, simply assuming that the West has security interests in keeping peace throughout Europe. In fact, as I explain below, Western security interests call only for rather narrow security guarantees that are designed to deter Russian expansion into Central Europe, but not to prevent all wars between the smaller countries of Central Europe. Furthermore, if making these security commitments would appear threatening to Russia, NATO should consider forgoing them entirely, since such a policy could be self-defeating. Other wars in Central Europe threaten primarily Western humanitarian interests, but not security interests. In these cases, the key question is not about appropriate institutional arrangements. If the West decides that protecting these interests warrants military intervention, a Western alliance would be adequate. Failure to intervene would most likely reflect inadequate Western concern, not inadequate means.

Purposes of a Security Structure: What Interests Are Threatened by War?

To lay the foundation for assessing security structures, I first address America's interest in European peace and next examine the types of European war that a security structure should be prepared to deal with.

America's Continuing Security Interest in European Peace

From an American perspective, a basic question is whether the United States still has security interests in Europe. The end of the Cold War is fueling calls for American withdrawal from Europe, adding arguments to the already extensive debate over American grand strategy.[2] Isolationists believe, now more than ever, that whatever dangers might threaten Europe will not threaten the United States.[3] During the Cold War, the most serious challenge to the traditional case for American involvement flowed from the nuclear revolution, which undermined geopolitical arguments for opposing a European hegemon. Isolationists now add that we can be confident that Western Europe will be free from military conflict, because the passing of the Soviet Union has eliminated the only serious external threat, and relations within the West are so good that military conflict is virtually unimaginable.

However, although the lack of an imminent Soviet threat eliminates the most obvious danger, U.S. security has not been entirely separated from the future of Western Europe. The ending of the Cold War has brought many benefits, but has not eliminated the possibility of major power war, especially since such a war could grow out of a smaller conflict in the East.[4] And, although nuclear weapons have greatly reduced the threat that a European hegemon would pose to U.S. security, a sound case nevertheless remains that a major European war could threaten U.S. security. The United States could be drawn into such a war, even if strict security considerations suggested it should stay out. A major power war could escalate to a nuclear war that, especially if the United States joins, could include attacks against the American homeland. Thus, the United States should not be unconcerned about Europe's future.[5]

Hedging Against a Resurgent Russian Threat to the West

The probability of a resurgent Russia launching a deliberate attack against the West in the foreseeable future is now generally believed to be extremely small: probably most important, Russian goals, unlike those of the Soviet Union, do not threaten the West. In addition, Russia's capability for threatening the West is significantly reduced, because it is laboring under the weight of economic and political turmoil and because its conventional forces are being reduced and withdrawn from Central Europe. Nevertheless, most analysts believe that such a war is more probable than a war within Western Europe, since they see the latter possibility as virtually non-existent for the foreseeable future.

Whether the probability of eventual Russian attack is sufficiently large to warrant Western efforts to insure against it is another question, however. Some analysts believe that the probability is so low that the West should ignore it completely. The more prudent policy, however, is for the West to buy insurance until the on-going transformation of the former Soviet Union has run its course. If Russia's growing economic troubles or intensifying nationalist interests bring leaders to power who favor more assertive foreign policies, the West will be glad that it continued to keep up its guard. If, on the other hand, Russia evolves into a stable peaceful democracy, the West can reconsider its insurance policy.

In addition to providing adequate deterrence and defense, Western military policies for dealing with the possibility of a resurgent Russia should satisfy two criteria. First, to encourage continued improvement of political relations with Russia, the West should be careful not to threaten the military capabilities that Russia believes are necessary for its defense. Increasing Russia's insecurity could create pressures for an expansionist foreign policy, in turn straining its relations with the West. Paying attention to these military considerations may appear unimportant today, when Western economic cooperation and diplomatic policies are likely to play a more important role in influencing Russia's future foreign policy. If relations ever begin to sour, however, Western military policies that appear threatening to Russian leaders could fuel growing tensions. This dimension of hedging is just as important as making sure that the West is not caught militarily unprepared.

Second, the West's insurance policy will have to be far less expensive than its Cold War defense policy, so that the costs of defense are more in line with current risks. Policies designed to deal with a vague future possibility of a Russian threat will be politically sustainable only if they are far less expensive than those that were required during the Cold War to deal with a clear-cut, immediate Soviet threat.

Preventing War in the East, or Avoiding Western Involvement

Whereas many observers consider the possibility of a resurgent Russia threatening the West to be more hypothetical than real, wars are already raging in the East.[6] The dissolution of the Soviet Union has added to the possibilities for war that already existed within Central Europe; tensions and disagreements between Russia and Ukraine highlight the possibility of a major power war in the East.

Whether to extend security guarantees to the East is now the key security question facing the West. Because war in the East is likely, Western commitments would likely be put to the test. Western intervention could carry substantial risks. Intervention in a Central European war could involve the West in a war that becomes unexpectedly large, including the possibility of an unintended clash with Russia. The probability of such a clash, although small, is likely to be larger than the probability of a NATO–Warsaw Pact war during the Cold War.

The question is still more important because there is apparently extensive American discussion about extending security guarantees to the East. For example, a high-level draft of the 1992 Defense Planning Guidance identified possible military responsibilities for American forces in the East: "The U.S. could also consider extending to the east-central European states security commitments analogous to those we have extended to Persian Gulf States. . . . Should there be a threat from the Soviet Union's successor state, we should plan to defend against such a threat in Eastern Europe, should there be an alliance decision to do so."[7] Although the document was quickly disowned by the Bush administration once leaked to the press, it was the unilateral tone of the document and the cost of preparing for ambitious military missions that caused controversy; the possibility of expanding Western commitments into the East did not excite much opposition.[8] In addition, according to news reports, the United States signaled willingness to discuss limited military cooperation with Ukraine once it resumed movement toward denuclearization.[9]

Western offers of security guarantees would likely be welcomed by Eastern countries, which have expressed interest in joining NATO or at least receiving its protection. Ukraine has noted that once all of its nuclear weapons have been sent to Russia—which it agreed to do, under pressure from the West—its security will require "some guarantees from the world community."[10]

In assessing the dangers posed by war in the East, and therefore the appropriate Western response, the West should distinguish between types of wars: at one end of this broad spectrum are wars between smaller states, such as the war involving states of the former Yugoslavia; at the other end are wars in which Russia fights a medium-to-major power, such as Ukraine.

To assess the danger that these types of war would pose to Western interests, it is useful to distinguish Western security interests from other Western interests, which include humanitarian and economic interests. The type of interests that are at stake influences the costs and risks the West should be willing to run to protect them. For example, protecting security interests tends to justify risking large-scale military conflict, whereas accomplishing humanitarian objectives may warrant the investment of Western resources, but rarely extensive military casualties.

Security interests. Western security might be threatened by war in the East in three principal ways; however, only the last of the three poses a major danger. First, fighting in the East could spread to the West; that is, once involved in an Eastern conflict, a participating country might decide to attack the West. However, although the term "spread" suggests that this type of expansion would occur through some natural unavoidable process, why and how an Eastern war should spread to the West is actually far from obvious. As long as the West makes clear its intention not to intervene, the warring states would have little incentive to attack the West to protect their ability to achieve war aims in the East. Moreover, if the West maintains adequate deterrent capabilities, these states should not see the war opening possibilities for opportunistic expansion into the West.[11]

Second, fighting in the East could draw in the West; that is, Western countries could decide to intervene to protect their interests. However, most wars in the East—especially wars between smaller states, and civil wars—would not directly threaten Western security interests; in such cases, the West could stay out of the war without jeopardizing its security. Thus, these wars pose a security threat only if the West might intervene for non-security reasons and if, following Western intervention, the war could expand further, resulting in a clash between the West and a major power (or several of them) in the East.[12] For example, if the West might intervene to stop a war between Hungary and Rumania, to save lives or to reduce the influx of refugees, and if then Russia or Ukraine might intervene on the opposite side, then a war between Hungary and Rumania would pose an indirect threat to Western security. The possibility of this type of escalation should count against Western intervention for humanitarian or economic reasons, an issue I turn to in the next section. On the other hand, if the West might nevertheless intervene for these non-security reasons, then these indirect security dangers increase Western incentives for trying to prevent these Eastern wars.

Third, war in the East could increase the military threat to the West. For example, if Russia were to conquer Ukraine and then in another war further extend its control over Central Europe, Western Europe could face a conventional threat that more closely resembles the one it faced during the Cold War than the greatly reduced threat it faces today. This military capability would be all the more worrisome, since Russian aggression would be taken as clear testimony of its malign objectives.

Consequently, the West has security interests in preventing Russian expansion into Central Europe, and might therefore want to make extended deterrence commitments to protect these countries from Russian attack.[13] Although this logic could support Western guarantees to prevent Russia from conquering Ukraine and Belarus (since these moves could constitute the first step in westward expansion), the West has grounds for choosing not to extend guarantees to former Soviet republics, while extending them to, for example, Poland, the Czech Republic, Slovakia, and Hungary. The rationale for this distinction would be two-fold: the West's security interests in the former Soviet republics are smaller, since they are further from the West; and the risks of extending these guarantees are greater, since relations between the republics of the former Soviet Union are still evolving, tensions between them are greater, and Western involvement is especially likely to irritate and provoke Russia.

In short, most wars in the East would not threaten Western security and, consequently, extending security guarantees in these cases would not be justified by standard security considerations. The key exception appears to be wars launched by Russia to reestablish the subjugation of Central Europe. This line of argument suggests that the West might offer conditional security guarantees to some of the countries of Central Europe—the West would offer to protect them against Russia, but not each other. . . .

Non-security interests. Although Western security interests would not be directly jeopardized by the Central European wars that are most likely, the West has other interests in preventing these wars and in reducing death and destruction if they occur. Probably most obvious are humanitarian interests. In addition, war in the East could increasingly damage Western economic interests, especially German interests, as Western direct investment and trade with the East grows. War in the East could also increase immigration to the West, straining Western economies and generating domestic turmoil.[14] Such non-security interests in some combination appear more likely to draw the West into smaller Eastern wars than do security interests. . . .

Preventing Major Power War in the West

The third broad category of war that the West should consider is a war between Western Europe's major powers, which could also include major powers from the East. This type of war is generally believed to be far less likely than the types discussed above. With NATO countries enjoying good political relations that matured during the forty-five years of the Cold War, and with the countries of the European Community committed to increasing the economic and political integration of Western Europe, the possibility of a major war in the West strikes many observers as too unlikely and distant even to consider. In contrast, more pessimistic analysts worry that this harmony fostered during the Cold War might not last far beyond its end. From this perspective, Europe is still in transition, propped up by institutions—like NATO—that will cease to function as Cold War arrangements are gradually brought into line with the transformed Europe.[15] Then, once again, serious tensions could begin growing within the West.

One does not, however, need to be convinced that the pessimists are correct to conclude that some effort to insure against bad outcomes is desirable. Because war within the West would be so costly, efforts to preserve currently good relations are appropriate, unless one is entirely confident about the peaceful future of Western Europe.

However, such efforts will not command political support if they are too expensive, since large investments in a hedge against distant and seemingly unlikely events will be unappealing. Moreover, policies designed explicitly to deal with conflict in the West promise to be difficult to sell because acknowledging the possibility of security competition within the West would clash with on-going efforts to expand Western European integration. Consequently, security arrangements that are warranted by other dangers, and can be explained as such, but that also help to preserve good political relations in the West, are likely to be most feasible. The obvious analogy is the Cold War NATO—officially justified entirely by its value for balancing against the Soviet Union, but widely if unofficially recognized as playing a valuable role in eliminating security tensions within the West.[16]

Security Structures

Having laid out the basic types of war that the United States and Western Europe must be concerned with, we are prepared to assess alternative security structures. This section assesses five significantly different security structures: NATO, the WEU, collective security, concerts, and defensive unilateral security. Implicitly, it also compares them to a sixth possibility—Europe without a security structure.[17] Virtually no one has advocated a complete end to coordination of Europe's national security policies, but some analysts worry that the lack of clear military threats could convince Europe's major powers that their interests are best protected by *ad hoc* coordination arranged when specific problems arise.

All of these security structures should be judged in terms of: (1) their ability to provide the military capabilities the West requires to protect its interests, by deterring war and, if necessary, fighting; (2) their ability to preserve or improve political relations, most importantly by moderating the security dilemma;[18] and (3) their political and military feasibility.

NATO

To evaluate the effectiveness of NATO, this section assesses NATO's ability to deal with the three types of war described above.

Resurgent Russia. A Western alliance—either NATO or a purely Western European alliance—is the obvious choice for dealing with the danger of future attack from the East. This was NATO's mission in the past, and if the only direct threat to the West were a deliberate attack from the East, a Western alliance would still be the best form of protection. When the source of the threat is known, balancing is the appropriate solution. A balancing coalition would insure that the West has the military capabilities required for deterring a major power, while spreading the costs of hedging across Western countries. (The relative merits of NATO and the WEU are addressed in the next section.)

A common argument against preserving NATO is that excluding Russia from the Western security structure will decrease Russian security, which will strain the West's political relations with Russia and eventually fuel conflicts that increase the probability of war. However, being excluded from the Western alliance should increase Russian insecurity only if, as a result, the West poses a larger military threat. This need not be the case. The West can reduce whatever military threat it might pose and engage in extensive arms control while retaining necessary defensive capabilities, even if it does not include Russia and other Eastern states in a continent-wide security structure. For example, Western conventional forces could be designed to have little capability for launching an offensive into the former Soviet Union.[19] Germany would forgo nuclear weapons for the foreseeable future, since, as discussed in a following section, the insecurity they would initially generate in the East could fuel problems that more than offset the security they might provide to Germany. Finally, American strategic nuclear policy could be designed to ensure that Russia retains confidence in its nuclear retaliatory capabilities, since this increases confidence in its ability to deter Western conventional attack, which in turn reduces pressures for Russian expansion in Central Europe.

Another common objection to prescribing NATO as a hedge is that the Russian threat is now too small to hold the Western alliance together. Some observers believe that with the Soviet threat first greatly reduced and now dissolved, the threat from the East is not great enough to sustain a balancing coalition—NATO has lost its mission and, therefore, it is only a matter of time until the alliance dissolves.[20]

However, whether states should join an alliance depends on both the magnitude of the threat and the magnitude of the costs—primarily economic—of continuing the alliance. If the danger posed by the Soviet Union or Russia has steeply declined but not permanently disappeared, then there is a sound case for maintaining a Western alliance as an insurance policy, if the cost is not too great. Thus, this case for buying insurance can be strengthened by greatly reducing the costs of maintaining the alliance, which is certainly possible given the greatly reduced military potential facing the West. NATO has already begun such a transformation.

Preventing war in the East. In assessing NATO's utility for preventing wars in the East, consider first the wars that pose a potential security threat to the West, specifically, wars launched by Russia into Central Europe or certain republics of the former Soviet Union. This case closely resembles the case of a resurgent Russia addressed above. As argued there, when the threat is a known major power, a balancing coalition is the obvious solution. Thus, if the West concludes that its security interests warrant extension of security guarantees against Russian expansion into Central Europe, NATO is well matched to this danger.

Consider next wars that do not threaten Western security, that is, wars between smaller states, but in which the West might intervene to protect non-security interests. In these cases, NATO is less important as a balancing coalition, since the United States and the major powers of Western Europe could each afford military capabilities sufficient to significantly influence smaller wars. Nevertheless, acting together—under NATO or the WEU— could achieve important efficiencies. Collective action spreads the risks of military intervention in the East across many countries, thereby increasing the willingness of Western countries to participate in peace-making missions. Countries that might see benefits in humanitarian intervention, but which were unwilling to incur the costs of maintaining capabilities for intervention or the risks of intervening on their own, would be more likely to intervene in a collective action. In addition to these benefits, foreign policy coordination could reduce the probability of political strains within the West; I discuss these potential benefits below in the section on concerts.

Preventing war in the West. NATO can play a major role in hedging against the growth of security competition in Western Europe by preserving America's role as a "defensive balancer." NATO enables the United States implicitly to promise to protect all countries of Western Europe against one another. Probably most important, this American role would make whatever offensive potential remains in Europe less threatening, since countries would expect the United States to come to their defense. By moderating the security dilemma that Western European countries might eventually face, the United States can reduce or eliminate the insecurity that pessimists believe is bound to generate security competition in Europe. In addition, the United States can contribute to deterrence, if this ever becomes necessary. Combined with the forces of the attacked country, the conventional capabilities of the United States and its even greater military potential should be sufficient to thwart any European expansionist.

Maintaining America's military commitment would have the additional advantage of reducing pressures for nuclear proliferation, which could strain relations within the West, as well as the East. More specifically, by increasing German security, America's European commitment should reduce German incentives for eventually acquiring nuclear weapons. If it lacked an American nuclear guarantee, Germany might conclude that it required nuclear weapons, especially if Russian foreign policy became more aggressive. Although this proliferation might provide some benefits (as discussed below), it will be unnecessary so long as German security remains high.

To meet these responsibilities, the United States would require capabilities for intervening in Europe. However, the United States could meet its commitment while appearing far less threatening than any European country that possessed comparable military forces. America's distance from the continent greatly reduces how threatening its conventional capabilities will appear. Distance increases the time it would take to bring these forces to bear, making it harder to launch offensive operations but possible to guarantee a difficult war of attrition. In addition, America's historical commitment to fighting in Europe only to oppose European hegemons reduces the prospect that the United States will come to be viewed as a threat to European security. As a result, adding American capabilities is not simply adding another pole to European multipolarity. Instead, because Western Europeans are likely to continue to view American capabilities as essentially defensive, the United States can increase political stability among the major powers across the entire continent.

To reduce doubts about its commitment to intervene in a European war, the United States should continue to deploy forces in Europe. Otherwise, with the United States safely separated from Europe, Western European states would be inclined to worry that a risk-taking aggressor would be especially likely to question whether the United States would run the risks of this intervention. These forward American forces would be valued more as a concrete symbol of America's commitment than as an essential component of its fighting capability. Consequently, American military deployments in Western Europe could be relatively small. The credibility of the U.S. commitment would depend, however, on its ability to deploy much larger forces to Europe in a timely fashion.

Keeping American forces in Europe will be politically infeasible if the principal justification were that Western Europe requires a defensive balancer. However, as argued above, there is a solid case for preserving NATO as a low-cost insurance policy against a resurgent Russia and as a means for achieving other Western objectives in the East. Fortunately, these other purposes of NATO can provide unofficial cover for an American presence that helps preserve good political relations in the West. Wide, if unofficial, recognition of this role for NATO should help build support for maintaining the alliance.

A Western European Alliance

In the Maastricht Treaty of December 1991 the EC, as part of its plan for moving toward a common foreign and security policy, decided to make the WEU the instrument of its increased defense cooperation.[21] Although WEU members supported WEU "as a means to strengthen the European pillar of the Atlantic Alliance," we need to consider how effective the WEU would be without NATO: as the Cold War becomes more distant, judgments about the effectiveness of Western European security cooperation could influence both American and Western European determination to preserve NATO.[22]

Resurgent Russia. Would not an alliance of Western European countries be as effective as NATO in hedging against a resurgent Russia? The first concern is that the prospects for developing an effective WEU in the post-Soviet world are probably worse than the prospects for maintaining a restructured NATO. The problem is not one of resources—Western Europe possesses resources that are more than sufficient to balance effectively against Russia, especially now that Russia is judged both less able and less likely to challenge the West.[23] Rather, the question is whether the WEU can effectively draw on these resources. Judging in structural terms, the WEU faces the same challenge facing NATO: as Josef Joffe argued recently, "if NATO has lost its rationale along with its rival, why should the EC/WEU do better?"[24] In fact, NATO probably has somewhat better prospects for survival, since American participation reduces the costs to Western European countries of buying insurance. Judging from an organizational perspective, even though NATO is in the midst of a major restructuring,[25] its well-established institutions and success in alliance cooperation appear to favor it over developing an essentially new military organization. Judging in terms of leadership, there is no clear leader for a Western European alliance, but differences in the military and foreign policy inclinations of the major Western European powers are sufficiently large to suggest that leadership will be required. Although the U.S. role in NATO will and should decline, NATO can continue to benefit from American leadership.[26] Overall, the case is not overwhelming, but if the choice were one or the other, NATO is the safer bet.

The second concern is that removing the United States from the alliance would increase the probability that Germany would decide it needs nuclear weapons, which could in turn strain relations within the West, which could undermine the cohesion of the WEU. As discussed above, proliferation becomes more likely if Germany loses the extended nuclear deterrence which the United States presently provides. Germany might decide that French and British nuclear guarantees, even if offered, were inadequate for a variety of military and historical reasons.

War in the East. For deterring Russian attacks into Central Europe, NATO has an advantage over the WEU, in addition to the advantages discussed above. The military potential that the United States contributes to NATO is likely to be more valuable for extending deterrence to Central Europe than for deterring direct attacks against Western Europe. Protecting a country in Central Europe is militarily more difficult than defending the West; Western Europe might be able to protect itself with high confidence, but not to protect countries in Central Europe. Russian doubts about Western European capabilities could be especially problematic, since extended deterrence threats are generally less credible than threats to protect one's own homeland, given the defender's greater interests in defending its homeland.

With regard to smaller wars in Central Europe, the case for NATO over the WEU is not as strong. Western intervention for non-security reasons appears to be the clearest mission for an expanded WEU that is prepared to act separately from the United States. Non-security intervention appears to be the category in which Western European and American interests might diverge most,[27] since Western Europe will have larger economic investments and trade links with the East and possibly stronger ethnic ties to populations that would be vulnerable.[28] European proponents believe that a European defense identity is necessary because divergences between Western European and American interests could create situations in which Western Europe needs to act on its own.[29] Moreover, this is the case in which the military capabilities offered by the United States would be least valuable, since Western Europe can certainly afford the capabilities required for this type of intervention.

War in the West. The WEU, without NATO, lacks America as a defensive balancer, and therefore cannot make NATO's contribution to the preservation of good political relations within the West. Western Europe would have to develop other means for hedging against strained relations and moderating the effects of the security dilemma. However, as following sections demonstrate, the alternatives are not promising.

In sum, the WEU has important shortcomings compared to NATO. NATO's relative advantages include the prospect of better survival in the post-Soviet world, of enhanced extended deterrence commitments to oppose Russia in the East (if the West decides they are warranted), and of maintaining the United States as a hedge against strained relations in the West. The WEU could, however, complement NATO, supporting a common EC defense policy and providing political flexibility for Western Europe to launch non-security interventions on its own.

Collective Security

The term "collective security" is often a source of confusion, and compared to standard alliances its logic is more complicated and its effectiveness more contentious. I will use "collective security" narrowly to refer to arrangements in which each member state commits itself to oppose any aggressor from within the system. This description of collective security, as a system of all-against-one, allows for a spectrum of organizational possibilities, of varying institutional arrangements and geographical scope.[30] However, much of what is frequently clustered under the label of collective security does not properly qualify, including standard alliances—like

NATO—and certain forms of collective action, such as cases in which a number of countries join together on an *ad hoc* basis to oppose a specific aggression.[31] . . .

Proponents of collective security identify three reasons why collective security is preferable to leaving Europe without formal security arrangements between states.[32] First, collective security enhances deterrence by promising more effective balancing against aggressors. Specifically, it enhances the probability that an aggressor will face a coalition of opposing states that possesses preponderant power. By comparison, without collective security, aggressors are likely to expect at most roughly equal opposition.[33]

Second, proponents argue that collective security will establish institutions that themselves encourage conditions favorable to continuing peace: by providing information useful for reducing concern about other states' expansionist intentions, and by providing international fora for sharing ideas and strengthening shared values.

Third, collective security is said to moderate the security dilemma. States require less offensive capability, since all states will contribute offense to defeat an aggressor. The transparency provided by collective security institutions helps here, reducing uncertainty about states' capabilities, thereby reducing misperceptions of intentions and pressures to build potentially more threatening forces.

The most commonly noted shortcoming of collective security is that states will fail to meet their commitments—states not directly threatened will stand aside, thereby permitting an aggressor to face less than the promised full opposition of the system.[34] However, although this danger exists, the criticism does not deal a lethal blow to collective security. If the point of comparison is a system without all-against-one commitments, then although the magnitude of increased participation in balancing is hard to assess, its sign is unlikely to be negative.

Nevertheless, whether collective security would enhance deterrence is harder to determine. If states expect to be protected by an all-against-one response, they will under-prepare for their own defense, possibly leaving themselves vulnerable if other states then stand out the war.[35] On the other hand, if states do not under-prepare, then a combined effort becomes less necessary and therefore somewhat less likely, and collective security does less to moderate the security dilemma.

The other key criticism is that collective security is feasible only when it is also unnecessary. A standard requirement for establishing and maintaining a collective security system is that all members are willing to accept the political status quo,[36] and each is equally likely to pose a threat to the status quo at some time in the future. Critics hold that under these conditions collective security is unnecessary since peace is already ensured by good political relations between all states in the system. Proponents, pointing to the value of institutions and moderation of the security dilemma, counter that this criticism ignores the potential of collective security to promote conditions that are conducive to peace.

This summary suggests significant doubts about the effectiveness of collective security. The following subsections identify further shortcomings: I argue that collective security's basic logic is poorly matched to the West's interests and capabilities for dealing with a resurgent Russia and wars in the East; its logic is better matched to the danger of war between the West's major powers, but collective security nevertheless suffers a variety of shortcomings in that case.

Resurgent Russia. Collective security would not offer the West any clear advantages in dealing with a resurgent Russia: if the threat to the West were known to originate from a major power in the East, then the West should balance specifically against it; under these conditions, there is no reason to establish an organization designed to deal with a more diffuse set of threats and dangers. A Western alliance is ideal for performing this balancing mission.

Proponents counter that collective security is desirable because including Russia in a continent-wide system will increase Russian security, while excluding Russia will decrease its security. As discussed above, although the West should try to reduce the threat it poses to Russia, this does not require establishment of a collective security system. Extensive arms control and unilateral Western restraint is possible without collective security. Moreover, even though proponents claim that collective security will reduce Russian insecurity, as discussed in more detail below a collective security system could require the West to deploy military capabilities that would appear more threatening than the capabilities that NATO would require.

War in the East. Collective security suffers two shortcomings with regard to Eastern wars. First, a continent-wide collective security system would commit the West to intervene in conflicts that it should stay out of, or at least that it will want to consider on a case-by-case basis. As we have seen, unlimited commitments to the East go far beyond the West's interests. Discussions of collective security tend to overlook this issue by simply assuming that the West has security interests in keeping peace throughout Europe. Proponents of collective security respond that a looser system—a concert—provides leeway to intervene selectively, while providing a forum for consultations between Europe's major powers.[37] However, as I argue below, concert-like arrangements would be useful, but they are not best thought of as a loose form of collective security.

Second, even where the West's interests warrant security commitments, collective security will not provide large benefits. Regarding Eastern wars in which Russia is fighting to reassert control over some or all of Central Europe, a Western alliance is the best solution. Regarding Eastern wars that do not threaten Western security, while preceding sections have identified reasons for pursuing collective action—for example, to spread the costs and risks of intervention—we should not confuse these rationales with those for developing a collective security system. The opposition of all-against-one, which collective security calls for to generate preponderant deterrent capabilities, is unnecessary when major powers are intervening in a war between smaller powers. If NATO decides intervention is justified, its capabilities would certainly be more than adequate. Contributions from other European countries might help spread further the costs and risks of deterrence and peacemaking, but are unlikely to be decisive either in determining whether the West will intervene or determining whether intervention would be successful.[38] Moreover, although the lack of a collective security commitment might somewhat reduce the probability that other countries would contribute to intervention, it would not preclude their involvement and, when appropriate, NATO could encourage them to participate.

War in the West. By elimination, a strong case for collective security depends on its ability to deal with the danger of war in the West, possibly joined by other powers. In addition to the potential shortcomings summarized in my basic description of collective security, here I argue that collective security suffers two additional shortcomings: first, proponents have exaggerated its potential to preserve good political relations; second, implementing anything more than a symbolic system in today's Europe will be politically infeasible.

Ironically, collective security could play a role in undermining political relations between Europe's major powers. Contrary to the claim that collective security arrangements moderate the security dilemma, the result could be just the opposite. To meet their collective security obligations, states might have to deploy military forces with greater offensive capability than under other arrangements. For example, a state that planned to rely entirely on its own resources—without the help of allies—might deploy less offensive capability than it would be required to deploy to meet its collective security obligations.[39] If the offense-defense balance favors defense, states should often find that a defensive strategy provides the greatest security.[40] In these cases, pursuing collective security over other options could increase offensive capability in the system.

To better understand the nature of the problem, consider the offensive capabilities that effective European collective security would demand. Russia would be expected to come to the aid of France if France were attacked by Germany. This is likely to require Russia to have the ability to attack Germany effectively, requiring the ability to project massive conventional capabilities across much of the continent.[41] Providing Germany with confidence that these capabilities would be employed only in reaction to its aggression could be difficult, if not impossible. Similarly, if Germany is to offer protection to Russia, from attack by say Japan or China, Germany would require massive power projection capabilities of its own. Similar capabilities would be required if Germany were going to offer protection to Ukraine. These capabilities could generate security concerns for Russia and quite possibly Germany's Western European neighbors. German capabilities could be planned on the assumption that France and Britain, and possibly the United States, would also contribute to the offensive against Russia, thereby reducing the offensive requirements of each country and possibly resulting in no more offensive capability than if NATO planned to defend Ukraine. Nevertheless, Russia might view these forces as an overall Western capability, not individual countries' capabilities.

Offensive capabilities will not have these undesirable political effects as long as Europe's major powers remain confident about each others' benign intentions.[42] However, if political relations begin to deteriorate—which is when the military features and the deterrent potential of a collective security system would matter—the threatening appearance created by offensive military capabilities would then be likely to contribute to further worsening of European relations.

At a minimum, the political problems that collective security arrangements could generate create a trade-off with any supposed contribution to enhancing deterrence. Even if collective security is the best way to maximize deterrence, it might not be the best way to preserve peace. The probability of major power war will depend on two sets of considerations: first, the quality of political relations—if relations stay as good as they are today, then preponderant deterrent capabilities will be unnecessary; second, on the quality of deterrent capabilities—assuming that countries' motivations for war do not change, the probability of war decreases as the quality of deterrent arrangements improves. Strained political relations, fueled by the offensive capabilities required by collective security, could create incentives for war that exceed the greater credibility and military effectiveness that collective security might provide. This possibility is especially worrisome, since as today's political relations are good enough to ensure peace among Europe's major powers, a primary objective of a European security system should be preserving these good relations.

Compounding this shortcoming are serious doubts about feasibility. There appears to be little chance of implementing a collective security system in which Western European states take their obligations seriously. The threat from within Western Europe is now believed to be too small for the countries of Western Europe to restructure their forces to bring them into line with the requirements for opposing aggression from within the West. However, simply declaring a collective security system, without adjusting military strategy and forces accordingly, will do very little to moderate the security dilemma. Thus, agreeing to join a continent-wide collective security system is likely to have little effect on political relations or security in the West. The good news is that the declaration would not damage these currently good relations; the bad news is that it would leave the West without an effective hedge. If political relations do take a turn for the worse, the countries of Western Europe would find themselves poorly cushioned from the security dilemma.

In short, collective security as a means of reducing the probability of war between Europe's major powers can play little more than a symbolic role. A collective security system could be declared, but would not significantly influence countries' force deployments. The key exception would be if the West decided to plan to protect Ukraine against Russia, in which case it might require larger offensive capabilities. However, if this is what collective security would amount to in practice, then the West should focus more directly on whether and how to make this commitment and not get confused by the additional complexities that necessarily accompany collective security arrangements.

Concerts—Foreign Policy Coordination Among Europe's Major Powers

The end of the Cold War has led many authors to declare that Europe is now prepared for a new Concert of Europe.[43] Although a concert is often understood as a limited form of collective security, concerts do not include the basic commitment of all-against-one that defines a collective security system and produces its benefits, and therefore are best not included in this category.[44] A concert strives to tap and to increase the willingness of the major powers to constrain and coordinate their foreign policies, thereby avoiding strained relations, misperceptions, and otherwise unforeseeable political and military clashes.[45] Compared to collective security, the operation of a concert is not as easily defined by a single feature. Among the most basic features of a concert are the "rules of the road" designed to moderate competition between the systems' major powers.[46] Whereas collective security focuses on providing overwhelming deterrent capabilities, a concert focuses on preserving good political relations through diplomatic means.

An example of rules that could establish a concert, and which are especially relevant to post-Soviet Europe, are understandings to coordinate any intervention that is designed to protect smaller powers and to terminate conflicts between them. Major powers could agree to intervene only under specific conditions, for example, only if all major powers were willing to participate in the intervention; or only if all powers agreed that it was acceptable for one or more powers to intervene; or, if the major powers agreed that certain of them had greater interests in intervention (or non-intervention) in specific cases, the decision on whether to intervene could be transferred to a sub-group. Arrangements for coordination would be designed to constrain the major powers while at the same time providing flexibility commensurate with the diversity of their interests.

This coordination by the major powers could provide two types of benefits. First, essentially barring independent unilateral intervention eliminates an important potential source of tension between the major powers. If it intervened unilaterally, a country could generate fears that it was trying to advance its own foreign policy interests and gain advantages relative to other major powers, even if it were actually pursuing more acceptable goals, such as preventing a regional conflict from spreading, or protecting humanitarian interests. Such fears might then fuel concerns about the intervening country's broader intentions, thereby giving impetus to more competitive policies. Multilateral intervention, or unilateral intervention approved by the relevant major powers, could reduce, if not eliminate, these concerns. Second, consultation and coordination prior to intervention could reduce the probability of unanticipated escalation— clashes between major powers resulting from their intervention on opposing sides of a regional conflict. Prior consultation increases the prospects for understanding why other states might object to intervention and how they might react, and for modifying policies accordingly.

A concert increases the prospects for coordination that already exist as a result of countries' shared interests. By increasing consultation between the major powers, the concert provides information that reduces the probability that a country would act unilaterally without recognizing that other major powers will object. In addition, by establishing the expectation that intervention will be coordinated, the concert increases the political costs that would follow uncoordinated intervention.

The prospects for a successful concert depend on the stakes involved. If the stakes are relatively low, compared to the value the major powers place on preserving good relations, then countries should be more willing to make compromises on intervention. For example, a major power is more likely to agree to forgo a humanitarian intervention than to forgo intervention motivated by national security concerns, since the latter would generally provide larger (often much larger) national benefits. Countries' willingness to coordinate is also likely to increase with the quality of their political relationship. Good relations reduce the risks of attempting to coordinate. The expectation, for example, that other countries will honor their commitment to exercise restraint makes one's own restraint more acceptable. In addition, the costs of failed cooperation would be smaller, since damage to one's credibility and reputation are less costly when the opposing country is less dangerous.[47]

Two potential costs of entering into a concert should be raised. First, as already noted, breaking a commitment to coordinate could be more damaging to relations than pursuing the same action without having made such a commitment. In the former case, the intervening country is likely to be seen as acting in bad faith, in addition to pursuing an action that is potentially threatening on its own terms. Thus, whether a concert is desirable depends on estimates of how likely its members are to meet their commitments. Second, agreeing to coordinate intervention could reduce the effectiveness of extended deterrent threats, since major powers are less likely to meet their deterrent commitments if all major powers, or even a subset of them, must agree before intervening.

The following discussion examines the potential of concerts for dealing with wars in Central Europe. A concert in post-Soviet Europe could not play much of a direct role in the other types of war I have identified, since it would focus on coordinating the major powers' policies toward third areas, not on changing their policies toward each other.

War in the East. Post-Soviet Europe might benefit from two sets of concert-like arrangements—coordination within the West and coordination between the West and Russia. However, cast in these more specific terms, this coordination may seem less grand than the term "concert" suggests. The considerations addressed above suggest optimism about the prospects for concert-like cooperation in Europe: the major powers enjoy good political relations and their stakes in most Central European conflicts will be limited.

A coordinated Western policy for intervention in the East could reduce the probability of political strains within the West.[48] For historical and geographical reasons the country of greatest potential concern is Germany. Although German economic strength is now creating fear about German economic dominance of the continent,[49] Germany's relatively smaller military capability and its reluctance to employ these capabilities outside its borders have so far dampened the growth of security fears among its neighbors. However, unilateral independent German military intervention in the East, for example for purely humanitarian reasons, could undermine confidence in German goals and intentions, even if such undermining were unwarranted. These strains could be the early seeds of security fears within the West, fueling concern about German military capabilities and potential. To insure that intervention in the East does not generate these strains, Western countries could agree to intervene only in coordination with each other and to integrate their military capabilities for intervention.[50] In fact, EC plans for establishing a common foreign and security policy have set this degree of coordination as an eventual goal.

The prospects for Western countries accepting restraints on non-security intervention should be greater than for security intervention, since the benefits are smaller. Thus, we expect that the West will have better prospects for coordinating restraint in intervention in wars between Central Europe's smaller countries than in wars that pose some security threat to Western Europe, most obviously a war involving Russia and also possibly Ukraine.

NATO or the EC/WEU are the obvious organizations for establishing Western coordination. A Western concert therefore does not require a new organization, but rather adds (or maybe simply clarifies[51]) another role for these organizations. The key to a coordinated Western policy is probably coordination within Western Europe. If only because of geography, the divergence of American and Western European policies is likely to create smaller problems. For example, the United States would be glad to see Western Europe effectively take the lead on humanitarian intervention, as U.S. policy toward the war of Yugoslavian disintegration has made clear.

The West might also want to develop concert-like arrangements with Russia, coordinating its decisions on non-security intervention with Russia, both to avoid generating Russian insecurity and to reduce the probability that Western intervention would escalate unpredictably to a clash with Russia. For example, the West might agree to consult with Russia before intervening in the East. Alternatively, the West could pursue more restrictive coordination, agreeing not to intervene without Russian consent, or to intervene only in coordination with Russia. In return, Russia would be expected to accept similar restrictions.[52] Although the more stringent restrictions would grant Russia a veto on Western actions, this might be warranted when Western intervention would be especially threatening or likely to lead to escalation. Western efforts to coordinate with Russia deserve careful attention, since the most probable path to major power war in Europe may well be through major power intervention in wars started by smaller powers.

There is presently not an organization tailored for this coordination between the West and Russia. However, by turning to the United Nations Security Council, the West has enabled the Security Council to serve many of these functions—providing among other things a forum in which Russia could veto Western proposals for intervention. Of course, the West could always choose to act without a UN mandate. However, use of the Security Council—in the Gulf War and more recently in the war in the former Yugoslavia—may be establishing expectations that will discourage independent Western action.[53]

Defensive Unilateral Security

In the fifth and final security structure I assess—defensive unilateral security—countries agree to defend themselves by defensive means. The motivation and design of a defensive unilateral security structure is guided by the advantages of moderating the security dilemma—avoiding the negative political consequences that can flow from threatening military postures—while recognizing countries' continuing need to defend themselves.

Defensive unilateral security applies best when countries are highly uncertain about the source of future threats.[54] Under this condition, arranging standard balancing alliances is difficult, since countries are unsure who to oppose. Thus, defensive unilateral security and collective security apply in similar situations, but are guided by different priorities: collective security gives priority to maximizing deterrence by guaranteeing that aggressors will face overwhelming opposition, whereas defensive unilateral security gives priority to preserving or improving good political relations by moderating the security dilemma.

Defensive unilateral security calls for the major powers to reduce their offensive capabilities to a minimum.[55] States would try to reduce their requirements for offense through unilateral means and multilateral arms control. Arms control agreements would limit offense, thereby shifting the balance of deployed forces toward defense, and provide for extensive monitoring of military capabilities.[56]

Is defensive unilateral security effective if deterrence becomes necessary? Defensive unilateral security leaves states to fend for themselves; states' security will therefore depend partly on the offense-defense balance. If the aggressor attacks without first breaking out of the arms control agreement, and if the balance of deployed forces favors defense, the attacker will have poor prospects for prevailing in a short war.[57]

If, however, the aggressor first launches a military buildup before attacking, then arms-race stability matters, making the offense-defense balance of *available* technology (distinguished from *deployed* technology) more important. When defense has an advantage, good monitoring and response capabilities should enable states of comparable size to continue to protect themselves effectively by launching a defensive buildup. On the other hand, when defense lacks a clear advantage over offense, potential victims will need help.

One solution is a security arrangement in which states commit themselves to break out of the defensive regime if another state violates it, and to join against the violator if it launches an attack. In a certain sense this is really only a disguised form of collective security, since when offense has the advantage each state is depending partly on the combined effort of others to deter aggressors.[58]

This important similarity, however, should not be allowed to obscure the significant difference between these approaches. By pushing offensive capabilities far into the background, defensive unilateral security makes military capabilities less likely to generate negative political consequences. Year in and year out, major powers would lack effective offensive capabilities. By continuing to meet the arms agreement's ban on building offensive capabilities, countries would signal goals consistent with the agreement's status-quo objectives.[59] Thus, keeping offensive capabilities in the background should be quite different politically, as well as militarily, from actually deploying them.

A basic criticism claims that defensive unilateral security cannot meet its primary objective of preserving good political relations. According to this argument, good political relations are at least as likely to be damaged by the emergence of a greedy country—one motivated to expand for reasons other than increasing its security—as by a highly insecure state. Defensive unilateral security is not well matched to this case because it gives priority to preventing war by reducing insecurity. If peace is most likely to be challenged by the rise of a state primarily motivated by greed, then a security system should emphasize the overriding determination and capability of its members to crush aggressors.

In this case, collective security, based on offensive capabilities dedicated to countering aggression, is more likely to succeed, not only because it holds out the possibility of overwhelming opposition, but also because it threatens to make losing a war very costly.[60] Ideally, this combination of high risks and the clear futility of aggression might also stop greedy states from developing in the first place, for example by increasing the domestic opposition against proponents of opportunistic expansion. Thus, proponents of defensive unilateral security should be confident either that insecurity is the primary threat to peace, or that defense has a large advantage over offense.

In theory at least, defensive unilateral security could be implemented in two complementary ways—shifting to non-offensive conventional postures, and proliferating nuclear weapons.

Non-offensive conventional defense. States relying on conventional forces would deploy forces that could effectively defend their borders, but provide little capability to project power far beyond them. This approach could build on plans for non-offensive defense that were developed in the context of the NATO–Warsaw Pact confrontation. According to proponents, although no effective conventional posture could be made purely defensive, limiting those weapons which are especially valuable for offensive operations could significantly shift the balance of deployed capabilities toward defense. Although a consensus did not exist, tanks, mobile air defenses, and bridge laying equipment were commonly cited as prime targets for severe limitation. By comparison, anti-tank weapons, close-support aircraft, and rapidly deployable barriers were generally believed to favor defensive operations.[61] Skeptics, however, argued that the conventional forces required for defense and for offense were quite similar, making non-offensive defense militarily infeasible, even if countries could reach highly restrictive agreements.

Plans for non-offensive conventional postures in a multi-polar Europe confront complications that did not exist in the simpler bipolar division. If all major European powers are assumed to be equally likely to fight each other, there exist a large number of dyads that must be balanced.

Making matters worse, countries might want confidence that their forces would work against a coalition of other powers. If so, they will be dissatisfied even with plans that manage to balance all of the dyads.

These concerns are evident in the current debate. A recent proposal for transforming the conventional military postures of all European countries combines a variety of quantitative and qualitative limits to create defensive advantages.[62] Using an estimate of the average density of forces required to protect a given distance of border, the total size of each country's forces would be based on the length of its border. Offensive potential would be further constrained by limits on types of forces, logistical support, and the movement and concentration of forces.

But critics have already argued that this plan (and probably any plan that does not rest on specific assumptions about the composition of future coalitions) suffers serious problems. For example, countries with long borders end up with forces that have extensive offensive potential; this problem is exacerbated by thin force-to-space ratios, which increase the prospects for successful offensives; and countering this problem by allowing high force-to-space ratios results in larger conventional forces than were deployed during the Cold War, which is politically infeasible.[63] Whether these problems can be overcome by different plans is a question that awaits further study.

Nuclear Weapons

A second possibility is to rely on nuclear weapons to provide the major powers with highly defensive military postures.[64] Whereas designing an effective defensive conventional posture faces a variety of military-technical difficulties, nuclear weapons are commonly believed to have brought a revolution in favor of defense for countries that possess the wealth and expertise to deploy survivable arsenals.[65] Nuclear proliferation in Europe, however, could increase some states' insecurity. Thus, despite the merits of the nuclear revolution argument, proliferation is not a straightforward solution.

A country with a survivable nuclear arsenal possesses a powerful deterrent to attacks against its homeland, since the aggressor is vulnerable to devastating nuclear retaliation in response to full-scale conventional aggression. Even when the aggressor also possesses a survivable nuclear arsenal, nuclear weapons are likely to favor the defender. Although the risks of nuclear war would be shared, the defender is likely to have greater resolve, since, unlike the aggressor, its political survival is immediately at stake.

Because the forces required for retaliation need not threaten other countries' nuclear retaliatory forces, all the major powers could simultaneously maintain nuclear postures dedicated to primarily defensive missions.

An arms control agreement could insure easy maintenance of retaliatory capabilities: agreements would limit counterforce capabilities, while allowing arsenals sufficiently large to insure that no combination of countries could acquire a significant damage-limitation capability.

Nuclear weapons eliminate two of the potential shortcomings of defensive unilateral security relative to collective security. First, because defense overwhelmingly dominates, nuclear weapons eliminate the need for states to rely on each other if the arms control agreement breaks down. Second, unlike conventional denial capabilities, nuclear retaliatory capabilities threaten extremely high costs; by making aggression extremely risky they increase the prospects of deterring greedy states.

Since four of Europe's five current major powers (including the United States) currently have nuclear arsenals, in effect this approach calls for Germany to deploy a survivable arsenal of its own.[66] Other countries, such as Ukraine, might emerge as major powers or face security problems that cannot be solved with conventional forces, and conclude that they also deserve or require nuclear weapons.[67]

The case for proliferation as the means for providing defensive postures is not, however, as clear as this discussion so far suggests.[68] Even retaliatory/countervalue nuclear weapons are not purely defensive under all conditions. Whether the proliferation of survivable nuclear capabilities increases security throughout the system depends on the military status quo. If all countries are going from non-nuclear to nuclear status, then the defensive advantage of nuclear weapons could increase all countries' security. On the other hand, if some countries already have nuclear arsenals, then the addition of new nuclear powers could decrease the security of old nuclear powers.

Both military and political considerations could fuel this insecurity. The military logic is straightforward: the original nuclear powers could see the emergence of new nuclear powers as reducing their ability to deter conventional attacks. It would remain true, as argued above, that a defender's nuclear arsenal would continue to contribute to deterrence of conventional war following the proliferator's acquisition of nuclear weapons. Nevertheless, proliferation is likely to reduce the defender's confidence that its deterrent threats are sufficiently credible. The political logic follows along a similar track: the new nuclear arsenal, because it reduces the effectiveness of the defender's deterrent, appears to the defender as offense and could therefore suggest malign intentions.[69] In short, increasing the number of nuclear states is not necessarily an across-the-board shift toward enhanced deterrence and, therefore, toward defense.

Consider, for example, German acquisition of nuclear weapons. This could appear threatening to the republics of the former Soviet Union and possibly to Germany's Western European neighbors. Facing a non-nuclear Germany, Russia can count on its nuclear weapons to deter conventional attacks against its homeland and possibly against other former Soviet republics and, to a lesser extent, against other countries in Central Europe. Russian leaders might therefore see German acquisition of nuclear capabilities as reducing Russia's ability to deter German conventional attacks, especially attacks that did not immediately reach into Russian territory.[70]

Of course, over time these new nuclear powers could become part of the accepted political and military status quo. Especially if proliferation of nuclear weapons were combined with a shift toward non-offensive conventional postures—which would make any reduction in the effectiveness of nuclear deterrents less worrisome—tensions and fears should fade as the new eqilibrium is fully established.

Resurgent Russia. A shift to defensive unilateral security has no clear advantages for dealing with the danger of a resurgent Russia. Although reducing the military threats that face Russia might reduce the probability that Russia would resort to expansionist policies, implementing conventional defensive postures in all Western countries is unnecessary. Instead, as discussed above, the West can achieve this objective by making sure that the *overall* Western capability poses little threat to Russian security. It is true that German acquisition of nuclear weapons could enhance its ability to deter Russia, but this would be unnecessary if U.S. nuclear guarantees are preserved in NATO.

War in the East. The benefits offered by unilateral defensive security depend on the type of Eastern war. Consider first Russian attacks into Central Europe. The key potential threat to Russian security will be from the West, since Russia's size and nuclear force should enable it to maintain confidence in its ability to defend against its Central European neighbors, especially if they do not acquire nuclear arsenals.[71] Of course, Russia might exaggerate and misperceive the conventional threat posed by its larger neighbors,[72] for example Ukraine, but even these fears should be greatly moderated by Russia's military advantages. Thus, adding defensive postures in Central Europe to an already defensive NATO would do little to reduce Russia's insecurity. In addition, defensive restructuring of Russia's military is unlikely to reduce the insecurity of its Central European neighbors significantly. Russia's overall power is simply too great to be converted into a force that is unthreatening. Eliminating its neighbors' insecurity would be valuable, since the insecurity might provoke reactions—like building nuclear weapons—which would threaten Russian security. Unfortunately, a shift toward defensive conventional force postures almost certainly cannot meet this challenge.

Consider next the case of war between smaller powers in Central Europe. Some proponents have argued that defensive postures could play a valuable role here, especially if the country most likely to have revisionist objectives (consider Hungary versus Rumania) is the smaller country.[73] Although the military possibilities for establishing effective defensive capabilities have to be studied on a case-by-case basis, the situation does appear to be politically ripe for pursuing defensive postures; relations are good enough to allow cooperation but the potential for intensified tensions and future conflict is generally recognized.

A potential shortcoming of continent-wide conventional defensive security is that, if it were highly effective, it might leave the major powers without the ability to intervene in Central Europe. A solution might be to permit multi-national power projection forces designed specifically for intervention in wars between smaller powers, while leaving the major powers with little capability to intervene on their own or to attack each other.

War in the West. Although plans for defensive unilateral security are in many ways well matched to the situation in the West—characterized by uncertainty about which country might eventually adopt expansionist policies, and the importance of preserving good political relations—they nevertheless suffer numerous shortcomings. Regarding conventional force postures, beyond the questions about military feasibility addressed above, there must be added grave doubts about the current political feasibility of non-offensive defense. A full-scale restructuring of the conventional forces of individual Western European states would probably require large investments at a time when NATO countries are significantly decreasing defense spending. Furthermore, the whole idea of investing in forces to protect against other Western European states would appear entirely out of step with the on-going plans for deepening the political integration of Western Europe, even taking into account doubts generated by recent troubles with the Maastricht agreement. Finally, although less basic, implementing defensive conventional postures would probably conflict with current NATO plans for establishing multi-national corps, and could therefore strain the alliance. In short, although the case for conventional defensive unilateral security is logically sound—calling for a highly conservative hedge—the effort required is out of proportion to its distant and uncertain benefits.

These military-technical and political problems suggest that, at most, plans for transforming all of Europe to non-offensive conventional postures should be put on the back burner. They are worth studying, but have little prospect of being implemented until relations in the West begin to sour. At that point, if militarily feasible, there might be time to implement conventional military policies that would slow the growth of insecurity and tensions between Western Europe's major powers.

The case against using nuclear proliferation to achieve defensive postures is quite different. Germany would have good prospects for developing a survivable nuclear deterrent. However, as discussed above, German acquisition of a nuclear arsenal might generate more insecurity in Russia, and possibly the rest of Europe, than it would provide security to Germany. At least during the transition period, relations between Europe's major powers would probably deteriorate, not improve. Thus, although limited nuclear proliferation might be a good long-term strategy for insuring European stability, security arrangements that avoid this disruption are preferable, at least until the on-going transformation brought by Soviet disintegration is complete and good political relations between the West and Russia, as well as relations within the West, are firmly cemented. Also counting against nuclear proliferation is the virtual lack of political support in Germany (and the rest of Europe) for such a move, although this might change if the United States were to withdraw from Europe.[74]

Implications for Today's Europe

Systematic assessment of the dangers and responsibilities for which the West should prepare, and measurement of the ability of different security structures to meet these objectives, reveal a multi-faceted case for preserving NATO. NATO can play a valuable role in hedging against a resurgent Russia; if warranted by Western interests, NATO can effectively extend security guarantees to countries in Central Europe and intervene for humanitarian purposes; and, by preserving the American presence in Europe, NATO can insure against the possibility that security concerns will begin to divide Western Europe's major powers. Because a resurgent Russia might be motivated by insecurity, the West should avoid policies that could appear provocative and fuel misperceptions of its intentions; NATO can achieve this objective without expanding its membership to include Russia in a continent-wide security organization.

A Western European alliance could meet the first two of these responsibilities, but not as effectively: without the United States, Western European security guarantees to protect Central European states from Russia would probably be less credible; and American participation can increase the prospects that a Western alliance will survive in the post-Soviet world. Probably more important, the WEU could not substitute for NATO in hedging against deteriorating relations *within* the West: it eliminates America's role as a defensive balancer in Western Europe; and American withdrawal from Europe increases the probability of German nuclear proliferation, which could generate security concerns in both East and West. Thus, although the WEU can complement NATO—providing flexibility for Western Europe to act militarily on its own—a Western European alliance would be an ineffective substitute for NATO.

In addition to these purposes, NATO or the EC/WEU can serve valuable concert-like functions, providing the institutional arrangements for coordinating Western policy in Central Europe. The West should also co-ordinate these policies with Russia, which will require developing shared understandings and expectations for intervention in Central Europe.

The other basic alternatives—continent-wide collective security and defensive unilateral security structures—turn out to be of interest primar-ily for dealing with conflict in the West. However, in anything more than symbolic form, both are now infeasible for political reasons; and conven-tional defensive security may be infeasible for military-technical reasons as well. Moreover, there are strong reasons for doubting whether a conti-nent-wide collective security structure would be the best way to preserve good political relations in Europe. . . .

Notes

The author would like to thank Anne-Marie Burley, George Downs, Lynn Eden, Matthew Evangelista, James Fearon, Barbara Koremenos, Charles Kupchan, John Mearsheimer, Andrew Moravcsik, Jane Sharp, Stephen Walt, Stephen Van Evera, and Barbara Walter, and participants in the PIPES seminar at the Univer-sity of Chicago for their helpful comments on earlier drafts. Kenneth Yao provided valuable research assistance. A similar version of this article will appear in George Downs, ed., *Collective Security Beyond the Cold War* (University of Michigan Press, forthcoming). Research for this volume was supported by the Pew Charita-ble Trust.

1. Some observers believe that Europe requires multiple, interlocking institu-tions, including not only NATO and the WEU but also the CSCE, the UN, and re-gional security organizations. See for example Hans Binnendijk, "The Emerging European Security Order," *Washington Quarterly,* Vol. 14, No. 4 (Autumn 1991), pp. 71–81.

2. Evaluating alternative American grand strategies during the Cold War is Stephen M. Walt, "The Case for Finite Containment: Analyzing U.S. Grand Strat-egy," *International Security,* Vol. 14, No. 1 (Summer 1989), pp. 5–49.

3. Recent arguments for isolationism include Christopher Layne, "Tragedy in the Balkans," *New York Times,* June 5, 1992, p. 15; Earl C. Ravenal, *Designing De-fense for a New World Order: The Military Budget in 1992 and Beyond* (Washing-ton, D.C.: CATO Institute, 1991); and Eric A. Nordlinger, "America's Strategic Im-munity: Tne Basis of a National Security Strategy," in Robert Jervis and Seweryn Bialer, eds., *Soviet-American Relations After the Cold War* (Durham, N.C.: Duke University Press, 1991).

4. For a range of views on these dangers see Sean M. Lynn-Jones, ed., *The Cold War and After: Prospects for Peace: An International Security Reader* (Cam-bridge, Mass.: MIT Press, 1991).

5. For more extensive discussion of America's continuing security interests in Europe see Stephen Van Evera, "Why Europe Matters, Why the Third World Doesn't: American Grand Strategy After the Cold War," *Journal of Strategic Studies,* Vol. 13, No. 2 (June 1990), pp. 2–12; Robert J. Art, "A Defensible Defense: America's Grand Strategy After the Cold War," *International Security,* Vol. 15, No. 4 (Spring 1991), pp. 5–53; and Charles L. Glaser and George W. Downs, "Defense Policy: U.S. Role in Europe and Nuclear Strategy," in Kenneth A. Oye, Robert J. Lieber,

and Donald Rothchild, eds., *Eagle in a New World: American Grand Strategy in the Post–Cold War Era* (New York: HarperCollins, 1991), pp. 72–78.

6. On the tensions and potential for conflict in the Balkans see F. Stephen Larrabee, "Long Memories and Short Fuses: Change and Instability in the Balkans," *International Security,* Vol. 15, No. 3 (Winter 1990/91), pp. 58–91.

7. Patrick E. Tyler, "U.S. Strategy Plan Calls for Insuring No Rivals Develop," *New York Times,* March 8, 1992, p. 1. Prominent analysts have suggested a similar expansion of NATO's responsibilities. See for example Samuel P. Huntington, "America's Changing Strategic Interests," *Survival,* Vol. 33, No. 1 (January/February 1991), pp. 11–13. On the growing ties between the West and East see Stephen J. Flanagan, "NATO and Central and Eastern Europe: From Liaison to Security Partnership," *Washington Quarterly,* Vol. 15, No. 2 (Spring 1992), pp. 141–151.

8. Patrick E. Tyler, "Lone Superpower Plan: Ammunition for Critics," *New York Times,* March 10, 1992, p. 10; and Tyler, "Senior U.S. Officials Assail A 'One Superpower' Goal," *New York Times,* March 11, 1992. A couple of months later, the final version of this document gave greater prominence to cooperation with allies and the role of international organizations. See Tyler, "Pentagon Drops Goal of Blocking New Superpowers," *New York Times,* May 24, 1992, p. 1.

9. Thomas L. Friedman, "The U.S. Takes a Serious Look at Ukraine," *New York Times,* April 19, 1992, p. E5. Another example is offered by reactions to the wars in the former Yugoslavia. Although the West has so far rejected a peace-making role, early calls for American military intervention reflected serious interest in expanding the West's military responsibilities. See, for example, editorial, "Shame in Our Time, in Bosnia," *New York Times,* May 21, 1992, p. 28; editorial, "The World Watches Murder," *New York Times,* June 24, 1992, p. 14; and editorial, "Silence Serbia's Big Guns," *New York Times,* July 22, 1992. As this article was in press, the West appeared to be on the verge of a significant increase in its use of force in Bosnia. See Gwen Ifill, "U.S. Is Considering Making Air Strikes on Bosnian Serbs," *New York Times,* April 24, 1993, p. 1.

10. "Four Ex-Soviet Republics Agree on Atom Arms," *New York Times,* April 29, 1992, p. 4; see also Steven Erlanger, "Ukraine and Arms Accords: Kiev Reluctant to Say 'I Do'," *New York Times,* March 31, 1993, p. 1.

11. For related points see Gregory F. Treverton, "Elements of a New European Security Order," *Journal of International Affairs,* Vol. 45, No. 1 (Summer 1991), p. 102.

12. On this possibility see James E. Goodby, "Peacekeeping in the New Europe," *Washington Quarterly,* Vol. 15, No. 2 (Spring 1992), pp. 154–155. War in the former Yugoslavia is suggestive of the complex ways in which a war could draw in the West. A commonly suggested scenario worries that Serbia might attack Kosovo and Macedonia, which could draw in Albania, Turkey, and Greece, which could create additional pressures for broader Western intervention and Russian counter-intervention in support of Serbia.

13. Another rationale for extending deterrence is to prevent nuclear proliferation in Central Europe and the republics of the former Soviet Union. According to this argument, extending deterrence can prevent proliferation by increasing countries' security, thereby reducing their need for nuclear weapons. If nuclear proliferation in the East poses a security threat to the West, then the benefits of slowed proliferation must be weighed against the risks of involvement that are discussed in the text.

14. If, however, stopping immigration were the sole reason for intervention, then the West could probably better achieve its objective by closing its borders. On

immigration see F. Stephen Larrabee, "Down and Out in Warsaw and Budapest: Eastern Europe and East-West Migration," *International Security*, Vol. 16, No. 4 (Spring 1992), pp. 5–33.

15. See especially John J. Mearsheimer, "Back to the Future: Instability in Europe After the Cold War," in Lynn-Jones, *The Cold War and After*.

16. On NATO's role in facilitating European integration see Josef Joffe, "Europe's American Pacifier," *Foreign Policy*, No. 54 (Spring 1984), pp. 64–82; and Joffe, *The Limited Partnership: Europe, the United States and Burdens of Alliance* (Cambridge, Mass.: Ballinger, 1987).

17. Even in this case, Europe could rely on the United Nations, which is taking on more ambitious peacekeeping operations and is considering military intervention for peacemaking (distinguished from peacekeeping); however, these peacemaking operations would not be effective in wars involving major powers. See Boutros Boutros-Ghali, *An Agenda for Peace* (New York: United Nations, 1992). On the strengths but also the limitations of UN intervention see William J. Durch and Barry M. Blechman, *Keeping the Peace: The United Nations in the Emerging World Order* (Washington, D.C.: The Henry L. Stimson Center, 1992).

18. For a general discussion of this issue see Charles L. Glaser, "Political Consequences of Military Strategy: Expanding and Refining the Spiral and Deterrence Models," *World Politics*, Vol. 44, No. 2 (July 1992), pp. 497–538. See also Robert Jervis, *Perception and Misperception in International Politics* (Princeton, N.J.: Princeton University Press, 1976), chapter 3.

19. Paul K. Davis and Robert D. Howe, *Planning for Long-Term Security in Central Europe*, R-3977-USDP (Santa Monica: Rand, 1990), argue that this should be relatively easy because of the "strategic buffer zone" that now lies between Western Europe and the Soviet Union (now Russia).

20. Analysts disagree on the prospects for retaining NATO. On the poor prospects see Mearsheimer, "Back to the Future," pp. 141–142; arguing that the prospects are much better are Van Evera, "Primed for Peace," pp. 202–203; Jonathan Dean, "Is NATO's Past Also Its Future?," *Arms Control Today*, Vol. 22, No. 1 (January/February 1992), p. 54; and Elizabeth Pond, "Germany in the New Europe," *Foreign Affairs*, Vol. 71, No. 2 (Spring 1992), pp. 121–123; for a detailed assessment, see Richard L. Kugler, *NATO Military Strategy for the Post–Cold War Era*, R-4217-AF (Santa Monica: RAND, 1993), pp. 46–56.

21. Alan Riding, "Europeans Agree on a Pact Forging New Political Ties and Integrating Economies," *New York Times*, December 11, 1991, p. 1; and Treaty on European Union (Maastricht), Provisions on a Common Foreign and Security Policy. After Maastricht the WEU offered membership to other EC states, and associate membership to other European members of NATO. David White, "Europe's New Muddle Army," *Financial Times*, May 21, 1992, p. 14.

22. For the most part, even strong proponents of a greatly enhanced European defense identity have also stressed the importance of preserving strong trans-Atlantic links. An exception is Hugh De Santis, "The Graying of NATO," *Washington Quarterly*, Vol. 14, No. 4 (Autumn 1991), pp. 51–65. Britain and the United States, however, have worried that the WEU could weaken NATO. On the one hand, an effective WEU could make NATO appear less necessary, thereby supporting American calls for withdrawing from Europe; on the other hand. if the WEU deploys forces of its own, it risks making the simultaneous maintenance of commitments to NATO appear too expensive. Concern about the latter possibility increased when some observers worried that France was interested in keeping the recently established Franco-German corps—intended to serve as the foundation for a WEU force—separate from NATO. The French position on the relationship

between NATO and the WEU has been murky, and some observers believe France would like to see the WEU replace NATO. For a range of views see David S. Yost, "France and the West European defense identity," *Survival,* Vol. 33, No. 4 (July/August 1991), pp. 327–351; Michael Clarke and Jane M.O. Sharp, "Defence and Security in the New Europe," in David Miliband, ed., *A Perfect Union? Britain and the New Europe* (London: Institute for Public Policy Research, 1992), pp. 31–58, who suggest that France, until recently, preferred that the WEU replace NATO; and Steven Philip Kramer, "The French Question," *Washington Quarterly,* Vol. 14, No. 4 (Fall 1991), pp. 83–96, who argues that France is anxious to maintain the U.S. military presence in Europe; for a similar analysis of French policy throughout the Cold War see A.W. DePorte, *Europe Between the Superpowers: The Enduring Balance* (New Haven: Yale University Press, 1979), pp. 229–242.

23. Before its disintegration, the Soviet Union produced approximately 15 percent of gross world product, while NATO Europe produced approximately 20 percent; Van Evera, "Why Europe Matters, Why the Third World Doesn't," pp. 6–7. Western economic advantages are now clearly greater, since the Russian economy is smaller than the Soviet economy and is struggling with a difficult economic transformation.

24. Josef Joffe, "Collective Security and the Future of Europe," *Survival,* Vol. 34, No. 1 (Spring 1992), p. 47.

25. Major developments include: 1) promulgation of a new strategic concept, including redefinition of the challenges facing the alliance and changes in its military doctrine; see "The Alliance's New Strategic Concept," NATO, Press Service, Press Communique S-1(91)85, Brussels, November 7, 1991; and 2) development of the North Atlantic Cooperation Council (NACC), which is designed to open new channels of interaction between members of the alliance and countries of Eastern Europe, thereby reducing misunderstandings and building trust; see "Rome Declaration on Peace and Cooperation," NATO, Press Service, Press Communique S-1(91)86, Brussels, November 8, 1991; Flanagan, "NATO and Central and Eastern Europe"; and Kugler, *NATO Military Strategy for the Post–Cold War Era.*

26. On leadership, see Joffe, "Collective Security and the Future of Europe," pp. 45–46.

27. We should note, however, that this does not appear to have been the case in recent major events—the Gulf War and the war in the former Yugoslavia. See Trevor C. Salmon, "Testing Times for European Political Cooperation: The Gulf and Yugoslavia, 1990–1992," *International Affairs* (London), Vol. 68, No. 2 (April 1992), pp. 233–253; and Goodby, "Peacekeeping in the New Europe." But see also Francois Heisbourg, "The Future of the Atlantic Alliance: Whither NATO, Whether NATO," *Washington Quarterly,* Vol. 15, No. 2 (Spring 1992), p. 133, who argues that these difference are less important than the fact that there was a single EC policy.

28. However, see Larrabee, "Down and Out in Warsaw and Budapest," who explains that immigration will significantly reduce the number of ethnic Germans in the East.

29. However, some analysts argue that American leadership is required if the West is going to become involved in the East. See, for example, Goodby, "Peacekeeping in the New Europe," pp. 163, 168; and Jane Sharp, "If Not NATO, Who?," *Bulletin of the Atomic Scientists,* Vol. 48, No. 8 (October 1992), pp. 29–32.

30. For a useful description of the spectrum of possibilities and citations to key sources, see Charles A. Kupchan and Clifford A. Kupchan, "Concerts, Collective Security and the Future of Europe," *International Security,* Vol. 16, No. 1 (Summer 1991), pp. 116–124; other recent discussions include Gregory Flynn and David J. Scheffer, "Limited Collective Security," *Foreign Policy,* No. 80 (Fall

1990), pp. 77–101; Richard H. Ullman, *Securing Europe* (Princeton: Princeton University Press, 1991). Critical discussions include Joffe, "Collective Security and the Future of Europe," pp. 36–50; and Richard K. Betts, "Systems for Peace or Causes of War?: Collective Security, Arms Control and the New Europe," *International Security,* Vol. 17, No. 1 (Summer 1992), pp. 5–43.

31. On the misuse of collective security terminology, see Inis L. Claude, Jr., *Swords into Plowshares: The Problems and Progress of International Organization* (New York: Random House, 1972), pp. 246–248; see also Joffe, "Collective Security and the Future of Europe," p. 36.

32. The following summary draws heavily on Kupchan and Kupchan, "Concerts, Collective Security and the Future of Europe," pp. 125–137.

33. This claim is more contentious than it initially sounds. Some analysts have argued that under multipolarity (but not assuming collective security) aggressors are likely to face an overwhelming balancing coalition, compared to bipolarity which offers only a roughly equal balancing coalition. See Stephen Van Evera, "Primed for Peace: Europe After the Cold War," in Lynn-Jones, ed., *The Cold War and After,* p. 222. This overwhelming opposition may be hard to explain in terms of balance-of-power logic, but does flow directly from "balance of threat" logic. Developing the latter set of arguments in a different context is Stephen M. Walt, *The Origins of Alliance* (Ithaca: Cornell University Press, 1987). Proponents of collective security go beyond balance of threat arguments, holding that under collective security states whose vital interests are not directly threatened will nevertheless join the opposing coalition. Their case draws on regime theory, especially states' concern for reputation, and on sanctions for non-participation; see Kupchan and Kupchan, "Concerts, Collective Security and the Future of Europe," pp. 126, 132. The problem with these arguments is that when cooperation or participation means joining a major power war that is otherwise avoidable, the costs of participation will overwhelmingly dominate the costs of damaged reputation and sanctions. As I discuss below, the prospects for coordinated policies in a major-power concert are greater because the issues at stake are less immediately vital.

34. A good recent statement of this view is Joffe, "Collective Security and the Future of Europe."

35. Whether this is in fact the case would depend on whether the aggressor also had less capable military forces as a result of its participation in the collective security system.

36. On this point see Kupchan and Kupchan, "Concerts, Collective Security and the Future of Europe," p. 124. In fact, it may be sufficient that all the powers prefer the status quo to a costly war required to change it and to changes in the status quo that favor one or more of the other major powers. This qualification is important because it relaxes the criteria that determine when collective security is feasible, and thus weakens the argument that it is feasible only when unnecessary.

37. See Kupchan and Kupchan, "Concerts, Collective Security and the Future of Europe."

38. Some NATO planners, however, have questioned NATO's ability to field 65,000–70,000 soldiers to help the UN enforce a settlement in Bosnia, and have raised the possibility of seeking help from former Soviet-bloc countries. "U.S. Official Affirms a 40% Cut in Troops Based in Europe by '96," *New York Times,* March 30, 1993, p. 6.

39. In general, this will depend on geography and the offense-defense balance.

40. Kupchan and Kupchan, "Concerts, Collective Security and the Future of Europe," p. 136, argue that anarchy tends to produce robust offensive capabilities and that collective security reduces states' need for offense, but neither of these claims should be true in general.

41. The possible exception would be if countries could come to the aid of the attacked country with defensive capabilities. This possibility appears to be less likely for collective security than for alliances. The political relations that characterize collective security—specifically, wide uncertainty about which state which will next challenge the system—are less conducive to stationing foreign troops on members' territory. The geography of Europe also cuts against relying on transportable defensive capabilities, since the collective security system would include major powers that could only reach the attacked country by crossing the territory of the aggressor state. On when extended deterrence requires offense, see Stephen Van Evera, "Offense, Defense and Strategy: When is Offense Best?," paper presented at the APSA annual meeting, September 1987.

42. We should recall (see note 36) that these are not necessary conditions for establishing collective security arrangements. When collective security is established under less promising conditions, effective offensive capabilities could create problems from the very beginning.

43. For example, Richard Rosecrance, "A Concert of Powers," *Foreign Affairs,* Vol. 71, No. 2 (Spring 1992), pp. 64–82; and Philip Zelikow, "The New Concert of Europe," *Survival,* Vol. 34, No. 2 (Summer 1992), pp. 12–30.

44. For related observations, see Betts, "Systems for Peace or Causes of War?," p. 25, who notes in this regard that a concert system is hard to distinguish from traditional balance-of-power politics; and Zelikow, "The New Concert of Europe," footnote 2.

45. Paul Gordon Lauren, "Crisis Prevention in Nineteenth-Century Diplomacy," in Alexander L. George, with others, *Managing U.S.-Soviet Rivalry* (Boulder, Colo.: Westview, 1983), p. 35, explains that the Concert of Europe "sought to coordinate relations, minimize friction, avoid misperceptions and miscalculations. . . . Various kinds of rules, regulations, norms, agreements, understandings, and procedures established a sophisticated and highly differentiated array of regimes designed to prevent the outbreak of serious crises." See also Richard B. Elrod, "The Concert of Europe: A Fresh Look at an International System," *World Politics,* Vol. 28, No. 2 (January 1976), pp. 159–174.

46. Lauren, "Crisis Prevention in Nineteenth-Century Diplomacy," provides a useful description of other elements that might be included in a concert: agreements to create buffer zones and demilitarized zones—designed to reduce the threat that major powers pose to each other—and approaches for preventing crises in third areas, thereby making intervention unnecessary.

47. For related points see Robert Jervis, "From Balance to Concert: A Study of International Security Cooperation," in Kenneth A. Oye, ed., *Cooperation Under Anarchy* (Princeton: Princeton University Press, 1986).

48. In addition to the benefits in the West, from Russia's perspective, multilateral Western intervention would likely appear less threatening, since it would reduce the ability of countries to use non-security intervention as a cover for pursuing self-interested foreign policy objectives. The opposite is also possible, however—Russia could be more threatened because the intervention was backed up by greater overall capabilities. Walzer, *Just and Unjust Wars,* p. 107, notes, in addition, that a coalition may be as likely as an individual state to have mixed motives.

49. See, for example, "Voices of Europe: Need for Germany Far Outweighs Any Fears," *New York Times,* September 29, 1992, p. 6.

50. Of course, as noted above, the downside of requiring consensus to intervene is that the West might altogether fail to act. Zelikow, "The New Concert of Europe," argues that EC decisions made at Maastricht, which require unanimous agreement for action, will undermine Western Europe's ability to act effectively.

51. Alliances often have a restraining role that is not explicit in their official descriptions; see Paul W. Schroeder, "Alliances, 1815–1945: Weapons of Power and Tools of Management," in Klaus Knorr, ed., *Historical Dimensions of National Security Problems* (Lawrence: University Press of Kansas, 1976).

52. On shortcomings of restrictive arrangements, see Van Evera, "Managing the Eastern Crisis: Preventing War in the Former Soviet Empire," p. 370.

53. On U.S. modification of its position on UN policy for ending the war in Bosnia in reaction to Russian requests see Paul Lewis, "UN Postpones Enforcing Ban on Serb Flights," *New York Times,* March 25, 1993, p. 3.

54. My analysis of other security structures recognizes the benefits of moderating the security dilemma under other conditions—for example, when discussing cases in which balancing is appropriate, I stress the importance of NATO avoiding force postures that threaten Russia.

55. However, even when feasible, this shift to defensive postures would usually not protect small states against large ones.

56. Transparency provided by monitoring might be even more valuable under defensive unilateral security than under collective security, since a buildup of offensive forces would more clearly violate the arms control agreement.

57. Countries' size and wealth also matter: even if defense has the advantage, small states may be unable to protect themselves against much larger or richer states.

58. One objection is that a defensive unilateral security regime reinforced by the system's potential for offensive rearmament will fail because member states will not rearm in response to violators of the arms control agreement. Although this failure to meet commitments is certainly possible, the problem of non-participation seems no more severe than in a standard collective security arrangement in which states not directly threatened by an aggressor decide to stand out the war.

59. A possible analogy may be found in nuclear non-proliferation. Although many powers have the ability to build nuclear weapons, which they have not exercised, countries do not view these non-proliferators as though they have built nuclear weapons and are nuclear weapons states. A Germany that has the potential to build nuclear weapons is not viewed in the same way as a Germany that has deployed an extensive nuclear arsenal. By raising this analogy I do not mean to suggest that proliferation is necessarily bad or that nuclear forces are necessarily offensive. As discussed below, their implications are partially dependent on context.

60. On the deterrent value of conventional retaliatory offensive capabilities in the NATO–Warsaw Pact context, see Samuel P. Huntington, "Conventional Deterrence and Conventional Retaliation in Europe," *International Security,* Vol. 8, No. 3 (Winter 1983–84), pp. 32–56; see also Barry R. Posen, "Crisis Stability and Conventional Arms Control," in "Arms Control: Thirty Years On," *Daedalus,* Vol. 120, No. 1 (Winter 1991).

61. Useful discussions include Anders Boserup and Robert Neild, eds., *The Foundations of Defensive Defense* (New York: St. Martin's Press, 1990); special edition on non-offensive defense in the *Bulletin of the Atomic Scientists,* Vol. 44, No. 7 (September 1988); Davis and Howe, *Planning for Long-Term Security in Central Europe,* pp. 35–37; and Jack Snyder, "Limiting Offensive Conventional Forces: Soviet Proposals and Western Options," *International Security,* Vol. 12, No. 4 (Spring 1988), esp. pp. 67–71. For a more skeptical view of conventional arms control see Posen, "Crisis Stability and Conventional Arms Control."

62. Paul B. Stares and John D. Steinbruner, "Cooperative Security in the New Europe," in Paul B. Stares, ed., *The New Germany and the New Europe* (Washington,

D.C.: Brookings Institution, 1992); see also, Steinbruner, "Revolution in Foreign Policy," in Henry Aaron, ed., *Setting National Priorities: Policy for the Nineties* (Washington, D.C.: Brookings Institution, 1990). Ted Hopf, "Managing Soviet Disintegration: A Demand for Behavioral Regimes," *International Security,* Vol. 17, No. 1 (Summer 1992), pp. 44–75, prescribes a similar plan for keeping peace within the former Soviet Union, but recognizes that differences in size will prevent former Soviet republics, including Ukraine, from being able to defend themselves against Russia.

63. Betts, "Systems for Peace or Causes of War?," pp. 31–34. On defending at low force levels, see Stephen D. Biddle, project leader, *Defense at Low Force Levels: The Effect of Force to Space Ratios on Conventional Combat Dynamics* (Arlington, Va.: Institute for Defense Analysis, 1991).

64. The case for limited proliferation in Europe, based on the defensive advantage created by nuclear weapons, is made by Mearsheimer, "Back to the Future," pp. 167–176; and Van Evera, "Primed for Peace," pp. 198–200.

65. Robert Jervis, "Cooperation Under the Security Dilemma," *World Politics,* Vol. 30, No. 2 (January 1978), p. 199; Shai Feldman, *Israeli Nuclear Deterrence* (New York: Columbia University Press, 1982); Stephen Van Evera, "Causes of War" (unpub. Ph.D. dissertation, University of California at Berkeley, 1984); and Charles L. Glaser, *Analyzing Strategic Nuclear Policy* (Princeton: Princeton University Press, 1990).

66. Requiring each country to maintain survivable retaliatory capabilities of its own, under the full range of attack scenarios, could also require improvements in current Western European arsenals. Although politically unrealistic today, this would be especially demanding if British and French arsenals had to be survivable against all of America's counterforce.

67. On Ukraine's growing reluctance to accept non-nuclear status, see Erlanger, "Ukraine and Arms Accords: Kiev Reluctant to Say 'I Do'."

68. In addition to the issues discussed below, proliferation raises a variety of other concerns not dealt with here. For example, acquisition of nuclear forces by major European powers could undermine efforts to slow proliferation by smaller European powers that are not well equipped to maintain secure and survivable capabilities. Nuclear weapons would provide far less security under these conditions. Vulnerable forces and vulnerable command and control can create incentives for preemptive and preventive war and can fuel competition between states already competing for security. Second, the dissolution of the Soviet Union is providing a disquieting reminder that the security provided by nuclear weapons depends on stable and clear-headed political regimes. Current political turmoil in the former Soviet Union raises the possibility of nuclear weapons that are not under strict political control and that might be inadequately protected from theft and diversion. See Kurt M. Campbell, Ashton B. Carter, Steven E. Miller, and Charles A. Zraket, *Soviet Nuclear Fission: Control of the Nuclear Arsenal in a Disintegrating Soviet Union,* CSIA Studies in International Security No. 1 (Cambridge, Mass.: Center for Science and International Affairs, Harvard University, 1991). The security provided by nuclear weapons also depends on responsible leaders who do not suffer extreme misperceptions about either threats to their country's security or their ability to conquer other countries. To the extent that over the very long term other powers are going to experience severe political upheavals or severely confused leaders, there is additional risk in relying increasingly on nuclear weapons.

69. This example highlights the importance of the status quo. Although starting from superiority and moving to mutual vulnerability can damage relations, it is

also true that when starting from mutual vulnerability, efforts to gain superiority require offensive policies, which are likely to damage political relations. See Glaser, *Analyzing Strategic Nuclear Policy,* chapter 5.

70. While the Soviet Union still existed, Jack Snyder offered a domestic political argument supporting this point; see Snyder, "The Transformation of the Soviet Empire: Consequences for International Peace," in Oye, Lieber, and Rothchild, *Eagle in a New World,* pp. 262–263.

71. Although three former Soviet republics, in addition to Russia, have nuclear forces deployed on their territory, they agreed in a protocol to the START Treaty to become non-nuclear states. Barbara Crossette, "4 Ex-Soviet States and U.S. in Accord on 1991 Arms Pact," *New York Times,* May 24, 1992, p. 1; however, Ukraine has not yet ratified the accord (see note 67).

72. On the potential for misperceptions and possible solutions see Hopf, "Managing Soviet Disintegration: A Demand for Behavioral Regimes."

73. Snyder, "Averting Anarchy in the New Europe," pp. 132–133.

74. On Germany's nuclear policy, see Jeffrey Boutwell, *The German Nuclear Dilemma* (Ithaca: Cornell University Press, 1990), esp. chap. 7.

9

The Conditions for Success in Peacekeeping Operations

Paul F. Diehl

The gradual abandonment of a collective security strategy [has] led the U.N. to seek other means to insure international peace and security. The Suez Crisis presented the United Nations with a difficult problem. Observation forces were insufficient to ensure disengagement and collective enforcement action would risk a confrontation between four world powers. The solution was to create the United Nations Emergency Force (UNEF) to facilitate withdrawal of troops, prevent a recurrence of hostilities, and act as a barrier separating the protagonists. A new strategy of "peacekeeping" had been created. . . .

The primary goal of a peacekeeping operation is to halt armed conflict or prevent its recurrence. It achieves this goal by acting as a physical barrier between hostile parties and monitoring their military movements. A secondary purpose of peacekeeping is to create a stable environment for negotiations, which could lead to resolution of the underlying conflict. The operation can defuse tensions between the parties by giving each side time to "cool-off' without fear of imminent attack. In theory, this should make them more willing to negotiate and offer concessions.

If peacekeeping operations are effective, they can help resolve conflict without bloodshed—a valuable accomplishment indeed. Nevertheless, no approach to peace is ideally suited to every situation. One approach may be a complete success under one set of conditions, but a total failure under another. Variations in the implementation of a program can also influence success rates. The purpose of this paper is to identify and analyze the conditions that contribute to the effectiveness of peacekeeping operations. Our initial focus is on the characteristics of the operations themselves; the elements of organization, impartiality, and logistics, among others, are considered. Secondly, the level of cooperative behavior exhibited by interested

Edited and abridged with permission from *Political Science Quarterly*.

parties is assessed, as is its impact on the operations' effectiveness. From an analysis of this multiplicity of factors in a comparative case study, we hope to gain a more complete picture of when and how peacekeeping operations should be used. . . .

We have decided to concentrate on six peacekeeping operations, including the earliest and most recent examples: The United Nations Emergency Force, with operations conducted after the Suez Crisis (UNEF I) and following the Yom Kippur War (UNEF II); the United Nations Operations in the Congo (ONUC); the United Nations Peacekeeping Force in Cyprus (UNFICYP); the United Nations Interim Force in Lebanon (UNIFIL); and the Multinational Force of American, British, French, and Italian troops stationed in Beirut (MNF).

The selection of these cases was guided by a number of principles. First, we wished to focus on those operations that were deployed to maintain cease-fires with military interposition forces. Consequently, we ignore observer and other civilian forces. In the instances, the performance of those missions played only a minor role in the maintenance of peace. Secondly, we looked only at operations that were sent to conflicts prior to final resolution of the dispute between the parties. Because some significant conflict remains, we are better able to assess the impact of the operations on conflict reduction and peace maintenance. Finally, we purposely ignored operations that resembled occupying forces more than peacekeeping troops and whose purpose was to preserve the hegemony of a regional power. Examples of such operations were the InterAmerican Peace Force (IAPF) in the Dominican Republic and the Syrian intervention in Lebanon following the 1975 Civil War. We are then left with the six operations noted above that are consistent with our purposes. Besides confining our analysis to those operations that neatly correspond to the goals of preventive diplomacy, we have chosen our sample so that it has a number of attractive features.

First, the sample enables the analyst to consider international intervention in two different settings: civil and interstate conflict. The sample cases include operations sent into an area wrecked by internal instability, as well as those that concerned themselves primarily with the separation of warring states. Another feature of the sample is that different operations within the same geographic area (the Middle East), involving many of the same protagonists, can be compared. In effect, the environmental context is held constant to some extent, and the effect of differences in the conduct of the operations can be assessed. Indeed, two different segments of the same operation (UNEF I and UNEF II) make for almost a perfect analysis of this kind.

Finally, comparisons are possible between operations conducted by an international organization and one conducted by a multilateral grouping of nations without international sanction. Whether peacekeeping should become a primary option in national foreign policy or whether such operations should be exclusive to international bodies can be judged.

It should be noted that estimating a peacekeeping operation's success is a difficult problem. It seems to us, however, that a successful operation should achieve two things in particular. First, the operation should prevent a renewal of armed hostilities between the disputing parties. Maintaining the cease-fire is its primary function and a prerequisite to attempts at reconciling the protagonists. Secondly, the peacekeeping operation should facilitate a final, peaceful resolution to the dispute. This often can be a monumental task, and the blame for failure cannot always rest solely on the operation itself. Nevertheless, unless the underlying sources of conflict are resolved, the threat of renewed war is always present. Thus, in evaluating each operation, we focus primarily on the first criterion of success, but [still] recognize the importance of the second. . . .

Internal Factors

In this section, we look at the internal operations of the peacekeeping mission and determine their effect on its success or failure. It is not our intention to focus on all aspects of a peacekeeping operation, but rather to concentrate on the non-trivial elements that could affect whether the mission's purpose is achieved or not. The five factors below are those most frequently cited in reports, debates, and scholarly works on preventive diplomacy. In addition, our analysis of the six cases indicates that these factors deserve consideration, if only to dispel or confirm some of the conventional wisdom surrounding peacekeeping.

Financing

Peacekeeping operations can be quite expensive; money is needed for supplies, equipment, salaries, and various administrative costs. In the United Nations system, peacekeeping operations are not funded from the regular budget. They require a special authorization from the organization or rely on voluntary contributions. When groups of nations form a peacekeeping mission, appropriations are dependent upon each national contribution, subject to the constraint of domestic political forces. Financing is a problem for any collective action, particularly when the coercive mechanism to enforce contributions is weak.[1] A peacekeeping operation could be terminated prematurely if its source of funding were cut off. Its area of operation or its efficiency could also be severely limited if funds were insufficient.

Almost all of the U.N. operations studied here had difficulties with financing. Operating expenses exceeded expectations, and there was a persistent problem with nations refusing to contribute their assessed share.

Attempts to rectify the problem have failed. In 1964, the United States attempted to suspend non-contributing members under Article 19 of the Charter. When the U.S. withdrew its effort, the only legal means of pressuring recalcitrant members was effectively abandoned for political considerations. The MNF endured threats of a cutoff of funds by the Congress of the United States, but was apparently unaffected by the financial actions of other countries in the consortium.

Although the operations experienced financial difficulties, these did not seem to adversely affect the conduct of missions. Large deficits did not prevent the U.N. from continuing the operations and the consequences of the financial problems were minor. For example, UNEF II was unable to purchase certain mine-sweeping equipment because of financial constraints. The U.N. operations benefitted from large voluntary contributions from some nations. These tended to hold down the deficits and allowed the operations to continue. A notable exception among the operations was ONUC. It was a very expensive operation, and the high cost produced constant pressure to complete the mission. It may be that this pressure encouraged the U.N. to use military force against Katanga and thereby complete its mission. Financial considerations were certainly important in the decision to withdraw from the Congo even though some analysts thought it wise to continue the mission for a little while longer.

Overall, finances were an irritating problem for peacekeeping missions, but in no case were any of the operations seriously hampered by the difficulty. Financial support of a peacekeeping operation is, to some degree, a barometer of the political support for the operation. Financial problems themselves apparently will not jeopardize the effectiveness of preventive diplomacy, but they could be the official cause of death were enough political support withdrawn.

Geography

Another consideration in the success or failure of preventive diplomacy is the locus of development. Where the operation is located can influence the effectiveness of its patrols. If the size of the area is great, the monitoring of conflicting parties' actions could be problematic; the margin for error in detection and verification would increase. The vulnerability of the peacekeeping forces to hostile fire also could damage their effectiveness and possibly draw them into the military struggle.

In our six cases, geographic considerations were important in the success or failure of each operation. The most successful operations had certain geographic advantages. The two UNEF missions were located in mostly desert terrain in sparsely populated areas. This allowed for easy observation of military movements and infiltration attempts. This advantage clearly outweighed the minor problems encountered with desert transportation. UNFICYP was fortunate to be located on an island separated from Greece and Turkey, who might have more easily instigated trouble had they been contiguous by land to Cyprus. In these three instances, geography assisted in the prevention of conflict.

A number of general rules can be derived by looking at those missions that were less than successful. First, when the peacekeeping troops did not separate the combatants by a significant distance, the results were adverse. The French troops in the MNF were stationed at the so-called Green Line separating East and West Beirut. Their presence was not enough to halt sniper fire or artillery attack over their heads. The buffer zone was much too narrow to effectively separate the rival militias. UNIFIL encountered a similar problem over a larger geographic area as political considerations prevented it from taking its desired positions. They were unable to prevent rocket attacks or retaliatory raids by either the Israelis or the Palestinians as each side was still close enough to do damage to the other.

Another geographic problem concerned logistics. If the area of deployment did not permit easy observation of the combatants, problems could arise. UNIFIL had to patrol a very rural portion of Lebanon, and it was rather easy for guerrilla fighters to infiltrate the area. ONUC operated in such a large geographic area that it was difficult to monitor all the activities around them, much less supply their own troops in an orderly fashion. A final rule is that the vulnerability of peacekeeping positions to attack can undermine their neutrality and complicate their mission. The MNF forces of the Americans and French were located in areas open to attack. The French position has already been mentioned. The American position was at the Beirut airport on low ground and subject to attack from the surrounding hills. The attacks on French and American positions led them to take an active role in combat, contrary to the basic principles of preventive diplomacy.

In general, geographic considerations were important to the success of peacekeeping missions. It appears that the peacekeeping forces ideally should be placed in an area that is relatively invulnerable, yet is easy to patrol and separates the combatants at a distance capable of preventing armed exchanges. Nevertheless, a favorable location is no guarantee that the mission will turn out well (as is evident from the remainder of the paper). At best, one might hope that a particular deployment will prevent violent incidents that could escalate and renew the warfare.

Clarity of the Mandate

A frequently cited problem, especially in light of the truck-bomb tragedy in Lebanon, is the absence of a clear mandate for a peacekeeping mission.[2]

A clearly defined mandate restricts the latitude of action given the mission, thereby limiting both the controversy of possible actions and the potential manipulation of the force by interested parties. A clear mandate also may generate greater public support in that the populace can identify and understand the purpose of the operation.

In practice, the most successful missions have begun with clear mandates. Nevertheless, the causal links between mandate clarity and operation success are not clear. Some missions had problems emanating from their mandates, but it is not evident whether these were sufficient to do serious damage. The MNF had very few guidelines to follow in its second deployment.[3] American forces had no clear idea of what to do beyond holding down positions around the airport.[4] This not only undermined public and congressional support, but perhaps led the force to undertake military actions that were inconsistent with the concept of peacekeeping. ONUC also experienced some problems because of its mandate. The Secretary-General was granted enormous power in the conduct of that operation, and his actions led to an erosion of support for the mission among U.N. members. Furthermore, the ONUC mandate was modified several times, leading to confusion and additional erosion of support.

It is evident from these six cases that a clear mandate is useful for a peacekeeping operation. Yet, that clarity is often only a reflection of the underlying political consensus on the mission. A clear mandate often can generate little support in the deliberative bodies that authorize such operations. In controversial situations, some operations would never have taken place without a vague mandate. The operations that had a vague mandate can attribute their major problems to something other than the mandate itself. In short, the importance of a clear mandate is probably overestimated as it is merely a surrogate for the political consensus underlying it.

Command and Control

Any organizational program needs to have a smooth method of operation. A peacekeeping mission can be jeopardized if it makes mistakes, cannot carry out its duties effectively, or lacks coordination. The most common command and control problem in over six cases was language. By organizing forces from many different nations, it was often difficult for commanders to communicate on a one-to-one basis (much less in any larger aggregation) with their subordinates.

A central command can solve coordination problems, and four of our sample operations were set up in this fashion. ONUC was somewhat disorganized because it lacked a central command.[5] It did, however, have a coordinating body to ensure the forces were not working at cross purposes. ONUC's only problem occurred when it was unclear who gave orders for a particular maneuver during the operation. The MNF was linked only through liaison officers. The sharing of intelligence and the mapping of joint strategy correspondingly suffered.

Most peacekeeping operations have run smoothly, with command and control problems affecting the efficiency, but not the overall success, of the missions. Language problems can be cumbersome, but there is an inherent tradeoff in making a peacekeeping force representative versus making it efficient. Most of the command and control problems should dissipate in the future.[6] From the benefits of experience, the U.N. can now send trained personnel into the field and choose from among many experienced individuals to direct the peacekeeping units. Should any collective effort be launched by a group of nations, they too should learn from the mistakes of the MNF. Other than an unprecedented case of complete incompetence, command and control problems are unlikely to ruin a peacekeeping operation.

Neutrality

An essential component of the preventive diplomacy strategy is that the forces should not work to the benefit of either side. Historically, military personnel from nonaligned countries were used to guarantee this neutrality. Two informal rules have arisen in choosing troops for the peacekeeping force. The first is to never allow forces from a state involved in the conflict to participate in the operation. A second rule is to bar troop contributions from major power nations (or their allies). In these ways, it was hoped that the conflicting parties would regard the peacekeeping forces as unbiased and disinterested. Because the host state's consent is necessary to deploy peacekeeping forces, the failure of the host state to approve a particular force composition prevents that operation from taking place.

In our sample, those operations that were staffed almost entirely from disinterested, non-aligned nations had the least difficulty. Nevertheless, we found the Cyprus operation was equally effective, despite being composed primarily of troops from NATO countries, including those of ex-colonial power Britain. This seems to indicate that troops from non-aligned countries are not a prerequisite for success. Nevertheless, they are no guarantee of it either; Israel claimed UNIFIL was guilty of aiding the Palestinian cause and took violent action. The MNF operation had terrible difficulties arising from the perceived unfairness of the troops. Many of the factions in Lebanon regarded U.S. troops as supporters of their two principal enemies in the dispute, the Gemayel government and Israel. This immediately subjected the forces to distrust and later to hostile fire. These suspicions seemed to be confirmed when the United States helped train Lebanese government troops and shelled surrounding villages. The French encountered a similar response from the militias. The Italian contingent was regarded as neutral by all sides, owing to its behavior during the operation (which included numerous humanitarian acts) and the political stance of its government. As a result, they generally were not the subject of protest or attack.

Overall, drawing peacekeeping personnel from non-aligned countries is desirable, but is not a necessary condition for successful completion of the mission. Neutrality in peacekeeping is determined more by behavior and situation than by force composition. To the extent that the troops' behavior is perceived as biased and undermines the cooperation between conflicting parties, the peacekeeping mission could be ruined. Furthermore, troops supplied by a given country may be regarded as neutral in one situation (e.g., Tanzanian troops in Latin America), but not necessarily under a different scenario (e.g., the same troops in Namibia). All things being equal, however, a non-aligned force is more desirable than any other. The non-aligned force is more likely to be accepted by all sides and will be less likely to take actions that may be interpreted as unfair by one or more of the parties.

Relevant Actors

Common sense and the previous analysis tell us that the manner in which a peacekeeping operation is conducted is not the sole determinant of success or failure. In this section, we consider the behavior of a number of relevant actors, with an eye to estimating their impact on peacekeeping operations. First, we investigate the actions of the primary disputants or host state(s) in the conflict. We then consider other states, which may be regional powers or neighboring countries that take an active role in the conflict. Because peacekeeping operations often deal with instability in the host state(s), we also analyze the behavior of sub-national groups. Finally, the policies of the superpowers are weighed. They have the global power, not to mention a dominant role in the Security Council, to dramatically influence a peacekeeping mission.

Primary Disputants

Before peacekeeping troops are deployed on a nation's territory, they must have the consent of that nation's government. If it is an interstate conflict, the other disputant(s) must usually agree to refrain from military force. A successful peacekeeping operation, however, depends on more than this initial level of cooperation. It would seem that the conflicting states also must not try to exploit the peacekeeping troops for their own advantage and refrain from incidents that could lead to a return of open warfare. If one side is not sincere in its support of peacekeeping or changes its policy over the course of the operation, the mission could be doomed.[7]

In practice, the maintenance of cooperation between the primary disputants has not been a severe problem. In both UNEF operations, Egypt was generally cooperative with the peacekeeping forces. Israel demonstrated a less cooperative attitude, but at no time did they initiate violent opposition. The disagreements were minor disputes concerning the use of troops from nations that did not recognize the Israeli state. The other operations had similar results, as the host state(s) usually did little to hinder the mission. In one instance, the Cyprus National Guard blocked access to certain areas, but this problem was short-lived. The major exception to this pattern of cooperative behavior was Israel's actions toward UNIFIL. Israel initially refused to turn over territory where the UNIFIL forces would patrol. Their subsequent behavior, including the 1982 invasion, showed a complete disregard of the force and its mission.

We tend to agree with David Wainhouse that "where cooperation of the parties is not sustained and whole-hearted, a positive result will be difficult to obtain."[8] Nevertheless, the initial level of agreement needed to establish the force has usually persisted; problems from the primary disputants have not been empirically important in the failure of the missions. Our analysis has discovered that while cooperation from the disputants is a necessary condition for success, it is not a sufficient one. This is particularly relevant when the host state has a very weak government. Although the Congolese government supported ONUC, the split among factions prevented it from fully aiding the operation. The Lebanese government support for UNIFIL and MNF had little impact because that government did not have *de facto* control over the areas where the troops were deployed. To identify the sources of failure for peacekeeping, it is necessary to consider the behavior of other actors.

Third Party States

Third party intervention can play a prominent role in international conflict. Allies of the conflicting parties may take certain actions (e.g., supplying arms, diplomatic pressure) that may assist or hinder resolution of the conflict. Peacekeeping operations are subject to these same benefits and constraints. Neighboring states or regional powers may have a stake in the outcome of the conflict and consequently may take actions in support of or contrary to the goals of the peacekeeping mission.

Among our sample cases, five involved significant intervention by third party states. UNEF II was the only operation that was not significantly affected by the actions of a third party state. It may be coincidental, but this mission not only kept the peace, the conflict was resolved by treaty. The other operations all experienced negative effects from the actions of other states. UNEF I was terminated after Syria and Jordan pressured Egypt into joining their military action against Israel. It is unlikely without that pressure Egypt would have expelled the peacekeeping force and gone to war with Israel at that time. In the Congo, Belgium encouraged the secessionist movement, and Belgian mercenaries joined in the armed struggle. A similar situation occurred in Cyprus as Turkey promoted the founding of a secessionist Turkish-Cypriot state on the island. On various occasions, they also made threats against the Greek majority there. The peacekeeping operations were severely jeopardized or complicated in each case.

Not surprisingly, the failed missions (MNF and UNIFIL) faced strong opposition from neighboring states. Syria played a critical role in each operation's downfall. Syria supplied weapons and other support to PLO fighters in southern Lebanon, helping them to infiltrate UNIFIL lines and attack Israeli positions. Syria opposed MNF through its allies among the factions in Beirut. They supplied weapons and pressured the Shi'ite and Druse factions not to accept a solution involving the MNF. There is also some indication that Syria, Iran, and possibly Libya had a hand in supporting terrorist attacks against the peacekeeping forces. Given its influence in Lebanon, Syria could have been a positive influence for MNF, but its actions were a major factor in the mission's failure.

It was difficult to detect any positive pressure in support of peacekeeping from this kind of analysis. Third party intervention was primarily negative and proved critical in damaging certain operations. Yet, this noncooperation from third party states is not automatically fatal to a mission. For example, UNFICYP survived despite the actions of Turkey. A peacekeeping operation can be destroyed if the third party state encourages violence from another state or sub-national group and/or undertakes violence itself. A large portion of the blame for the UNIFIL and MNF failures must be borne not by the primary disputants, but rather by hostile third states.

Sub-national Groups

Just as other states might influence peacekeeping operations, so too might sub-national groups in the host or neighboring states. The behavior of these groups could be particularly important when peacekeeping forces are thrust into areas of internal instability. Preventive diplomacy may be viewed unfavorably by groups seeking to topple the government of the host state; preservation of peace and the status quo favors the established government.

Sub-national groups played little role in either UNEF operations, but were detrimental in the other operations. The PLO never really accepted UNIFIL, claiming that Palestinians had a right to operate in the disputed area. Consequently, they smuggled weapons into UNIFIL's patrol area and launched attacks against Israeli targets. Following the 1982 invasion, UNIFIL has continued to have difficulty dealing with uncooperative local

militias, particularly the SLA. ONUC faced problems from the Katanga independence movement and various tribal groups that supported factional
leaders in the central government.

Perhaps the best example of how sub-national groups can destroy a
peacekeeping operation is the tragedy of the MNF. Lebanon consisted of
a large number of competing factions, none of which actually supported
their presence. Even the Christian Phalangists were less than enthusiastic
about the operation, as they continued battles with Moslem factions. The
Shi'ite and Druse factions opposed the MNF; they felt the MNF was a
shield for the Gemayel government. Part of their demands for a resolution
to the conflict was a withdrawal of the peacekeeping forces. Terrorist
groups were at times just as damaging as those of third party states. When
those states and sub-national groups acted in unison to undermine the operation, not even the support of the host state could save the operation.
Whether peacekeeping is even an appropriate mechanism for resolving internal conflict is questionable.

Superpowers

An analysis of peacekeeping success should not ignore the behavior of another group of third parties—the superpowers. The United States and the
Soviet Union (along with the other three permanent members of the Security Council) have the power to veto a resolution that initially authorizes
a U.N. peacekeeping operation. Because the initial authorization is usually
for a specified time period, the operation and its mandate will again be
subject to that power if renewal is necessary. Beyond their powers in the
United Nations, the superpowers can use their political, economic, and
military power to influence the actors in the area of conflict. In these
ways, the superpowers have the potential to rescue or destroy peacekeeping operations.

The United States has proved quite helpful to the cause of preventive
diplomacy. Its political support was often the driving force behind the creation of peacekeeping operations. Later, the United States provided logistical support and other voluntary contributions to keep the operations running smoothly. Its support of the MNF troops, through the bombing of
suspected terrorist bases, proved counter-productive as it increased hostil-
ity against the operation. The Soviet Union was reluctant to offer political
and financial support for ONUC and other operations, but demonstrated
little active opposition in the way of military action or vetoing resolutions.
It did resupply Syria during the MNF's operation and vetoed a resolution
authorizing a U.N. force to replace MNF. Yet, the MNF was too badly
damaged already to say that the Soviets' actions were decisive.

It is easy to attribute a great deal of influence to the superpowers in any
area of world politics. Nevertheless, in the U.N. peacekeeping operations

studied here, their actual influence was less than conventional wisdom might predict. The superpowers clearly played an important role in setting up some of these operations.[9] Of particular note was their ability to halt the 1973 Mideast war and install UNEF II forces. The success of the operations once in place, however, was only marginally affected by superpower behavior. At best, they helped supply the operations and gave them some political support. At worst, they complicated an operation's efficiency and increased its controversy. The superpowers have a great potential to do good or harm to peacekeeping. While their behavior must be considered in any evaluation of peacekeeping, we have found that thus far, their actual influence has been overrated.

Conclusions

International peacekeeping has had a mixed record of success over the past thirty years. The main reason for the failure of peacekeeping operations has been the opposition of third party states and sub-national groups. By refusing to stop violent activity and in some cases attacking the peacekeeping forces, these two sets of actors can undermine a whole operation. The failure of UNIFIL and MNF can be attributed to this as can many of the problems encountered by other operations. This leaves us with something of a tautology: peacekeeping is successful only when all parties wish to stop fighting. Peacekeeping forces can do certain things (e.g., remain neutral) to ensure that the desire for peace continues. Nevertheless, peacekeeping will fail or be severely damaged if peace is not initially desired by all parties.

Although the primary disputants and the superpowers each had a great deal of power to destroy a peacekeeping operation, our study revealed that neither group generally took strong action in opposition to the operation. To set up a peacekeeping force, the host state(s) must grant its (their) approval, indicating some desire to stop fighting. If the peacekeeping force was organized by the United Nations, the Security Council would likely have to approve it; superpower acquiescence is the minimum requirement for this. Therefore, once a peacekeeping operation is authorized, there is already confirmation that it is not opposed by the primary disputants or the superpowers. Operations opposed by either of these two groups will likely never come into being.

The internal characteristics of a peacekeeping operation were generally found to have a relatively minor impact on the mission's success. A clear mandate was useful, but hardly critical in determining the outcome. When the mandate was vague, the underlying political consensus was already shaky, and the mission experienced support problems with the various interested parties. The same conclusion is appropriate with respect to the financing and organization of the peacekeeping force. Problems with funding and command structure served to make the operation less efficient, but not necessarily less successful. Budget deficits were ameliorated by voluntary contributions or ignored. Command and control difficulties were never serious enough to jeopardize any of the operations.

Two aspects of the operations did have an impact on their success: geography and neutrality. Peacekeeping operations performed best when their areas of deployment adequately separated the combatants, were fairly invulnerable to attack, and permitted easy observation. The absence of these conditions undermined confidence in the operation and allowed minor incidents to escalate. The neutrality of the peacekeeping forces was also significant. If the peacekeeping force is perceived as biased, support from interested parties was likely to be withheld or withdrawn. As we have seen, this is enough to ruin the operation. Neutral behavior is not always linked with non-aligned force composition. The likelihood, however, that a force composed from non-aligned countries will take action favoring one party (or be perceived as doing so) is much less.

From these findings, we can draw a few guidelines regarding the use of a preventive diplomacy strategy.[10] Peacekeeping is most appropriate in a conflict in which all parties are willing to halt hostilities and accept a peacekeeping force. Consideration must be given to more than just the primary disputants; other interested states and sub-national groups deserve attention. If these latter two actors oppose the operation, then the peacekeeping option might be reconsidered unless the opposition is minor or would not involve violent activity. This criterion may confine peacekeeping operations to conflicts that involve relatively few actors, as the probability of consensus will decrease as the number of interested parties increases.

Implementation by an international organization is to be preferred to a multilateral grouping of nations. The U.N., in particular, now has extensive experience with peacekeeping and is more likely to conduct an efficient operation. More importantly, however, an international organization will be better able to acquire consent from the host state(s) and approval from interested parties.[11] It is not that a multinational peacekeeping force cannot succeed, but rather problems with perceived bias (justified or otherwise) will be more likely and its moral authority will not be as great.

Once it has been established that the relevant actors will support a peacekeeping operation, the U.N. command should give special attention to taking a proper geographic position as well as continuing their policy of neutral force composition. Although the issues of mandate, financing, and command should not be ignored, neither should problems with them hold up the operation.

The findings of this study do more than confirm conventional wisdom about peacekeeping, although in some cases they do that too. The importance of the mandate and the role of the superpowers is considerably less than has been assumed. Analysts have also probably overestimated the importance of the primary disputants and the operation's command structure once there is an agreed-upon cease-fire. Yet, as is prominent in the literature on conflict and peacekeeping, the importance of third parties, neutrality, and geography is reaffirmed. Regardless of whether the guidelines laid down here conform to prior expectations about peacekeeping, they bear repetition. We know that policymakers too often ignore or forget these guidelines, with the MNF being the most recent example of neglect. According to these guidelines, the number of peacekeeping operations would be limited, but the rate of success should be positively affected. . . .

Some Final Notes

As final notes, we offer a few caveats and considerations on this analysis of preventive diplomacy. We are limited in anticipating how and where the peacekeeping strategy might be applied next. The superpowers did not play a critical role in the five U.N. operations studied here, but this is not to say that they can not or will not in the future. In addition, a multinational operation sponsored by non-aligned countries (such as Finland or Sweden) may offer a more desirable alternative than those offered here. Without empirical referents, such a judgment is premature. The future may breed new variations of peacekeeping that overcome the difficulties cited. It is our sincere hope that it does.

Finally, we have seemed to imply that no peacekeeping operation is better than an unsuccessful one. But, is this really correct? If peacekeeping can halt fighting and stop bloodshed, even for a short time, is this enough to justify a peacekeeping operation? The answer requires a value judgment. How a failed mission affects future operations is an empirical question. Both deserve serious consideration.

Notes

1. The classic analysis of this problem is given in Mancur Olson, *The Logic of Collective Action*. Cambridge: Harvard University Press, 1965.

2. For example, both Naomi Weinberger, "Peacekeeping Options in Lebanon," *The Middle East Journal,* 37, 3 (1983): 341–369 and Richard Nelson, "Multinational Peacekeeping in the Middle East and the United Nations Model," *International Affairs,* 61, 1 (Winter 1984–85): 67–89, give primary importance to this factor.

3. Unlike a U.N. operation, there is no authorizing resolution stating the mandate of MNF's operation. The closest one comes to a statement of the mandate came from Deputy Press Secretary Speakes:

"The MNF is to provide an interposition force at agreed locations and thereby provide the MNF presence requested by the Government of Lebanon to assist it and Lebanon's armed forces in the Beirut area" (quote taken from *Public Papers of the President of the United States: Ronald Reagan.* Book II, Washington: GPO, 1983: a 1202).

This is still vague and quite in contrast to the first deployment of MNF, when the guidelines for supervising PLO withdrawal were fairly specific.

4. Problems with the mandate were complicated by the lack of training in peacekeeping measures for the military personnel. MNF troops were primarily combat personnel, unaccustomed to holding down a defensive position without firing at an enemy force. For a description of peacekeeping training, see Richard Swift, "United Nations Military Training for Peace," *International Organization,* 28, 2 (1974): 267–280.

5. An elaboration on ONUC's problem in this regard is given by Lincoln Bloomfield, "Political Control of International Forces in Dealing with Problems of Local Instability," in Arthur Waskow, *Quis Custodiet?: Controlling the Police in a Disarmed World.* Washington: Peace Research Institute, 1963: Appendix E.

6. An excellent operations manual detailing the mechanics of setting up and conducting a peacekeeping operation is International Peace Academy, *Peacekeeper's Handbook.* New York: Pergamon Press, 1984.

7. Of course, if the host state formally withdraws consent, the space operation is terminated. This occurred in 1967 as Egypt asked UNEF I forces to leave. Despite some suggestions to the contrary by members of the international community, U Thant complied with this request. See Jack Garvey, "United Nations Peacekeeping and Host State Consent," *American Journal of International Law,* 64, 1 (1970): 241–269.

8. David Wainhouse, *International Peace Observation.* Baltimore: Johns Hopkins University Press, 1966: 557.

9. Nathan Pelcovits and Kevin Kramer, "Local Conflict and U.N. Peacekeeping: The Uses of Computerized Data," *International Studies Quarterly,* 20, 4 (1976): 533–552 reports a strong correlation between superpower intervention in a conflict and the use of peacekeeping. This demonstrates that the superpowers are also an indirect stimulus for peacekeeping operations, beyond their more direct role in the U.N. Security Council.

10. Although we look at peacekeeping operations as presently constituted, there have been many proposals for improvement. Representative of these efforts and ideas are Indar Jit Rikhye, *The Theory and Practice of Peacekeeping.* New York: St. Martin's Press, 1984; and Alastair Taylor, "Peacekeeping: The International Context," in Canadian Institute of International Affairs, *Peacekeeping: International Challenge and Canadian Response.* Ontario: Canadian Institute of International Affairs, 1968: 1–40.

11. Certain nations, such as Israel and South Africa, may object to peacekeeping operations directed by the United Nations, owing to the perceived bias of that institution toward their interests. In that event, a multinational force may be more appropriate. In general, however, its advantages over a U.N. force are minimal; see Frank Gregory, *The Multinational Force: Aid or Obstacle to Conflict Resolution.* Conflict Study, no. 170. Institute for the Study of Conflict. London: Eastern Press, 1984.

10

Second Generation
Multinational Operations

John Mackinlay & Jarat Chopra

The end of the Cold War marks the rebirth of the United Nations (UN)
and the start of its second generation as an institution. Incapacitated
for its first 40 years by a deeply divided Security Council, the UN is re-
discovering its original mandate as it faces the demands of a new era. With
fewer political constraints in the Council, the UN is able to address a much
wider range of tasks, which tend to be under the sobriquet "peacekeeping."
Many of these tasks, however, although they fall short of enforcement, are
more demanding than peacekeeping.

In a rejuvenated UN, nowhere is the need for change more acute than
in the area of peacekeeping. A Cold War expedient that overcame some of
the disabling effects of superpower rivalry, peacekeeping has hitherto relied largely on a token UN presence and the consent of the opposed forces
rather than on any effective military capability. The inadequacy of this
doctrine in the post–Cold War era is likely to be tested by the UN forces
now deploying to Cambodia[1] and Yugoslavia,[2] which are the largest multinational UN forces mobilized since the 1964 Congo operation. Local consent to their activities is demonstrably less than universal, and they will
have to hope for a best case scenario because neither force will have the
capability to restore law and order, even if they encounter only a limited
breakdown.

It has become clear that the UN's resourcefulness as a mediator has
outstripped its capability as a military organizer and that a more effective
military response is now required by the newly defined tasks of the second
generation of UN activity. Peacekeeping cannot be adapted any further to
perform these tasks. A more practical instrument is needed.

Reprinted from *Washington Quarterly,* Vol. 15, No. 3 (1992), pp. 113–131, John
Mackinlay and Jarat Chopra, "Second Generation Multinational Operations," by
permission of MIT Press.

In January 1992, the Security Council heads of state appeared willing to tackle this problem when they called for better organized and more effective UN multinational operations.[3] It is still not clear, however, whether this will lead to more than streamlining the UN Secretariat's management and rearranging existing structure. Delivering a UN force that is more than symbolic will require something of a revolution: in the Secretariat, which must develop a credible capability to direct military operations, and among the UN's most powerful members, who will have to forgo their inclination for unilateral foreign policy options and be prepared to subordinate their effective military assets to a multinational command.

This article explains how a more effective UN instrument for assuring peace and security could be developed. It argues that a humane, but more proactive, concept of operations can be developed from existing doctrine and demonstrates how military command and political control should flow from the Security Council, through the secretary general, down to the commander in the field. The problems raised by the contingencies of the future can be overcome, but will the major powers in whose hands the solution lies be willing to facilitate a stronger system for maintaining peace?

Cold War Peacekeeping

Drafting in the wake of Nazi aggression, the authors of the United Nations Charter were preoccupied with conflict between states. Their vision of a returning scourge was another Hitlerian war, state against state, Clausewitzian in scale, in which victory would be measured by territorial gain. The language of the Charter refers to "aggression," "self-defence," and "armed attack," in which force is used by conventional armies.

They envisaged two pillars upholding the Charter and safeguarding the world against this threat: pacific settlement of disputes under chapter VI and, where that failed, chapter VII enforcement. The use of collective force would rely on a level of accord among the world powers comparable to that achieved to defeat the Axis expansion, as well as a degree of military cooperation reminiscent of the huge multinational landings on the Normandy beaches. In the Charter world, wars erupt across frontiers; the UN's mandate does not clearly extend to maintaining peace within a state.

The drafters did not anticipate the nature of the conflict that developed or the political structures that emerged as a consequence of the rise and decline of world powers. During the Cold War, the Security Council failed to agree on collective enforcement mechanisms, and a lesser instrument, peacekeeping, was developed to guarantee the agreements successfully negotiated under UN auspices. Peacekeeping, therefore, was an expedient of a divided Security Council that lacked the consensus for collective action but could agree to use a less powerful instrument that would not impinge on the superpower zero-sum game.

As a result, peacekeeping had several characteristics that proscribed its wider use. The confidence and full support of the Security Council were essential prerequisites. A peace force could only deploy with the consent of all local parties in conflict, and particularly of the host nation in which the force would be stationed. To achieve an international balance, participating nations had to represent a spread of regional interests. Permanent members of the Security Council did not, as a rule, contribute to peacekeeping forces except with strategic movement and logistic support, which were seldom stationed in the area of operations. Finally, peacekeepers could use force only in self-defense.[4]

Under these conditions, peacekeeping became a narrowly constrained activity. Unless the zone of conflict under consideration met with the stringent preconditions for their use, UN forces could not be deployed. Unlike a combat unit, peacekeeping forces could not often create the conditions for their own success;[5] they acted rather in the role of an umpire or a referee. The referee's success relied on the consent of the players and their understanding of the rules of the game but never on the pugilistic skills of the referee himself.[6]

Being lightly armed and impartially disposed was a benefit to the peacekeeper. It protected him on the battlefield and allowed him to move freely and negotiate dispassionately. His military role was mainly reactive. He could only operate when hostilities had ceased. He could not enforce a solution or drive away an aggressor. Veteran peacekeepers stressed the value of being regarded as impartial and nonthreatening. Many saw the aggressive efficiency of powerful armies as an obstacle to acceptance by local parties. In this way, peacekeeping achieved many successes in the Cold War period. In their role as referees or custodians of UN agreements, peacekeepers developed a range of useful techniques to reassure fighters, disarm violence, and stabilize the battlefield.

In terms of the UN's institutional effectiveness, however, there was a price to pay. The organization and control of peacekeeping bypassed the Military Staff Committee (MSC). Because peacekeepers, in principle, had no enemies in their area of operations, there was little pressure on them to be militarily effective. In the field, there was no need for total operational reliability by day and night,[7] and gaps in logistic arrangements were tolerated because they did not diminish results. This in turn removed pressure on the Secretariat to maintain an effective staff capability in New York. There was seldom any need, or facility, to maintain elaborate map rooms, with 24-hour vigilance and daily situation briefings. When the need arose, contingency planning could be carried out by co-opted staff officers who came and went on an ad hoc basis. Operational lessons were lost,[8] UN equipment became obsolete,[9] and military functions were largely conducted by a largely civilian Secretariat. Although the deployment of each new peacekeeping force began with minor blunders,[10] once the modus operandi was established, lessons were soon forgotten. With the Cold War stalemate in the Security Council, member nations had no incentive to improve military competence.

After the Cold War

The end of the Cold War established new parameters and removed many political tensions that had limited the scope and application of peacekeeping. Although the national interests of the superpowers were still vigorously maintained, their destructive zero-sum game was abandoned in many theaters. Clandestine support for proxy forces in Cambodia, Angola, Afghanistan, Central America, and the Horn of Africa was reduced or withdrawn. Insurgent forces, which for years had eschewed attempts to negotiate peace settlements, succumbed to international pressures that were augmented by their own inability to sustain operations without external support.

The Soviet position on peacekeeping shifted in 1988 with Mikhail Gorbachev's statements to the press and the UN General Assembly in which he called for improvements in the UN's peacekeeping role.[11] He offered to provide a contingent for future operations, a suggestion that not only signaled an end to the unwritten principle of superpower nonparticipation in peacekeeping but also put pressure on the United States to think seriously about peacekeeping as a likely military contingency.[12] Previously, the Soviet Union had viewed the arrangement and conduct of peacekeeping with a degree of intransigence. Now that the Soviets were supportive of peacekeeping and had made efforts to resuscitate the MSC, it was unfortunate that other members of the Security Council backed away from it. Nevertheless, the end of the zero-sum game in many war zones opened the prospect of direct superpower involvement in UN multinational forces.

With a new collegiality in the Security Council, the UN's ability to negotiate was greatly enhanced. Since 1988 peacekeepers and observers have deployed to nine trouble spots.[13] This surge in demand exhausted the capacity of the middle nations[14] that habitually provided contingents, including Australia, Austria, Canada, Ireland, the Nordic countries, Poland, and Fiji. Not only was there now a need to expand the pool of peacekeepers to include armies with more sophisticated assets, but also it was no longer morally acceptable for the major military powers to stand back and allow a group of smaller nations to pay the price, in casualties as well as national resources, for their long-standing involvement in what should have been an international effort.[15]

Prior to the Persian Gulf War, peace-negotiating successes in the UN were already beginning to outstrip the willingness of members, and the capacity of the small Secretariat staff, to provide and organize adequate multinational forces to supervise these new and complex agreements. Within the UN, member nations insisted on a ponderous system of authorization and funding that hampered the launching of UN peace forces to such an extent that in some cases only leading elements could be made available at the critical early stages of a cease-fire.[16]

The widening gap between the UN's growing list of negotiated agreements and its ability to underwrite them with effective forces was revealed during the early stages of the Gulf confrontation. Although the UN had become the focal point at which the international community coalesced its support for some form of effective military action against Iraq, it soon became clear that the Security Council could in no way conduct a dynamic military campaign on the scale required. The collective membership, in some cases under pressure from the United States, had set aside their national and domestic interests to authorize the use of collective force under Security Council Resolution 678, but the forces that formed the coalition never seriously considered the idea of submitting themselves to a UN command. Whether or not this reluctance stemmed from a desire to impose a *pax Americana* in the Persian Gulf, there was no capability in the UN structure to take on such a military responsibility. Institutionally, the UN had since the onset of the Cold War abandoned developing the machinery of enforcement procedures under chapter VII.

Second Generation UN Operations

Practitioners developed a narrow and precise definition of peacekeeping over time, but today the word is misleading because it is used to describe the whole range of UN-authorized military activity. In reality a second generation of UN military operations is already emerging, outside the parameters of traditional peacekeeping, to cope with the new commitments of a more effective Security Council. The enlarging span of legitimate military tasks can be depicted as a continuum: at one end are the lowest intensity operations, involving the smallest number of assets and the least risk of conflict to UN contingents; at the opposing end conflict level is high and involves commensurately larger military assets. In escalating order, this UN continuum could now include the following tasks.

[a] Conventional observer missions.   Unarmed officers monitor and supervise a tense situation or stalemate in which the potential level of conflict may be high but the assets deployed by the UN are minimal.

(b) Traditional peacekeeping.   Lightly armed multinational contingents, with the prior agreement of opposed conventional forces, interpose themselves along a linear cease-fire line, establish an area of separation, and facilitate the conduct of life-sustaining activities that help to stabilize a war zone.

(c) Preventive peacekeeping.   Lightly armed or unarmed monitors representing a powerful selection of member states are stationed along a threatened border to warn an impending aggressor that further menacing action will not be tolerated.

(d) Supervising a cease-fire between irregular forces.   Armed multinational troops, with the prior agreement of the *majority* of involved parties, organize an area-wide cease-fire between a number of opposed regular and irregular forces. The endemic conflict level may be lower than in a traditional war zone, but the tasks of the multinational troops are more dangerous, complicated by the possibility that not all parties will necessarily cooperate with their arrangements.

(e) Assisting in the maintenance of law and order.   Multinational troops, under a UN-appointed caretaker government or similar form of interim authority, "assist" local security forces in maintaining law and order, while a referendum or election is held free from intimidation. The likelihood of violence occurs when the writ of the authorized local security forces fails to extend to every corner of the state. This task may in future include the protection of minority groups and refugees in states where ethnic violence has erupted. Violence in this case may be intense locally, involving intercommunal slaughter.

(f) Protecting the delivery of humanitarian assistance.   A joint (air, land, and sea) multinational force establishes corridors for the passage of aid or a protected area to provide life-sustaining assistance for a threatened population. (Humanitarian assistance is considered here in a peace-threatening context.)

(g) The guarantee of rights of passage.   A powerful joint multinational force convenes to protect traffic through a threatened air route or sea lane. This action might involve naval minesweeping activities as well as the setting up of air defense zones.

(h) Sanctions.   Firmly within chapter VII of the UN Charter are the operations that enforce economic sanctions under article 41. These will require the sophisticated coordination of military operations in the air and

at sea. Although it does not amount to an operation of war, enforcing sanctions can be a demanding and dangerous undertaking.

(i) Enforcement. At the farthest end of the continuum, to denote their intensity and scale, are the operations of collective enforcement under article 42 "by air, sea, or land."

Several considerations qualify this tentative continuum of second generation tasks. The order in which tasks are shown along the spectrum of intensity is not fixed. It is possible, for example, that a sanction task (h) may turn out to be an extremely dull and undemanding exercise, such as the British navy's blockade of Beira that prevented the passage of oil into Rhodesia. Arranging a conventional cease-fire (b), by contrast, may be fraught with every kind of physical danger and complexity, such as the UN contingents faced in Suez. The order is only a guide to the scale of UN forces involved and the possible complexity and intensity of the operation.

Although success in Cold War peacekeeping was largely dictated by the effectiveness of the preceding political agreement between the parties and not by the capabilities of the military force, in a second generation continuum this immutable principle becomes less steadfast. The requirement that sound political decisions precede or underwrite a successful UN mandate is still paramount, but in the execution of tasks the importance of military effectiveness grows as the intensity of the operation increases until, at the threshold of collective enforcement, it becomes the overriding key to success. Although an enforcement action on the scale of the Persian Gulf War will be exceptional, the operational focus is already moving toward the center of the continuum, into the areas of maintaining law and order (e) and the protection of humanitarian assistance and refugees (f).

Because operations have already moved away from the constrained parameters of Cold War peacekeeping, military contributors and humanitarian relief agencies are put in a quandary. Removal of political constraints has opened a widening spectrum of operational requirements under the increasingly elastic sobriquet of peacekeeping, but UN contingents are still constrained by their own Cold War peacekeeping rules in the field and by ad hoc military organization in the UN Secretariat. Peacekeeping cannot be stretched any further to meet second generation contingencies. There is pressing need for a new category of international military operations somewhere between peacekeeping and large-scale enforcement.[17] At present, the search for a new tactical approach is stalled by middle nations that do not wish to become involved in military tasks lying beyond the limitations of traditional peacekeeping, by peacekeeping cognoscenti who assert that it is not possible to operate beyond Cold War limitations, and by the apparent reluctance of powerful nations to support anything more than token forces.[18]

Keeping the Peace During Decolonization

While peacekeeping was developing in the UN in the 1950s, a military technique known as "keeping the peace" began to take shape for entirely separate reasons among the armies of the British Commonwealth and Europe during decolonization. Confronted with serious threats to internal security, they faced contingencies ranging from largely spontaneous outbursts of intercommunal slaughter to the carefully orchestrated tactics of insurgency.

The breakup of colonial regimes released a tide of violence, similar to the intercommunal violence now erupting in Yugoslavia and in the former Soviet Union in the wake of its collapse. The root causes were similar; they included the desire to expel colonial regimes, frictions caused by differing ideology, race, and culture, and economic deprivation. Much of the violence was internal to the state and took the form of rioting, intercommunal fighting, and the use of revolutionary warfare, which became more widespread than conventional war.

All the principles for the use of mass armies that had given the allies their success in Europe were rudely overturned by what came to be known as the "war of the flea." The potency of firepower and sophistication was diminished; small but energetic forces could now challenge more powerful adversaries by using an entirely new range of tactics. Revolutionary warfare was not only used in this way against withdrawing colonial powers, but also between communities within states, and later between states. In rural areas, it followed Maoist principles of the people's war,[19] and in the cities the tactics of the urban guerrilla.[20]

As a result of continuous requirements to maintain law and order during, or directly after the transfer of power to fledgling local governments, these armies developed a well-tried formula for operations to restore order when faced by insurgents and in event of serious intercommunal strife. This required them to abandon many of the advantages of mass and fire power and compete directly with the insurgent for the support of the people. Although many UN members may still find the practices of the colonial era repugnant, it would now be a calamitous waste to allow this to become a reason to disregard the basic military lessons that were derived from the hard-won experiences of the colonial run-down. At a practical level, the forces involved, which in each successful case included a substantial element of local security forces, developed a formula for maintaining a satisfactory level of calm and internal security to allow daily life to resume.

Broadly speaking, their doctrine was not far removed from the concepts for using force that are developing under the sobriquet of peacekeeping. In their developed form, practiced by the British Commonwealth armies, the underlying principles for military forces in operations to keep the peace were the following.

- There is no purely military solution; the military contribution is only one element in the interrelationship of civil and military functions.
- Security forces act only in support of the civil government.
- The operational level of response is not fixed; it can swiftly escalate or deescalate.
- Cooperation is essential between the [multinational force] and the local security forces.
- All operations must be conducted within the law of the country where the operations are taking place and must be seen to be within the law.
- A commander must never use more force than is strictly necessary to achieve his immediate military aim.
- Minimum force does not imply minimum troops; a large presence correctly used may enable a commander to avoid using force at all.
- Both commanders and troops must be aware of the constraints of civil law on the use of force.
- Popular support is a prerequisite of success in internal security operations.[21]

In keeping-the-peace operations under these guidelines, control was delegated to districts in a structure of committees that at each level of government integrated military assets into a political strategy. Troops were required to understand arrest procedures and the importance of evidence. Techniques were developed to protect key personnel, road convoys, and rail movement and installations. In violent urban areas, there were procedures to reduce the opportunities for rioting and intercommunal violence. In addition to crowd control, the troops had to be able to cope with determined and experienced partisans and terrorists. This demanded more proactive searching, close surveillance, and explosives disposal procedures to cope with bomb threats in crowded areas and against vital installations. It is a misconception that a military unit can only exercise one function in civil disorder. In practice, a well-trained unit will have an escalating range of options; using force in an indiscriminate manner is not one of them.

These apparently simple procedures, however, needed trained and experienced troops to be successful. Training a military force in the breadth of capabilities from using a side arm safely but surely in a crowded urban area to understanding the complexities of arrest turned out to be a very expensive business. It militated against the use of part-time soldiers, who had barely gained this expertise before they were returned to civilian life. It required the establishment of expensive training schools and urban ranges where the stress and complexity of urban conditions could be reproduced. It was essential that the armed soldier should not carry out these procedures for the first time in the actual dispersal of a crowd.

Beyond Peacekeeping

How do these military lessons relate to problems of using multilateral forces in the second generation of UN tasks? In the continuum, the tasks that fall between traditional peacekeeping and chapter VII enforcement, drawing on our earlier list, are: (d) a cease-fire between irregular forces; (e) maintenance of law and order; (f) protection of humanitarian aid delivery; and (g) guarantee of rights of passage. The characteristic that distinguishes these from peacekeeping is the extent to which local parties have consented to the presence of a third party multinational force.

In peacekeeping, the principle of consent is an operational sine qua non. Moving along the continuum, however, away from the strict parameters of peacekeeping, this condition becomes less absolute. In some cease-fires and transfers of power, it may not be possible to gain the consent of all parties, either because they are so remotely deployed that they cannot be consulted, or because they do not *want* to be consulted. In the case of Lebanon, it was too difficult to identify all the parties. In the delivery of humanitarian assistance, the absence of consent is conspicuous because the aid will oppose an effective local force using access to food and other supplies as a weapon. In the guarantee of rights of passage, hostile actions may already have been taken to lay mines or attack aircraft, and the task will be to remove these threats. Although some tasks, particularly cease-fires and election supervision, will resemble classic peacekeeping, there is an important distinction in the degree of local consent. This distinction dictates a very different operational approach.

A second generation force needs to be capable of exercising a wide range of military responses as situations escalate and deescalate. In the best scenario, the task is carried out unopposed. The presence of an overwhelming multinational force (as in the case of Operation Provide Comfort in northern Iraq) may avert confrontation with the opposed local forces. But if a small and unrepresentative local force unlawfully challenges the writ of the UN, the integrity of the mandate should not be eroded by compromise.

The price of deploying a small token force for a second generation task was illustrated by the United Nations Transition Assistance Group

(UNTAG) in Namibia. When forces of the South West Africa Peoples' Organization (SWAPO) began to cross the Angolan border on April 1, 1989, UNTAG was both operationally unprepared and tactically incapable of exercising a military response. Unavoidably, the task of securing the border area was passed to the South African Defense Forces (SADF), who very quickly killed 350 SWAPO insurgents with a significant lack of prisoners and walking wounded. Setting aside the legality of SWAPO's action and the abdication of security control to South African forces, would it not have been a more humane solution to exercise a keeping-the-peace option under UN command?

To be successful, a second generation force will need operational presence and tactical flexibility, in addition to its normal characteristics as a UN-mandated initiative. The range of its capabilities is suggested in the following example:

- After intercommunal violence, the parties in an intrastate conflict observe a cease-fire and conduct peace negotiations under an interim UN authority.
- A multinational force is deployed to assist in the maintenance of law and order during the peace process, supervise safe conduct of refugees, and deliver humanitarian assistance.
- Security during the process is the responsibility of each party in its own district, but ethnic cleavages may not conform to district boundaries.
- The multinational force deploys statewide, concentrating in each district at the headquarters of authorized militia forces. A powerful multinational mobile reserve remains available to the force commander for deployment.
- The tasks of the multinational force are primarily to observe, monitor, and supervise the provisions of the mandate. In the event of a local breakdown of law and order, its secondary task will be to restore local security, and in particular to protect threatened minorities. It may be assisted in its secondary task by the swift deployment of the mobile reserve.
- The force commander may be subordinated at state level to a special representative of the secretary general. The actions of the multinational force would be governed by new UN standard operating procedures, including rules of engagement, as well as local emergency regulations as defined in a status of forces agreement.
- The multinational force will not be able to maintain law and order in face of a widely supported breakdown of security, but in the event of a limited disturbance its task would be to uphold the force mandate and protect the population against attacks by an unrepresentative minority.

In this example, the second generation force has intervened in response to the appeal of a majority of the local people. Its distinguishing characteristic is its ability to provide an effective multinational military *presence* and, if necessary, to take the initiative if the mandate is threatened. The "tactical flexibility" to achieve this is provided by a powerful mobile reserve. Further along the continuum, a larger force may intervene, for instance, to protect the rights of a minority. Acting contrary to the will of a majority, this presence could be maintained only for a limited period of time and would require better organization and a more effective force.

Organization and attitudes must change before this type of intervention could become a safe or realistic UN option. The pool of potential force commanders must be widened to include general officers from armies with a wider experience of low intensity conflict. Rules for their maximum age and professional qualifications must be rigorously applied. Command experience at formation level must now be a sine qua non; it is too late to find out in the teeth of a crisis that a force commander has no experience of command. At the peacekeeping end of the continuum, force commanders will be chosen from traditional sources; further along the continuum of intensity, commanders with wider experience will be essential.

During negotiations, greater understanding must be shown for the military requirements of mounting an effective force. In the past, successful negotiators handed agreements to the Secretariat for immediate execution, regardless of the need to allow time for preparation of a viable force to underwrite the process. In most cases, these disadvantages have been endured by the military in the interest of maintaining the impetus of the political process. But in future, when the military operations could be more dangerous and crucial to success, there has to be a greater sense of balance between the immediate desires of negotiators and the conditions required for a successful military deployment.

In the UN Secretariat, planning capability will have to learn unfamiliar doctrines currently the métier of North Atlantic Treaty Organization (NATO) armies, which are poorly represented in New York. In addition to the UN experts from the middle nations who enjoy a preeminent position in UN contingency planning due to their long-standing peacekeeping experience, staff from armies with wider skills will be needed. To achieve a more flexible capability, member nations will have to face the unpalatable truth that they cannot keep calling for a more effective UN response without actively supporting a commensurate improvement in the Secretariat staff. Armies that have wider experience, including keeping the peace and law and order operations, will have to take a greater interest in applying their expertise in this field; to do so they may have to convince a recalcitrant international audience of the validity of some new doctrinal principles.

Even with these new tools, the Secretariat will have to establish its credibility as a multinational force manager. In the past, there was no need for doctrinal creativity. The participants brought with them the essential ingredients of a peacekeeping formula, which produced a mixture of national procedures at force level. Standards of professionalism varied between forces. Each combination comprised a different matrix of military and national characteristics, and the Secretariat lacked the professional knowledge and authority to enforce a common military standard. Future UN military operations cannot be driven by ad hoc doctrines. In addition to improving its administrative capabilities. the Secretariat must be concerned with developing a future doctrine and ensuring its new standards are maintained in the field. Any laxity in a second generation operation will be extremely dangerous. If, for example, national interpretations of the use of force are allowed to assert themselves in a multinational force, an overreaction by inexperienced troops may set back the development of a new option by several decades. Preparing a multinational force with a wider operational capability will take months rather than weeks and will involve intensive work-up training in the simulation units that are currently the monopoly of the major armies.

These enhancements to the UN capability carry an unacceptable price in the present parsimonious climate in New York. A fuller consideration of this increasingly important problem is unfortunately beyond the scope of this article; the following points, however, are essential to our argument. In the past, cost cutting by the Security Council and the failure of members to pay their dues had a debilitating, but not emasculating, effect on some UN initiatives. Very often the token nature of peacekeeping allowed tactical flexibility to be reduced below a workable minimum level on the assumption that because a force would meet with universal consent in the field, a best case scenario was likely. As the UN begins to take on tasks where universal consent cannot be assumed, however, a workable level of tactical flexibility becomes essential. The folly of being unprepared for unexpected contingencies was demonstrated in Namibia. At the time of writing it remains to be seen whether history will repeat itself in Cambodia and Yugoslavia.

The cost-cutting exercises imposed on these recently established forces demonstrate that the Security Council is still not anxious for the UN to deploy effective military forces to underwrite its increasingly complex peace initiatives.[22] It could be argued that the development and use of such a UN instrument might jeopardize the unilateral options of major powers; cost cutting that amounts to force cutting becomes an important controlling mechanism. Efforts to redistribute the burden of these costs could reduce the controlling ability of the permanent members and have not met with much enthusiasm. Compared to defense research and development costs, the price of peacekeeping is small and could be met outside the UN from commercial borrowing or insurance financing. No effort has been made to develop these ideas, which might support the suggestion that an independent funding mechanism would wrest an important element of control from the hands of the Security Council.

Because the UN costs are comparatively small and shortfalls could be remedied outside the five permanent members of the Security Council, a prolonged attempt to obstruct the development of effective UN forces by financial strangulation could be outflanked in the General Assembly. It is to be hoped that these financial constraints will be removed and a better instrument allowed to develop before a serious military debacle involving UN forces spells out the need for supportive action by the major powers.

Assuming that their euphoric declarations on January 31, 1992, will in due course be accompanied by action, there is plenty for the major powers to do. The commendable efforts of the Special Committee on Peacekeeping Operations have raised many questions in addition to the issues discussed here.[23] In fact, there is wide disparity in members' attitudes on fundamental issues that has not surfaced in the comparatively relaxed confines of a peacekeeping operation. There are known disagreements on the use of force, intelligence, the maintenance of law and order, powers of arrest, and the principles of logistic support. There will be serious problems of equipment interoperability. There are enormous differences in members' military experience and competence. Several important major powers and middle nations will be politically unable to participate in UN operations that have a greater capacity to use force. In addition, the fundamental question is whether member nations are ready to subordinate their national assets to a UN command. These problems do not constitute an overwhelming reason to abandon the development of a more effective instrument to uphold the Charter, but they do lead to a formidable dilemma on the question of how a second generation force should be controlled and directed.

Command and Control

Operation Desert Storm has opened a huge debate on the control mechanisms for collective enforcement. For NATO contributors, there was no realistic military alternative to a U.S. command, however politically uncomfortable that option may have been for their wider diplomatic responsibilities. Most nations, however, would support the view that

> No single country, not even one as powerful and rich as the United States can or has the right to play the role of global policemen. No one country, even the smallest and weakest, would agree with the idea of restraining the violators of order in the world if the restraining were done by a single power.[24]

The universal dismissal of a single-nation structure for future enforcement operations is understandable, but it leaves unresolved the problem of

how a future operation in this category should be controlled. Many support
the Russian call to resuscitate the MSC. Because the United States, France,
and the United Kingdom have so far opted, however, for the single-nation
structure, it is hard to see how a more effective MSC can become a reality
without the support of its sophisticated military members. Even if the un-
stated lack of support by three out of five of its members were overcome,
it is questionable whether the Security Council could swiftly develop a cooperative modus operandi as well as a staff capability of its own.

There is also the proposal for a standing UN force, even contract
peacekeepers, which at a superficial level seems to solve the problem of
relying on single-nation military capabilities. Assuming that widespread
reluctance to contribute to such a force were to be overcome, the dilemma
for all standing forces is that, until they are convened in one place, they
cannot solve the problems of coordinating multinational units into a single
force. If they are successfully convened, running costs to keep them pro-
fessionally alert and operationally viable will be more than many countries
could contribute. Although the cost of war is much greater, unfortunately
most countries prefer to skimp on their premiums and take the risk that it
is unlikely to happen to them.

With no evidence of an impending resuscitation of the MSC, the universal dismissal of the single-nation option, and proposals for a standing
force overwhelmed by their own impracticalities, the international community seems to be steering much the same course as before on the question of controlling enforcement operations. In Brian Urquhart's estimation,
the currently practiced "sheriff's posse"[25] continues to be the highest form
of military cooperation; but this probability does not address the question
of how multinational force operations at the high intensity end of the continuum will be directed in the future. Unless the international community
is continuously threatened by global crises, it is unlikely in the short term
that either the MSC or the relevant echelons of the Secretariat will be dis-
mantled and reorganized in pursuit of a radical solution. It is probable,
however, that over time new parameters will emerge and the institution
will evolve toward a better system.

How will this proceed? In the short term, the UN Secretariat will continue to organize operations under the sobriquet of peacekeeping. It is to
be hoped, however, that the secretary general, assisted by an enhanced military staff, will consider with much greater precision the new parameters
of peacekeeping and as a result, with the full support of the Security Council, begin to develop a better instrument that has an appropriate measure of
tactical flexibility. The move away from the hitherto staunchly maintained
limitations of peacekeeping will start modestly, unnoticed by the majority
of members. In terms of hazard and complexity, it may have already
started with the mandates for Cambodia and Yugoslavia, although the
expected threats in the field have not been met with a commensurate

enhancement of force capability. At the high intensity level of the operational continuum, multinational forces will probably continue to deploy under a single-nation command structure. The majority of member nations will continue to express their dismay, but given the dire circumstances that usually initiate such an extreme response, the expedient will be regionally acceptable.

In the long term, by gradually moving toward proactive operations, the UN Secretariat may begin to build up a military capability similar to a national government's department of defense. A concept of operations may be developed by an expanded military staff. Its tenets will be uniformly imposed, so that all UN forces gradually achieve the same standards of professionalism. A UN staff college, under the direction of the MSC and not the UN Institute for Training and Research (UNITAR), may be established, and large-scale UN military and humanitarian relief exercises organized. All these thresholds will have been imperceptibly crossed, raising no alarm among members but at the same time conferring on the UN a sense of operational credibility. In the same gradual manner, the governance of the secretary general, in real terms, will begin to move across the operational continuum, taking on tasks that were formerly the province of military alliances. By this means, in the long term, when the call comes for an enforcement operation, the Secretariat will have established the credibility it lacked in August 1990.

It is hard to discern the precise nature of the relationship that will have to develop between the Security Council, the UN secretary general, and the force commander. It may follow one of several models. In NATO, there is a similar linkage between the NATO Council, the Supreme Allied Commander, Europe (SACEUR), and the national army corps. In NATO, however, the operational plans have been written, agreed, and frequently exercised, which reduces decision making and political canvassing and creates a high degree of institutional continuity. In most governments, there is the interface between elected ministers and the professional civil servants who execute their directives in a department of defense.

What will be the UN model? Given the inadequacy of the "sheriff's posse," the impracticality of the MSC, and rejection of the single-nation option, there is a middle possibility that borrows from national institutions a clear separation of powers. *Political* control and *military* command are fundamental tenets of democracies, but in the UN this relationship is imbalanced. It is not clear where this line ought to be drawn because the Charter offers direction only in the context of the ideal collective security system. One option, given the political capacity of the UN and the military expertise of states, is to divide control and command. Although this is a more effective arrangement than peacekeeping and a functional alternative to the MSC, it dangerously resembles the single-nation option. It differs fundamentally, however, in that effective and final authority is vested in the UN, and it is underwritten by a Charter-based legitimacy in keeping with the principles of the organization. This distinction is apparent in the examination of legal provisions for second generation operations below.

Legal Aspects of Second Generation Operations

The legitimacy of second generation forces rests on "devising a satisfactory system of political control."[26] The Persian Gulf War opened a wide debate in which two views predominate. One postulates a linear progression between chapters VI and VII, and although peacekeeping was the furthest point reached along this continuum during the Cold War, the eventual goal was always to develop the ideal collective security mechanism envisioned by the drafters of the Charter. This has been the goal of renewed calls for resuscitating the MSC and strengthening the role of the secretary general. The U.S. war coalition arrangement, therefore, was a detour, and the world community ought to return to the original road to chapter VII. The other view holds that the ideal of chapter VII is still too unrealistic, and that coalition forces authorized by the UN provided the best opportunity for action, even if its collective character could be questioned. These opinions represent a conflict over who should and can command and control collective actions.

During the Gulf War, it was a widespread misconception that the U.S.-dominated model constituted a collective basis for action. There has since been controversy over the gap between what some member states understood Security Council Resolution 678 to authorize and prosecution of the war in the field, particularly the unexpected degree of force used.[27] "Collective" must mean the subordination of control of sovereign armed forces to a centralized instrument, authorized to act by the larger community in the event of a crisis. Action through an international organization, or multilateralism, is distinct from multinational action, which amounts to individual states independently cooperating in a loose federation, effectively as a form of self-help. Particularly, collective action is conducted according to standard operating procedures that are devised and agreed prior to a crisis and are consistently applied whatever the subjective interests of community members. The importance of "collective" is not necessarily in the operation, which may be executed by one or two or many states; international will must be represented in the decision to act as well as the continued direction of the operation.[28]

Legitimate second generation operations must be collective actions, which can be distinguished from purely enforcement measures. Although both are collective in authority, second generation operations and enforcement measures differ in their objectives and character. Second generation forces can only be authorized by the UN Charter. To represent an international will legitimately, they must be constituted on a truly collective basis. Article 1(1) states that a purpose of the UN is "To maintain international peace and security, and to that end: to take effective collective measures for the prevention and removal of threats to the peace, and for the suppression of acts of aggression or other breaches of the peace." It has been argued that the authority to establish UN forces is implied in this provision.[29]

Centralizing control will not, however, mitigate the practical problem of the UN's military competence to conduct these operations. The two views emerging from the Gulf War represent old thinking about multinational forces, in which only peacekeeping and enforcement are options. Just as there is a potential third category of operations, it is possible for the Charter to authorize a collective action beyond peacekeeping that is not carried out by the permanent UN force originally envisioned, provided three conditions are met.

In this arrangement, individual states act as UN representatives and execute decisions arrived at collectively. Under article 7(2) of the UN Charter, the principal organs of the organization, including the Security Council, can appoint an agent or establish "such subsidiary organs as may be found necessary." The Charter nowhere defines "subsidiary organ," but it may include a collegiate body, a single individual or member state, or a group of members.[30] This raises the question of whether the Security Council can delegate to "subsidiary organs" the execution of measures strictly within its purview that would be unlawful for states acting independently. Although the Charter is unclear, it would seem that the answer is affirmative conditionally. First, it should be clear that the state or group of states is acting on behalf of the world organization and that the link between the two is direct. Second, given that the command of the operation is not functionally part of the UN, instructions to its agent—the appointed force—must be clear, specific, and incontestable. Finally, the agent must be directly responsible to the authority of the UN.[31] Inability to regulate U.S. coalition forces following resolution 678 has made imperative the formalization of procedures to delegate command to multinational forces undertaking second generation operations.

UN instructions to its forces will need to be carefully balanced. If they are too specific, they may lack the flexibility required by a force commander in the operational area to match rapidly changing conditions. For this reason, a designated force or subsidiary organ may be reluctant to accept detailed direction in principle and for practical purposes. On the other hand, general or vague instructions may leave too much room for interpretation and even abuse. Reference in resolution 678 to "all necessary means" failed to restrict the use of force in the Persian Gulf and some believe restrictions on sanctions, such as proportionality,[32] were lost in the prosecution of the coalition's military objectives.

This arrangement, therefore, requires a clear separation of powers. The political decision making and strategic executive capacities are vested in the Security Council and the secretary general, respectively, and the local operational powers in the force commander. Although it is difficult to define where these sources of authority separate, it must be done to avoid the confusion of powers evident in the Gulf War. The force commander must be directed by the secretary general as the executive agent of the collective will of the international community represented by the Security Council. The task of translating broad directives from the Security Council would fall between the Secretariat (including the MSC, were it resuscitated) and the force commander. The powers of the body exercising political control would be to:

- Appoint and dismiss the commander;
- Circumscribe the authority of the commander in the statute and regulations for the force;
- Determine the size and composition of the force;
- Determine movements of the force across international boundaries; and
- Require the commander to submit full and periodic reports on the force and its activities.[33]

Reporting has become an acute concern given the absence of effective reporting procedures in the Persian Gulf, so there will be pressure on force commanders to provide full and timely situation reports.

Turning strategic direction into a military plan, on the other hand, must be an exclusive responsibility of the force commander if the military principle of unity of command is to be maintained. That is, there may be control by committee, but command must be by a single hand. In second generation operations, given the politico-military tasks in the continuum, there is likely to be both a civilian and a military field commander. In this case, the force commander will be responsible to the special representative or his equivalent. Furthermore, his "authority would not include a right to initiate armed action, except in self-defence,"[34] unless clear rules of engagement for the use of minimum force had been previously authorized by the political directorate.

The reluctance of contributors to subordinate their assets to the UN for tasks beyond peacekeeping raises the issue of whether *political* direction of operations can be delegated to a group of states or regional agents as a means of soliciting their participation. Enforcement actions through regional arrangements were envisaged by chapter VIII of the UN Charter, but article 53 categorically states that the Security Council retains final authority and, therefore, political control. Furthermore, most of these organizations are limited in scope, dominated by a regional power, not universal even by regional standards, or grew out of East-West or other tensions. They are invariably perceived as partisan, and there would be extreme opposition from UN member states if they were to control "forces in the name of the United Nations operating outside the territories of their own members, and probably also even if designed to meet a situation internal to the regional organization itself." Divested of its political control, the UN would be unable "to ensure that the political objectives of the operations remained those of the United Nations and not of that particular group of States."[35] On balance, this is not a lawful solution to the problem of effective command and control.

Furthermore, collectively constituted forces have the authority and legitimacy to operate in the absence of host state consent. Once properly constituted, "there is no Charter requirement that permission for the movement of such forces be obtained" from host states.[36] Article 2(5) and particularly article 25, by which members "agree to accept and carry out the decisions of the Security Council," have been construed as an advance form of consent.[37] Article 49 may also be cited in the same spirit, although it refers to "measures" of the Security Council and would imply it is meant to cover enforcement actions. As argued earlier, second generation forces may have to operate without local consent; such authority provides indispensable legitimacy in face of local criticism and protest. Key to this legitimacy is the degree of universal will underwriting the action that is represented by the United Nations.

Conclusion

In the earlier sections of this article we explained why after the Cold War a need emerged for a much more effective instrument to underwrite the authority of the UN. The global forecast of violence demands the development of UN forces that are more than symbolic, forces that can restore order in face of local opposition and perform an increasingly varied range of tasks by land, sea, and air. This revolution can only be delivered by the major powers. It will require them to abandon their unilateralist tendency in conflicts where a multilateral UN solution has been agreed. They must demonstrate their support by unconditional subordination of an appropriate element of their effective military assets to an integrated UN command system. Above all, it will require them to pay the full price of these improvements and refrain from exercising financial control mechanisms in pursuit of national interests.

Notwithstanding the January 1992 declaration, there is little evidence that the major powers are planning to meet these requirements. Of all peacekeeping initiatives since the Congo, the UN forces destined for Cambodia and Yugoslavia will be least likely to face best case scenarios. A degree of tactical flexibility will be an essential factor in success or failure in both cases. Nevertheless, cost cutting by the major powers has limited the forces to all but the essential units required to carry out the mandate under optimum conditions. As these contingents deploy, it is clear that conditions at their destinations are far from ideal. Even if they return successful and unscathed, the message from the major powers seems clear: for the time being UN forces will continue to be a military presence without a capability for effective operations. But the unhealed wounds of recent history, the forecast of impending conflict, and the proliferating arms threat all argue loudly and uncompromisingly for a better system. The leaders of the world must now deliver one.

Notes

1. See further, "Report of the Secretary-General on Cambodia," UN Doc. S/23613, February 19, 1992.

2. See further, "Further Report of the Secretary-General Pursuant to Security Council Resolution 721 (1991)," UN Doc. S/23592, February 15, 1992.

3. "Note by the President of the Security Council," UN Doc. S/23500, January 31, 1992, pp. 3–4.

4. The internationally recognized principles of peacekeeping are enumerated in "Report of the Secretary-General on the Implementation of Security Council Resolution 340 (1973)," UN Doc. S/11052/Rev. 1, October 27, 1973.

5. Alan James, "Painful Peacekeeping: The UN in Lebanon 1978–82," *International Journal* 38 (Autumn 1983).

6. John Mackinlay, *The Peacekeepers: An Assessment of Peacekeeping Operations at the Arab-Israeli Interface* (London: Unwin Hyman, 1989), p. 14.

7. *Ibid.,* p. 151 and note 33, p. 159.

8. F. R. Henn, "Guidelines for Peacekeepng," *British Army Review,* no. 67 (April 1981), p. 36; Indar Jit Rikhye, "The Problems of International Peacekeeping," Royal United Services Institute lecture, London, September 29, 1976.

9. UN stockpiles of military equipment were World War II surplus. Although useful until the mid-1970s, by 1980 the whole inventory was obsolete and much of it unfit for service.

10. F. R. Henn, "UNTAG Shambles," *Daily Telegraph* (London), April 20, 1989, letters; Emmanuel A. Erskine, "Establishment of UNIFIL," International Workshop on UNIFIL, Oslo, July 1–4, 1986; Mackinlay, *Peacekeepers,* p. 12.

11. Mikhail Gorbachev, "Reality and the Guarantee of World Security," *Pravda,* September 17, 1987; and *Mikhail Gorbachev: Address at the United Nations, New York, December 7, 1988* (Moscow: Novosti Press Agency Publishing House, 1988).

12. New procedural documents on peacekeeping were developed both in the officer staff training syllabi and in the doctrine development centers. See, for instance, U.S. Joint Chiefs of Staff, "Joint Tactics, Techniques, and Procedures for Peacekeeping Operations," Joint Pub 3-07.3 (Washington, D.C., November 1991).

13. Afghanistan and Pakistan (1988), Iran-Iraq (1988), Angola (1989), Namibia (1989), Central America (1989), Iraq-Kuwait (1991), Western Sahara

(1991), Cambodia (advance mission 1991, main body 1992), and Yugoslavia (1992).

14. "Middle nations" refers to an ill-defined group of nations that are not major economic powers, or members of the UN Security Council, or militarily powerful. The only factor they all have in common is that they habitually contribute to peacekeeping.

15. Marianne Heiberg, "UN Peacekeeping in the New World Order," lecture at the NATO Defense College, Rome, May 1991; Johan Jørgen Holst, "Enhancing Peace-keeping Operations," *Survival* 32 (May/June 1990), p. 265.

16. For example, in Namibia UN action was delayed by budgetary authorization and late reductions in force size, and in Cambodia the UN force is facing the reluctance of permanent members to commit financial contributions that are needed to underwrite the political agreement they have brokered.

17. Brian Urquhart interview by Helga Graham, "UN Can Be Real Peacemaker in the Brave New World Order," *Observer* (London), January 26, 1992.

18. John Mackinlay, "Why the British Army Should Take Peacekeeping More Seriously," *British Army Review,* no. 78 (August 1991), p. 16; and "Toward a New Look for the UN," *Providence Journal,* March 1, 1992.

19. Mao Tse Tung, *Basic Tactics* (London: Pall Mall Press, 1966); Richard Clutterbuck, *The Long War: The Emergency in Malaya, 1948–1960* (London: Cassel, 1967).

20. Martin Oppenheimer, *Urban Guerrilla* (London: Penguin, 1968); Carlos Marighela, *For the Liberation of Brazil* (London: Pelican, 1971).

21. U.K. Ministry of Defence, *Land Operations,* vol. 3, *Counter-Revolutionary Operations* (London: Ministry of Defence, 1977), pt. 1, chap. 5, sec. 17.

22. See, for instance, on Yugoslavia, Security Council Resolution 743 (1992) of February 21, 1992, para. 4.

23. See UN General Assembly Docs. A/44/301, June 9, 1989, A/SPC/44/C.6, October 27, 1989, and A/45/212, May 8, 1990.

24. Eduard A. Shevardnadze, *Working Together* (Providence, R.I.: Thomas J.Watson, Jr., Institute for International Studies, 1991), p. 13.

25. Brian Urquhart, "After the Cold War: Learning from the Gulf," in *Toward Collective Security: Two Views* (Providence, R.I.: Thomas J. Watson, Jr., Institute for International Studies, 1991).

26. D. W. Bowett. *United Nations Forces: A Legal Study* (London: Stevens & Sons, 1964), p. 353.

27. Burns H. Weston, "Security Council Resolution 678 and Persian Gulf Decision Making: Precarious Legitimacy," *American Journal of International Law* 85 (1991), pp. 516–535. See also, Stephen Lewis, Clovis Maksoud, and Robert C. Johansen, "The United Nations After the Gulf War," *World Policy Journal* 8 (Summer 1991), pp. 537–574; and Brian Urquhart, "Learning from the Gulf War," *New York Review of Books,* March 7, 1991, pp. 34–37.

28. This definition is from Jarat Chopra and Thomas G. Weiss, "Sovereignty Is No Longer Sacrosanct: Codifying Humanitarian Intervention," *Ethics and International Affairs* 6 (1992), p. 114. See also Inis Claude, *Swords Into Ploughshares* (New York: Random House, 1964), chap. 12.

29. John W. Halderman, "Legal Basis for United Nations Armed Forces," *American Journal of International Law* 56 (1962), pp. 972ff. on article 1(1). On implied powers see: *Reparation for Injuries Suffered in the Service of the United Nations* case, Advisory Opinion, *I.C.J. Reports,* 1949, p. 174; *Certain Expenses of the United Nations* case, *I.C.J. Reports,* 1962, p. 151; and Rahmatullah Khan, *Implied Powers of the United Nations* (New Delhi: Vikas Publications, 1970), p. 72.

30. Hans Kelsen, *The Law of the United Nations: A Critical Analysis of Its Fundamental Problems* (London: Stevens & Sons, 1950), p. 138. See also discussion of issues that follows, as well as pp. 149ff. on states and individuals as UN "organs."

31. For a more detailed analysis of these conditions that compares the Gulf with enforcing sanctions against Rhodesia and UN action in Korea, see Thomas G. Weiss and Jarat Chopra, *United Nations Peackeeping: An ACUNS Teaching Text* (Hanover, N.H.: Academic Council on the United Nations System, 1992-I), pt. 2, sec. E.

32. For the applicability of proportionality as a restriction on enforcement action in the Gulf, see Oscar Schachter, "United Nations Law in the Gulf Conflict," *American Journal of International Law* 85 (1991), pp. 465–466; Eugene V. Rostow, "Until What? Enforcement Action or Collective Self-Defense?" *American Journal of International Law* 85 (1991), p. 514; and Weston, "Security Council Resolution 678," pp. 525–528.

33. See further, Bowett, *United Nations Forces,* p. 359.

34. *Ibid.,* p. 353.

35. *Ibid.,* p. 338.

36. Halderman, "Legal Basis," p. 972.

37. Bowett, *United Nations Forces,* chap. 12, sec. I.

Part 5

ECONOMIC ISSUES

FOLLOWING World War II, the international economic system was redefined by the agreements at Bretton Woods. The Bretton Woods system came to rest on three pillars: the International Monetary Fund (IMF), the World Bank, and the General Agreement on Tariffs and Trade (GATT). The IMF was designed to deal with currency exchange and balance of payments problems stemming from international trade. The World Bank was created to assist in the development process of member states, specifically to arrange for loans to facilitate economic projects. GATT was the mechanism by which states could resolve disputes and increase the volume of international trade through the lifting of national restrictions.

There have been several important changes in the Bretton Woods system in the last forty years. For example, floating currency exchange rates have replaced fixed rates pegged to gold, and the IMF and World Bank now perform some of the other's original functions. The negotiating rounds of GATT have been formalized under the structure of the World Trade Organization (WTO). Nevertheless, the Bretton Woods system remains largely intact. The major debates in international organizations center on whether that system should be changed further and in what ways. The Bretton Woods system was designed by Western and, for the most part developed, states committed to the principles of capitalism; most Third World states had not yet even achieved independence. The institutions underlying the system are still largely controlled by the Western economic powers, either through formal voting procedures or by virtue of their collective power in international economic relations. Third World states have argued that the current system is, at worst, designed to perpetuate the dominance of the Western countries or, at best, not designed to meet the needs of less developed states. It is the disagreement between the states of the North and the South that has increasingly dominated the agendas of international economic bodies during the past quarter century.

In order to understand the North-South conflict, it is appropriate to consider the changes in the system advocated by the Third World. Many of these demands for change have been lumped into what has been called the New International Economic Order (NIEO). Rather than a set list of policies or a definitive program, NIEO is a loose collection of often vaguely defined ideas and proposals on how the international economic system might be altered to meet Third World needs. In the first article of Part 5, Craig Murphy traces the history of the NIEO movement and in his words "what the Third World wants." The rest of the articles in Part 5 at least implicitly refer back to the bases of Murphy's piece.

The International Monetary Fund and the World Bank, for better or worse, have perhaps been the most influential international organizations over the last three decades in the economic issue area. They certainly have been among the most controversial with their policies coming under sharp criticism from many Third World states. The two organizations have changed dramatically since their inception, when their purposes were, respectively, to stabilize world trade and rebuild Europe after World War II. Richard Feinberg details a more recent evolution in the two organizations, such that they now have somewhat overlapping functions. Beyond surveying the evolution of these organizations and their functions, the author presents a series of recommendations for more efficient and effective coordination and distribution of functions between these two Bretton Woods pillars.

As a response to the perceived inhospitable climate of the international economic system and its organizational structure, some poorer states have looked to regional groupings to strengthen their trading positions or to promote economic development. Such regional blocs may better reflect the peculiar needs of the states in a given geographic area. One such institution is the Inter-American Development Bank (IDB). Enrique Iglesias reviews the economic problems of Latin America and then discusses the role that the IDB has played or will have to play in meeting those concerns. Not only does his analysis show the multitude of ways that a regional organization can promote economic development, but he argues strongly that such organizations must also deal with socioeconomic conditions such as poverty before real progress can be made in development.

11

What the Third World Wants:
An Interpretation of the Development
and Meaning of the New International
Economic Order Ideology

Craig N. Murphy

In this article I argue that the New Order ideology results from 'consciousness raising,' and the recognition of real problems. It further suggests that Third World leaders came to their views responsibly and that international regimes can be transformed through the opening of communications that responsible global negotiations would assure. Such negotiations would in themselves serve to test the model further. . . .

The Core of the
New International Economic Order Ideology

The story about what Third World governments want to achieve through their support of the NIEO ideology logically begins in the 1940s. Even though Asian, Latin American, and African states agreed with many of the principles underlying the 'new economic order' that was then being created, many of the Third World's views about post-war regimes were not taken into account in the formation of that 'new order.' During World War II, and immediately before, most of the independent governments of Latin America and the semi-autonomous local governments in Asia and Africa pursued development plans supported by interventionist foreign economic policies, including a whole range of trade and currency restrictions.[1] During the War and at its end, however, what would later be Third World governments preferred a vision of post-war international economic institutions that would allow national regulation of international economic relations while seeing to it that those national regulations conflicted with each other as little as possible.[2]

Reprinted from the *International Studies Quarterly,* Vol. 27, No. 1, 1983, with permission of the International Studies Association, Byrnes International Center, University of South Carolina, Columbia, S.C. 29208.

In the 1940s, this vision of the post-war institutions was, if anything, the dominant view worldwide. Representatives of the national government of Argentina and the native government of India could find what Fred Block (1977) calls 'national capitalist' spokesmen from countries like Britain and Australia agreeing that international institutions should approve of national regulation of the economy and should only serve to make the regulations that different governments desired, compatible. And, of course, Soviet officials, representing an economy that required regulation, sang the same tune.

That tune was not pleasing to the most powerful people in the most powerful country at the end of the War. The most significant American policy makers imagined post-war economic institutions as agencies that would aim to abolish national restrictions on the international economy rather than merely regulate them (*see* Gardner, 1964: 195).

The American vision became the blueprint for the institutions. Socialist states whose economies required regulation never became active members of the post-war system. Other states that had been wealthy prior to World War II went along with the development of increasingly liberal regimes because the United States assured the liberal system work by giving the previously rich market states the opportunity to reconstruct their economies.[3] Latin America and the independent and colonial areas in Asia and Africa went along with the system, while unconvinced of its value for them. But without any alternative for managing some of the global money, finance, and trade problems that they, as much as the Europeans or North Americans, felt should be managed globally, they conceded to the American vision.

The key problem confronted by Asian, African, and Latin American policy makers in the late 1940s, the problem that led to the adoption of the ideas that became the core of the New Order ideology, was how to argue for and justify those restrictions upon strictly liberal international exchange that they had used in the past and might want to continue to use as part of their industrial development policies.

The ideological milieu of the 1940s, especially within the international organizations and meetings on economic matters, really provided only two possible justifications.

1. A 'scientific' principle. If it could be shown that such economic restrictions would be the most efficient way to achieve specific economic goals, like national industrial development, then those policies could be justified by principles of economic science alone. It was to this sort of principle that Keynes and many other economists appealed when they supported the 'national capitalist' vision of post-war regimes (Block, 1977: 7–8).[4]
2. The other justification was based upon notions concerning the rights of sovereign states and their duties toward one another.

These ideas were new; they had been developed during international discussions about the creation of the United Nations and the operation of the wartime 'United and Associated Nations,' the antifascist alliance.

Unlike appeals to economic science, appeals to various economic rights and duties of states never required that they be understood as the most rational principles possible; those policies had only to be the ones that could achieve some set of goals that governments were said to have the sovereign right to formulate for themselves. Supporting those goals could even be considered the *duty* of other states. The most significant version of the economic rights and duties of states formulated at the end of the War was expressed by officials of the United Nations Relief and Rehabilitation Administration (UNRRA). They argued that each state had the duty to aid the economic development of every other state, that this aid should be given no matter what political and economic disagreements a country might have with another country's economic ideology or economic policies (e.g., it was the duty of a capitalist state to aid the economic development of socialist states), and that the material extent of this obligation was directly proportional to the material differences in life from one country to another; every state had duties to aid all those states where people were materially less advantaged.[5]

In the late 1940s, Latin American, Asian, and African officials invoked the principles of states' economic rights and duties rather than the scientific principle. They made this choice because the notions about the rights and duties would not only suggest that they had a right to employ illiberal policies, those ideas could also justify Latin American, Asian, and African claims for direct international material aid for their industrial development plans, aid similar to that given to the previously wealthy war-torn nations through UNRRA and the American Marshall Plan (Brown, 1950: 136; the *Economist,* 8 May, 1948: 782). At the earliest meetings of the United Nations, and throughout the 1940s and 50s, representatives from what would become the Third World argued both for new international economic regimes that would regulate rather than abolish national interventions *and* they argued that aid similar to that being given to Europe should be given to Asia, Africa, and Latin America, because such aid was required of wealthy states as their duty to poorer states. They justified both claims by citing UN statements defining states' rights and duties and by citing the short-lived UNRRA precedent. Latin American officials, in particular, argued that it was only fair that aid be given to them because they had contributed to European reconstruction through UNRRA in response to American appeals to the economic rights and duties of states.[6]

Thus, the core of the NIEO was formed in the 1940s when the pre-war 'Third World' goal of achieving national industrial development by using as wide a range of national economic policy tools as possible appeared to be thwarted by the liberal international economic regimes that were being created. At the same time, Third World governments had available to them a particularly attractive justification for the policies that they wanted to pursue. That justification had been treated as a legitimate one by the supporters of the liberal order when they created UNRRA and later aid systems. And, more significantly, that justification suggested that other states had *moral* obligations to aid the industrial development plans that Third World states advocated. By 1950 this moral justification was already being reiterated at every international meeting on economic matters attended by delegates from Asia, Africa, and Latin America. Around it grew the entire New Order ideology.

Analysis of the World Economy: Response to Unanticipated Problems

Almost any conversation about the growth of the Third World's NIEO ideology brings up Raul Prebisch, his ideas about terms of trade shifting against products produced in the Third World, and his ideas about the structures of the global economy impeding Third World industrial development. Prebisch's analysis of the world economy has been invoked for the past 20 years by almost every Third World government spokesman on international economic matters. As such, his analysis was the first major addition to those simple precepts that formed the core of the NIEO ideology.

The best way to understand why Prebisch's ideas became so important is to look at what most Third World policy makers were concerned with when they first started talking in the terms of that analysis. Although Prebisch wrote his seminal work (1950) in the late 1940s, examination of General Assembly Second (Economic) Committee debates shows that Prebisch's ideas did not become a consistent topic of general UN debate until the mid-1950s. And they did not become 'the Third World position' in the General Assembly, until the early 1960s. This timing is significant: Prebisch's ideas were not adopted as the Third World position earlier simply because they were completely compelling in their own right.

Third World governments began to adopt Prebisch's views when they first faced specific problems that those ideas helped them understand. The first time Prebisch's ideas entered the General Assembly debate they were linked to something Prebisch hardly would have been able to discuss in 1949—the effects that the formation and (later) depletion of strategic stockpiles of raw materials in the North had on Third World economies. Yet, those Northern, Korean War era policies certainly represented an example of the situation that Prebisch wrote about: institutions at the core of the world economy having more influence on the world economy than institutions in the periphery.[7]

By the early 1960s, the Third World's trade problems included others similar to those associated with the North's use of strategic stockpiles. Since the War, while worldwide trade had expanded at unprecedented rates and had fueled world economic growth, just as the founders of the post-war system had intended, the Third World's percentage of this trade had declined. That was, if anything, just the opposite of what was expected (Pincus, 1965: 126–27). By the early 1960s most Third World governments felt cheated out of the trade-induced growth that the rich nations enjoyed just as some of the same officials had felt cheated out of the growth that could have been encouraged by continuous trade in raw materials at stable prices had it not been for the Northern stockpiling.

In response to the problem of the declining Third World trade share, most Third World representatives in the General Assembly and in GATT[8] began to articulate their resentment in the language of Prebisch's analysis. This ideological package brought with it some additional ideas like the notion that the relative value of Third World trade with the North had been declining for some time (a notion that proved to be debatable). But Prebisch's ideas certainly were not the only ones available at the time. Southern officials could have explained their economic problems in terms of the 'cultural constraints on development' popularly cited by many early Northern development economists (e.g., Rostow, 1953, 1960: 12). Instead, Third World representatives appealed to the economic rights and duties of states, and held that every government had a right to choose an economic development plan compatible with its cultural context, and that all nations should support such plans. For the South, the idea that the international community should identify 'cultural impediments to development' was ridiculous. Third World governments could have looked to domestic structures impeding development, such as those identified by Gunnar Myrdal (1956), and many states did. But such domestic structures could not become the *shared* Third World explanation for their trade income problem simply because other shared principles allowed any Southern government to reject such an explanation as being applicable to *its* domestic economy.

More significantly, Third World leaders now had an alternative *global* explanation of the source of their problems. And while supporters of the post-war system were just as upset about the declining Third World trade share, the GATT's 1958 report on the problem, written by liberal economist Gottfried Haberler, directly blamed the developed states for the declining Third World share of trade (Friedeberg, 1969: 53–56). Northern trade policies, like those associated with strategic stockpiling, created tariff and non-tariff barriers to increasing the Third World's share of trade. The free trade system was not to blame according to the GATT report, but the exceptions to the system, which had been granted mostly to Northern states, were.

Why did the Prebisch thesis rather than the 'Haberler thesis' become the center of Third World New Order policy analysis? The answer has little to do with the comparative accuracy, sufficiency, or elegance of the two theses. In fact, both theories explained that key issue in exactly the same way: it was the result of the West's greater power to influence international economic relations. A new manifestation of an old pattern, said Prebisch. A violation of recently achieved liberalizations that should benefit all, said Haberler. Both theses provide sufficient explanation of the declining Third World trade share. Haberler's 'saves' liberal trade theory, easily one of the most elegant ideas any social scientist has ever invented. And Haberler's thesis certainly identifies the immediate problems of the 1960s in a more concrete way than Prebisch's ideas, invented to explain 50 years of Latin American underdevelopment, do. Why, then, did the Third World reject the Haberler thesis? Apparently Prebisch's ideas were preferable to Haberler's simply because they did not contradict the core of the New Order ideology. They were compatible with the notion that national regulation of international economic exchange was desirable. Haberler's ideas were not.

Of course, a supporter of Haberler's point of view could argue, as many did and still do, that the core of the Third World's new ideology was irrational and that an increasingly liberal world economic system was better for everyone than a system of internationally regulated national regulations of the world economy, but someone from the Third World could counter that such a fact had never been proved: the system the Third World wanted had never been tried, and the operating system was not total liberalism, but only a partial liberalism, and only one part of a system that even liberals admitted discriminated against the Third World because power was concentrated in the North.

The Group of 77 and the
Democratization of International Relations

Prebisch's analysis of the world economy had become the official position of the growing Third World alliance by the first UNCTAD in 1964. The South presented a set of 'trade principles' based on Prebisch's views, and the vote on these demonstrated the sharp division between North and South (Moss and Winton, 1976: 43–51). Adding Prebisch's views to the Third World's ideological consensus meant more than adding an explanation of some of the unanticipated problems experienced by the Third World, it meant adding a primarily political analysis of what should be done about Third World economic problems.

The logical starting place of Prebisch's analysis, the most significant independent variable in his model of the world political economy, is the difference between the power to influence economic decisions in the center and in the periphery of the world economy. People in the center can influence most global economic decisions; people in the periphery cannot.

Accepting Prebisch's thesis meant constantly searching for *new* Third World powers to influence economic relations. It meant, for example, considering the creation of producer's alliances as a legitimate way to carry out some international economic policies[9] and it meant actively and self-consciously pursuing Third World unity not only through the regional economic development schemes Prebisch's followers then supported (Cardoso, 1977), but also through more conscious development of the alliance's ideology.[10] In short, accepting Prebisch's ideas meant looking for ways to change institutions that structured and governed international trade by shifting the power over those institutions to the South.

In the late 1960s then, the South articulated its desire to gain more power over international institutions in a 'political analysis,' a view of how international economic regimes can and should be changed. Third World governments argued for the 'democratization' of international relations, meaning by that two very different, and somewhat contradictory things.

1. On the one hand, Third World officials meant that international institutions should be used to 'energize' public opinion in developed countries to support Third World goals.[11]
2. On the other hand, Third World governments argued for making more, binding international decisions 'democratically,' that is, on the basis of a one-nation, one-vote principle.[12]

The apparent contradiction of the Third World position lies in the contradictory justifications that *could* be used for these two different 'democratic' policies. Stressing the importance of public opinion suggests that popular sovereignty legitimates political decisions. Popular sovereignty could lead to very different decisions than rules based on the principle of the equal sovereignty of states, the principle that could be called upon to justify the other half of the Third World's plan for 'democratizing' international relations.

This apparent contradiction can be explained by the fact that the desire for these 'democratizing' policies reflected only a Third World desire for greater power over international economic relations and not prior principles about how decisions can be made justly. It was an extension of a policy analysis which said that the Third World should try to get more power over international economic relations in order to achieve those truly central goals of economic development. These were simply two different ways to get more power.

The mercantilist version of the American common wisdom correctly identifies this 'structural power interest' in the Third World but the common wisdom is wrong about where this interest comes from. It is not the result of some permanent inherent interest that states or individuals have in gaining or maintaining power over others, an interest that perhaps would best be masked by more pleasant ideas like 'popular sovereignty.' The conscious Third World desire for greater power over international economic decisions came as part of the analysis they adopted to help them understand and cope with a real, practical problem. Even when Third World officials in the United Nations argued that the organization should try to influence Northern public opinion, very few Southern representatives invoked 'popular sovereignty' as a justification (or mask). Most only said that they believed public opinion actually influenced decisions made by Northern governments and that they wanted the majority of the states in the United Nations to have indirect influence over those decisions.[13]

Certainly, Third World governments justified the one-nation, one-vote and UNCTAD conciliation decision-making procedures on the basis of the equal rights and duties of states, the only principles that have been at the core of the Third World ideology since it was first invented. But that does not mean that arguments for such 'democratic' forms of decision making are merely a mask for the South's interest in collectively developing the power to structure international economic relations. If the South were looking for a mask under which to hide such a power interest there are principles more appealing to the North than one-nation, one-vote that could be used. For example, the South could have argued for greater influence by invoking the old claim of democratic theory mentioned earlier—the claim that greater Third World input would have assured that more of the potential problems with economic regimes could have been anticipated and avoided. Southern states did not invoke that argument because Third World governments were not *only* seeking more collective power over international economic relations. They were also still seeking that world where states would have those equal economic rights and duties, the world they had wanted since the end of World War II. And they remained quite willing to justify their proposals with their fundamental principles despite the fact that Northern governments rejected their moral force.

Reiterating the Moral Basis for the NIEO: Response to Unanticipated Opportunities

The early years of the Third World's self-conscious attempts to gain greater power over international economic relations hardly suggested that the alliance gathered under the new ideology would ever achieve its goal. By the late 1960s the alliance had begun to fragment.

The alliance reunified between 1971 and 1974, seizing the opportunities created by the breakdown of the Bretton Woods system to patch-up an ideological split. In doing so, the South added a final, significant (and most often misunderstood)[14] notion to their collective ideology. This was the notion that Northern states owe something to the South as backpayments for past colonialism.

That notion was hardly new in 1971. It had split the alliance ever since more radical African governments, such as those of Guinea (UN, 1961: 49) and of Nkrumah's Ghana (UN, 1960: 35) first took it up. If restitution for colonialism were to be the only grounds for reforms in international economic institutions, then those Third World states that did not have a long experience of colonialism (e.g., Ethiopia, Liberia, or Argentina) could claim no right to have the institutions changed to serve their own national interests. If restitution (even for both colonialism and neocolonialism) defined the only duties of wealthy states, then some states where people were wealthy probably had *no* duty to aid poorer nations; it would be hard to identify a significant level of colonialism or neocolonialism practiced by (say) Norway, Finland, or Poland.[15]

By 1970 the debate over restitution helped split the South into 'radical' and 'moderate' camps. The radical camp included mostly Asian and African nations, non-aligned states, states that were recently independent, and other states that supported the restitution ethic. The moderate camp tended to be Latin American, aligned with the West, and included some states that had been independent longer, where people were relatively better off and whose governments rarely talked about the need for restitution for colonialism.[16]

By 1975 the issue was resolved: In the 'Charter of Economic Rights and Duties of States' (Moss and Winton, 1976: 902–06) Third World governments agreed, as they had in the 1940s, that the equal rights and duties of states made it incumbent upon all states to aid the economic development of every other state along the path chosen by its government. Nevertheless, in the debate over the NIEO, *all* Southern states began to tell former colonizers and 'neocolonialists' that they were required, by a principle of restitution, to *negotiate* the creation of a New Order.[17]

This manipulation of justifications and the resulting reunification of the Third World behind all elements of its long-standing ethic was not the result of some individual's brilliant solution to a logical problem, nor was it the result of direct bargaining and exchanges of concessions among those Third World governments that had different interests. Certainly some individuals were important—perhaps the Mexican delegate who appears in UN records as the first to raise the idea that certain Northern policies made it incumbent upon the North to negotiate a new order (UN, 1971: 79) and certainly Mexico's President, who put the 'Charter' itself on the Third World agenda. Nonetheless, those individuals could not have acted without having contemplated the political opportunities created by the first signs that the post-war global economic institutions were breaking down.

Those institutions started to break down, as Block (1977) illustrates, because of a series of problems affecting the wealthy market states, problems that the founders had not been able to anticipate and problems severe enough to lead the United States to renounce part of its leadership role in monetary matters and apply some trade restrictions universally in order to try to get some other wealthy states to bear some of the burdens of regime maintenance. These American actions, taken at the end of the summer of 1971, allowed the unity of the Third World to reemerge with a vengeance in that autumn's General Assembly session when both radical and moderate Third World governments claimed rights to receive compensation from the United States for the adverse effects of the new American economic policy. Third World governments expressed their demands not as calls for simple material transfer, but said (echoing the Mexican delegate) that because the United States had ended the effective life of the post-war economic regimes, it now had a responsibility to the Third World to negotiate the creation of new regimes (UN, 1972: 27–98).

At the same time, individual oil producers and, later, OPEC as a whole, seized upon the West's growing oil dependence on some Third World states to make greater exactions. This was something not taken into account by the architects of the post-war institutions, even though the dependence of their nations on Third World oil was created, in part, by the post-war prosperity that the system helped create. With the unity of the Third World already reaffirmed, the oil price increases of 1973 and 1974 were met with enthusiasm across the South, much to the surprise and chagrin of policy makers in the North who had predicted Southern responses based on the common wisdom and knowledge of immediate Third World economic interests which were, in fact, disastrously affected by the rising prices (Singh, 1977: 6–9).

The oil price increases created a Western interest in discussing some reforms of international economic regimes with some Third World countries. The Group of 77 used that opportunity to present its entire package of proposals for a New Order once again. Surprised by the coherence and unity of Third World support for that presentation at the United Nations in 1974, many Westerners for the first time started to try to figure out what it was that the Third World wanted.

Appropriate Political Action in
Response to Third World Demands

What *does* the Third World want? This reading of the way the New Order ideology developed suggests that the Group of 77 wants more power over international economic regimes in order to assure that Third World countries get all the advantages of trade-induced growth that they can. Third World governments want to take part in the creation and maintenance of stable international economic regimes which would coordinate, rather than abolish, national regulations of foreign economic relations. The South believes that such national regulations are sometimes necessary, or at least useful, ways to encourage industrial development, but it also believes, just as firmly, that stable, effective international regimes are essential as well. Of course tensions and differences of opinion divide Southern governments. Now, as has always been the case, when richer Third World states face no immediate economic crises that might make them want to use trade restrictions, they still remain interested in having the global system of coordination move toward greater liberalism. They want the North to reduce barriers to Southern industrial exports. All Third World governments, it seems, argue that international coordination of current development-related economic restrictions is a must.

One way to test these conclusions would be for Northern supporters of current regimes to unite with other states in the North and actively engage Southern governments in serious debates about how existing international economic regimes should be reformed. The history offered here of how the South came to its views, while not suggesting those views are fully justified or that the process of their development was wholly rational, does indicate that those views developed in response to real problems and that they are held in good faith. Those social theorists who provide the best arguments for recognizing the role that ideology can play in shaping social history suggest that, when we are confused about what someone means while still believing that he is acting competently and in good faith, the most efficient way to understand his interests is to ask him and to clarify them while at the same time demonstrating our willingness to cooperate with him to do things to our mutual interest.[18] That means negotiating.

Camps and Gwin's (1981) proposals for reforming international economic regimes, written under the auspices of the Council on Foreign Relations, suggest both a good idea for a new international economic order that might be acceptable to the Third World and the Northern states, and a good idea for a reasonable attitude that Northern policy makers might take toward Third World proposals. Camps and Gwin note, for example, that a vision of a world without national restrictions on international economic exchange has proved to be too optimistic, and will probably remain so. Thus, even those with a commitment to international liberalism must accept that truly effective international economic regimes should be more widely recognized as legitimate, and more justly coordinated with respect to national attempts to regulate than present regimes are. The United States' position on this fundamental issue has grown a lot closer to the Third World's, and the chances for real cooperation are that much better for it.

Of course, those who believe the liberal version of the American common wisdom about the New Order ideology would not trust Third World governments to negotiate with wisdom and in good faith. Assuming that all governments should, and do, act 'rationally' on the basis of simple power and economic interests, the incompetence of Third World governments—'proven' to liberals by Southern attachment to imperfect economic analyses—means that Third World states would be unreliable partners in any new international economic order. The deviousness of many Third World governments—'proven' to liberals by Southern calls for 'democratizing' and 'equalizing' international economic relations while they were unwilling to democratize and equalize domestic economic relations— shows they could not negotiate in good faith.

We need not be so pessimistic. As mercantilists Krasner (1981) and Tucker (1977) both say, Third World governments have fairly good reasons for the New Order positions they have adopted. We can go even further: the history of the adoption of those beliefs suggests that those good Third World reasons are not just tactical. The theories embodied in the New Order ideology may not explain the underdevelopment of the Third World as coherently as other theories do, and they may have been adopted under the ideological constraint of prior consensus, but Third World advocates of the New Order were trying to understand real problems and they selected one of a number of equally flawed theories to do so. Likewise, even if some Third World states do advocate popular sovereignty and greater economic equality among individuals, those positions have no more been part of the ideology shared by the *alliance* which is dedicated to creating the New Order than they were part of the ideology of the alliance which created the United Nations system in the first place. Lack of concern for social democratic values may mean a government is inegalitarian or authoritarian. It need not mean a government is devious.

The mercantilists who think the Third World has good reasons for its New Order ideology, yet still maintain that the North should avoid New Order discussions, may be right. But their argument must be based on their assumptions about the ways international regimes work most effectively and not on their interpretations of Third World views. But those assumptions are also open to question. As yet, no one has done the research necessary to find out who is really right: the statists who relate the stability of international regimes to the degree they accurately reflect an underlying power structure, or those who think learning and shared ideas are more important.

Notes

1. On Latin America *see* Gardner (1964: 109–32, 195–216) and on countries in the British Empire and Commonwealth, Bell (1958: 260–63).

2. Rothschild (1944) gives a prescient Keynesian justification for the poorer states' views. American trade negotiator Clair Wilcox's book (1949) remains the most readily available discussion of the post-war economic conferences where the Asian, Latin American, and few free African states began to state shared views.

3. Such, at least, was the view the London *Economist* took in the name of Europe after the Marshall Plan was developed (17 July, 1948: 90) and after having ridiculed the United States throughout the months between the end of the War and the development of the Plan *(see* the *Economist,* 26 Oct. 1945: 652; 22 Nov. 1947: 828).

4. Keynes's speech at the first World Bank/IMF governors' meeting exemplifies the argument (Horsefield, 1969: 123).

5. *See* UNRRA Director Fiorello La Guardia's defense of these principles (UN, 1946: 51).

6. *See* e.g. Argentina (UN, 1946: 8); Brazil (UN, 1946: 89); India (UN, 1947: 46); in a speech by later UNCTAD official and Pearson Commission member Roberto de Oliveira Campos: Brazil (UN, 1948: 168–69); and George Hakim in proposing the outline of what would become proposals for the Special UN Fund for Economic Development: Lebanon (UN, 1949: 9). As these citations demonstrate, and Wilcox affirms (1949: 42), in the 1940s the Third World tended to be 'led' by the larger and wealthier states from each region. Later the most ideologically committed governments in the South would be more active and thus also appear to lead, joining but not displacing the large and wealthy states (Hart, 1982: chapter 4).

7. *See* e.g. Brazil (UN, 1950: 138), Egypt (UN, 1951: 19).

See Nwekwe's (1980: 94–107) discussion of the politics in the GATT. Nwekwe, a Nigerian, calls his discussion of the Third World response in the GATT to falling trade shares 'The Nigerian Initiative of 1961' and notes (p. 99) that Gosovic and Ruggie (1976) were apparently unaware of how the Nigerian action in the GATT was a direct antecedent of the calls for a New Order in 1974. Nwekwe's claim of Nigerian initiation of the New Order debate, while uncharacteristically simplistic, is evidence of the degree to which New Order ideas are taken very seriously by many scholars and public officials from the Third World and serves as an example of a growing genre—statements by Third World nationalist leaders and scholars attributing a special role to their particular country in creating the NIEO ideology.

8. *See* e.g. Saudi Arabia (UN, 1960: 100) and Colombia (UN, 1960: 114).

9. A statement made by Alfonso Patino of Colombia in 1963 is typical:

Against blind respect for those (market) forces and against anachronistic trade restrictions imposed by the strongest against the weakest ranges the vigorous new ideology which inspired the convening of the (UNCTAD) conference. That ideology, which we must specify further, will constitute a new phase in the age-old struggle for the liberation of peoples and respect for human dignity (UN, 1963: 27).

10. E.g. Indonesia (UN, 1968: 2) and Tanzania (UN, 1969: 30).

11. See the Cairo Declaration of 1964 (Moss and Winton, 1976: 94) and Gosovic (1972: 57).

12. Only one state in the General Assembly challenged these proposals. Sudan objected, but only because they might not work (UN, 1969: 19). Nonetheless, an inter–Third World debate on democratic principles would have been possible. Chinweizu's (1975) account explains why (say) Sudan and Tanzania would have had different views about whether domestic democracy was good in 1969 while illustrating why few Third World governments would have then agreed with the Sudanese who were unusual in asserting that public opinion was not a major force shaping the policies of developed market states.

13. *See* e.g. MacPhee's (1979) response to Bronfenbrenner's (1976) article. Bronfenbrenner had (incorrectly) argued that the Third World position was based

on an ethic of reparations. MacPhee (correctly) points out that this view has never been central to the South's position but then (incorrectly) goes on to say that the reparations argument had never been raised by UNCTAD.

14. MacPhee (1979) notes that the most important states accepting this reparations notion are Eastern European (*see* Moss and Winton, 1976: 204–07, 310–14).

15. Compare the Asian-African dominated declaration of the nonaligned (Moss and Winton, 1976: 194–205) to the Latin American influenced plan for the 1970s development decade (Moss and Winton, 1976: 856–67).

16. For a humorous account of this position *see* Ul Haq, 1976: 140–41.

17. Habermas writes about the basic efficiency of dialogue as a means of resolving confusions in his long essay on scientific methodology (1971), and in his later discussions of communication and the development of society (1979). Perwin's (1975) critique of the first essay correctly points out that for dialogue to work the people engaged in it must have faith in each other and, moreover, need to be involved in a real, concrete relationship, acting together and not just talking.

18. While Camps and Gwin's view would be compatible with much of the NIEO Ideology and with the views of many Northern governments many issues would remain to be debated and bargained over before there could be a NIEO. A New Order resulting from such negotiations would, by no means, signal the end of basically liberal economic relations among nations or the end of a basically capitalist world-system. These are points that can perhaps be brought home best by reviewing Shoup and Minter's (1977: 264–72) radical critique of the earliest published version of Camps's argument and by noting the degree to which what she argues for is similar to what Third World spokesmen demand. Within the framework of the capitalist world-economy as a whole, the ideas behind calls for a NIEO constitute a reformist ideology and not a revolutionary one, despite what both some of the New Order's advocates and some of its conservative critics sometimes say. The compatibility of New Order views with many of Camps's views neither suggests that the New Order is merely a Third World elite sell-out, as some radicals would believe, nor that people like Camps and Gwin are sellouts to the Third World, as some American conservatives claim. Rather, that compatibility may suggest that both New Order advocates and Camps and Gwin, as well as others with similar views, like the Brandt Independent Commission (1980) or former World Bank official Paul Streeten (1981), are doing just what they say they are doing: looking for the best North-South compromise now possible.

References

Bell, P. (1958) *The Sterling Area in the Post-War World.* Oxford: Oxford University Press.

Block, F. (1977) *The Origins of International Economic Disorder.* Berkeley: University of California Press.

Bronfenbrenner, M. (1976) 'Predatory Poverty on the Offensive: The UNCTAD Record.' *Economic Development and Cultural Change* 24: 825–31.

Brown, W. A. Jr. (1950) *The United States and the Restoration of World Trade.* Washington: Brookings.

Camps, M. and C. Gwin (1981) *Collective Management: Reform of Global Economic Organization.* New York: McGraw-Hill.

Cardoso, F. (1977) 'The Originality of a Copy: CEPAL and the Idea of Development.' *CEPAL Review* 2nd Half: 7–40.

Chinwizu (1975) 'The Cult of Liberal Democracy,' in *The West and the Rest of Us.* New York: Random House.

Friedeberg, A. S. (1969) *UNCTAD 1964: The Theory of the Peripheral Economy at the Center of Global Discussion*. Rotterdam: University of Rotterdam Press.

Gardner, L. C. (1964) *Economic Aspects of New Deal Diplomacy*. Madison: University of Wisconsin Press.

Gosovic, B. (1972) *UNCTAD: Conflict and Compromise*. Leiden: A. W. Sifthoff.

Gosovic, B. and J. Ruggie (1976) 'On the Creation of the New International Economic Order: Issue Linkage and the Seventh Special Session of the United Nations General Assembly.' *International Organization* 30, 2: 309–45.

Habermas, J. (1971) 'Knowledge and Human Interests: A General Perspective,' in *Knowledge and Human Interests*. Boston: Beacon.

Habermas, J. (1979) *Communication and the Evolution of Society*. Boston: Beacon.

Hart, J. (1982) *Political Forces in the Global Economy: Explaining Negotiations for the New International Economic Order*. London: Macmillan.

Horsefield, J. K. (1969) *The International Monetary Fund: 1945–1965*. Washington: IMF.

Independent Commission (1980) *North-South: A Programme for Survival*. Cambridge: MIT Press.

Krasner, S. (1974) 'Oil Is the Exception.' *Foreign Policy* No. 14: 68–83.

Krasner, S. (1980) 'The United Nations and the Struggle for Control of North-South Relations.' Unpublished paper. Department of Political Science, University of California, Los Angeles.

Krasner, S. (1981) 'Transforming International Regimes: What the Third World Wants and Why.' *International Studies Quarterly* 25: 119–48.

MacPhee, C. (1979) 'Martin Bronfenbrenner on UNCTAD and the GSP.' *Economic Development and Cultural Change* 27: 357–63.

Moss. A. and H. Winton (1976) *A New International Economic Order: Selected Documents, 1945–1975*. New York: UNIPUB.

Myrdal, G. (1956) *Development and Underdevelopment*. Cairo: National Bank of Egypt.

Nwekwe, G. A. (1980) *Harmonization of African Foreign Policies 1955–1975: The Political Economy of African Diplomacy*. African Research Studies No. 14. Boston: African Studies Center, Boston University.

Perwin, C. (1975) 'Habermas and Psychoanalytic Epistemology.' Paper presented at the annual meeting of the Southern Political Science Association.

Pincus, J. (1967) *Trade, Aid, and Development*. New York: Council on Foreign Relations.

Prebisch, R. (1950) *The Economic Development of Latin America and Its Principle Problems*. Lake Success: United Nations.

Rostow, W. W. (1953, 1960) *The Process of Economic Growth*. Oxford: Oxford University Press.

Rothschild, K. W. (1944) 'The Small Nation in World Trade.' *Economic Journal* 54: 26–37.

Shoup, L. H. and W. Minter (1977) *Imperial Brain Trust*. New York: Monthly Review Press.

Singh, J. S. (1977) *A New International Economic Order*. New York: Praeger.

Streeten, P. (1981) 'Constructive Responses to the North-South Dialogue,' in Edwin Reuben (ed.), *The Challenge of the New International Economic Order*. Boulder: Westview.

Tucker, R. W. (1977) *The Inequality of Nations*. New York: Basic Books.

Ul Haq, M. (1976) *The Poverty Curtain*. New York: Columbia University Press.

UN General Assembly (1946–1974) *Summary Records of the Meetings the Second (Economic) Committee*.

Wilcox, C. (1949) *A Charter for World Trade*. New York: Macmillan.

12

The Changing Relationship Between the World Bank and the International Monetary Fund

Richard E. Feinberg

A t one time, the division of labor between the World Bank and the International Monetary Fund seemed straightforward. The Fund was responsible for short-term stabilization programs that concentrated on monetary variables and demand management, while the Bank took a longer term perspective, analyzed "real" variables, and was oriented towards increasing supply-side efficiency and stimulating productive investment. While there was always some interdependence among these various factors, the Fund's focus on providing immediate balance-of-payments lending to support macroeconomic reform and the Bank's concentration on slowly maturing, discrete projects allowed their respective staffs to carry on their labors with only occasional interaction.

This simple world has been erased by the multiple shocks that have destabilized the global economy over the last two decades, and that have stimulated the Bank and Fund to alter their basic programs and approaches in fundamental ways. Each institution has adopted reforms gradually, and often without fully taking into account their relation to the work of the other Bretton Woods agency. While many of these reforms have improved the institutions' ability to respond to the needs of developing countries, they have also produced a blurring of responsibilities. The time has come for a full-fledged review of Bank–Fund relations, to determine where the responsibilities of one institution end and the other begin, where overlapping jurisdictions are appropriate, and when and how the two institutions should collaborate to maximize their joint effectiveness while preserving the rights of member states.

Reprinted from *International Organization,* Vol. 42, No. 3, Summer 1988, pp. 545–560—Richard Feinberg, "The Changing Relationship Between the World Bank and the International Monetary Fund," by permission of MIT Press.

This article reviews the thoughts of the Bretton Woods founding fathers regarding the division of labor between the Bank and Fund, and explains how these lines have gradually been lightened over time, most recently by the creation of the Structural Adjustment Facility (SAF). I then examine the controversial issue of linkage between the conditions imposed on loans by the two agencies ("cross-conditionality") and suggest several new categories for defining Bank–Fund interaction. I conclude with a series of recommendations on ways to redefine the two institutions' responsibilities, and to assure that increased interagency collaboration yields additional financial flows for member countries.

Origins of the Bretton Woods Institutions

The World Bank and the International Monetary Fund have been bedeviled since their common creation over how to define their areas of specialized competence, and how to interact in areas of overlapping jurisdiction. Both the leading American and British representatives at the Bretton Woods conference were aware of these problems, and argued against suggestions that a single institution ought to be created to deal with international finance and development, while at the same time recognizing that two separate institutions would have to work closely together. In his draft plan for the Bank and the Fund, Harry White wrote:

> Doubtless one agency with the combined functions of both could be set up, but it could operate only with a loss of effectiveness, risk of over-centralization of power, and danger of making costly errors of judgment. The best promise of successful operation seems to lie in the creation of two separate institutions, linked together by one or two directors in common.[1]

In a rarely cited passage, White noted the common purposes of his proposed Bank and Fund, while seeking to underscore their distinctiveness:

> The objectives of the Bank, it will be noted, are similar in some respects to those of the Fund, but a careful examination will reveal that in their most important aspects they are different. The Fund is designed chiefly to prevent the disruption of foreign exchange and to strengthen monetary and credit systems and help in the restoration of foreign trade, whereas the Bank is designed chiefly to supply the volume of capital to the United Nations and Associated Nations that will be needed for reconstruction, for relief, and for economic recovery.[2]

Elaborating on their similarities of purpose, White wrote of the "combined operations of the Bank and the Fund" that would seek to restore confidence in the continued stability of exchanges, and suggested that "both Fund and Bank must seek to develop those conditions in which trade and productive capital movements can be expected to prosper."[3]

In his early thinking, John Maynard Keynes toyed with allowing close financial collaboration between the two agencies, suggesting that his proposed International Currency Union set up a clearing account in favor of the international body charged with post-war relief and reconstruction, to supplement the resources received by this latter body from other sources.[4] Keynes also suggested that his proposed Union "be closely linked with a Board for International Investment." Later, however, Keynes reacted negatively to a suggestion that the United States appoint the same person to both Bank and Fund boards:

> [It] seems to me a thoroughly bad idea. Different qualities are required, and the range of activities of the two would be widely divergent. It must be doubtful, therefore, whether one man can efficiently perform both functions. I should like to see the Board of the Fund composed of cautious bankers, and the Board of the Bank of imaginative expansionists.[5]

In the public debate that followed the Bretton Woods conference, the American Bankers Association (ABA) was impressed with the potential overlapping powers of the two proposed agencies, and warned of "the prospect of divided authority and the likelihood of jurisdictional conflicts."[6] The ABA argued instead for a single agency, with the Bank absorbing the functions being delegated to the Fund.

The founding fathers' preference for two separate institutions prevailed. The Bank and Fund were given separate legal charters, sources of funds, staff, and management. The two institutions' Articles of Agreement do not directly address the division of labor between them, and the only explicit cross-reference is that membership in the Fund is a prerequisite for membership in the Bank. The two charters do, however, contain identical wording directing each agency to "cooperate within the terms of this Agreement with any general international organization and with public international organizations having specialized responsibilities in related fields."[7] Clearly, this language was meant to encourage cooperation between the Bretton Woods siblings.

A Division of Labor:
The "Primary Responsibilities" Rule of the 1960s

Keynes' distinction between "cautious bankers" and "imaginative expansionists" insightfully captured the differences in style and function that developed between the Bank and Fund. The Fund came to focus on short-term stabilization, on correcting imbalances in external accounts, and on fighting inflation by restricting fiscal deficits and domestic credit expansion. The World Bank provided long-term capital for investment in capital-intensive projects, especially in the energy, mining, and transportation sectors.

In a 1966 memorandum, the Bank and Fund sought to further clarify their respective functions by assigning "primary responsibilities" to each agency. The Fund was accorded jurisdiction "for exchange rates and restrictive systems, for adjustment of temporary balance of payments disequilibria and for evaluating and assisting members to work out stabilization programs as a sound basis for economic advice."[8] The Bank was given "primary responsibility for the composition and appropriateness of development programs and project evaluation, including development priorities." On a given issue, staff were instructed to learn the views of the institution with primary responsibility "and adopt those views as a working basis for their own work."

The Fund thus asserted its hegemony over the vital matter of exchange rates. The assignment of short-term stabilization to the Fund and development projects to the Bank was unexceptional. More interesting was the memorandum's recognition of substantial overlapping responsibilities, including the structure and functioning of financial institutions, the adequacy of money and capital markets, the actual and potential capacity of a member country to generate domestic savings, the financial implications of economic development programs for the internal financial position of a country and for its internal debt program, foreign debt problems, and so on.[9]

Already it was becoming apparent that distinctions between such areas as balance of payments correction and domestic investment, stabilization programs and development priorities, and exchange rates and projects' rates of return were difficult to draw with great clarity. Nevertheless, in the relatively healthy global economic environment of the 1960s that enabled most developing countries to expand, the "primary responsibility" rule worked reasonably well, and Bank and Fund staff were able to go about their own business while only occasionally crossing each other's paths.

The Drift Towards Ambiguity

The collapse of the Bretton Woods system of fixed exchange rates and the first oil shock in 1973 suddenly created a more uncertain and difficult international climate for many developing countries. The Fund took note of economies "characterized by slow growth and inherently weak balance of payments positions" and of economies "suffering serious payments imbalances relating to structural maladjustments in production and trade."[10] In establishing the Extended Fund Facility (EFF) in 1974 to provide members with more time and money to adjust, the Fund recognized that the more adverse international environment made it harder to correct payments imbalances, and that the "inherent" weaknesses of some economies required special treatment.

The Fund's executive directors called on the staff to "pay particular attention to the policy measures that the member intends to implement in order to mobilize resources and improve the utilization of them" through EFF activities. This mandate for a medium-term stabilization program explicitly recognized the links between balance of payments adjustment and resource mobilization, and between stabilization and production, and edged the Fund more directly into the realm of traditional World Bank expertise.

The division of labor further blurred when the Bank announced its program of structural adjustment lending in 1979. Responding to the second oil price shock, the Bank offered medium-term balance of payments support, "in order that the current account deficits of many developing countries do not become so large as to jeopardize seriously the implementation of current investment programs and foreign exchange-producing activities."[11] The Bank conditioned its structural adjustment loans (SALs) on measures that addressed the underlying, structural causes of members' balance of payments deficits. While there had been precedents in "program" loans often designed to meet the immediate consequences of crises, and project loans had often carried conditions regarding output prices and other related variables, in their boldness and breadth the SALs represented a major policy shift. The Bank moved away from its nearly exclusive emphasis on discrete projects to the provision of non-project, balance of payments loans aimed at broader economic reform.

With the establishment of the Extended Fund Facility and structural adjustment lending, the Fund and the Bank were now both providing balance of payments loans, tranched over one to three years, with medium-term amortization periods. Both programs supported macroeconomic and microeconomic adjustments, and focused on improving both external and internal accounts. The degree of overlap between the two institutions had greatly increased.

More recently, the Fund has allowed the EFF to fall into disuse. The Fund was disappointed in the early EFF programs, finding it too difficult to design multi-year programs in the midst of great international variability. The Fund could not see far enough ahead and targets were in need of constant revision. (Critics contend that EFF programs had only superficially addressed supply-side issues and that Fund staff had impatiently expected quick results.) Instead, the Fund has preferred a succession of one-year stand-by arrangements. Nevertheless, the EFF's emphasis on resource mobilization and utilization has survived and has emerged with even greater vigor under the aegis of "supply side," growth-oriented measures. In earlier years, the Fund would have concentrated on financial variables and the management of aggregate demand, leaving "real" variables and the productive sector to the World Bank. Today, authoritative Fund staff firmly state that "demand-side and supply-side policies are closely interrelated," and policy packages "must be designed to reduce the level of aggregate demand and simultaneously to cause a shift in its composition away from current consumption and toward fixed capital formation."[12] While Fund stand-bys still imperfectly internalize these redirections, the change in rhetoric is striking.

The Fund can readily cite its Articles to justify its new emphasis on achieving a sustainable improvement in the balance of payments through an expansion of domestic supply and exports. The purposes of the Fund include assisting members "to correct maladjustments in their balance of payments without resorting to measures destructive of national or international prosperity [and to contribute] to the promotion and maintenance of high levels of employment and real income and to the development of the productive resources of all members as primary objectives of economic policy" (Article 1).

Table 12.1 compares the variables addressed in Bank structural and sector adjustment loans and in Fund-supported programs during the 1980s. Both institutions now claim some responsibility for an extremely wide range of instruments, policies, and objectives. The Bank is currently concerned with many variables central to Fund stabilization programs, and has developed an acute interest in exchange rates—a variable deemed in 1966 to be the "primary responsibility" of the Fund. For its part, Fund-supported programs address variables of great interest to the Bank. For example, between 1980 and 1984, energy prices were addressed in 46 percent of Fund-supported programs, the mobilization of domestic savings in 54 percent, investment planning and execution in 37 percent, and divestiture of enterprises to the private sector in 29 percent.[13] Increasingly the Fund is not simply incorporating Bank inputs but is undertaking its own analyses of the structural elements in its programs.

This increased recognition of the interrelatedness of economic variables is a welcome development. Both Bank and Fund staff are made more aware of the need to construct programs that are consistent across variables, that identify trade-offs among objectives, and that reconcile short-term and long-term targets. The result could be advice for developing countries that is more sophisticated and coherent.

The increasing overlap in responsibilities has generated a sharp increase in collaboration between the staffs of the Bank and the Fund.[14] Staff working on the same region more regularly exchange draft papers for comment, participate in each other's missions, and attend each other's board meetings. The depth and success of such cross-fertilization (which by

Table 12.1 Characteristics of World Bank Structural Adjustment Programs and Fund-supported Adjustment Programs

World Bank	International Monetary Fund
Trade Policy	*Exchange and Trade Policies*
Exchange rate policy	Liberalization and reform of exchange rate
Tariff reform and import liberalization	Liberalization and reform of trade system
Export incentives	Export promotion measures
Improved institutional support for exporters	
Specific programs for major export or import saving sectors	Import and export duties
Sector Policies	*Sector Policies*
Pricing policies in industry and agriculture	Review or increase sector prices in industry, agriculture, and so forth
Energy policy and pricing	Petroleum prices and taxes
	Capping or reductions in subsidies for food, petroleum, fertilizers
Industry incentive system	Partial or general wage restraint policies
Agricultural institutional support	Review price control systems
Public Investment Program	*Public Sector Policies*
Revision and review of sectoral priorities	Bank credit to public sector and specific state enterprises
Strengthening of institutional capacity to formulate and implement public investment program	Improved expenditure control mechanisms; investment planning and execution procedures
Public Sector Enterprises	*Public Sector Enterprises*
Financial performance	Improved price structuring for public enterprises
Institutional efficiency	Control of state enterprises' operating expenses
	Overall management and control
	Privatization
Resource Mobilization	*Monetary and Financial Policies*
Budget policy	Restraint on central government expenditures
	Tax reform
Interest rate policy	Interest rate and financial system reforms
Debt Management	*External Debt*
Strengthening of institutional capacity to manage external borrowing	Control of level and maturity of external debt

Note: The order of the characteristics of IMF programs has been rearranged to match the World Bank listing, but wording has remained true to the original tables as published by the Bank and Fund.

Source: Pierre M. Landell-Mills, "Structural Adjustment Lending: Early Experience," *Finance and Development* (December 1981), p. 19; and "Fund-Supported Programs, Fiscal Policy, and Income Distribution," *IMF Occasional Paper* 46 (September 1986), pp. 42–45.

itself certainly does not constitute formal cross-conditionality) has depended heavily on the personal chemistry of the respective staff members.

Enhanced collaboration is clearly justified in the two institutions' Articles, and is required by their current programmatic choices. At the same time, the blurring in institutional responsibilities has potential risks. It could well result in duplication of efforts, wasted talent, delays in program design and implementation, and conflicts over bureaucratic turf. Certainly, the programs both of the Bank and Fund have changed dramatically since the concordat of 1966, and a new set of mutually agreed upon guidelines that define the primary responsibilities of each institution is necessary. In response to the widened programmatic responsibilities of both agencies, these updated guidelines need to be more specific and detailed.

Another danger arising out of the widening responsibilities of both institutions and the consequent blurring of jurisdictions is the increased potential for cross-conditionality.

Cross-Conditionality

Both the Bank and the Fund claim that despite the evident increasing overlap in program design and their ever-closer collaboration, they have avoided "cross-conditionality" and should continue to do so.[15] The Group of 24 has repeatedly stated its concern that cross-conditionality not arise, while favoring enhanced cooperation between the Bank and Fund. In its report, "The Functioning and Improvement of the International Monetary System," the G-24 remarked:

> Developing countries consider that coordination between the IMF and the World Bank should not lead to cross conditionality but should help further their mutual objectives of providing resources to developing countries. Closer contacts between the managements and staffs of the two institutions could help foster understanding of each other's points of view. However, it would not be advisable to seek some kind of uniformity of advice. Such a step would be counterproductive, could lead to cross conditionality, would dilute the respective responsibilities of the two institutions, and could become a means of exerting a concerted pressure on borrowing developing countries. Any policy advice by these institutions would therefore have to be in keeping with their respective roles. If there were to be a coordination of policy advice on a country, it would be essential to obtain the country's consent in this process.[16]

While it appears that no generally accepted or official definition of the term exists, Sidney Dell has suggested the following four examples of "formal" cross-conditionality:

1. If either of the Bretton Woods institutions exercised, or sought to exercise, a veto over a loan under consideration by the other or over a drawing against an existing loan.
2. If there were a formal understanding between the two institutions that neither would make a loan to or an arrangement with any member country, or with a particular member country, except with the concurrence of the other institution.
3. If there were a formal understanding between the two institutions that neither would allow member countries, or a particular member country, continued access to a previously agreed loan or arrangement except with the concurrence of the other institution.
4. If a formal action, notably a declaration of ineligibility by the Fund were, by previous arrangement between the two institutions, to interrupt access to a Bank loan.[17]

This is a strict, highly legalistic definition, which places great weight on the words "veto," "formal understanding," and "formal action." Yet decisions in the Bank and Fund are often made through less structured procedures. There is a preference for consultation and consensus, informal bargaining, and flexible decisionmaking. Moreover, many decisions are taken by management and staff outside of the formal board frameworks (especially in the more decentralized Bank but also in the Fund). Consultations between the Bank and Fund generally occur at the staff level, between regional directors, between the Bank's senior vice president for operations and the Fund's deputy managing director, or between the Bank's president and the Fund's managing director. These "consultations" can tie the two institutions' decisionmaking tightly together without recourse to formal vetoes, votes, or written memoranda.

The most obvious example of what might be termed *consultative cross-conditionality* is the close linkage between World Bank structural and sector loans ("policy-based" lending) and Fund stand-by arrangements. . . . Only three of all the World Bank sector loans signed during fiscal years 1979–85 occurred in countries not engaged in Fund programs. The three exceptions indicate that the World Bank does not have an iron-clad rule requiring members seeking policy-based loans to sign stand-bys. But it is also apparent that the approval of policy-based loans has been associated with the existence of a Fund program. There have been at least several incidents where the Bank delayed or refused a policy-based loan pending a member's reaching agreement with the Fund on a stabilization program. The Bank argues that without consistent macroeconomic policies designed to correct external equilibrium by restoring a more sustainable balance between aggregate supply and demand, a structural adjustment program will fail.

Consultative cross-conditionality has also occurred during rounds or bargaining between either of the Bretton Woods institutions and a member state, when one Bretton Woods agency withholds new credits in order not to reduce the other's bargaining leverage. The Bank and Fund generally seek to avoid being played off against each other by member nations. They particularly seek to avoid the appearance of "inconsistent" behavior.

Another form of linkage might be termed *interdependent cross-conditionality:* when the Bank and Fund each consider the same policy variable or variables to be critical for their programs in a member state. With increasing frequency both institutions consider the adoption of a "realistic" exchange rate to be a *sine qua non.* This variable does not necessarily appear centrally in a sector loan document, nor might it be a formal performance criterion in a Fund stand-by; rather, exchange rate adjustment may be a "prior" condition, or an "understanding." Nevertheless, refusal by a member to correct its exchange rate can simultaneously deprive it of financing from both the Bank and Fund.

There seem to be cases where cross-conditionality has approached Dell's formal definition with regard to exchange rate regimes. In describing two industrial and trade policy adjustment loans provided to Morocco in 1984–85, the Bank noted:

> The loan program was implemented concurrently with an IMF stabilization program initiated about six months before the loan was approved. A 10% devaluation of the exchange rate had taken place in line with the Fund's stand-by arrangement. One condition of the loan was the government's continued commitment to a flexible exchange rate to maintain profitability of exports.[18]

Interdependent cross-conditionality can also occur through the broader, vaguer avenue of "creditworthiness." The Bank and Fund undertake their own studies to determine members' creditworthiness; in that sense, there is no formal cross-conditionality. But a country judged uncreditworthy by the Fund is unlikely to receive a favorable rating at the Bank. Bank and Fund economists increasingly exchange information and analyses, and the Bank and Fund seek to avoid public disagreement on controversial cases. Furthermore, the Fund's declaration of "uncreditworthiness" is to a degree self-fulfilling, depriving the member not only of Fund credit but also worsening the member's standing before other sources of finance. With less credit available, the member's economy may deteriorate and become, ipso facto, less creditworthy.

Where Bank and Fund lending is significant in relation to a member's economy, funding decisions can result in what might be named *indirect financial linkage.* If the Fund withholds credit, the member may find itself without the counterpart funds needed to proceed with Bank projects. The Bank and Fund can also find themselves tied together through "third-party" indirect financial linkage. Take the case where commercial bank loans are conditioned on the borrower meeting its quarterly stand-by targets. If the Fund judges the borrower to be in noncompliance, the banks may halt disbursements. The loss of sizable commercial bank credits could undermine the borrowers' creditworthiness, destroy its ability to proceed with Bank-supported structural reforms, or leave it unable to finance Bank-supported investment projects. Or take the case where, as is beginning to occur, commercial banks enter into parallel or cofinancing arrangements, and condition their loans on the World Bank certifying progress on sector loans. A negative Bank finding could disrupt commercial bank credit and adversely affect the borrower's budgetary revenues, credit policies, and exchange reserves, causing it to fail to meet Fund program targets.

Traditionally, most interdependencies have tied the Bank to Fund decisions and policies. World Bank structural adjustment loans, and sometimes project loans, may await the borrower's accord with the Fund, whereas Fund stand-by negotiations have not generally been dependent upon Bank attitudes. The withholding of Fund credit may injure a member's budget sufficiently to disrupt funding for a Bank-supported project, but the smaller size of Bank project disbursements has made the reverse process much less likely. However, this asymmetrical interdependency is becoming more equilibrated, as the World Bank augments the size of its own and associated disbursements, and makes judgments on members' compliance with sector loans. Increasingly, a negative Bank finding could disrupt the borrower's finances and cause the Fund to have to reconsider its own evaluation of the member's progress.

These three novel forms of Bank–Fund interaction—consultative cross-conditionality, interdependent cross-conditionality, and indirect financial linkage—go well beyond what is usually implied by "collaboration," yet do not necessarily fall under a narrow, strict definition of cross-conditionality.

The Structural Adjustment Facility

The establishment by the Fund in March 1986 of the Structural Adjustment Facility (SAF) marks a significant new phase in Bank–Fund collaboration. The SAF will make approximately SDR 2.7 billion in Trust Fund reflows available to low-income countries which face protracted balance of payments problems and are currently eligible for IDA resources. Interest rates will be one-half of one percent per annum over ten years with five-and-a-half years grace period. To gain access to the SAF, a member must develop a "policy framework describing the member's medium-term objectives and the main outlines of the policies to be followed in pursuing these objectives."[19] Significantly, the policy framework paper is to be developed *jointly* with the staffs of the Fund and the Bank. The framework should describe the "general outlines" of a three-year adjustment program including structural measures, and delineate in "broad terms" the expected path of macroeconomic policies. An assessment of the country's financing need and of indicated levels of financing from the SAF and the World Bank Group will also comprise part of the program.

The policy framework papers are discussed but not voted upon by a committee of the World Bank executive board, whose comments are then "taken into account" when the Fund's executive board passes on the paper. This arrangement was a compromise between some members who wanted the Bank board itself to review the framework paper, and developing countries who objected to the Bank board discussing the macroeconomic strategies of members.

By requiring the preparation of joint country papers for review by senior management and executive directors, the SAF clearly adds an important element to Bank–Fund collaboration. For developing countries, it has the advantages of providing highly concessional finance, and potentially of yielding more consistent policy advice from the Bank and Fund.

The SAF may also serve to generate more resources for eligible members from other sources. The confidence of lenders might be enhanced by a process that provides borrowers with coherent economic policies blessed and financed by both Bretton Woods agencies. A framework paper that includes external financial requirements could play an important catalytic role in Consultative Group meetings. The SAF can also stimulate more World Bank lending by helping to overcome Bank reticence to increasing its lending to nations where repurchases are making the Fund a net recipient of resource transfers.

On the other hand, developing countries note that the SAF carries more conditionality than did the Trust Fund, and have expressed concern about the potential for cross-conditionality, urging that the policy framework procedure not be extended to other Fund and Bank facilities. According to the Group of 24:

> any Fund–Bank collaboration in this regard should avoid cross conditionality, with the institutions limiting their advice to areas of their respective expertise and competence and with full respect for the sovereignty of members requiring assistance.[20]

Since the Fund only "takes into account" the opinions of the Bank executive directors, the SAF seems to have avoided formal cross-conditionality in the sense of giving one institution an explicit veto power over the other's decisionmaking. Reinforcing the traditional asymmetry of interaction between the Bank and Fund, the Fund has taken the lead in preparing many of the papers, which seem so far basically to recapitulate existing

Fund and Bank programs. According to Fund officials, there has not yet been a case where the Bank expressed strong reservations to a framework paper.

The SAF clearly has the potential to link more tightly decisionmaking on Fund stand-by arrangements and Bank structural adjustment lending. The developing countries sought to avoid tying the SAF directly to these programs by requiring the framework papers to delineate macroeconomic policies only in "broad terms," and adjustment policies in "general outlines." It remains to be seen whether these guidelines are observed.

Certainly the SAF will increase the probability of consultative and interdependent cross-conditionality. If the SAF has been structured to avoid giving the Bank a formal veto over the use of Fund resources, the real test will come if the Bank's executive directors voice strong objections to a policy framework paper which is acceptable to the Fund and the member nation. The Bank might want to delay the signing of an SAF agreement in order to increase its own bargaining position vis-à-vis a borrowing country. For its part, the IMF has good reasons for not permitting Bank objections it either disagrees with or considers of secondary importance to block SAF disbursements. In addition to wanting to maintain its institutional independence and integrity, the Fund has a strong self-interest in providing SAF monies to members having difficulty in servicing Fund debt. Indeed, a cynic might suggest that a primary purpose of the SAF is to recycle Fund credit, and to restructure it on terms more appropriate for low-income countries. To the extent that the Fund has an institutional interest in disbursing SAF monies, its willingness to impose strict conditionality may be diluted.

Summary of Main Conclusions and Recommendations

Since their twin birth, the World Bank and the International Monetary Fund have faced dilemmas over how to define their areas of special competence, and how to interact in areas of overlapping jurisdiction. The institutions' founding fathers and charters intended to establish two separate, independent agencies, but ones which were clearly meant to collaborate closely when their respective activities took them into related fields.

In response to changing global economic conditions, the Fund and Bank have established, respectively, the Extended Fund Facility and structural adjustment lending, and most recently the Fund has created the Structural Adjustment Facility (SAF). These programs share the objective of adjustment with growth, and have greatly increased the degree of overlap between the two institutions, both of which now claim some responsibility for an extremely wide range of policy instruments. Consequently, both Bank and Fund staff are gradually becoming more aware of the need to construct programs that are consistent across variables, that identify trade-offs among objectives, and that reconcile short-term and long-term targets. This increased recognition of the interdependency among economic variables is a welcome development. At the same time, the blurring of institutional responsibilities threatens to result in duplication of efforts, wasted talent, and delays in program design and implementation. The formation of a creditor cartel would also place undue pressures on developing countries bargaining in isolation.

The Bank and Fund claim to have avoided cross-conditionality in the narrow, legalistic sense of exercising vetoes or requiring formal concurrence on each other's loans. More relevant are three novel forms of Bank–Fund collaboration—termed here consultative cross-conditionality, interdependent cross-conditionality, and indirect financial linkage—that go well beyond what is usually implied by "collaboration," yet do not necessarily fall under a strict definition of cross-conditionality. Consultative cross-conditionality occurs as a result of the routine association of Bank policy-based loans with Fund stand-bys. Close consultations between staff produce joint policy positions that are coordinated in a common bargaining posture. Interdependent cross-conditionality occurs when the Bank and Fund each consider the same policy variable or variables to be critical for their programs in a member state, or when the Bank is heavily influenced by the Fund's determination of a member's creditworthiness. Indirect financial linkage occurs when either institution's withholding of credit affects the programs of the other.

The time has come for a full-fledged review of Bank–Fund relations, to determine where the responsibilities of one institution end and those of the other begin, where overlapping jurisdictions are appropriate, and when and how the two institutions should collaborate to maximize their joint effectiveness while preserving the rights of members states. To arrive at such a new division of labor, the following suggestions are made:

1. Bank and Fund research staff should seek to develop consistent models that reconcile the differences in their current analytical approaches, and that can assist countries pursuing stabilization with growth. Furthermore, when economists produce divergent country economic assessments, which can lead to contradictory and confusing advice, Bank and Fund staff should attempt to reach a genuine consensus. However, when a harmony of views is not possible, staff should make clear to the member country the underlying assumptions and methodologies that account for the different outcomes. Bank and Fund management ought not to enforce an artificial uniformity of views on country economists.

2. In seeking a new demarcation of primary responsibilities, the Fund should restrict its stand-by arrangements to key macroeconomic issues. The Fund should strive to make its programs consistent with

growth, but without unduly broadening its scope. For its part, the Bank should concentrate on sectoral and microeconomic targets in its lending programs.

3. The Bank and Fund should focus their loan conditionality on a few select variables that must be resolved if progress is to be made toward the broader goals of the entire program, avoiding long lists of requirements.

4. The Bank and Fund should discourage automatic, contractual linkages that tie a country's progress on Fund and/or Bank programs to its access to commercial bank finance. In cases where multiple sector loans are associated with private finance, the Bank might periodically issue a single report that would indicate the Bank's assessment of the country's overall progress.

5. The Bank and Fund should maintain separate decisions on ineligibility. The Fund needs to seek more flexible and creative ways to bring countries with extended arrears in from the cold. Rather than reflexively lining up behind the Fund to pressure a member declared Fund-ineligible, the Bank should attempt to maintain a policy dialogue that helps reintegrate the country into the Bretton Woods system.

6. Bank decisions on whether to fund projects should not be tied automatically to Fund programs or to general creditworthiness evaluations. Many projects can succeed even in an adverse macroeconomic environment.

Resource transfers to many developing countries will have to increase substantially if their adjustment programs are going to succeed. Even if significantly increased, the resources of the two institutions will clearly have to be supplemented by other donors and the international private sector. The Bank and Fund should establish joint mechanisms for approaching other sources of official and private capital, perhaps by appointing joint committees and by establishing unified procedures for interfacing with the international private markets. Furthermore, to assure that private capital markets do not undermine adjustment programs, the Bank and Fund might consider establishing country-by-country target figures for reducing the resource drain that is afflicting many developing nations. The country targets should be consistent with the rates of economic expansion anticipated in Bank and Fund programs.

Notes

This article draws heavily from a report commissioned by an UNCTAD/ UNDP project for submission to the Intergovernmental Group of Twenty-Four on International Monetary Affairs (G-24), as background for its report on "The Role of the International Monetary Fund in Adjustment with Growth" (March 1987). I thank the many executive directors and staff at the Bank and Fund who assisted in the preparation of that report. The views expressed herein are, of course, solely my own, and do not necessarily reflect those of the UNCTAD Secretariat, UNDP, or the G-24.

1. J. Keith Horsefield, ed., *The International Monetary Fund 1945–65: Twenty Years of International Monetary Cooperation* (Washington, D.C.: IMF, 1969), vol. 3, p. 39.

2. Robert W. Oliver, *International Economic Co-operation and the World Bank* (New York: Holmes and Meier, 1975), Appendix A, pp. 297–98. Interestingly, in this 1941 draft White gave the Bank the power to make short-term as well as long-term loans.

3. Ibid., pp. 298–99.

4. Horsefield, *International Monetary Fund 1945–65*, pp. 14–15.

5. Donald Moggridge, ed., *The Collected Writings of John Maynard Keynes, Vol. XXVI, Activities 1941–46* (London: MacMillan, 1980), p. 194.

6. American Bankers Association, *Practical International Financial Organization Through Amendments to Bretton Woods Proposals,* February 1, 1945. As cited in Sidney Dell, "The Question of Cross-Conditionality," mimeo, June 1986, note 20.

7. IMF, *Articles of Agreement,* Article X; and World Bank, *Articles of Agreement,* Article V, Section 8.

8. Cited in Edward S. Mason and Robert E. Asher, *The World Bank Since Bretton Woods* (Washington D.C.: Brookings Institution, 1973), p. 551.

9. Cited in Joseph Gold, "The Relationship between the International Monetary Fund and the World Bank," *Creighton Law Review* 15 (1981–82), p. 514, note 57.

10. IMF, *Selected Decisions of the International Monetary Fund* (Washington, D.C.: IMF, 1981), ninth issue, pp. 26–27.

11. World Bank, *Annual Report 1980* (Washington, D.C.: World Bank), pp. 67–68.

12. Moshin S. Kahn and Malcolm D. Knight, *Fund-Supported Adjustment Programs and Economic Growth* (Washington, D.C.: IMF, 1985), Occasional Paper No. 41, p. 4.

13. Ibid., tables 2, 3, and 7.

14. A review of some of the main issues can be found in Hiroyuki Hino, "IMF–World Bank Collaboration," *Finance and Development* 23 (September 1986), pp. 10–14.

15. *IMF Survey,* 28 October 1985, p. 309, para. 9(b).

16. *IMF Survey,* September 1985, p. 14, para. 137.

17. Dell, "Question of Cross-Conditionality," p. 6. Dell notes that in deriving this definition he sought the views of Joseph Gold, the Fund's former general counsel and director of the legal department.

18. *World Bank News,* "Sector Adjustment Lending," Special Report, April 1986, p. 11.

19. *IMF Survey,* 31 March 1986, p. 109.

20. *IMF Survey,* 21 April 1986, p. 121.

13

The New Latin America and the Inter-American Development Bank

Enrique V. Iglesias

After a painful decade of recession and retrenchment, Latin America is firmly embarked on the road to economic recovery. The region has entered an unprecedented phase of economic stabilization, adjustment, and structural reform that will lead to renewed economic growth and ultimate success in the fight against inflation. Moreover, Latin America is achieving these gains even in the face of declining world prices for its main commodity exports and an unsettled international economy.

Growing evidence clearly indicates that Latin America's economic reforms are working. The region's exports are burgeoning, and capital is once again flowing into the region in response to the new climate of confidence. Financial relations between the region's countries and their creditors are well on their way to being normalized.

These changes are in large measure the result of the emergence of a new generation of political leaders who, perceiving a critical historical juncture, have demonstrated the pragmatic spirit and political will to proceed with the necessary reforms. The Inter-American Development Bank (IDB) is supporting those reforms through an expanded lending and technical cooperation program.

The political leaders have achieved success by carrying out comprehensive structural reforms, opening up their economies, deregulating domestic markets, and implementing aggressive institutional reforms, including a redefinition of the public sector's role and its sphere of action. . . .

The region's progress on international financial relations—particularly in those countries that are further ahead in economic reform and have achieved more stability—is evidenced by the influx of foreign capital in the form of loans, bonds, and foreign investment. In 1991, these totaled

Reprinted from *Washington Quarterly,* Vol. 16, No. 1, 1993, pp. 115–125, Enrique Iglesias, "The New Latin America and the Inter-American Development Bank," by permission of MIT Press.

over $36 billion, nearly double the 1990 figure. Part of this capital represented direct foreign investment. A significant proportion of this amount resulted from debt-to-equity conversions involving the privatization of state-owned companies.

As a result of the increase in the flow of foreign capital, combined with lower interest payments, Latin America received a net transfer of funds of nearly $7 billion in 1991—the first net gain to the region since 1981. This marked a reversal of the tendency to transfer savings abroad during the 1982–1990 period, when resources of some $220 billion were diverted from the region.

This article offers a brief review of the factors leading to this remarkable transformation of the economic situation in Latin America. It then turns to the role of the international financial community, and especially of the IDB, in facilitating continued economic, political, and social reform. The essay concludes with some thoughts about the future of prosperity and democracy in the region.

The International Economic Context

Despite Latin America's achievements, the world economic environment continues to threaten the fruits of the aforementioned economic restructuring and the development processes set in motion in the region. Although a long-term view of the international economy augurs a widespread favorable economic transition, recent years have seen a high degree of vulnerability and uncertainty. . . .

Latin America has been adversely affected by fiscal imbalances in the major economies, through their influence on interest rates and international capital movements, as well as by instability and uncertainty on global financial and exchange markets. All these factors make for a context that is not favorable to sustained economic growth in the region and, in particular, to the consolidation of the structural reforms the countries have been pursuing with determination.

Although world trade has continued to expand more rapidly than production, it is undergoing structural changes that have troubling implications for Latin America. Recent decades have seen a trend toward high-technology products, frequently within a single sector, including trade between different parts of the same company. This has given rise to trade circuits that, while dynamic, are not easily accessible to developing countries. In addition, the emergence of trading blocs is generating anxiety and uncertainty.

This difficult, unfavorable international economic situation presents the Latin American countries with an urgent reason to proceed with domestic reforms and subregional integration. Instead of delinking from the world economy, the countries must continue to build upon encouraging progress in economic integration as a means of creating economies of scale that are crucial to their success in global competition.

Argentina, Brazil, Paraguay, and Uruguay [have created] the Southern Cone Common Market (Mercosur), [and] Mercosur also has concluded a framework trade agreement with the United States. In Central America, progress is being made on establishing a common external tariff. In the Caribbean, the English-speaking countries of the Caribbean Community (Caricom) have signed a framework agreement with the United States that would lead to a future trade agreement. Meanwhile, Venezuela has offered to open up its market unilaterally to Caricom for five years, after which the Caribbean states will progressively remove duties on Venezuelan goods during the next five years.

The countries of the Andean region are entering into a free trade pact. In addition, Colombia and Venezuela are forming a free trade area with Mexico. Chile signed a similar agreement with Mexico and is now seeking entry into the North American Free Trade Area (NAFTA). . . .

On a broader level, the Enterprise for the Americas Initiative offers a promising opportunity for Latin America and the Caribbean, one in which the IDB is pleased to be playing a major role, as discussed below. The Enterprise Initiative recognizes that Latin America's participation in the major trade circuits will depend not only on its economic reforms and the consequent increase in international competitiveness, but also on economies of scale, intercompany associations, and the spread of technology through economic integration movements.

The Burden of Poverty and Social Inequity

Today more than ever before, it is clear that the economic restructuring under way in Latin America will not be sufficient to ensure long-term growth unless it is accompanied by decisive action to tackle the social problems that Latin America's past development strategies have failed to correct. Improving social conditions and increasing employment will be major objectives in the IDB's future lending program.

Although poverty has always existed in Latin America, perpetuated by traditional growth patterns, it was aggravated by the crisis of the 1980s. Stagnation swelled the ranks of the so-called informal sectors of the region's economies, with the proportion of the poor rising from 41 percent to 44 percent over the last decade, affecting living conditions for nearly 183 million Latin Americans.

The economic growth that alone can reverse this trend has one prerequisite: a stable society. The sweeping economic reforms being implemented in Latin America will succeed only if they take place within a more integrated and equitable society, in which all groups are incorporated. A more integrated society can only enrich and foster the process of development in the long term, through the creativity and support of a larger number of economic agents partaking of its success. In the short term, however, it will be necessary to adopt specific policies to reduce extreme poverty. Achieving better social integration, together with a reduction in extreme poverty, is crucial to the viability of the development model being applied today by the countries of Latin America.

In its aim of furthering the region's development, the IDB has sought from the outset to link the economic and social spheres through its programs in borrowing member countries. Today that concern is stronger than ever as the region's countries, while beginning to enjoy the benefits of economic reform, have come to the realization that they can and must deal with the social question.

The task is to engage all ranks of society in the modernization of the structures of production and assure more effective provision of basic social services to disadvantaged social groups. The essential prerequisite for overcoming marginalization and poverty is for society as a whole to initiate a process of political participation, democratic consensus building, and stable, responsible, transparent government, in order to strengthen social cohesion, promote wide participation in the productive process, and achieve a more equitable distribution of the benefits of economic growth.

In the past there were wide discrepancies both in the relative importance given to social issues and in the way they were defined or approached. Most positions revolved around two extremes. At one extreme, the more traditional sectors took a one-dimensional view of the problem, in which growth and equity were considered somewhat incompatible, at least in the short term. According to this view, resources should not be diverted from economic growth to deal with social problems in the early stages, in the belief that they would be solved at subsequent stages through the trickle-down effect of growth-generated benefits. The contrary view held that, since the goal of development is to ensure social equality, distribution and equity should be made priorities from the very outset, although in practice this endangered economic equilibrium in many cases. Public policy has often wavered between these two positions in an attempt to achieve growth and distribution goals separately, giving rise to counterproductive dichotomies.

Beyond the theoretical controversy, and taking into account past experiences and current economic policy requirements, it is clear that social issues are not confined to extreme poverty and cannot be resolved by the trickle-down effect. They are an essential part of development and call for shaping new social infrastructure and policies to underpin economic reforms.

Improved social conditions are in fact a main prerequisite for growth, especially when considering that growth is driven today by creativity, technological innovation, the capacity for organizing social and economic activity along modern lines, open economies, and international competitiveness.

Latin America, with its human and natural resources, certainly has attractive potential to offer the rest of the world. But the region's relations with the world of today cannot be confined to merely exporting raw materials and low-cost labor. The region needs to enhance its human resources through training and development, scientific knowledge, and new technology.

In response to these problems of poverty and social fragmentation, countries in the region must take steps both to reduce extreme poverty and to move toward a more integrated society, involving all social groups in the modernization of productive structures. . . .

Alongside the compelling urgency of the problem of extreme poverty is the no less essential need to increase social integration, particularly by opening up new productive opportunities. Strengthening the region's entrepreneurial capacity requires first that the business base be broadened. The key here is to create an environment in which small and medium-sized businesses can flourish in our economies.

It is very clear from the successful experiences documented around the world that it is small and medium-sized businesses that provide the best channels for entrepreneurial creativity, are most effective at putting new technologies to use, and are most successful at creating new jobs.

The aim is not only to strengthen the existing business sector, but also to provide incentives for it to gradually assimilate Latin America's huge informal sector. Integral to this strategy are programs to support microentrepreneurs and the informal sector in general, including financial-sector reforms that create incentives and backing for financial institutions prepared to operate in the informal sector. Along with, and complementary to financial-sector reform is the creation of a network to provide technical assistance and expert advice to that same sector.

Of all measures designed to achieve better social integration and reconcile economic growth with equity, perhaps the most important is developing human resources, the second essential component of the social integration process. Success on the economic front hinges on the ability of the region's countries to upgrade the labor force and to modernize educational and training systems.

Worker training programs should not be designed only for the young; they should provide people with opportunities for updating their skills throughout their productive lives. A Latin American working person today has access, on average, to just five weeks of training in his or her entire working life, and this is clearly inadequate.

Because the available resources are so scarce, it is essential to continually identify the changing work-force requirements being created by the process of development and to create an educational system that is flexible and responsive to those demands. This includes raising the level of professionalism of the providers of training, using the latest instructional methods, and assuring broader access to new training programs by all segments of society.

An efficient state is the third component in social integration. Although the countries in the region are more aware today that they can and must tackle social problems, it will not be enough for them to redouble their efforts in the same ways and with the same programs as in the past. It is not a question of doing more of the same. In addition to overcoming widespread budget constraints by putting in place an adequate fiscal system, these countries need to improve the objectives, mechanisms, and effectiveness of social programs.

Public-sector action must be improved precisely in the traditional areas of social policy, such as health, nutrition, and education. Sweeping changes will be needed to improve the delivery of social services and to better target their benefits. Also in need of strengthening are other areas of public-sector action, such as combating violence and the administration of justice.

Improving the efficiency of the public sector in the social sphere must be part of a larger goal: that of comprehensive public-sector reform. Such reform would include, on the one hand, a strengthening of the tax system by broadening the tax base, bringing evasion under control, and ensuring an equitable tax burden, and, on the other hand, an overall review of public spending. A reassessment of priorities—including military spending—and the mobilization of domestic savings in support of privatization efforts are other requirements for efficient public-sector action in the social sphere.

The Role of the IDB

For the Inter-American Development Bank, the scope of the present challenge is matched only by the size of the individual and collective efforts needed to meet it.

The IDB is today in a stronger position than at any time in its history to take on this challenge. The Bank has resumed its traditional role as the major source of multilateral financing in the region, one it has fulfilled consistently for most countries—particularly the least developed—and is fulfilling today for the region as a whole. . . .

The IDB is stepping up its financing for technical cooperation, an activity of vital importance for ensuring the ability of the countries in the region to carry out investment projects and prepare future ones. Approvals for new IDB operations rose to $140 million in 1991, more than double those of the year before. Cofinancing operations, though still restricted to official sources, reached $861.8 million, three times the amount posted in 1990.

Another welcome development for the Bank, and an additional piece of evidence that the crisis years of the 1980s may be behind us, is that those countries that had previously been ineligible to receive loan disbursements and new loan approvals have completed the task of normalizing their relations with the international financial community. This achievement came as the result of complex negotiations in which the IDB played a leadership role.

Clearly, the process of reform and internal reorganization launched by the Bank in 1989 is now bearing fruit. The IDB's strengthened programming process has enabled the Bank to work more closely with the appropriate institutions in each borrower country to help them define priorities, select projects, and improve their quality. In 1991 alone, the IDB sent programming missions to 19 countries.

One of the Bank's major challenges, and an area where it has had a particularly encouraging record of success, has been in supporting the economic reform efforts of its member countries through fast-disbursing policy-based loans.The IDB's governors have taken the steps needed to enable the Bank to mount sector operations in a new area: improving the investment climate in borrowing member countries.

Through its loans for investment-sector reform, the IDB has provided key support to the Enterprise for the Americas Initiative, in particular that portion of the initiative that provides for the reduction of United States bilateral debt with Latin American and Caribbean countries. To qualify for debt relief under the Enterprise Initiative, a country must first have in place major investment reforms in conjunction with an IDB investment-sector loan or otherwise be deemed by the Bank to be taking the necessary steps to create an investment climate favorable to private-sector growth.

There has been substantial demand for investment-sector loans. The Bank has approved four so far, for Bolivia, Chile, Colombia, and Jamaica. The Bank's governors are now addressing the issue of how the IDB can best support the economic adjustment process in the coming years.

One of the Bank's principal concerns has been to help improve the lives of the least fortunate people in its borrowing member countries. As countries once again begin investing in human resources and social services, opportunities will increase for the IDB to finance programs to help ensure the efficiency of these investments.

There are two compelling reasons for the IDB to give priority attention to helping its member countries address the problem of poverty. The first is the obligation to help people in need and to bring about social justice. The second, equally important, is to create the conditions for putting the country's economic reforms on a solid footing.

One way the IDB participates in the fight against poverty is by financing projects that directly benefit low-income groups. Since the Bank's founding in 1959, the institution has sought to link the social and economic aspects of development, financing not only productive projects, but also social projects in the areas of sanitation, health, education, human resource training, urban development, and others. . . .

Beyond financing for social projects and microenterprise, the IDB benefits low-income people through its sector reform programs, in which governments commit themselves to a broad series of policy changes in key areas of the economy. The economic reforms supported by the IDB through these sectoral programs benefit the poor, often rapidly, when, for example, inflation takes a smaller bite out of salaries and income. Macroeconomic reforms, the creation of economic and employment opportunities, and poverty alleviation are mutually complementary objectives.

The Bank's governors have repeatedly urged that the IDB strengthen its antipoverty efforts. Given the limited capacity of the region's less-developed countries for absorbing new loans on conventional terms—whether for economic reforms or for projects in the social sectors—the governors have emphasized the need for strengthening the IDB's capacity to make concessional loans. . . .

As mentioned earlier, a key precondition in Latin America's ultimate success in modernizing its economies and in creating employment will be the strengthening of the region's human resource base. This will be a principal objective of the Multilateral Investment Fund, to be administered by the IDB within the Enterprise for the Americas Initiative. This new fund will provide grants and loans for worker training, for strengthening institutions, and for developing small businesses and microenterprises. The 24 donor countries that signed the agreement establishing the fund have announced contributions that so far total $1.3 billion. Most of the fund's support will be in the form of grants, but some will also be through "revolving" loans and equity investments.

One arm of the fund will provide grants for studies to identify constraints on investment and needs for new legislation and regulatory measures. A particular priority will be to help governments establish the firm prudential safeguards that are the foundation for a stable financial system.

The fund will also provide grants for the design and implementation of privatization programs and for the development of financial systems and business infrastructure. Grants will also finance efforts to restructure work forces, improve vocational education, and provide management training, in this way helping countries to transform their state-directed economies into open market systems. At present, workers laid off as a result of a shrinking public sector generally cannot afford the costs of retraining and relocation.

A final objective of the fund will be to provide grants to improve the basic business skills of smaller enterprises to enable them to grow and avail themselves of financial services. It will also create an investment fund that will provide seed capital for creating or expanding small enterprises and developing financial institutions that can meet their needs.

As the Multilateral Investment Fund implicitly recognizes, jobs are the key issue that bridges the twin objectives of economic modernization and poverty alleviation. Throughout Latin America, small enterprises have become a major source of employment and income for the poor, and particularly for women and minorities. But despite their growing economic importance, small enterprises are severely handicapped by lack of both skills and access to financing. As a result, they are unable to develop as businesses, apply for working capital and other financing, or obtain licenses and contracts from the government. The investment fund will provide the support to help small enterprises to join their countries' economic mainstreams and thereby increase their contribution to economic development.

The Bank will be helping to promote other changes in Latin America as well, among them restructuring and modernizing essential services, not only to promote equity, but also to decentralize government decision making to the local level and increase support to the private sector. The Bank will continue supporting the region's movement toward economic integration and export-led growth, and, closely related to this, it will help the region to strengthen the role of technology in production to increase the competitiveness of the region's industries.

Another area of special emphasis is the environment and the protection of natural resources. The creation of the Bank's Environmental Protection Division in 1990 laid a solid institutional base for planning, preparing technical experts, and training the Bank's professional staff, both at IDB headquarters and in the field. Among other things, this has resulted in a system in which all IDB operations are reviewed for environmental impact. This system enables the Bank to intervene at the earliest stages of the project cycle, making adjustments to prevent adverse environmental consequences and, even more important, requiring that all Bank-financed operations—regardless of their primary objective—include specific actions to protect and enhance the environment. . . .

Substantial progress has also been made in the area of women in development. A three-year action plan has been approved and is being implemented. It includes an ongoing dialogue with member countries to ensure comprehensive treatment of women's issues in all of the Bank's operations. The socioeconomic studies done by the Bank on borrowing countries now include an analysis of the situation of women, thereby opening up the possibility of linkages with projects, especially those for microenterprise and social investment funds. . . .

The IDB's Role in
Central America and the Caribbean

The IDB continues to give special attention to the compelling needs of the countries of Central America. . . . The IDB's special commitment to Central

America will grow as all of Latin America, and the international community as a whole, celebrates the end of fratricidal conflicts there, and as possibilities for true progress emerge for the area's long-suffering people.

The countries of Central America view economic integration as the central instrument of their individual and collective development strategies. At the urging of their leaders, the IDB has organized a Regional Consultative Group in support of the countries' integration efforts and is funding a program to enhance the ability of Central American institutions and organizations, both public and private, to contribute to the formulation and analysis of policy options in areas of critical interest to the region's governments.

To assist the integration efforts under way in the Caribbean region, the Bank is planning to intensify its relations with the Caribbean Development Bank, as well as to continue to fund regional programs such as one recently approved for strengthening the University of the West Indies. The Bank has been supporting the West Indies Commission in its efforts to provide the region's heads of state with technical advice to speed up Caribbean integration. Proposals under discussion include allowing unrestricted movement within the region by Caribbean nationals, examining the possible adoption of a common currency, renewing the investment process, establishing a Caribbean common market, and forging stronger ties between the countries of the Caribbean and their Latin American neighbors.

An issue of particular concern for the countries of both the Caribbean and Central America is the difficulty the IDB is facing in meeting its overall lending goal for its smaller and less-developed member countries. The constraints include the limited capacity of these countries to formulate and carry out projects, as well as the burden placed on IDB staff in processing an increasing number of smaller loans.

The scarcity of concessional resources provides another constraint. The smaller countries already have significant debt exposure to the IDB, and their potential for export growth is limited, making concessional lending particularly important for them. The demand for these "soft" resources, however, already exceeds the amounts the IDB has available. . . .

Latin American thinkers have frequently said that, by virtue of its traditions and culture, their region is obsessed with the past. Leaving behind a development model that prompted both the region's growth in the postwar period and the painful crisis of the 1980s has, for the region's countries, meant overcoming the past in order to begin building for the future clearsightedly, free of prejudices, creatively, and with unshakable resolve. In the same spirit, the IDB must in turn be prepared to contribute to building that future by coming up with innovative ideas, developing new facilities, and cooperating generously with all agents and institutions at present engaged in that ambitious endeavor.

Part 6

SOCIAL AND HUMANITARIAN ACTIVITIES

THE most varied and yet least known activities of international organizations are in the social and humanitarian issue area. Many goals such as those of universal literacy, adequate nutrition, and proper health care are widely shared. The methods of implementation are also considerably less controversial than operational activities in the security and economic issue areas. States are less inclined to disagree over the promotion of sanitary facilities than they are over international trade barriers. Consequently, support for these efforts is generally high. The World Health Organization (WHO) is almost universally applauded for its efforts at eradicating disease. The United Nations High Commissioner for Refugees has twice been awarded the Nobel Peace Prize for its work. Some of the most effective work of international organizations takes place in this issue area.

Even though there is consensus on many such international organization activities, controversy is not absent. The most prominent example of conflict is the withdrawal of several states from the United Nations Scientific, Educational, and Cultural Organization (UNESCO). As that organization questioned the value of full press freedom and acted on other issues with political overtones, some Western members objected that the organization had gone beyond its original mandate of promoting literacy and cultural exchanges. Indeed, the same cleavages that are apparent in the economic realm manifested themselves in UNESCO. Other social issues also generated conflict between member states. A recent UN conference on population problems produced a heated debate over the use of abortion to limit further population growth. In another instance, various meetings on the status of women have produced bitter debate as states seek to reconcile differing cultural perspectives on the role of women in society.

The social and humanitarian issue area is also one in which nongovernmental organizations (NGOs) have a prominent, and in some cases primary, role. NGOs do not have the independent military capacity nor the economic strength to be major actors in either security or economic affairs.

(It is important to note that NGOs technically are different from transnational organizations, such as multinational corporations, who of course are also important global actors.) Within the issue area of concern here, NGOs may have the expertise or the legitimacy that many international governmental organizations (IGOs) lack. Furthermore, NGOs may be able to operate without all the political constraints imposed on member-state organizations in several of the more controversial areas such as human rights.

The five selections in Part 6 cover a representative range of international organization activities on key problems in the world: human rights, hunger, humanitarian emergencies, environmental protection, and the status of women. Ramesh Thakur describes how IGOs and NGOs can work in complementary ways in addressing social problems, here human rights. He considers how the United Nations and perhaps the most famous NGO—Amnesty International (AI)—perform different functions in the global pursuit of human rights protection and enhancement. Human rights violations are still a common practice in many states of the world today. Yet, it must be remembered that prior to World War II, little or no international standards of human rights conduct existed. Given also that it takes several generations for norms to become embedded in international society, it is surprising how much real progress has been made in this area. The relative advantages of AI and the UN complement one another and facilitate, under difficult political circumstances, norm creation, compliance monitoring, and the enforcement of those standards.

Ross Talbot and H. Wayne Moyer examine the structure and governance of four international agencies concerned with alleviating hunger and promoting agricultural development: the Food and Agriculture Organization (FAO), the World Food Council (WFC), the World Food Programme (WFP), and the International Fund for Agricultural Development (IFAD). Each has experienced problems in meeting the goal of a minimum standard of nutrition and living among the world's poorest people, although one must not forget the many lives that have been saved by their efforts. The authors conclude by considering some possible alternative arrangements for the four agencies, including consolidation or dissolution.

The four international agencies noted in the article by Talbot and Moyer are for the most part concerned with the long-term problems of hunger and agriculture. Yet many problems are less endemic and require more immediate attention from the international community. Complex humanitarian emergencies often involve food shortages or even mass starvation. Exacerbating such problems may be patterns of human rights abuses, large flows of refugees, and war; at the extreme, the state affected may become a "failed state" that implodes. The synergistic character of these problems make them very difficult to address; problems in Ethiopia, the Sudan, and Somalia over the past two decades are indicative of the complexity of the problems and their high costs in human life. Andrew Natsios looks at how the United Nations and various NGOs intersect in their efforts to address complex humanitarian emergencies. He concludes that the partnership across the organizations involved, including NGOs such as the International Committee of the Red Cross (ICRC), is far from optimal; their strengths and weaknesses may not be as offsetting or complementary as the organizations noted above in the human rights field.

An increasingly important issue on the global agenda is environmental protection. The United Nations Conference on Environment and Development (UNCED) held in Rio de Janeiro in 1992 was a major effort to achieve consensus on a global strategy that would address environmental concerns, such as ozone depletion, while not inhibiting states' abilities to develop economically. Harold Jacobson and Edith Brown Weiss explore the factors associated with national compliance with international environmental accords, many of which were drafted under the auspices of international organizations. The potential and limitations of global governance are illustrated well by attempts to create effective international environmental standards when some national interests may dictate otherwise. The authors discuss how IGOs and NGOs influence compliance behavior, but they also correctly note a number of other influences (information, the actions of other states, etc.) that can provide equally important incentives or disincentives for state compliance. These influences are largely out of the control of international organizations—another reminder that the successes and failures of the global community in addressing problems of common concern are not wholly attributable to international organizations, as idealists and cynics both may assume.

A final social problem in which international organizations have become increasingly involved is the second-class status of women around the globe. There are a number of dimensions to this problem, including economic, political, health, and human rights. Redressing the problem has been difficult at the global level, in large part due to cultural and religious practices that reinforce a lower status for women, but also because women have not been empowered at the international level to bring this issue to the agenda and compel states to take action. Ellen Dorsey traces the development of the global women's movement and especially the central role that the United Nations and affiliated organizations have played in that struggle. The special UN conferences on women held every ten years have been catalysts for action and have led to the creation of more formal structures that deal with women's issues. Once again, the importance of NGOs in the process is revealed. Although Dorsey sees significant progress over the last several decades, she identifies several significant obstacles to further change.

14

Human Rights:
Amnesty International and
the United Nations

Ramesh Thakur

Human Rights and Peace Research

The award of the Nobel Prize is the most prestigious recognition for services to world peace. The list of Nobel peace laureates, including Aung San Suu Kyi in 1991 and Rigoberta Menchú in 1992, reveals a clear acknowledgment of the link between international peace and human rights. A wider conception of security has received recognition from responsible political leaders in some countries, for example New Zealand (Graham, 1992; Marshall, 1988). Scholarship, too, has attempted to broaden and deepen the definition of security. While this has always been true, it has gathered fresh momentum with the end of the Cold War (Kolodziej, 1992a). Security studies which ignore the normative questions associated with the control, threat, and use of organized violence rest on shallow foundations and are isolated from the central question of its legitimation (Kolodziej, 1992b, p. 429).

One example of the trend to marry normative inquiries to strategic studies is the recently revived interest in the proposition that democracies do not go to war against one another (see Doyle, 1986; Gleditsch, 1993; Lake, 1992). Democracies also promote human rights better than alternative regimes (a proposition that is less keenly contested after the Cold War because of the demonstrable hypocrisies of the former communist regimes and disillusionment with the results of one-party states in the Third World; (see Gleditsch, 1993, p. 301). Putting the two propositions together, we can conclude that increasing democratization will lead simultaneously to an enhancement of human rights and a more peaceful world. A concern with human rights should be of interest to peace researchers also because it can lead to violent conflict in any one (or all) of three ways. The groups whose rights are being abused can resort to arms in retaliation; the conflict can entangle neighbouring countries; the scale of the human rights abuses can lead to international involvement and intervention. The ongoing crisis in Bosnia-Herzegovina is a perfect illustration of all three dangers.

The most important intergovernmental organization (IGO) charged with the responsibility for maintaining world peace is the United Nations (UN). Its peace-keeping forces were awarded the Nobel peace prize in 1988. But it does not have an exemplary record in defending human rights. The best known nongovernmental organization (NGO) in the field of human rights is Amnesty International (AI), which is itself a former recipient of the Nobel peace prize (1977). AI and the UN work together in the area of human rights. The complementarity of the roles played by IGOs and NGOs remains a neglected dimension of international relations scholarship (notable exceptions including Jacobson, 1979; Taylor & Groom, 1989). In this article, I hope to begin the process of filling this gap. The purpose of comparing AI and the UN is to analyse the complementarity of IGOs and NGOs in the issue-area of human rights on the three dimensions of norm-generation, monitoring, and enforcement. Their variations in performance (the dependent variable) may be explained by the diverging characteristics of the two units of analysis (the independent variables), most importantly their nongovernmental and governmental attributes. The analysis will also challenge us to theorize about NGOs: their roles, the implications for the state-based realist edifice of international relations scholarship, and the inviolability of sovereign territory behind which human rights can be abused with impunity.

Universalism versus Relativism

A *right* is a claim, meaning that it lies in the domain of entitlements: it may not be granted or denied by anyone else (Wasserstrom, 1964, p. 632). This carries two further connotations. First, as distinct from a mere demand, a right is justified or legitimate. Second, it is a claim against some entity or person. A theory of rights can be postulated alongside a *doctrine of logical correlativity,* that is, the association of the rights of one person with the duties of another. (This is different from the doctrine of *moral correlativity,* which holds that in order to enjoy rights one must be able and willing to perform reciprocal obligations.) Legal positivists might argue that the only true rights are those that are set out and enforceable in law. Others would embrace as moral rights those that merit recognition by an enlightened conscience.

With these qualifications in mind, by a human right I mean one which is:

- universal, owing to every person simply as a human being;
- held only by human beings;
- held equally by every person, since it is available to anyone qua person;
- not dependent on the holding of any office, rank, or relationship, such as political leader, teacher, aristocrat, parent, or creditor;
- claimable against all governments. That is, if someone asserts a human right against the Government of China, then that right is equally assertible by that person against the Government of New Zealand or vice versa.

Such a definition is immediately controversial. An international theory of human rights must confront the vexed dilemma of cultural relativism. The existence of universal human rights is asserted by human rights advocates; its possibility is denied by cultural relativists. Many universalists escape the need for justification by assuming the validity of culture-invariant rights. Conversely, many relativists aver that because moral standards are always culture-specific, there can be no cross-cultural universals in the field of human rights. Yet the second part of the statement does not follow logically from the first. Murder is proscribed in all moral systems; but few if any proscribe the act of killing absolutely under all circumstances. The definition of murder therefore has to be understood within the confining coordinates of time and place. Within any one society at different periods of time, or between different societies at any given time, such activities as war, capital punishment, and abortion may or may not be morally permissible.

Human beings do not inhabit a universe of shared moral values. Instead, we find diverse moral communities cohabiting in international society. Article 16(2) of the Universal Declaration of Human Rights proclaims the right to marriage 'only with the free and full consent of the intending spouses'; the clause contravenes the widespread practice of arranged marriage which many societies regard as perfectly consistent with their moral systems. Political rights (freedoms of speech, press, and assembly; political and legal equality) are rights held by the individual against the state. By contrast, socialist regimes view human rights as benefits secured by the state for collective groups such as workers; individuals owe obligations to society.

The notion of individual human rights provides a subset of the larger dilemma of locating justification outside particular moral frameworks. In many societies the individual as a person is a social construct: individual beliefs, religions, world-views, language, gestures, mores are all shaped by and products of society and culture. Consider the case of a cross-clan murder in some kinship systems. If a chiefly person has been killed by a commoner, then the revenge death of the original killer may not be appropriate retribution, that of a person of chiefly rank may. The original killer can go scot-free, an outcome that is alien and abhorrent to the Western concept of individual guilt and responsibility. In most such societies with an eye for an eye and a tooth for a tooth philosophy, the underlying principle of retributive justice was a means of *limiting* violence: take your tooth and be done with it. A second mechanism for containing violence, which also horrified some Europeans, was blood money or the compensation principle: the kin-group which initiated the killing could escape retribution in kind by compensating the victim kin-group with appropriate payment.

In Marxist ideology, rights emerge historically and reflect class relations. Individual human rights are the expression of the class interests of the bourgeoisie. By contrast, collective rights are the foundation of human rights and the precondition for all individuals to enjoy all rights and freedoms equally. Moreover, human rights are not just abstract ideals. They are expressed concretely in the specific laws of various countries. Therefore they cannot be understood apart from a country's laws and institutions. Differences in national laws reflect the different conceptions of human rights: there is no universal human right which overrides national laws.

It might be argued that holding governments to international standards that they have voluntarily signed sidesteps the dilemma of cultural relativism. Not so. Signature and ratification of international conventions is decided on by ruling elites; their actions may not correspond to the views of most people in their home countries.

Equally, though, rejection of international human rights standards by a government may be based on political expediency that does not reflect majority views of ordinary people. We should be suspicious of the self-serving and spurious claims of ruling elites that their rejection of external criticism is based on an alternative social consensus. The UN General Assembly's Declaration on the Right to Development (Resolution 41/128, 1986) diluted and confused the human rights agenda and could be used by governments so inclined to legitimize violations of citizens' rights. The false dichotomy between development and human rights is designed to mask the fact that the tradeoffs 'are contingent political choices, undertaken for largely political not technical, economic reasons' (Donnelly, 1989, p. 306). The dichotomy is usually a smokescreen for corruption, cronyism, and personal aggrandizement.

If value relativism were to be accepted in its extreme form, then no government of any country—Stalin's Russia, Amin's Uganda, Pol Pot's Cambodia, the current government of Serbia—could be criticized by outsiders for any of its actions. Not many would be happy with such total value relativism. This is why many Western academics abominate relativism (Barnes & Bloor, 1982, p. 21). It is dismissed because, seemingly, it requires Westerners to project their liberalism universally on everyone else: everyone should follow the Western tradition of tolerance because it is the best. It is seen to require absolute tolerance and to negate the possibility of moral judgment. The proposition that 'all moral judgments are culture-specific' is also self-refuting in such a crude formulation. For, if true, then the proposition is itself not absolute but contingent on whether a particular culture subscribes to that belief. If it is contingent, then under certain circumstances it could be false. In a sense it is the equivalent of the philosopher's familiar paradox about two statements on either side of a page: (a) 'The statement on the next page is true' and (b) 'The statement on the previous page is false'. Cultural relativism entangles us in a similar ethnocentric circumlocution.

International relations is a domain of moral choice where diversity does not vitiate or preclude efforts at moral reasoning. There are four reasons why relativism need not necessarily lead us into the blind alley of rejecting the possibility of moral judgment. Action by a government is open to evaluation by the moral code of its own society.

Second, diversity does not rule out partial convergence. The internal standard may in fact be congruent with international conventions. Relativism does require an acknowledgment that each culture has its own moral system. This insight directs our attention to enculturation: the process by which cultural categories and standards are acquired and internalized by individuals. But the fact that moral precepts vary from one culture to another does not mean that different peoples do not hold some values in common. One attempt to reconcile relativism with universalism was organized around the proposition that all societies require retribution to be proportionate to the wrong done (Renteln, 1990). The justification for much of the AI movement could be anchored to this apparently simple universal principle. For, if true, then from this single principle we could derive the following propositions:

- A government may not punish a citizen who has done no wrong.
- Before a citizen can be properly punished, his or her guilt must be established.
- Since a society cannot make moral judgments on guilt or innocence in ignorance, the process of establishing guilt must be open and transparent.
- The establishment of guilt therefore requires fair procedures, that is, the institutions of free and fair trial.
- Since retribution must follow and not precede the establishment of guilt, no person may be tortured into confessions of guilt.
- Since retribution is required to be proportionate to the crime, a citizen who has neither preached nor practiced violence may not have violence done to his or her person.
- No one shall be deprived of life arbitrarily: summary executions and disappearances are morally impermissible in any society or political system.

- Every victim has the right to seek redress of grievance: retributive punishment should be imposed on officials or the state as a collective entity (e.g. by way of financial compensation) for wrongful acts of torture or killings. Nicholas Gage, in the moving story of his mother's torture and death at the hands of communists during the Greek civil war, writes of 'that pain which never sleeps': the pain of unfulfilled retribution against the perpetrators of inhuman cruelty (Gage, 1983, p. 447).

The third riposte to relativism is that under certain circumstances we can still criticize actions which violate our codes, even if they are morally permissible by the domestic code of another government. This can occur, for example, when the government of that country appeals to our sense of charity in seeking humanitarian or developmental assistance. This is, if you will, a variant of moral correlativity. If our moral code imposes a duty on us to assist you, then the same code also permits us to impose a reciprocal duty on you.

Fourth, we can turn cultural relativism on its head. Precisely because moral values are culture-specific, outsiders are unable to determine congruence of governmental actions with internal moral codes. All that outsiders can do is to presume, however imperfectly, that adherence to international conventions does reflect societal consensus on or elite commitment to international community norms. And, as outsiders, all we can judge is the consistency of governmental actions with such international conventions.

Standard-setting and Norm-generation

In general, the most appropriate forum for efforts to reconcile divergent moral traditions into common public policy is the United Nations as a universal IGO. The international moral code is embodied in the UN Charter. Civil-political human rights are an outgrowth of Western liberalism; the United Nations is a meeting ground for all the world's civilizations.[1] Human rights puts the welfare of individuals first; the UN puts the interests of member-states first. AI is of, by, and for individuals; the United Nations is of, by, and for governments. AI is a single-purpose NGO; the UN is a general-purpose IGO.

IGOs are held to be more important than NGOs because, in the global political system, authoritative policies are more frequently made in and applied by governmental than nongovernmental institutions (Jacobson, 1979, p. 8). Power is the capacity simply to enforce a particular form of behaviour. Authority signifies the capacity to create and enforce rights and obligations that are accepted as legitimate and binding by members of an all-inclusive society. International society exists to the extent that states observe limits on their freedom of action in pursuing national interests and acknowledge the authority of these limits (Nardin, 1983, p. 309). It denotes, not a universal society of individuals governed by natural law, but a distinctive society of states that acknowledge formal rules of accommodation. To be viable, international society must establish a generally accepted body of procedural rules which specify the office-holders of rule-maker, rule-interpreter, rule-enforcer, and rule-changer. For international order to be maintained, certain decisions pertaining to international behaviours must be accepted simply because some person or body, specified by rules of procedure, has made them.

Today, UN resolutions are the most commonly cited and widely acceptable code of conduct and metric of state compliance with internationally prescribed behaviour. The reconciliation of divergent interests by the UN has procedural as well as representational legitimacy: it is authenticated by the procedures that have been freely accepted by the authorized representatives of world society. Conversely. a single-issue NGO like Amnesty International is an inappropriate forum for such reconciliation. A significant illustration of AI's distance from universalism lies in its total opposition to the death penalty.[2] While no civilization or culture proclaims the virtues of torture, many countries have less compunction in defending the death penalty as an instrument of state policy.[3]

The central normative instrument of the international human rights regime is the Universal Declaration of Human Rights (1948). The 1966 International Covenants on Civil and Political Rights (ICCPR), and on Economic, Social, and Cultural Rights, add force and specificity. Collectively, the three products of the UN system comprise the International Bill of Rights. (Such a labelling of the trinity imparts an American flavour, which is politically unfortunate in the context of the debate on relativism.) The UN has also adopted some 50 other legal instruments on human rights, including declarations and conventions on genocide, torture, racial discrimination, and discrimination against women. The 1966 covenants assume that human rights may need to be restricted if they begin to interfere with the rights of others. And the ICCPR permits a state to limit or suspend the rights in cases of officially proclaimed public emergencies—that is, precisely when they are most needed. This is a stark illustration of how, in a state-based IGO, reasons of state triumph over rights of individuals.

Monitoring and Verification

United Nations

Human rights activities of international organizations can be divided into three categories. The UN has been impartial and remarkably successful in a standard-setting role; guilty of bias and only selectively (in regard to both rights and regimes) successful in monitoring human rights abuses; and feeble and ineffectual in enforcement. Governments, if they permit formal international review of state practice at all, will agree to review only by IGOs. Responsibility for human rights oversight was given to the Economic and Social Council under the general auspices of the General Assembly. ECOSOC set up a Commission on Human Rights in 1946. The United Nations has also set up special committees to oversee implementation of the human rights covenants.

Socialist and many Third World member-states were lukewarm and hostile to international human rights control and monitoring mechanisms. They subordinated considerations of UN effectiveness to the principle of non-interference. While the United States too, with its strong tradition of isolationism, has generally been suspicious of expansive interpretations of UN power, most Western governments supported the adoption of such devices as individual complaints systems and enhanced monitoring procedures. International teams have little formal power to monitor or carry out independent investigations (such as spot-checks and on-site verifications with unfettered freedom of movement for UN inspectors) of state compliance with UN norms. The UN 'monitoring' machinery is little more than a system of international information exchange, some of which can be plain farcical. The result has been characterized as 'normative strength and procedural weakness' (Donnelly, 1986, p. 614).

The modesty of UN achievement should not blind us to its reality. Human rights activists and NGOs are able to use the International Bill of Rights as a concrete point of reference against which to judge state conduct. The utility of the covenants lies in the requirement imposed on signatories to submit periodic reports on the human rights situation in their countries. Therefore, ratifying and bringing the covenants into force does not simply connote acceptance of internationally proclaimed standards of human rights. It also entails the creation of long-term national infrastructures for the protection and promotion of human rights.

Amnesty International

The UN Charter begins with the words 'We the peoples'. Unfortunately, the UN remains a creature of member governments. Above everything else, human rights means putting people first. AI too puts people first: both externally, in relation to human rights, and internally, in relation to its own organization and activities. AI reports carry a ring of authority, because the organization—not being a voluntary association of governments—has not been wilfully myopic in the UN mould in investigating and judging human rights abuses around the world without discrimination on grounds of race, religion, or ideological belief. Thus, in May 1992, Amnesty reported that there has been harsh repression and long-standing human rights violations in Tibet (AI, 1992a, pp. 88–91)—an issue from which the United Nations has gingerly but persistently shied away.

The United Nations is a multipurpose organization. This means that many considerations in addition to the human rights record have to be taken into account in deciding what to do about the errant behaviour of a member-state. As a permanent member of the Security Council, China can veto any draft resolution critical of its human rights records. It can also veto other resolutions where its help may be urgently needed, as in the Gulf War. Such broader considerations of tradeoffs are extraneous to the decision calculus of a single-issue NGO like Amnesty International.

The Amnesty decision calculus involves an initial placement of the person concerned into one of three categories meriting investigation: prisoner, disappeared, other. Its activities have had to change to reflect the changing nature of human rights abuses and the changing understandings of the concept of human rights. In the AI structure, decision-making on the role of the NGO is the responsibility of the biennial International Council Meeting. The 1991 Council meeting, held in Yokohama, extended the organization's mandate in several areas. One of the most important policy shifts was the decision to include human rights abuses committed by armed political opposition groups within the scope of AI monitoring, reporting, and action. Without such extension of the AI mandate, the organization's activities were becoming vulnerable to the charge of imbalance. In a sense the new policy permits AI to take some action to protect individuals against abuses by armed political groups (for example killings or hostage-takings of innocent civilians) when governments have failed to do so.

Another extension concerned the types of human rights abuses. People who are imprisoned solely because of their homosexuality, for example, are now considered to be prisoners of conscience. AI has been engaged in defending the rights of refugees to asylum as set out in the Universal Declaration on Human Rights. The Yokohama meeting expanded AI's role by including opposition to involuntary exile. In addition, AI opposes any forcible relocation of a people to a particular area of their own country, if this is based solely on religion, ethnic identity, language, and so on.

The strength and assets of AI are complementary to those of the UN. Unlike the latter, AI has managed to maintain a scrupulous neutrality with respect to international ideological conflicts. During the Cold War, it did this by using its own version of the principle of equitable geographical representation which permeates the UN system. Its prisoner of conscience campaign selected one prisoner from the industrialized, communist, and Third World group of countries for simultaneous focus by each AI group.

Amnesty International has investigated and censured governments of all political persuasion. Its neutral stance has been helped by the deliberate tactic of precluding AI chapters from investigative and lobbying activities in home countries. The campaign for the release of US citizens jailed for refusing to serve in Vietnam, for example, was led by Swiss members of Amnesty International.

This is most useful in reducing the prospect of AI chapters becoming the targets of hostile attention from home governments. It also enhances detachment and objectivity and so builds up credibility over time. Governments are notably frustrated when they cannot dismiss allegations against them as politically motivated. Who is going to believe China's protestations that AI is a tool of Western capitalism, when AI has a long and proud record of opposing the use of the death penalty in the United States and investigating human rights abuses in Northern Ireland?

Members of AI have a dual role. The most obvious is that they work to protect victims of human rights abuses in other countries. But, despite being prevented by AI rules from investigating or taking action in respect of abuses in their own countries, they also have an internal role. They contribute to the development and promotion of a human rights culture in their own country. This then assists in the prevention of human rights abuses by their governments in the future through promotion of social commitment and enactment of appropriate laws reflecting the more enlightened human rights culture.

The United Nations has been harnessed to the cause of serving state interests and has become a creature of member governments. Its agencies and committees—even those dealing with human rights cases—are staffed by civil servants, politicians, lawyers, economists, and so on. Invariably, they owe their jobs to national governments (or IGOs, which in essence come to the same thing). By contrast, AI remains a people's movement. Its heart and soul are the millions of volunteers in addition to the 1.1 million membership engaged in the various campaigns to secure the release of political prisoners, the welfare of political refugees, the raising of human rights consciousness and funds.

UN diffidence stems in part also from a reluctance to become embroiled in controversies. The periodic storms of controversy that swirl around AI show that governments are indeed sensitive to impartial and accurate criticisms of their human rights records.

There is another necessary consequence of linkage to peoples and not governments. AI had the foresight to reject any financial help from any government body. Financial independence has in turn ensured political independence of governments. It has also made AI dependent on direct contributions from the public. As a result AI has remained close to the people: their beliefs, their concerns, their agendas. The intensely personal nature of AI campaigns means that it remains a grass-roots international movement. This too has helped to keep AI honest.

The comparison with the UN is again striking. UN activities have been severely affected by the fluctuations of its finances, the refusal of major member-states to pay their assessed share of costs, the refusal of some to pay for particular UN activities or agencies which offend their political sensibilities, the insistence of others that they be given a larger say in some decisions. It is inconceivable, for example, that the UN could contemplate investigating human rights abuses by the US government, which pays 25% of its budget.

Impartiality is buttressed with veracity. The long-term credibility of AI would be badly damaged if its reports and statements could be shown to be false. The entire structure of the AI movement is designed to collect, distribute, and use information that has been cross-checked and will withstand determined efforts by governments to discredit it: about the identity of prisoners, cause of imprisonment, trial procedures, prison conditions. The chain of pressure built up in any particular instance by AI is only as strong as the weakest link in the information in that case.

In short, AI adopts a case-work approach to the human rights campaign. Information collected by AI researchers, for example on prisoners of conscience, is used in four different ways. First, it is analysed and digested. Second, it is used to make judgments on the reasons for imprisonment. Third, it is communicated to appropriate AI chapters. And fourth, it is used to organize a campaign on behalf of the prisoners.

The good fight is usually worth fighting for itself. But it helps if it can be shown to be efficacious at least some of the time. Otherwise the army of AI campaigners and activists could be forgiven for being so discouraged as to give up the fight. The viability of AI as a movement is due to the belief that its work 'is both worthwhile in general terms and is effective in specific cases' (Ennals, 1982, p. 82).

Compliance and Enforcement

Where the goal is to set inviolate standards for the domestic conduct of governments, only the United Nations as an all-embracing IGO can create new rules by such means as legally binding conventions. While the UN is better qualified to set international human rights standards, Amnesty International is better able to investigate human rights abuses at the grass-roots level. Measuring success is difficult, perhaps even impossible. No government is going to admit having given in to external pressure. In many cases there may well be several influences at work simultaneously on a government. For the UN or AI to claim success could be boastful, only partially true, and possibly counterproductive in future cases. The fact that AI cannot demonstrate success in every instance does not diminish the worth of its efforts. In this instance, it is better for reach to exceed grasp, for ambitions to exceed resources.

The doctrine of national security has been doubly corrosive of human rights. It is used frequently by governments, who are charged with the main responsibility for the welfare of their citizens, to diminish the security of their peoples by subjecting them to gross human rights abuses. The grossest violence to the proper relationship between the authorities and the citizens occurs when the military takes over the reins of government and establishes a repressive regime. For then the instrument to protect a people against attack from without is turned into the means of coercing a people from within. The second respect in which the doctrine of national security has undermined human rights is its use to justify a policy of doing nothing to those regimes that are guilty of human rights abuses but which might be present or prospective allies.

As the last comment suggests, human rights have traditionally been relegated to a lowly position in the hierarchy of foreign policy objectives of governments. While reaffirming a commitment to democratic ideals, officials or politicians will invoke geopolitical, geostrategic, or commercial considerations for suppressing outrage at human rights atrocities (Greenfield, 1989, p. 84). Consider for example how loath governments have been to condemn China for its brutality in Tiananmen Square in June 1989, or for its record in Tibet since the 1950s. Many ordinary people refuse to accept such rationalizations and demand a more forceful and robust response from their own governments.

Perhaps governments empathize with one another more easily than is commonly realized. Even for the major democracies, public opinion is a nuisance to be managed by governments, not for the voice of sweet reason to be heeded. Protestors are regarded as an ill-informed and rag-tag lot who are always out to create trouble and sometimes manage to jam the smooth running of affairs of state, be these domestic or international. . . .

Another argument invoked for a policy of See Nothing, Hear Nothing, Do Nothing is that an activist concern would merely worsen the situation of the victims. Interestingly, victims do not subscribe to this point of view. The number who have made forceful declarations to the contrary are legion. Some even beg for open, vociferous demonstrations of support from the outside. It seems rather important to prisoners to know that they have not been forgotten totally, that others care. Lack of open support is grist to the propaganda mill of repressive governments. The *Beijing Review* declared that 'the proper, rational and lawful actions of a sovereign nation' in Tiananmen Square were 'understood and supported by most countries in the world' (Yi, 1989).

Having said that, since the end of the Cold War governments have been more prepared to impose political conditionalities in granting foreign aid. The UN too has been expanding its concerns and becoming somewhat more assertive in defence of human rights. For example, the UN peace-keeping mission in El Salvador, ONUSAL, was required, among other tasks, to verify the 1990 agreement on human rights between the government and the armed opposition concluded under UN auspices. Security Council Resolution 794 of 3 December 1992 authorized military action under enforcement Chapter 7 in order to establish a secure environment for humanitarian relief operations in Somalia.

Other examples from the 1990s illustrate the twin thesis being developed here, that AI and the UN play complementary roles, and the AI is more willing to investigate possible human rights abuses by any government while the UN confines itself to selected governments. On 12 November 1991, Indonesian security forces opened fire on a group of demonstrators in Dili in East Timor, provoking an international outcry and threats of suspension of foreign aid. The government at first claimed that 'only 19' people had been killed, but then an inquiry commission concluded that about 50 had been killed. In August 1991, Amnesty International made an oral submission to the UN Special Committee on Decolonization alleging serious human rights abuses in East Timor, including extrajudicial executions and disappearances. In November, the organization appealed to the UN Secretary-General to initiate a prompt and impartial international investigation into the incident (AI, 1992a, pp. 141–144). As it happened, the UN Special Rapporteur on Torture was in Dili during his first visit to East Timor on the day of the shootings. On 11 March 1993, the UN Human Rights Commission voiced concern at reports of continuing violations by Indonesian forces in East Timor and criticized light sentences imposed on the soldiers involved in a massacre of pro-independence demonstrators in November 1991. The resolution was approved by a vote of 22–12, with 15 abstentions. Most Western governments voted in favour; most Asian governments either voted against or abstained (*Otago Daily Times,* 13 March 1993).

On the second point, the UN Human Rights Commission established a Special Rapporteur to investigate the human rights situation in Kuwait during the period of Iraqi occupation. AI drew the attention of the Commission to reports of human rights violations by Kuwaiti authorities after the withdrawal of Iraqi forces, but the Commission refused to extend the mandate of the Special Rapporteur to investigate allegations of post-occupation violations (AI, 1992a, pp. 34–35).

The tragic crisis in ex-Yugoslavia is a good example of how ineffectual action by the United Nations leads to disillusionment about its role. The Security Council first acted on the crisis by adopting Resolution 713 on 25 September 1991. On 13–14 August 1992, the 53-member UN Human

Rights Commission held an extraordinary session in Geneva to examine events in former Yugoslavia. This was the first exceptional session in the Commission's history. It adopted a resolution strongly condemning the policy of forced expulsions or 'ethnic cleansing' by Bosnian Serbs (*UN Chronicle,* December 1992, p. 22). By the end of 1992 the Security Council had adopted more than 20 resolutions on the crisis censuring bad behaviour, demanding compliance, and imposing sanctions, all to no discernible effect. On 25 May 1993 the Council voted unanimously to set up an 11-judge war crimes court at The Hague to try people accused of murder, rape, torture, and ethnic cleansing. The success of this operation remains to be seen.

By 1993, governments and the UN were being forced to be seen to be doing something in response to public pressure that had built up with the crisis in Bosnia-Herzegovina having become the focus of a media blitz. But human rights organizations were instrumental in generating and sustaining the initial public interest in the tragedy. Between October 1992 and January 1993, AI issued three reports on widespread human rights abuses in Bosnia-Herzegovina. While all warring parties were guilty of abuses, Amnesty International had concluded that most of the blame lay with the Serbs (AI, 1992c, 1993a, and 1993b).

One reason for the lack of progress could be cynicism towards the statements made on behalf of the United Nations. On 4 August 1992, for example, the Security Council expressed deep concern at continuing reports of widespread violations of international humanitarian law in the former Yugoslavia, in particular regarding imprisonment and abuse of civilians in camps, prisons, and detention centres. The President of the Security Council condemned such violations and abuses and demanded that relevant international organizations should be granted immediate, unimpeded, and continued access to all such places *(UN Chronicle,* December 1992, p. 23). The Serb leaders would have noted that the Council president was Li Daoyu of China. Such clear hypocrisy and double standards do little to enhance the behaviour-regulating authority of the world organization.

Theoretical Implications

International human rights policy is not the exclusive domain of government officials. Instead, it is what I shall call a 'pluralist resultant' of a lengthy process of interaction and consultation between politicians, officials, and private transnational groups. Even in a major international forum like the UN, AI has access to national delegates and Secretariat officials, provides a range of information from a broader cross-section of sources, and lobbies for its preferred solutions. The degree of influence exerted by AI depends partly on its internal organizational attributes (size, funding, structure, etc.) and partly on the salience of human rights as an international issue. But the last in turn depends to some extent on the success of AI and other human rights NGOs, success which makes it correspondingly more difficult for governments to deny consultative access to them.

Roles of NGOs

NGOs, like AI, can serve as focal points for the mobilization and articulation of interests shared by many people living in different countries. They play five distinct roles in international relations: consciousness raising or value promotion; agenda setting; lobbying to shape the terms of the instructions given to delegates at multilateral and IGO forums, and to implement international commitments; monitoring; and direct action (for example, Greenpeace boats obstructing the entry of nuclear ships into New Zealand ports). AI eschews direct action, but does engage in the other four types of activities.

Amnesty International is a limited actor in its own right. The United Nations is a *sovereignty-bound* actor; Amnesty International is a *sovereignty-free* actor.[4] The lofty proclamations of human rights in the UN Charter suggest an expansive interest; the enabling clauses reveal a more restrictive authority. The powers of NGOs like AI, although no more extensive, can be utilized more effectively because they are free of some of the types of inhibitions that impede the functioning of IGOs which are subject to 'capture' by member governments.

While IGOs and many NGOs deal with states' international behaviour, AI is concerned principally with a state's internal behaviour. AI representatives can activate the UN human rights monitoring process by entering the picture as complainants. So while the relevant UN watchdog bodies may exercise rule-supervisory functions, a complaint from AI can often initiate the exercise. Furthermore, AI is less constrained than the UN in holding states to norms that have been declared in forms other than legally binding instruments. Moreover, by such activities as participation in global conferences, NGOs contribute towards the enfranchisement of other relevant actors in the decision-making process on international issues (Taylor & Groom, 1989, p. 295).

By creating transnational coalitions that circumvent the policies of any individual state, AI acts as an international pressure group, publicizes the human rights problematique, and proposes solutions to them. The United Nations convened a World Conference on Human Rights from 14 to 25 June 1993. In an oral submission to the first session of the Preparatory Committee in September 1991, AI proposed that the UN should establish a standing mechanism of a coordinated, concrete, and rapid response to massive human rights violations (AI, 1992a, p. 33). Amnesty wanted the conference's final statement to commit governments to the ratification of international treaties, funding of human rights programmes, and the adoption of annual independent reviews of human rights.

In the event, the Vienna Declaration and Programme of Action was described as 'anodyne' (*The Times, 26 June 1993*). The conference, attended by 180 governments, got off to an inauspicious start by first refusing permission to the Dalai Lama to address an audience. Although this refusal was later rescinded, China did succeed in preventing NGOs from participating in the sessions on drafting the final declaration. The conference became a public squabble between West and East over the principle of universality. Rejected by US Secretary of State Warren Christopher as 'the last refuge of repression' (*The Times, 19 June 1993*), cultural relativism proved to be a successful rallying cry of many Asian nations (see Madhubani, 1993). Paragraph 26 of the final declaration seemed to make press freedom conditional on objectivity and responsibility (*The Times, 26 June 1993*). Far from being an occasion to make major progress on an international human rights regime, the Vienna Conference became a rearguard effort to preserve the gains of the past 45 years.[5]

NGOs can also act as systemic modifiers of state behaviour. In the late 1970s, the US government, in allocating economic assistance, began to take note of the human rights performance of governments as judged by such nongovernmental groups as Freedom House and Amnesty International (Jacobson, 1979, p. 362). Items are raised to the international agenda by non-state actors (Holsti, 1992, p. 70). It has been claimed that the launching of the International Decade of Women in 1975 by the United Nations was the result of NGO pressure rather than an initiative of states (Harrison, 1989, p. 243).

The process of implementing global conference declarations and the review mechanisms usually built into them act as stimuli to the international networking of NGOs. The enhanced networking capacity of NGOs helps to offset the imbalance in relative capabilities of states and international organizations. In the 1980s, IGOs were subjected to severe budgetary stringencies, while NGOs like AI and Greenpeace experienced growth in membership and subscriptions. AI membership increased from 700,000 in 1987 to 1,100,000 in 1991; its budget increased from GBP 7.4m to GBP 12.7m in the same period (AI, 1988, p. 278; AI, 1991a, p. 311). This has helped to redress to some extent the traditional imbalance in relative IGO-NGO capabilities.

It has also produced an expansion in the extent of AI activities. For example, the number of 'Urgent Action' appeals jumped from 373 in 1987 to 605 in 1991 (AI, 1988, p. 278; AI, 1992a, p. 311). When AI learns that someone has disappeared after being taken into custody, it can issue a call to Urgent Action. AI's Urgent Action network has about 50,000 participants around the world. Taking advantage of advances in communications technology, in particular faxes and electronic mail, the network can be mobilized within hours of information reaching the international secretariat.

Members of the Urgent Action network will then swing into action with letters, faxes, and telegrams on behalf of the victim.

Realism on the Retreat

The role of NGOs as 'soft' actors also poses a challenge to the realist paradigm in international relations. The state-centric approach can be so dominant that NGOs like Amnesty International do not even merit a mention in some textbooks (e.g. Kegley & Wittkopf, 1989; Stoessinger, 1986; Ziegler, 1990). True, state governments remain the focus of human rights activity by both the UN and AI. Both organizations are effective through changing government policy rather than by direct action. But this reduces realism to a formal, juridical conception more than a substantive one.

The ascendancy of realism provided a normative justification for a state-centric approach to international politics and security (Kolodziej, 1992a, p. 1). Even the traditional notion of international organizations viewed them as the results of agreements between governments. In this conception, only sovereign states could be the subjects of international law, had equal standing in international law, and were constitutionally self-contained (Archer, 1983, p. 38). By contrast, the above analysis confirms the following consequences that were predicted to flow from interdependence (Keohane & Nye, 1971, pp. viii–xvii): attitudinal changes among citizens, an increase in international pluralism by the linking of national interest groups in transnational structures, and the emergence of autonomous actors with private foreign policies. The complex interdependence model (Keohane & Nye, 1977) helps us to understand the inability of states to use their capabilities to change human rights and other international regimes: international coalition-forming ability becomes more important than power resources.

Similarly, the above analysis helps to resist the elision from the state-as-actor into state-as-unitary-actor. For it shows that the state consists of rulers and citizens whose interests can come into conflict. In such circumstances, the security interests of some citizens may coincide with the goals of international organizations like AI and the United Nations, in opposition to the security and political interests (regime maintenance) of national governments. By raising the twin questions of security against what (answer: inhumane governance) and for whom (answer: a state's own citizens), AI sensitizes us to definitions of security outside the realist framework of states and state interests.[6] . . .

Conclusion

The AI-UN complementarity can best be expressed as follows. Only governments can implement changes, so NGOs need governmental forums for the pursuit of their single-interest agendas. On the other hand, governments are unlikely to abdicate voluntarily their own powers in any field of human activity. Human rights claims are claims by citizens on governments. They can be abused most systematically, pervasively, and widely by governments. That is, the relationship between governments and human rights organizations is necessarily adversarial. This is why IGOs are so peculiarly ill-suited to the task of being the guardians of human rights, and why NGOs are so much better at monitoring human rights abuses and state compliance with international standards of human rights treatment.

The UN can proclaim the human rights values that we hold dear; AI can monitor compliance of state behaviour with these lofty proclamations. In fact there has been a complementarity of norm-generation and standard-setting in a different and very interesting sense. AI's impeccable record has helped it to establish the principle that states are responsible for the protection of the human rights of their citizens and internationally accountable for any failures to do so. Conversely, AI has also set the standard against which the UN's own efforts at censuring and preventing human rights abuses are measured. In other words, there is now a symbiotic relationship between the United Nations and Amnesty International in the establishment of new human rights standards and the implementation of existing ones.

Another respect in which the United Nations and Amnesty International are complementary is in annual reports on human rights practices by states. The superior administrative capacities of the UN mean that reporting requirements are better vested in the IGO than in an NGO. Similarly, the governmental character of the UN makes it a more substantial forum for formal investigation of serious human rights breaches by national governments. The United Nations collects almost overwhelming masses of information from member governments. Increasing bureaucratization is helpful to the reporting role but not to enforcement. Members produce their own official reports for UN committees. If the AI report is congruent with a government's version, then the latter stands internationally corroborated. If the government's claims are at variance with those of AI, then international plaudit is denied to the government (Williams, 1988, p. 123).

Being apolitical, AI is hostile to no government or political philosophy. Predicated on the belief that government policy can be changed by appeals to reason, AI uses the techniques of courtesy and reasonableness alongside firmness and persistence. The United Nations has the power to issue authoritative edicts to regulate state behaviour. AI has only the weapon of publicity and the threat of publicity. The whole movement rests on the simple idea that governments respond to public opinion. The moral authority of AI would be weakened in proportion to political bias and factual inaccuracies.

Between them, the United Nations and Amnesty International have chalked up some achievements in the field of human rights. National laws and international instruments have been improved, some people who were illegally imprisoned have been freed, and some victims of human rights violations have been compensated. The United Nations could perhaps do better by creating a new post of a UN High Commissioner for Human Rights, equivalent to the UN High Commissioner for Refugees, to complement the UN mechanisms and ensure a more coordinated and swifter UN response (AI, 1992b). An active High Commissioner would give the United Nations a far more public profile in this field, give a human face to the organization's concern with human rights, and enable a prominent and committed individual to monitor compliance with human rights requirements with the full authority of the world body. It is possible that member governments have shied away from establishing such a post for the very same reasons, since once again the primary focus of the High Commissioner would be allegations of misbehaviour by member governments.[7]

In the meantime, NGOs like AI continue to play a more effective role than the UN in human rights monitoring. Reasons for the relatively greater success of AI include the more intensely personal commitment of its members, its cost-effectiveness, and flexibility of management and structure. At the same time, liaising with the United Nations enables Amnesty International to maximize its own impact in world affairs, to express ideas and promote programmes to a wider audience and on a broader platform, and to believe that it is an integral part of a global network of decision-making structures.

The world needs NGOs so that they can operate outside the framework of the states-system in order to put pressure on states on a variety of fronts, such as human rights (AI) or the environment (Greenpeace). It would be difficult to dispute the claim that the world would be a less pleasant place to live in today had there been no NGOs holding governments to account over the past 50 years.

Finally, AI is living proof that individuals matter in international relations both as subjects and objects. Writing in *The Observer* on 26 May 1961, Peter Benenson called for a one-year campaign for the release of 'The Forgotten Prisoners'—people imprisoned for political or religious beliefs and then forgotten by the media, the public, and even the authorities. The campaign goes on. The first effort at neutral research into political imprisonment, the 1961 article sowed the seeds of an idea whose time had come. Sceptics doubted the impact of the John and Jane Smiths of the world writing directly to government leaders and expected the initial impetus to flag. Instead they have watched AI grow from an idea to an organization to an institution. Its continuance is made necessary by the persistence of human rights abuses by governments: its 1992 report listed human rights abuses in 142 countries. Abuses of human rights have been an enduring feature of human history everywhere. The continuing vitality of Amnesty International is proof that people, ordinary people, are no longer prepared to accept the abuses as a permanent blot on the human race anywhere in the world. Just one private citizen with a good idea can make a visible impact on world affairs by bringing joy to some and hope to many.

Notes

1. The Western-universal dichotomy, while analytically useful, should be qualified. Gunnar Fermann, in reviewing this article, noted that the UN Charter too is indebted both politically and philosophically to Western civilization: politically, due to the fact that the Western countries dominated the UN Conference in San Francisco in 1945; philosophically, in that the Charter embodies the dominant Western values of the time.

2. The basis of AI opposition can be distilled into four propositions: the death penalty is brutalizing to all who are involved in the process; its deterrent effect remains unproven and questionable; execution is irrevocable and can be inflicted upon the innocent; in practice it is inflicted disproportionately heavily on the poor, the minorities, and the oppressed.

3. The difference in wordings here between cultures and countries is deliberate, but should not be taken to imply that national cultures and states are homologues.

4. The terminology is borrowed from James N. Rosenau. However, Rosenau uses sovereignty-bound to refer to state actors, and sovereignty-free to refer to non-state actors. Thus, in his definition, international organizations are explicitly included in the sovereignty-free category (Rosenau, 1990, p. 36). I find his terminology useful, but not his usage. In the sense in which I am using it, the United Nations is constrained by the sovereignty of its member states, but Amnesty International is not so bound.

5. For example, Bosnia's Foreign Minister Haris Silajdzic pricked the conscience of many delegates with a passionate description of the horrors taking place in his country while they were busy extolling progress in human rights.

6. However, the writings of traditional realist thinkers like Hans J. Morgenthau and Robert E. Osgood were infused with broad normative concerns that were relegated by Cold War era 'scientific' realists and neorealists (Kolodziej, 1992b, p. 421).

7. The idea of a UN High Commissioner for Refugees was on the agenda of the Vienna Conference in June 1993. Staunchly backed by the EC, Japan, and the United States, the proposal was resisted by developing countries. In the end, rather than scuttle the conference on the issue, delegates entrusted the task to the UN General Assembly (*The Times*, 26 June 1993).

References

AI (Amnesty International), 1988. *Amnesty International Report 1988.* London: Amnesty International Publications.

AI, 1992a. *Amnesty International Report 1992.* London: Amnesty International Publications.

AI, 1992b. *Facing Up to the Failures*. London: Amnesty International Publications.

AI, 1992c. *Bosnia-Herzegovina: Gross Abuses of Basic Human Rights*. London: Amnesty International Publications.

AI, 1993a. *Bosnia-Herzegovina: Rape and Sexual Abuse by Armed Forces*. London: Amnesty International Publications.

AI, 1993b. *Rana u dusi—A Wound to the Soul*. London: Amnesty International Publications.

Archer, Clive, 1983. *International Organizations*. London: George Allen & Unwin. [Second edition, London: Routledge, 1992.]

Barnes, Barry & David Bloor, 1982. 'Relativism, Rationalism and the Sociology of Knowledge', pp. 21–47 in Martin Hollis & Steven Lukes, eds., *Rationality and Relativism*. Cambridge, MA: MIT Press.

Beitz, Charles R., 1979. *Political Theory and International Relations*. Princeton, NJ: Princeton University Press.

Benn, Stanley I. & Richard S. Peters, 1965. *The Principles of Political Thought: Social Principles and the Democratic State*. New York: Free Press.

Donnelly, Jack, 1986. 'International Human Rights: A Regime Analysis', *International Organization*, vol. 40, no. 3, Summer, pp. 599–642.

Donnelly, Jack, 1989. 'Repression and Development: The Political Contingency of Human Rights Trade-Offs', pp. 305–328 in David P. Forsythe, ed., *Human Rights and Development: International Views*. London: Macmillan.

Doyle, Michael W., 1986. 'Liberalism and World Politics', *American Political Science Review*, vol. 80, no. 4, December, pp. 1151–1169.

Ennals, Martin, 1982. 'Amnesty International and Human Rights', pp. 63–83 in Peter Willetts, ed., *Pressure Groups in the Global System*. London: Pinter.

Gage, Nicholas, 1983. *Eleni*. London: William Collins.

Gleditsch, Nils Petter, 1993. 'Democracy and Peace: Good News for Human Rights Advocates', pp. 287–306 in Donna Comien, ed., *Broadening the Frontiers of Human Rights: Essays in Honour of Asbjørn Eide*. Oslo: Scandinavian University Press.

Graham, Doug, 1992. 'Peace and Security in the Asia-Pacific Region: A New Zealand Perspective'. Address by the New Zealand Minister for Disarmament and Arms Control to the Asian Peace Research Association Conference in Christchurch, 31 January 1992. Text of the Minister's address supplied to the author by his office.

Greenfield, Meg, 1989. 'Beware of Geobaloney', *Newsweek*, 25 December, p. 84.

Harrison, Reginald J., 1989. 'Women's Rights: 1975–1985', pp. 226–244 in Paul Taylor & A. John R. Groom, eds., *Global Issues in the United Nations' Framework*. London: Macmillan.

Henkin, Louis, 1989. 'Use of Force: Law and U.S. Policy', pp. 37–69 in Louis Henkin et al., *Right v. Might: International Law and the Use of Force*. New York: Council on Foreign Relations.

Holsti, Kalevi, J., 1992. *International Politics: A Framework for Analysis*. Englewood Cliffs, NJ: Prentice-Hall.

Jacobson, Harold K., 1979. *Networks of Interdependence: International Organizations and the Global Political System*. New York: Knopf.

Kegley, Charles W. & Eugene R. Wittkopf, 1989. *World Politics: Trend and Transformation*. London: Macmillan.

Keohane, Robert O. & Joseph S. Nye, 1971. *Transnational Relations and World Politics*. Cambridge, MA: Harvard University Press.

Keohane, Robert O. & Joseph S. Nye, 1977. *Power and Interdependence: World Politics in Transition*. Boston, MA: Little, Brown.

Kolodziej, Edward A., 1992a. 'What Is Security and Security Studies? Lessons from the Cold War', *Arms Control,* vol. 13, no. 1, April, pp. 1–31.

Kolodziej, Edward A., 1992b. 'Renaissance in Security Studies? Caveat Lector!' *International Studies Quarterly,* vol. 36, no. 4, December, pp. 421–438.

Lake, David A., 1992. 'Powerful Pacifists: Democratic States and War', *American Political Science Review,* vol. 86, no. 1, March, pp. 24–37.

Madhubani, Kishore (Deputy Secretary, Ministry of Foreign Affairs, Singapore), 1993. 'Live and Let Live: Allow Asians to Choose Their Own Course', *Far Eastern Economic Review,* 17 June, p. 7.

Marshall, Russell, 1988. 'Comprehensive Security', pp. 35–42 in Ramesh Thakur, ed., *International Conflict Resolution.* Boulder, CO: Westview.

Nardin, Terry, 1983. *Law, Morality and the Relations of States.* Princeton, NJ: Princeton University Press.

Renteln, Alison Dundes, 1990. *International Human Rights: Universalism versus Relativism.* Newbury Park, CA: Sage.

Rosas, Allan, 1990. 'Democracy and Human Rights', pp. 17–57 in Allan Rosas & Jan Helgesen, eds., *Human Rights in a Changing East/West Perspective.* London: Pinter.

Rosenau, James N., 1990. *Turbulence in World Politics: A Theory of Change and Continuity.* Princeton, NJ: Princeton University Press.

Stoessinger, John G., 1986. *The Might of Nations: World Politics in Our Time.* New York: Random.

Taylor, Paul & A. John R. Groom, eds., 1989. *Global Issues in the United Nations' Framework.* London: Macmillan.

Thakur, Ramesh, 1990. 'Non-Intervention in International Relations: A Case Study', *Political Science,* vol. 42, no. 1, July, pp. 26–61.

Vincent, John, 1982. 'Realpolitik', pp. 73–84 in J. Mayall, ed., *The Community of States.* London: George Allen & Unwin.

Wasserstrom, Richard, 1964. 'Rights, Human Rights and Racial Discrimination', *Journal of Philosophy,* vol. 61, no. 20, October, pp. 628–641.

Williams, Andrew, 1988 'The United Nations and Human Rights', pp. 114–129 in Paul Taylor & A. John R. Groom, eds., *International Institutions at Work.* London: Pinter.

Yi Ding, 1989. 'Opposing Interference in Other Countries' Internal Affairs through Human Rights', *Beijing Review,* 6 November.

Ziegler, David W., 1990. *War, Peace and International Politics,* 5th ed. Glenview, IL: Scott, Foresman.

15

Who Governs the Rome Food Agencies?

Ross B. Talbot & H. Wayne Moyer

The purpose of this article is to analyse the structure of power in the four world food organizations headquartered in Rome, specifically the Food and Agriculture Organization (FAO), World Food Council (WFC), the World Food Programme (WFP) and the International Fund for Agricultural Development (IFAD). . . .

The FAO became an international organization in the 1943–45 period. It was a creature of the Allied powers, predominantly the USA, the UK and Canada, with the exclusion (by its own choice) of the USSR. Third World nations, excluding Latin America, were nearly all colonies at that time. The World Food Programme is a product of the 1960–63 period; sponsored by the US government, abetted by the FAO, supported by Canada and Australia, and somewhat reluctantly agreed to by the new and suspicious developing nations. Today, the European Economic Community has become a major contributor and Third World nations have acquired a power status nearing equality within the WFP. Both the World Food Council and the International Fund for Agricultural Development were the creations of the World Food Conference, which was held in Rome in November 1974 at a time when a worldwide food shortage seemed to be on the immediate horizon. But their configurations of power differ decidedly from each other, and from those of FAO and WFP. The World Food Council is primarily a policy innovator, a minor broker in superpower politics, with the USA, [Russia], and China as continuing members. IFAD has a unique configuration: OECD (Organization of Economic Cooperation and Development), OPEC (Organization of Petroleum Exporting Countries) and the Group of 77 (Third World nations). Process follows structure by and large and, as we will indicate, this means that the issue of 'who governs?'

Reprinted with permission from *Food Policy,* Vol. 2, Ross Talbot and H. Wayne Moyer, "Who Governs the Rome Food Agencies?" 1987, Elsevier Science, Ltd., Butterworth Heinemann Imprint, Oxford, England.

must often be answered differently over time. Using the FAO as an example, the structure of power within that IO changed during the 1945–85 period, and as a result the answer needs to be modified at particular points in time.

An International Triangle (Quadrangle) Model

We will speak to the question of 'who governs?' in turn, for each international organization. However, we were unable to formulate a single model which would explain both structure and process for all four organizations. Conceptually, an international triangle of power works fairly well for FAO and WFP. One side of the power triangle would be the OECD member states (i.e., the nations of Western Europe and North America, plus Japan, Australia and New Zealand) who are, by far, the principal funding actors; a second side would be the Third World nations, somewhat loosely organized into a political coalition called the Group of 77, who are the principal recipients of this funding; with a third side being the secretariats (the bureaucracy) of FAO and WFP, which have the crucial roles of policy innovator and mediator for promoting mutually acceptable agreements between those who fund and those who receive.[1] But the triangle-of-power concept has to be restructured into a quadrangle in order to explain the workings of IFAD: OECD, OPEC, Group of 77, and the IFAD bureaucracy. And for the World Food Council, the USSR and the Eastern Europe bloc have to be included, and OPEC becomes a part (unrealistically, in economic terms) of the Group of 77.

These schematic arrangements are useful in explaining how the world food organizations function. There is, to some extent, a commonality of interest. OECD nations (the North) have political, economic and cultural interests in assisting developing nations (the South) to emerge from conditions of poverty; the developing nations, obviously, have the desire to do so, but claim that a prerequisite is abundant development assistance. On the other hand, this agreement on goals and objectives often does not translate into an agreement on means and methods. North and South need each other, but the latter's demands are insatiable, while the former believes that the resources available for redistribution are limited. The respective international bureaucracies function as a kind of influential prime mover, inclining towards finding policies and means to meet the demands of the South, but understanding the limitations of their power to make a claim on the wealth of the North. Moreover, these bureaucracies have vested interests of their own. The result is compromise: incremental change which is presumed to be an optional arrangement by the major political actors at the particular moment.

Also, none of these power configurations takes sufficiently into account three other important considerations. One is the influence on the world food agencies of the United Nations itself and some of the other IOs—specifically, the United Nations Development Program (UNDP), the World Bank and the regional banks, and, to a lesser extent, such organizations as the World Health Organization (WHO) and the International Labour Organization (ILO). Secondly, the non-governmental organizations (NGOs), such as CARE, Catholic Relief Service and Church World Service, are secondary actors, but not without influence, in the policy making of each of the world food organizations. They are effectively organized, politically and functionally, in North America, Western Europe and Australia, and are closely associated with an international structure in Geneva—The International Council of Voluntary Agencies. Thirdly, in each international organization there is a director-general (or an executive director or president), who is certainly first and foremost in the bureaucratic hierarchy; jealous of his or her authority, suspicious of competitors, authoritarian (in varying degrees) in leadership style, although dependent on the imaginative insights, analytical expertise, personal and corporate loyalty, and administrative skills of the IO's professional and technical staff. Moreover, problems of organizational competitiveness and jurisdiction, always prevalent and occasionally of some magnitude, exist within and between the bureaucracies of these world food agencies.

In any respect, we could not develop a single model which describes the behaviour of all of these agencies, and the two variations we have offered are not without their defects, which we will later elaborate.

A Descriptive Explanation

We will attempt an answer for each of the world food agencies to our central questions: Who governs? Our presentation cannot be comprehensive but we will provide an overview based on the following outline. First, there will be a brief look at the constitutional-political basis of power of each IO. Those who study IOs tend to overlook the constitutional basis from which the agency must proceed; if this legal framework is abused or violated it is quite likely that serious political conflict will ensue, and little will be accomplished until those constitutional issues are resolved. Second, we will explain the budgetary-financial basis of each organization. An IO does not have the power to tax; even less does it have the power of the sword (i.e., exacting and enforcing penalties on the negligent or recalcitrant member state). But the questions of 'Who pays? Who receives?' always generate fundamental political and economic issues, the answers to which tell us much about who gets what, when and how. Third, we will sketch out the policy-making process, and do so by briefly explaining, where applicable, the internal power relationships which occur at the various stages of the policy cycle. We will use a frequently employed, five-state policy cycle: agenda building, formulation, legitimation, implementation and evaluation.[2]

What eventuates, in terms of policy decisions and their implementation, is what a reasonably knowledgeable person would suspect, based on [models of power]. That is, the policy process in the international organization is one of compromise and mutual accommodation, resulting usually in incremental change. Conflicts of interest and ideology do occur, of course, and the competing demands are decided on in an environment in which the principal actors must search for a consensus. One of the definitions of power offered by Keohane and Nye—'The ability of an actor to get others to do something they otherwise would not do (at an acceptable cost to the actor)'[3]—has come to have a special meaning in these IOs. The Third World nations have the votes, but not the resources; conversely, the have-nations have their own interests in maintaining a forum for continuing international cooperation which would not be served by withdrawal or persistent 'stonewalling.' The power of the actors (member states and bureaucracies) is so limited that, confronted with interests both common and conflicting, there is really no visible alternative other than a search for a mutually acceptable consensus.

Who Governs the Food and Agriculture Organization?

The Food and Agriculture Organization of the United Nations was created in 1945 as one of the autonomous specialized agencies of the United Nations system whose purpose was to promote cooperation among nations and encourage action on common problems, thus contributing to world peace. FAO actually predated the formal establishment of the United Nations, and was given a broad mandate under its constitution. It had four purposes.

- Raising levels of nutrition and standards of living under the jurisdiction of the member governments.
- Securing improvements in the efficiency of production and distribution of food and agricultural products.
- Bettering the conditions of rural populations.
- Contributing to an expanding world economy and striving to assure freedom from hunger.[4]

The organization which emerged reflected a compromise between those who wanted a strong action-oriented agency to foster agricultural development and those who wanted a more limited fact-gathering and advisory agency.[5]

FAO was established with an organizational structure fairly common for intergovernmental organizations. The supreme governing body is the Conference which holds regular sessions biennially and elects the Director-General and FAO Secretariat. The Conference also decides the scale of member contributions to FAO. Assessments have generally been made in accordance with the UN formula, with members contributing a percentage of the FAO budget proportionate to the relative size of GNP.

Another function of the Conference is to elect member countries to the Council which meets between conferences and serves as a second-level governing body. The membership of the Council has grown to 49 members. The USA has always been a member. Much of the substantive work discussed by the Conference and Council is carried out by committees. There are seven standing committees dealing with programme, finance, constitutional and legal issues, commodities, agriculture, forestry and fisheries. The Conference and Council also carry on their work through a number of *ad hoc* bodies such as the Committee on World Food Security and Commission on Fertilizers.

FAO has grown very significantly since its inception. . . . In FAO's early years, prior to decolonization, FAO was dominated by the Western industrial powers who took a rather restricted view of what the organization could accomplish. Primary emphasis was given to making technical studies, collecting and publishing statistics, conducting conferences, establishing technical commissions and dispatching occasional field study missions. In this period, the FAO budget grew slowly.

Independence for the former colonies led to a significant increase in the membership of FAO in the 1950s and 1960s and a shift in the voting balance to give the developing nations a significant majority in the Conference. New pressures were generated on FAO to change its focus from information gathering and dissemination to field activities in support of Third World agricultural development. An active field programme was developed by FAO, funded by extra-budgetary resources contributed primarily by UN agencies and national governments. However, the transition proceeded slowly. Change was resisted by the FAO bureaucracy and resistance developed, and continues, among the industrial nations to FAO becoming primarily a development agency.

The early 1970s saw the development of a world food crisis caused by global drought occurring in the context of Third World population explosion. FAO was severely criticized for not anticipating the crisis and for not having done enough to stimulate Third World agricultural development and thus limit the effects of the famine. The general dissatisfaction with FAO was an important factor leading to the 1974 Rome World Food Conference, which was held under UN rather than FAO auspices.[6] New international food organizations, independent of FAO, were established to accomplish missions which it was thought were not well carried out by FAO.

The Rome World Food Conference galvanized change in FAO. The sense of crisis forged a new consensus of OECD and Group of 77 countries, which led to the election of a dynamic Director-General, Edouard Saouma, committed to Third World agricultural development and widespread support for such reforms as the development of an extensive system of country representatives, the establishment of a Technical Cooperation

Programme with quick grants for short-term development needs, increased support for agricultural investment, and a considered effort to shift personnel resources from headquarters to the field. The crisis atmosphere facilitated mutual adjustment along with a rapid growth of FAO's budget and extra-budgetary resources.

As the world food crisis receded in the late 1970s, the consensus between OECD and the Group of 77 weakened and FAO's budget growth and innovations slowed down perceptibly. The USA, concerned about an increasing balance of payments deficit, among other reasons, began to exert cost containment pressures. Since 1983, FAO has operated with almost a no-growth budget.

The FAO policy process is a cumbersome one with a strong tendency towards incrementalism, as one would expect from an organization with 158 member governments and 6,600 staff. The programme of work is put together in the various divisions of FAO and the Director-General makes the final determination of priorities after consultation with the staff and member countries. Director-General Saouma has a decisive style and dominates the policy process. He has to walk a very fine line between meeting the demands of the Group of 77 countries for expanding FAO programmes without offending the OECD countries, which still provide the bulk of the funding. The Conference, in practice, is unwieldy and does not play a major role in planning or determining priorities. Its major function appears to be to ratify the decisions reached by the Director-General and staff. The Council is more involved than the Conference in FAO substantive matters, primarily as a sounding board for new proposals but still tends to defer to the Director-General and the Secretariat.

FAO is severely constrained in its policy autonomy in that its resources are primarily technical rather than financial. Unlike the World Bank and IFAD, FAO cannot carry out development projects, but can only provide technical support. Hence, FAO activities must remain very closely tied to the projects funded by the major lending agencies. FAO's dependence on extra-budgetary funding provides the regular assessed budget.[7] The remainder comes from a variety of grants and trust funds provided by international organizations and countries, and FAO must do what the donors want, if it is to retain access to this funding.

The Director-General gains support to legitimize his policies in a number of ways. He can use his discretionary authority to distribute Technical Cooperation Programme funds to gain support from Third World governments. He also has power to make staff appointments and can exert significant leverage on member governments by adroit use of his patronage power, at some cost, arguably, to the general technical competence of the FAO staff. He maintains influence internally through control of promotions and by placing 'his own people' in important positions.

FAO can implement its policies only to the extent that it has the support of the nations where it operates. Our sense is that FAO has gained a freer hand to function in Third World countries as the perceived need for agricultural development has increased. A more serious problem is the sensitivity of many governments to criticism. Hence, FAO has been slow to develop meaningful evaluations and in communicating the results of those evaluations it has made. Since the World Food Conference, FAO has developed a more rigorous evaluation process, though these assessments are still not generally available to outsiders.

Another obstacle to effective implementation is that FAO programmes need to be coordinated with the activities of other international organizations and of national governments. This was very difficult before the Rome World Food Conference when most of FAO's personnel were headquarters-based. Director-General Saouma has alleviated this problem somewhat with his system of 74 country representatives, who now serve 98 countries. These country representatives, under the direct control of the Director-General, are responsible for seeing that FAO intentions are carried out, and in coordinating FAO activities with those of host governments and other international organizations.

FAO has shown itself effective in adjusting to shifting international priorities. It responded well to the call of the Rome World Food Conference for an increased emphasis on agricultural production and investment and for the development of an agricultural early-warning system. It has also moved to extend its efforts to the peasant farmer by sponsoring the 1979 World Conference on Agrarian Reform and Rural Development (WCARRD), and by emphasizing small farmers in its recent programmes of work and budget. It has also given emphasis in recent years to food production in Africa, the region with the most serious problems. However, it is not possible to measure correctly the increased commitment to Africa and to agricultural reform by analysing FAO budget figures. The percent of the FAO budget for Africa only increased from 29.9% in 1978–79 to 30.7% in 1986–87.[8] One can surmise that the political balance is so delicate that it is difficult to make any significant policy changes in the absence of real budgetary growth.

Who Governs the World Food Council?

The World Food Council is a product of the World Food Conference of 1974. Resolution XXII, which was later ratified by the UN's Economic and Social Council, and then the General Assembly, designated the WFC as the highest political institution in the UN system dealing with world food policies and problems. It is not an operating agency, '. . . but rather a forum and mechanism for initiating ideas and for reviewing the work of other international organizations with operating programs.'[9]

The construction of the 36-member Council gives some political leverage to the Group of 77, whose members occupy 25 of the Council seats. But the Council has no funds for projects or programmes, only ideas and proposals. Its operating budget [is] sufficient to pay for an almost miniscule bureaucracy, consultants and internal programming.

The Council exists because, in the minds of many of the delegates at the World Food Conference, the Food and Agriculture Organization failed to fulfill its principal mission—that is, to foresee and, presumably, to prevent the world food crisis of 1972–74. This is likely an unfair and misdirected charge, but the FAO has suffered from, and has become embittered by, this perceived failure. The relationship between the two organizations, particularly at the highest levels, has generally been one of studied, brooding and mutual incompatibility.

The Council's Executive Director and (to a lesser extent) its elected President have provided the Council with dynamic and imaginative leadership. Its annual agenda has been dictated to a minor extent by desires made explicit at a previous Council session, but much more often Council proposals concerning 'what should be done' to alleviate world food problems are the brainchild of the Executive Director, his staff and their consultants. Searching for and exposing ways and means to improve food production, enhance world food security, and increase the flow of food aid constitute the Council's central objectives. The annual formulations of proposed strategies and programmes are contained in a set of documents drafted by the WFC bureaucracy, which heretofore have first been considered at the Preparatory Meeting, and then ratified (largely without revision) by the Council at its annual session, usually held in June each year in a different continent. The Group of 77, through the device of the Preparatory Meeting, has endeavoured to gain control of the Council's agenda in order to modify the secretariat's proposals in their favour, but the Executive Director has managed to maintain control. Indeed, in 1986 the Preparatory Meeting was simply abolished.

The Council is not an implementing agency, and has no formal mechanism for evaluating the activities and programmes of the other world food agencies. In establishing the Council, the World Food Conference envisaged high-level, policy-discussing annual meetings, composed not only of ministers of agriculture but also with some representation of those from finance, planning and development. But in 1975–76 the world food crisis began to slip from its status as high politics on the world scene, down to a kind of middle-level position as the crisis receded. Gradually, there developed the realization that the world food problem, at its core and conscience, was actually one of poverty. A massive redistribution, from rich to poor nations, would likely have to take place if this condition was to be attacked in a serious, concerted manner. The political environment simply did not (and does not) exist for that kind of revolutionary policy making to take place.

The World Food Council does not and cannot govern; it endeavours to pursuade (to use a prominent and current example) the Third World nations to formulate and implement a national food strategy which will, over extended time, enable that food-deficit nation to become food self-reliant. And simultaneously the Executive Director and his staff have persisted in their efforts to persuade the OECD nations that they, in turn, must support—financially and through non-protectionist trade policies—those Third World nations who are endeavouring to implement a national food strategy.

Not only does the World Food Council seek to be creative and innovative, but it must also be concerned with searching for the means whereby ideas can be transformed into effective policies and programmes. Over the past decade much has been heard of the concept of political will: that the international community could overcome the scourge of poverty—and the problems of food, shelter, ignorance and illness which follow in its wake—if the OECD and Group of 77 states displayed the political will to do so. Ideally, perhaps this is so, but the peroration has been essentially self-denying. This world, we would argue, is composed of many interdependent nation states, but they do not perceive of themselves as constituting a world community. From those according to their ability to those according to their need is not the dominant theme in world politics. The World Food Council endeavours to function as a policy innovator and political broker between those who have and those who have not. In that pursuit the Council has been successful to the extent that a North-South dialogue continues on major issues relating to agriculture and food, and many of these issues have been either initiated or enlightened by the endeavours of the Council.

Who Governs the World Food Programme?

Viewed constitutionally, the World Food Programme is a voluntary agency build upon an FAO Conference resolution passed in November 1961, and subsequent UN General Assembly resolutions enacted in 1961, 1965 and 1975.[10] The economic reality was that the origin of the WFP came about because of the growing burden of over-bountiful farm surpluses, especially in the USA. The political reality was two-fold: (1) the FAO bureaucracy had devised a programme whereby surplus agricultural commodities of rich nations could be utilized in Third World countries for rural development projects, welfare programmes, and food-disaster emergencies; (2) the Kennedy administration—more explicitly, the Food For Peace director George McGovern—seized the opportunity presented by the FAO scheme and proposed the establishment of a World Food Programme, financed predominantly by US agricultural commodities and dollars.

Over time the WFP has become a unique type of voluntary agency. In essence, it is financed primarily (80–90%) by OECD nations who contribute food, cash and services for the support of WFP-sponsored development and disaster relief projects. Every two years a pledging conference is held in New York. . . . This fund of food, cash and services is spent on both development and emergency projects in Third World nations. Development projects are broadly of two types—primarily for agricultural and rural development (e.g., land rehabilitation, soil conversion, irrigation), and to a lesser extent for human resource development (nutritional support for mothers, their infants and primary school children). . . .

Because the funding is voluntary, the policy-making process must be two-sided. Funding must first be volunteered, essentially by OECD countries; the expenditures are completely within Third World countries. Herein lies the international iron triangle, with the WFP bureaucracy occupying a prominent corner through its influence in the determinations of the project cycle. That is, projects are initiated and formulated by a Third World nation, sometimes with the assistance of the WFP Field Representative in the least-developed nations. The legitimation stage takes place in the Committee on Food Aid Policy and Programmes (CFA). In a sense, CFA performs a legislative function. Its 30 members—composed of OECD and Group of 77 members, in approximately equal numbers—discuss each project, and occasionally will influence the WFP staff to modify the terms of a project proposal. Small projects, costing WFP less than $1.5 million, may be approved by the Executive Director, then reported and justified to CFA. Since adequate food resources are available, projects are rarely denied, at either the formulation or legitimation stage. (Funds, however, are usually in short supply.) The implementation of an approved project is primarily the responsibility of the recipient Third World nation, although the WFP is gradually becoming more involved in the transportation and distribution functions within the recipient nations. The WFP has been a pioneer agency in the use of project evaluations, which must be reported periodically to CFA, and a final evaluation report is required after a project has been completed.

The answer to the question of who governs the WFP must therefore be somewhat complex. On the input side, the OECD nations have to make the major financial commitment, although agricultural surpluses in North America, Western Europe and Australia have meant that the opportunity costs of food aid have been quite low in recent years. On the output (project) side, the WFP staff and the proposing/recipient Third World nations play the dominant roles. Internally, emergency project proposals have to be approved by FAO's Director-General. Importantly, too, catastrophic events—such as Kampuchea, the Sahel, and the Ethiopian food crises—are an exogenous variable which mandate a positive decision. The WFP staff desires to be viewed as primarily a rural development agency, but Third World disasters (human-made and natural) impose an increasing and recurring responsibility. In 1985, for example, regular WFP assistance to Ethiopia cost over $211 million for 14 development projects and almost $70 million for 20 emergency operations.

As mentioned earlier, this triangular power configuration has to be modified, at least marginally, because of the desires and influence of the NGOs and other UN specialized organizations. But, in general terms and discounting the exceptions to the rule, we believe that the triangular model has significant descriptive power.

Who Governs the International Fund for Agricultural Development?

The World Food Conference's Resolution XIII states that 'an International Fund for Agricultural Development should be established immediately to finance agricultural development projects primarily for food production in the developing countries.' Implicit, too, in this resolve was that IFAD's projects should be aimed predominantly at the rural peasantry who live in conditions of abject poverty. The concurrence of the UN Secretary-General proceeded to initiate a search for voluntary pledges to finance IFAD's operations. Funding has constantly been one of its principal concerns. Probably no international organization has been accorded as positive, indeed enthusiastic, a public press as has IFAD, but none has been plagued by so many obstacles in the search for funds, at its inception and especially during the negotiations for replenishment.

Resolution XIII also set forth, in somewhat vague terms, the constitutional structure of IFAD: a Governing Board representing 'contributing developed countries [i.e., OECD], contributing developing countries [i.e., OPEC], and potential recipient countries [i.e., Third World nations].' Moreover, this representation was to be selected so as to ensure 'regional balance' and an 'equitable distribution.' After some difficult negotiations, a set of Articles of Agreement was drafted, and opened for signature by willing nation states. But a serious controversy between OECD and OPEC member states over funding was resolved only after difficult negotiations, and IFAD could not commence operation until 30 November 1977.[11] The Articles specified the establishment of a governing Council (all signatory countries) and a tripartite Executive Board with each part having one-third of the 1,800 votes. According to Section 6(b), '. . . decisions of the Executive Board shall be taken by a majority of three fifths of the votes cast [except for voting for suspensions or amendments], provided that such majority is more than half of the total number of votes of all members of the Executive Board.'

The realities of power within IFAD are quite different, however, from the constitutional requirements. Some 141 nations are now voluntary members of IFAD, and constitute its Governing Council. The Council meets annually; its authority is decidedly limited, but the Council formally elects a President (the first was from Saudi Arabia, the second from Algeria), who in turn selects a Vice President (thus far, an American). However, political power actually lies with an Executive Board of 18 members: six in Category I (OECD), six in Category II (OPEC), and six in Category III (Group of 77). Initially nearly all of IFAD's small bureaucracy were on secondment from other international or national aid agencies, although this is much less the situation today. The reputation of this bureaucracy has been consistently high: dynamic, experienced, resourceful, innovative.

IFAD's conundrum has been how to secure funding for projects which would increase food production in developing countries, and would also '. . . improve the nutritional level of the poorest populations in the poorest food deficit countries . . . [and] in other developing countries.'[12] In its origin as an idea, IFAD was probably the brainchild of the Secretary-General of the World Food Conference—Saved Ahmed Marei, the Egyptian Minister of Agriculture. The idea proved attractive to at least some members of OPEC, primarily because that organization was incurring sharp and increasing criticism from non-oil-producing Third World countries who had been subjected to a sixfold increase in oil prices. The OECD countries, and principally the USA, were opposed to the creation of new international organizations, but they were attracted to the idea of securing OPEC's financial contributions to aid food production in the Third World countries. In a nutshell, an 'equitable' contribution meant 50–50 to the OECD members, but the OPEC equity could be defined as no more than a 60–40 ratio, with OPEC on the lesser side. Finally, by late 1977, a compromise was agreed to: a 58–42 ratio, with the total pledged fund for 1978–81 amounting to just over $1 billion (actually $1,021 million, with Category III nations pledging $19 million). The contribution of the USA was $200 million.

IFAD's financial troubles began with the first replenishment, which was to be for the 1981–84 period. The target figure of $1.1 billion was arrived at without much difficult negotiation, with approximately the same ratios prevailing. But the USA arbitrarily cut its funding from $200 million to $180 million, and soon fell behind in its payments because of Congress's refusal to appropriate any funds, even in annual increments. However, other OECD countries finally agreed to fill in the deficit in the Category I pledge. On the Category II (OPEC) side, the Iranian revolution turned that nation into a non-contributor; then Libya defaulted, as did Iraq after the Iran-Iraq war began.

The second replenishment, for 1985–87, was even more complicated. Indeed, our sketch does little justice to its complexities. A dramatic reduction in oil prices put all OPEC contributions at risk, and President Reagan and the US Congress vied for honours in setting up replenishment obstacles for the US contribution. . . .

Despite this severe handicap, IFAD's record is noteworthy. In some eight years, IFAD has financed 177 projects in 87 developing countries at a total cost of almost $9.1 billion, of which IFAD's share has been $2.1 billion. For example, even in the African nations some 47% of the project costs were incurred by the recipient government, while 28% were co-financed (primarily, by the World Bank and regional banks).

The politics involved in IFAD's policy cycle are complicated. Our description and explanation are somewhat superficial, but hopefully sufficient to answer: who governs IFAD? The agenda of IFAD is clearly stated in its constitutional documents; for example, *Lending Policies and Criteria* (December 1978, Article 27) specifies that projects and programmes must '. . . normally . . . provide proportionately large benefits to the poorest segments of the population when compared with other groups.' Because IFAD has a remarkably small bureaucracy (84 professionals and 106 support staff, as of February 1986) the matter of identification and formulation of project proposals which are in accord with IFAD purposes and criteria has been a particularly difficult matter. Through the use of technical assistance grants and special programming missions IFAD has largely succeeded in influencing this process in a manner which enables the organization to function in accord with its objectives, at least in the view of IFAD's secretariat.

It is difficult to generalize about the legitimation stage. The Governing Council has almost no role; the Executive Board is influential in moulding and modifying project proposals, but to what extent and in what matter we are uncertain. Executive Board sessions are closed; minutes are kept, but (we are told) they are recorded only in terms of decisions, not verbatim. However, we do not desire to leave the impression that the IFAD President and staff govern. The Executive Board must primarily be a reacting institution, but interviews with some members of IFAD's secretariat caused us to believe that, on occasion, the Board's reactions have been critical, influential and demanding.

At the implementation stage, the limitations (in numbers) of the IFAD management staff again become apparent. Our impression, based heavily on a few interviews and a reading of IFAD's annual reports, is that the bureaucracy has been gradually gaining effective control over its implementation process. More accurately, the principal responsibility for implementation lies with the recipient Third World nation; IFAD's responsibility is '. . . to ensure timely and effective implementation of its projects,'[13] which it seems to be accomplishing. The IFAD staff has been especially active and innovative in the evaluation stage, again within the confines and constraints imposed by a shortage of professional staff. Robert Berg has recently commended IFAD: '. . . they set up monitoring authorities at the project level and strengthen evaluation at the ministerial levels [of the recipient country].'[14] And the UN's Joint Inspection Unit, in a 1985 report, noted that '. . . IFAD has continued to establish and strengthen monitoring and evaluation as a central element of its programme.'[15]

What does all of this mean in terms of IFAD as an organization of power? The current situation has evolved into a kind of political enigma. There is strong ideological support for IFAD, particularly from liberals in

OECD states, although IFAD is not without conservative support. On the other hand, IFAD continues to face serious funding difficulties. Nearly all of the media's adverse criticism has been directed at the Reagan administration because of its obstinacy towards the funding of IFAD. But most of the other OECD nations (and notably the major contributors to IFAD) and all the members of OPEC seem to be permitting the USA to receive the opprobrium for niggardliness which they would incur, too, if put into a situation where they would be committed to increase their financial commitment to IFAD. More will be said on this matter below.

The Rome Food Agencies, Towards 2000

We conclude with a brief foray into the hazardous field of forecasting. What do we guess the structure of power in the world food agencies will look like by the year 2000? We see four possible alternatives.

Unification

In a recent article, John Gerard Ruggie observed that '. . . it was not international bureaucrats but national governments that established . . . no fewer than four international agencies dealing with food and agriculture alone.'[16] Political scientists have a kind of abiding passion for advising against overlap and duplication in the structure and functions of governments, and the Rome food agencies, at least deductively, seem to be a logical target for reorganization and consolidation.

For over a decade there has been an unorganized but articulate anti–World Food Council contingent; some of them are quartered within the Food and Agriculture Organization, but by no means all of the dissenters are there. Based on a recommendation of the 11th session of the World Food Council (Paris, June 1985), an 'advisory group' of three was set up to investigate what the future role of the World Food Council should be. Their preliminary report has now been released, and the terse summary of their nine recommendations would be that the Council should be strengthened in its authority, funding and independence.[17] This report will not silence WFC's detractors, but our surmise is that the end result will be a marginally stronger Council.

Then there is the school of disbelievers concerning the IFAD. That is: Why do we need an IFAD when we already have an IDA (International Development Association—the soft-window, concessional arm of the World Bank) and three regional banks? There is no intrinsic need for a duplicative specialized agency; besides, the pie of development assistance is shrinking so a competitive structure is not only unnecessary but divisive and damaging, or at least inefficient. (So the anti-IFAD argument goes.)

There has never been much discussion regarding the abolition of the World Food Programme, at least to our knowledge, but there is concern (and notably so within the WFP) as to its increasing involvement in worldwide disaster relief. There is also some discussion about the future of the Committee on World Food Security, which was established by the World Food Conference to monitor and recommend regarding those concerns; it meets annually in Rome, and reports to FAO and the UN General Assembly.

There will be no unification of world food agencies by 2000; at least that is our forecast, and primarily for two reasons—one negative, one positive. On the negative side, the Food and Agriculture Organization is still suspect throughout much of the world food policy network. In our judgement, a considerable amount of the criticism of FAO has been unfair and misdirected. Nevertheless, its image has been blemished; it is improving, but the FAO continues to be viewed as a 'bureaucracy' in the pejorative sense of the term—overstaffed, overpaid, unimaginative, not at the cutting edge of current agricultural science and technology.

On the positive side, the other three world food agencies (with the World Food Council as somewhat problematical) have proven themselves. There are those who are opposed to food aid, multilateral and bilateral, and their disincentive arguments constitute a valid concern. But these criticisms have been heard and the necessary preventive measures factored into WFP policies. IFAD has yet to prove that its policies and programmes will enable those in rural poverty to improve their degraded condition, at least in substantial numbers, but there is considerable evidence that IFAD has a positive image within the world food policy network. To be sure, its funding problems are immediate and impairing, but they do not appear to be unresolvable.

Major Expansion of Authority

This is an unlikely alternative. Neither the World Food Council nor FAO will be permitted by the OECD, or even by the Group of 77, to become a World Food Authority. Lord Boyd-Orr's vision will continue to be unrealized. The World Food Programme will not be transformed into the world disaster agency; there are too many other international disaster agencies who would engage themselves with ardor and vehemence in that kind of turf fight. Besides, this would require a considerable reconstitution of the WFP as an institution; there is more to disaster relief than the supply of food, important as that is. Likewise, the World Bank's IDA is not going to be dissolved into an IFAD, although a considerable increase in oil prices would renew the appetites of OECD members towards finding ways to direct substantial amounts of those 'undeserving' profits into development assistance. In this kind of thinking, IFAD is not without growth potential, although one is sorely pressed to think of ways that would convince OPEC that the unpleasant is the necessary.

Dissolution

Cynics (or are they realists?) often conjecture that international bureaucracies, like those of the national variety, are rarely abolished and seldom tend to fade away. There are possibilities here, although we see the probabilities as quite high that no one of these world food agencies will be abolished. Our reasons can fairly well be extracted from the discussion concerning unification. If the World Food Council were to be abolished, who would assume its persuading, mobilizing, coordinating responsibilities?[18] The FAO would be the logical, but politically unviable, choice. . . . In the best of all possible worlds, food aid should become an anachronism, but that is a 21st century dream. Besides, the WFP is politically useful as a multilateral agency, performing functions that OECD surplus-producing nations would find to be awkward, perhaps embarrassing, and possibly counterproductive, if they had to be carried out exclusively within a bilateral framework. The USA's PL 480 programme and, to a lesser extent, the European Community's food aid programme, are vulnerable to the charges of self-serving, subtle bribery and undue influence, as viewed by Third World recipients. IFAD is a candidate for dissolution, but not realistically; the late 1980s may not be the heyday period for liberals, but we see IFAD as institutionally invulnerable because of its special rural-poor focus which the International Development Association does not have. However, IFAD's funding arrangements will continue to be the subject of hard negotiating.

Incremental Change

There will necessarily be policy changes, but we do not see them to be of a dramatic nature. Likewise, since their decision-making processes have not changed much in the last decade they are not likely to change much in the future. At its 1986 session in Rome, the World Food Council reverted, at least in part, to the format and agenda for which it was originally designed: a policy-innovation kind of arrangement orchestrated by the Council's Executive Director and his staff, at which ministers of agriculture, and a few of their money- and planning-oriented counterparts, would talk over what they are, might be, and could be doing. The final report constituted a kind of 'sense of the meeting,' experiential in content, rather than a politicized set of conclusions and recommendations. Whether these high-level, time-conscious political administrators will accept this format as both utilitarian and perception-broadening, and not just another cacophony of rhetoric, remains to be seen.

In this increasingly interdependent world there is a vital need for a Food and Agriculture Organization. And in several policy areas—food quality standards, plant and animal genetics, seed identification and preservation, the use and sale of pesticides, fungicides and rodenticides, among others—we believe that FAO's power and responsibility will be gradually increased.

The World Food Programme is now adjusting to its recent increases in authority, which were granted following the deliberations of the Joint UN/FAO Task Force on WFP Relationship Problems. WFP management 'won' more autonomy from FAO in internal matters involving personnel, finances and auditing. But that power struggle seems now to have been resolved, and WFP still does not have the status of an independent specialized agency. However, WFP will likely have incremental increases in its authority over the next few years—such as funding of programmes (rather than only projects), and multi-year funding.

Just how the funding difficulties of IFAD will be resolved (meaning alleviated; funding is never finally resolved) is unclear. The two principal actors in this matter seem to be the USA and Saudi Arabia. In our judgement, the USA—in its own interests and those of Third World nations—should retreat from two wrong-headed positions: that funding for IFAD must be niggardly and defensive, and that IFAD's staff needs are now being adequately served. We have no grandiose numbers in mind; perhaps a return to the original $1+ billion for a three-year period and a doubling of the management staff. But IFAD has earned its right to be treated with respect, and to adequate funding.

To conclude, our own intelligent perspective comes out of a kind of American Lockian tradition: 'Men [and women] are not angels and angels do not govern men'—'ambition must be made to counteract ambition'—'. . . experience has taught mankind the necessity of auxiliary precautions.'[19] Within that kind of a philosophical outlook, we view the international food organizations as useful and, to a considerable extent, necessary instruments to be used in the pursuit of justice and equity, for rich as well as poor nations. By and large, these organizations have functioned effectively, with some positive results. We view the four-organization structure as optimal in terms of balancing the interest of the competing factions, while at the same time facilitating some constructive action. That is, the present arrangement provides the various political blocs (OECD, OPEC, Third World, etc.) with multiple channels to pursue their varied interests. How these Rome food agencies are governed—by whom, for whom, in what manner, and with what results—are political matters of enduring consequence.

Notes

1. For an elaborate theoretical analysis of this proposition, see Robert O. Keohane, *After Hegemony: Cooperation and Discord in the World Political Economy* (Princeton, NJ: Princeton University Press, 1984), especially chapters 4–6.

2. Standard sources are: James E. Anderson, *Public Policy-Making* 3rd ed (New York: Holt, Rinehart and Winston, 1984) and Charles O. Jones, *An Introduction to the Study of Public Policy* 3rd ed (Monterey, CA: Brooks-Cole Publishing Company, 1983).

3. Robert O. Keohane and Joseph S. Nye, *Power and Interdependence: Politics in Transition* (Boston: Little, Brown, 1977).

4. See Ralph W. Phillips, *FAO, Its Origins, Formation and Evolution, 1945–1981* (Rome: FAO, 1981), 9.

5. Select Committee on Nutrition and Human Needs, US Senate, Staff Report, *The United States, FAO and World Food Politics: U.S. Relations with an International Food Organization* (Washington, DC: US Government Printing Office, 1976), 70.

6. Important, too, was the fact that the USSR was (and is) not a member of FAO.

7. Martin Kriesberg, *International Organizations and Agricultural Development,* Foreign Agricultural Report 131 (US Department of Agriculture, November 1984), 48.

8. Wayne Moyer, 'FAO Is a Structure of Power: The Reality of Its Limitations,' paper delivered at the annual meeting of the Midwest Political Science Association (April 1986).

9. Kriesberg, *op cit,* Ref 7, 121.

10. World Food Programme, *World Food Programme Basic Documents* 4th ed (Rome: WFP, September 1978), 55.

11. See the *Agreement Establishing the International Fund for Agricultural Development* (Rome: IFAD, 30 November 1977) and *Lending Policies and Criteria* (Rome: IFAD, December 1978).

12. *Articles of Agreement,* Article 7, section 1, [d], [i and ii].

13. International Fund for Agricultural Development, *Annual Report—1984* (Rome: IFAD, May 1985), 37.

14. Robert J. Berg, 'Donor Evaluations: What Is and What Could Be,' a paper prepared for the International Conference on the Role of Evaluation in National Agricultural Research Systems, held in Singapore, 7–9 July 1986, 25.

15. A report of the UN's Joint Inspection Unit, October 1985, 24.

16. John Gerard Ruggie, 'The United States and the United Nations: Toward a New Realism,' *International Organization* 39, no. 2 (Spring 1985), 353.

17. At the 1986 meeting of the World Food Council in Rome, a document issued for review and discussion was based on one section of the report of the advisory group: 'Recommendations and Suggestions for the Future,' WFC/1986/5 (14 March 1986).

18. A person who refereed this paper responded to our question as follows: 'No one. Would that leave a vacuum of the sort nature would abhor?'

19. John Locke, *Federalist Papers,* 10 and 51.

16

NGOs and the UN System in Complex Humanitarian Emergencies: Conflict or Cooperation?

Andrew S. Natsios

This article explores the evolving relationship between the United Nations (UN) system and nongovernmental organisations (NGOs) in responding to complex humanitarian emergencies, and describes the two sets of actors, their organisational cultures, governance and mandates. It examines why the two sets of organisations have been drawn into a closer collaboration in dealing with civil conflicts and famines, how that interaction is working from both an operational and policy perspective and whether both are suited as currently constituted to respond to ongoing challenges. What are the unique institutional competencies and weaknesses each brings to relief responses? How is the friction between the UN and NGOs manifested in their diverse missions, operational styles and organisational cultures?

This essay focuses on operational and organisational cooperation between NGOs and the UN system, but not on the role of the military or the media in the humanitarian response system, subjects that have been well covered elsewhere.[1] Although operational NGOs in particular have been increasing their activity in policy and advocacy work in complex emergencies, this essay also does not address this work, which would require another essay in itself.

In Africa, the Balkans, the Middle East and the former Soviet Union, the growing number of failed states has produced a widening level of chaos to which NGOs and the UN have tried to respond. However, even the most charitable assessment must conclude that their responses have had mixed results. These complex humanitarian emergencies are defined by five common characteristics: the deterioration or complete collapse of central government authority; ethnic or religious conflict and widespread

Reprinted from *Third World Quarterly,* Vol. 16, No. 3, 1995, by permission of the publisher. © 1995.

human rights abuses; episodic food insecurity, frequently deteriorating into mass starvation; macroeconomic collapse involving hyperinflation, massive unemployment and net decreases in GNP; and mass population movements of displaced people and refugees escaping conflict or searching for food. This instability does not respect national boundaries and frequently spills over into neighbouring countries, many of which are themselves unstable. The spreading chaos does not appear to be subsiding and presents the international community with a major challenge.

Some observers have argued that these emergencies have caused a shift of increasingly scarce resources away from sustainable development to life-saving humanitarian interventions. The amount of funding provided by the United States Agency for International Development (USAID) to UN organisations, the International Organization for Migrations (IOM), the International Committee of the Red Cross (ICRC) and NGOs for relief interventions in complex humanitarian emergencies has risen dramatically beginning in the late 1980s. In 1989 the Office of Foreign Disaster Assistance (OFDA) and Food for Peace (FFP), both USAID offices, provided $297 million in cash and food grants for humanitarian relief; by 1993 that had increased to $1.2 billion.[2]

Funding for relief work is derived from four US government accounts: the OFDA, Title II of P.L. 480, Section 416 food aid (from the Department of Agriculture), and the refugee programme budget (in the State Department). Much of the actual increase during this period has been in food aid, which would probably not have been used for development purposes, and which is now in precipitous decline. These funds would not have been used for sustainable development, which is not as politically popular as disaster relief in the US Congress or among the American people. This ambivalence over development assistance is reflected in Washington's relative contribution to relief efforts compared to other developed countries. The USA proportionally provides the tenth highest level of relief assistance among OECD countries, although it trails at 20th place in development assistance. It is not that relief funding is so high, it is that development assistance is so low.[3]

A complex response system has evolved to spend this money and respond to these emergencies, more by accident than design; it is composed of three sets of institutional actors: NGOs, UN organisations and the International Red Cross movement.

Nongovernmental Organisations

NGOs are perhaps the most complex and diverse of these three sets of actors, particularly those involved in complex humanitarian emergencies. Although there are 1,500 NGOs registered with the UN system as having observer status, only 400 are registered with USAID, a process necessary for them to receive US government grants.[4]

When Operation Restore Hope was deployed to Somalia in December 1992, there were 40 international NGOs working in the country. In November 1993, 76 NGOs had mailboxes at the UN High Commissioner for Refugees (UNHCR) offices at the Rwandan refugee camps in Goma, Zaire.[5] These NGOs were almost entirely based in the Western democracies. Although a mailbox in Goma is certainly an indication of some activity, these numbers are misleading. Many of these nongovernmental organisations provided services in Goma and Somalia on a modest scale for a few months and then left. Many others delivered gifts in kind—such as pharmaceuticals and clothing—to operational NGOs which then provided them to people in the refugee camps. Others are the national offices of the same international NGO: for example, Médicins Sans Frontières has national chapters in Spain, France, Belgium and the Netherlands, and members of these chapters worked together at Goma.

In short, most NGOs are not involved in relief. There are perhaps 20 in the USA and another 20 in Europe that work in complex emergencies. This work is sustained, technically sound and widespread enough to have an impact on the situation on the ground. Of these 40 NGOs, perhaps 10 UN and another 10 European NGOs receive 75% of all the public funds spent by NGOs in complex emergencies. The US NGOs received 76% of all cash grants to NGOs for relief purposes from the US government in fiscal year (FY) 1993 and over 87% of all food aid for relief purposes in FY 1993.[6] The European Union gave 65% of all relief grants to 20 nongovernmental organisations in FY 1994.

These relief NGOs frequently specialise in one or more of the five activities that are commonly understood to compose the relief discipline: food distribution, shelter, water, sanitation and medical care. To this may be added the rehabilitation efforts to bring a society traumatised by a complex emergency to minimum self-sufficiency: animal husbandry, agriculture and primary health care. Perhaps half of these NGOs perform relief work exclusively, whereas the other half work in both relief and development. The larger development NGOs (CARE, Catholic Relief Services, World Vision, Save the Children, and Oxfam/UK) have the added advantage in many complex emergencies of having had development programmes and staff to run them in the countries before the onset of the emergency. This advantage gives them a familiarity with the culture, ethnic groups and development programmes of the country as well as with indigenous staff.

Since the Ethiopian famine of 1985—a watershed event for most of the 10 major NGOs that work in relief—a quiet revolution has taken place in doctrine and practice between relief and development.[7] Traditional relief efforts were commodity-driven and logistically-based, with little programmatic, economic or developmental thought given to how the relief effort might be more than simply pushing down death rates and saving lives. Most NGOs, as a matter of policy, will now try to integrate into their relief work developmental components particularly focused in agriculture, microenterprise, primary health care, reforestation and road construction. This is done through food or cash for which recipients are assigned a specific project that community leaders have determined is of longer-term importance in the area. Much more effort now is spent on examining the economics of what is happening in famine, with the major food NGOs conducting household, food price and market surveys as a regular part of their relief interventions. A recent study of the USAID/OFDA effort in the Somalia emergency showed that 50% of its relief grants to NGOs contained developmental interventions.[8]

NGOs derive their financial support from both public and private sources. A few will accept no public sector money, while others get between 60%–70% of their income from donor governments.[9] Although UN funds and programmes have increasingly been making relief grants to NGOs, these grants do not yet approach the level of donor government grant assistance, a condition that may shortly change if present trends continue. NGO private funding resources come primarily from mass media appeals (most notably television), direct mail and major donor government contributions. US law requires an NGO to raise at least 20% of its aggregate resources privately to be eligible to apply for government funding. Most donor governments have created disaster relief offices—such as Agency for International Development's OFDA, Food for Peace and the European Community Humanitarian Office (ECHO) of the European Union— to provide grant assistance to NGOs, the ICRC and UN organisations.

How these NGOs are organised and governed affects their work. They have chosen four models to organise themselves internationally. First, all began and some remain with one headquarters based entirely in one country, even though they work internationally in others, for example, the International Rescue Committee and the International Medical Corps. Second, some have many autonomous national chapters with independent field organisations, each reporting back to the home offices. This means several offices may work independently of each other in the same country, for example Save the Children and Oxfam. Third, some have chosen to create many national fundraising offices that pool their collective funds and spend them through a single worldwide field organisation, which is indigenously staffed and managed, such as World Vision International and the International Federation of Red Cross and Red Crescent Societies. A variation of this is a hybrid of the second and third models, in which each national headquarters has its own field organisation but is assigned specific emergencies in which to work by a central international organisation to avoid competition in the same country, e.g. CARE. Fourth, others only work through indigenous local NGOs that are not part of their organisational

structure; they have no independent operational capacity in the field outside such indigenous partner agencies as the Church World Service,
Oxfam/US, and Christian Children's Fund.

Each model has particular advantages and drawbacks. The first model
tend to be the fastest in operations and decision making and the least bureaucratic; the second tends to be the most flexible, internally competitive
and, at times, organisationally contentious; the third tends to have deeper
community roots and capacity to aggregate large amounts of money
rapidly for a particular relief programme; and the fourth has the deepest
community roots but does not have a field staff that it may direct to a particular emergency and so lacks flexibility and quality control.

NGOs are governed by boards of directors that tend to reflect the particular culture, history and mandates of the organisations concerned. The
board of directors of the International Medical Corps, a US NGO that spe-
cialises in emergency medical care in conflict, for instance, has been dominated by the medical professionals who founded it. Catholic bishops serving on the board of directors of Catholic Relief Services is another
example. Since most NGOs raise money among a particular market segment of the American people, they must design their field programmes
around the interests of their constituency or they may not survive. Under
the NGO standards required by InterAction (the American nongovernmental organisation partnership association) of its 160 members, NGO bylaws
must provide for term limits to ensure rotation of board members, require
some racial and gender diversity, avoid appointing relatives of NGO ex-
ecutives, and limit the number of senior staff who serve on their boards.
A similar set of standards exists for European and Third World NGOs
which are members of the International Council of Voluntary Agencies
(ICVA), the European equivalent of InterAction. Most major relief NGOs
belong to either of these two associations and most try to conform to these
standards. Their boards of directors approve annual budgets; hire; review
and fire the chief executive officer; and control major corporate policy decisions. Some are involved in operations, approving, for example, each
new programme initiative and advocacy position on public policy taken by
the organisation.

The rash of recent emergencies has created the impression that NGOs
are in the business of ambulance chasing as they appear on the scene in
large numbers to provide assistance. This impression is somewhat accurate. To attract private contributions to run their programmes, the NGOs
must make use of news events and media coverage, which raise public
awareness in a way that no paid advertisement could ever achieve. The
more dramatic the event, the greater the media coverage, and the greater
the ease of fundraising around it. Overhead rates for nongovernmental organisations are one of the few constant measures of success used to judge
their worthiness as charities in the annual rankings of NGO efficiency in

such publications as *Money Magazine* and the *Wall Street Journal*. These rankings affect NGO fundraising success in a self-reinforcing cycle that ultimately puts a high premium on early and visible involvement in relief operations. Fundraising around highly visible humanitarian crises raises more money at a lower cost than any other form of advertising or publicity. Certain NGOs have been attacked for what some critics call 'relief pornography'—raising money by showing scenes of starving children that wrench the donor's heart and portray a sense of helplessness. This distorts an organisation's judgment on where to work and when, but it is not an easily addressed problem since without funding they cannot work at all.

Nongovernmental organisations are accountable to their boards, but accountability to their contributors and beneficiaries is more tenuous. Unlike a profitmaking business where customers can judge the quality of the service or product that they have purchased, the beneficiaries of the NGO contributions in a relief intervention have no regular way of registering individually their approval or dissatisfaction to donors of an organisation, or for that matter ICRC or UN performance. Likewise, private donors have no direct experience with the quality of the work that their contributions support. Good marketing does not necessarily ensure good programming. As a general proposition, NGOs make an effort in good faith—given the altruistic motivation of most of their workers and managers—to involve the people they serve in the field with how resources are spent. Community participation is an elemental axiom of NGO work. The wide variation in the quality of field programmes and the technical competence of staffs is a testament to the limitations of the existing system of accountability. Larger NGOs—the combined budgets of CARE, World Vision and Catholic Relief Services, the three largest NGOs, exceed $1 billion—have developed many of the management information, evaluation and control systems of private sector corporations to monitor quality in their projects.

Perhaps the most encouraging recent trend in the NGO community has been the growing presence of indigenous nongovernmental organisations working in their own countries to provide services during complex emergencies. In Liberia, during the worst period of chaos in the capital city, Monrovia, in the summer and autumn of 1990, all UN agencies, international NGOs, and even the ICRC had evacuated. The only Western presence at the time was a team of five operational staff from OFDA to run a relief effort to feed and provide medical care to 500,000 people in desperate conditions as four undisciplined militias fought for control of the city. The OFDA team enlisted the support of the local community to run the relief effort by forming an indigenous Liberian NGO that effectively distributed food, water and medical services. While the OFDA team withdrew six months later, the indigenous NGO did not and it continues its work today. The ICRC formed Somali women's committees to run hundreds of open air soup kitchens in Somalia in 1992, which fed hundreds of thousands of people during the worst of the chaos. These women's committees, in-dependent of the ICRC, resurrected the moribund school system of Mo-gadishu and put 500 teachers and 20,000 students back in the classroom by using ICRC food aid to pay the teachers. The World Food Programme (WFP) worked with CARE and gave grants of local currency generated by the monetisation of food aid in Somalia in 1993 and 1994 to local Somali NGOs, which from all reports were quite effective on smaller scale pro-jects. Bosnian Muslim NGOs have been the most effective in providing as-sistance during the conflict because they have been willing to take risks that international NGOs would never consider. Also they know the terrain and feel the suffering themselves. These indigenous NGOs are perhaps the fastest growing part of the relief response system and provide an intuitive understanding of local conditions that international NGOs could not hope to equal.

The UN System

Four UN organisations have become such visible players in most complex humanitarian emergencies that describing their functions and mandates will describe most if not all of the operational work of the entire UN sys-tem in relief operations. They are the World Food Programme, the Office of the United Nations High Commissioner for Refugees, the United Na-tions Children's Fund (UNICEF) and the United Nations Development Programme (UNDP). The first three are clearly the strongest and most in-dispensable. Although UNDP technically has the mandate to manage UN emergency operations in the field, it has been unwilling or perhaps unable to manage and technically fulfil its assigned role, and it has not distin-guished itself by the work it has done either in quality or speed. The cre-ation of the Department of Humanitarian Affairs (DHA) in the UN secre-tariat in December 1991 to coordinate UN work in complex emergencies is testimony to UNDP's failure—coordination had been the assigned task of the UNDP for two decades. A half dozen other UN agencies, seeing the movement of donor resources to complex emergencies, have flung them-selves into the organisational chaos, but they arguably lack serious opera-tional capacity or experience, and have only limited relief resources.

The WFP functions as the food aid agency of the UN system, provid-ing a central coordinating role in developing crop production estimates, food aid requirements and logistics planning for major relief operations. At $1.8 billion its annual budget is the largest of the big four. It signed its first worldwide NGO cooperative agreement for relief operations in February 1995 with Catholic Relief Services and it is now engaged in negotiations over similar agreements with three other NGOs. WFP has had only a lim-ited history of work with international NGOs, a historical reality that it is fast overcoming. Although WFP is organisationally subordinate to the United Nations and the Food and Agriculture Organization (FAO), it has become virtually independent since the 1991 reforms.

UNICEF's special mandate is to focus on the relief and development needs of women and children, which has made it the focal point among the big four UN agencies for emergency medical interventions, mass inoculation campaigns for children, water and sanitation programmes and therapeutic feeding programmes for severely malnourished children in emergencies. This work has placed it for some time in closer contact with NGOs at the village level than any other of the big four organisations. UNICEF is the only one of the UN entities with a substantial popular following in donor countries and a contributor base that provides significant private support for its work.

UNHCR has the longest history of the big four funds and programmes; its predecessor was created during the 1920s under the League of Nations. It also has the longest history of work with NGOs and spends the largest amount of money—at least $300 million annually—in grants to 130 NGOs, many of them indigenous. Although the bulk of its funding still goes to host governments to run refugee camps, the rush of events and the need for speed has made the NGO-UNHCR partnership more intimate and frequent in recent years, particularly in complex emergencies.[10]

UNDP, the development programme of the UN system, does only limited work with international or indigenous NGOs in emergencies. By tradition, as well as General Assembly guidelines, the UNDP resident representative in each country normally acts as the UN's resident coordinator with pre-eminent executive authority to coordinate other UN agencies. This authority also extends to disasters, although UNDP field representatives have been remarkably unprepared and unwilling to perform this function, with a few notable exceptions—for example Michael Priestley's strong leadership in Sudan during the civil war as UNDP resident representative was of consistently high quality. UNDP has occasionally funded certain public service projects in complex emergencies, such as managing airport facilities, city water and electrical systems, and other public services needed to support life, particularly in urban areas. The UNDP niche in the provision of public services in complex emergencies is the least developed and most needed of functions of the UN system.

The International Red Cross System

The International Red Cross movement arose out of the horrific conditions on the battlefield at Solferino in 1859, and its mandate has now been extended to alleviate suffering during conventional armed conflicts. The movement is the oldest, most disciplined and best organised of the three sets of actors of the international relief response system, with a worldwide budget of about $600 million. The ICRC also conveys family messages across conflict lines, reunites families separated by war and protects prisoners of war.[11] Its budget is primarily funded by annual block grants from donor governments, and to a lesser degree national Red Cross and Red Crescent societies, in much the same way as the UN funds and programmes obtain their funding. The ICRC operates under a set of inviolate principles that have been integrated into the nine governing principles of the national Red Cross and Red Crescent societies. These include absolute political neutrality in a conflict; indeed, the Red Cross symbol is the visual embodiment of the principle of neutrality in war. ICRC operating procedures require that they work on both sides of any armed conflict and that they respond to and practise complete transparency in all operations, notifying both sides each time a convoy departs, arrives or is delayed. These procedures sometimes put them at odds with NGOs and the UN agencies, and it encourages their insularity as an organisation, although their rules make it possible for them to work in armed conflicts where few other institutions dare go.

The age, doctrine, funding mechanism and mandates of the ICRC set it apart from both the UN system and the NGO community. Other than UNHCR, no other humanitarian relief organisation has a mandate assigned to it under international law, as are the cases of UNHCR under the UN Charter and the ICRC under the Geneva Conventions and Additional Protocols. The ICRC is an international organisation, not an NGO, and yet it is outside the UN system. As an international organisation, the ICRC more jealously guards its autonomy and prerogatives than any of the other institutional actors—UN or NGO—and resists coordination, but it shares information, sometimes reluctantly, and will attend organising meetings. For the most part, however, it must be discussed separately from either nongovernmental or intergovernmental organisations.

Collaboration of NGOs with the 'Big Four'

The collaboration of NGOs and the major four funds and programmes active in the humanitarian arena has increased dramatically over a short time. In most complex emergencies, host governments do not exist or exist in such anaemic form that they are ineffective as an interlocutor for the UN system, which deals with NGOs increasingly as the first responders. UN agencies have traditionally focused their attention on governments, their primary constituency, while NGOs focus on grassroots development at the village level and cooperate with developing country governments only at the regional or provincial level during emergency operations. Under this traditional paradigm, UN agencies viewed NGOs as subcontractors in a clearly subordinate position—paid for services performed—not as equal partners with unique capacities, particularly in humanitarian relief operations. This has caused the resentment by UN agencies of nongovernmental organisations when they do not act in the way expected, and by NGOs when they are treated as contractors rather than equal partners.

The UN system and the NGO community have made some progress at improved collaboration as the international humanitarian response system has matured. The Department of Humanitarian Affairs initiated monthly coordination meetings with NGOs in New York and Geneva to exchange information and discuss policy disputes in complex emergencies. UNHCR is well under way with its Partnership in Action (PARinAC) initiative to develop an operational and policy framework for working with NGOs. In complex emergencies, UN field offices have provided a natural coordination mechanism for nongovernmental organisations and UN organisations that has at least improved the exchange of information among the response agencies.

This recent UN and NGO marriage is more a relationship of convenience arranged by the press of events and overbearing donor governments than a passionate romance. The partners remain distrustful and moody when working together and are uncomfortable with the contrived arrangement. This discomfort is not based on an absence of familiarity with one another; they have good reason to be uncomfortable. The two sets of institutions compete for scarce donor government resources, speak to quite different constituencies that are frequently hostile to each other, recruit different kinds of people to work for them and move at distinctly different speeds. One institution measures success by whether host governments are pleased, the other by whether public and private donors are happy. One is more centralised, the other highly decentralised. NGO field directors generally have much more authority over the programme and management than their UN field counterparts, a situation about which many of the latter complain a great deal. One encourages risk-taking (some would argue cowboyism) and informality; the other advocates regular procedures and bureaucratic propriety. There are some overlapping functional claims between UN organisations and NGOs in complex emergencies, which means turf wars over competing roles and mandates. The UN system is more feudal then integrated, while the four agencies work essentially independently of one another.

While UN agencies and NGOs may wish for a discrete divorce or at least separation, in the chaos of complex emergencies they need each other more than they may want to admit. Each brings unique mandates and potential competencies to the relief response discipline, which are essential if collapsed societies are to be assisted in restoring some measure of self-sufficiency. The challenge now is to reach a consensus about who does what best to clarify institutional mandates and limitations, and better define roles.

As a general proposition, NGOs do their relief and development work at the grassroots level, which is labour intensive from a staff perspective, both expatriate and indigenous. Thus, they tend to have large field staffs that can carry out complex operations in remote areas. Philosophically, they are committed to empowering people at the lowest level of social organisation—the family and the village—to work collectively towards the sort of social and economic services that would typically be run by municipal government; however, NGOs are sometimes inconsistent in following their own ideology. Some services succeed more than others. These include community-based health care, primary and secondary education, agricultural extension work, water and sanitation projects, small-scale enterprise typically through cooperatives or small loans, road and bridge construction, and environmental programmes, particularly reforestation. These are the same operational and sectoral skills NGOs use in their relief response operations.

These strengths are at the same time weaknesses. The greatest single endemic weakness of NGOs is their reluctance to cede managerial or programme autonomy towards the goal of greater strategic coherence or managerial efficiency. Most lack either the will or the self-discipline to surrender autonomy and integrate their work with other actors. Their focus on the village and neighbourhood has been at the expense of dealing with national problems of governance, economic reform, planning and policy—which, when done badly, can cancel out overnight any grassroots successes their programmes may have enjoyed. NGOs have a problem of scale in their field programmes; they produce patches of green in barren landscapes, patches that are small, fragile and usually unconnected to each other.

UN funds and programmes are comparatively weak in field operations, with a modest presence usually in the country capital. They work under the UN Charter with the host government in each country. Most UN assistance then moves through host government ministries where UN organisations cultivate relationships with senior policy makers and managers. They are not heavily involved with grassroots organisations, with the possible exception of UNICEF because of the nature of its mandate. This means that the UN is much more familiar with central government bureaucracies and public services than most NGOs.

These two quite different sets of NGO and UN missions mean that when countries sink into civil war or ethnic conflict, their relief roles not unnaturally reflect their missions and unique competencies; they do what they know best. The UN tries to negotiate country-wide access in conflict areas, exemptions from customs duties for relief commodities and protection agreements for relief workers from the violence of the conflicts—essential tasks at which NGOs have little experience or success. UN agencies are reluctant to violate the sovereignty of any of the organisations' constituencies and member states. This recalcitrance is not merely a function of the UN Charter, but also the prejudice of some UN staff, who are drawn from the educated elites of developing countries and retain a suspicion of Western colonial ambitions reasserting themselves under the guise of humanitarian interventionism. Only when the Security Council has voted for resolutions permitting a violation of state sovereignty will the system respond. NGOs have fewer inhibitions, except where they are working on both sides of a conflict and risk censure or danger from the national government. In fact, NGOs have violated state sovereignty over extended periods of time in at least four civil wars in Africa, Iraq and Bosnia. This same paradigm functions with respect to advocacy on human rights and diplomatic issues: UN staff are hesitant to criticise publicly a member state during a civil war, while NGOs do this more often in the context of their normal advocacy efforts.

There have been four reform efforts over the past three years to force UN agencies to work in a more cohesive and integrated way in complex emergencies. These reforms may have the combined effect of encouraging the UN system to design a single defined strategy in each complex emergency. NGOs look, however reluctantly, to the UN or provide some measure of operational coordination during complex emergencies, and these reforms strengthen the UN's capacity for doing so.

This coordination function was the major rationale for the creation of the DHA, led by an under-secretary-general in New York, the first of these reforms. Although DHA has made some progress in fulfilling its mandate, there are intrinsic institutional limitations built into the UN system itself that make this task unenviable. Although the secretary-general (to which the under-secretary-general who heads DHA reports) has legal authority over the big four UN programmes, they do what they want in practice. Their policy, budgets, personnel and procurement are self-contained, controlled internally by these independent UN organisations. Their governing boards reflect donor and recipient country politics more than those of the central bureaucracy at the secretariat or of the secretary-general himself, which are not necessarily the same thing. The field offices of UN organisations in emergencies are not necessarily responsive to the special representative of the secretary-general or of the representative of DHA who is theoretically in charge of the coordination of the UN's relief operations in an emergency. These field offices report back to their organisational headquarters and not to DHA directors in the field. Agency field directors are not deliberately uncooperative. However, the DHA representative does not have the institutional authority to resolve any disputes over policy, management and strategy among the big four in the field except by intellect or personality. This is not easily remedied in the absence of unlikely changes in the basic authority of the secretary-general.

The second of these reforms was proposed by the Nordic countries and approved by the General Assembly in 1993. The reform gives the Economic and Social Council (ECOSOC) oversight over the policy, budget and management of the big four funds and programmes. This administrative innovation may begin to put some pressure on these agencies to work more intimately together in emergency situations and force some measure of accountability when they do not. It remains to be seen whether this innovation will have salutary operational or strategic consequences.

The third reform is now begin drafted within the UN secretariat. It would encourage a greater degree of information sharing, joint policy and strategy development, and overall management among the under-secretary-generals in charge of the political, military and humanitarian functions in the departments of Humanitarian Affairs, Peace-keeping Operations and Political Affairs during complex emergencies. There has been until now no formal mechanism for integrating these functions in headquarters, a situation that has not encouraged coordination among these three functions in the field. If this reform is successful, it may lead to the UN equivalent of Washington's National Security Council as a coordination and management mechanism for more coherent direction in field operations during complex humanitarian emergencies.

The fourth and perhaps most important innovation has been the creation of the Inter-Agency Standing Committee (IASC): a coordination mechanism chaired by the UN under-secretary-general for Humanitarian Affairs. Created in January 1992, it is composed of the 'big four' UN organisations: the World Health Organization; the Food and Agriculture Organization (which should not have been included in the group because of its lack of expertise and operational capacity in disaster response); the ICRC (the Federation of Red Cross and Crescent Societies); and the International Organization for Migrations; and representatives of the European and US NGOs. The IASC meets quarterly, but only its principals are allowed to attend. Between meetings, working groups do much of the staff work on specific issues. This mechanism has improved the flow of information, but has been unable to design comprehensive strategies or enforce discipline in the response system. It has two major weaknesses. The donor aid agencies that fund much of this work are not members, and DHA has not had the bureaucratic power to force integration of UN organisations. It is, however, a step in the right direction.

Conclusion

Perhaps the single most serious challenge to the international community is developing and implementing strategies for dealing with failed states or preventing their collapse in the first instance. There is by no means a consensus among donor governments, NGOs, the ICRC and UN agencies on the need for a unified strategy in each complex emergency. Some argue that a thousand flowers should bloom and every agency should do its own thing. Information is shared reluctantly if donors insist, but nothing more. Given the gap between resources and needs, resources need to be leveraged to increase their influence. Conflicting strategies and objectives, or their abysmal absence, in complex emergencies with multiple actors frequently cancel each other out. Conversely, a single coherent strategy could allow the aggregation of sufficient resources to change the course of a conflict. Without clear objectives, the managers of the international response system will never know whether they have achieved their goals. Such achievements could convince wary parliamentarians, media and public opinion in donor countries that the heavy investment of public funds in relief response serves some successful purpose other than just keeping people alive so that they can die later. Given the declining donor resources for development and reconstruction after conflicts, as many developmental components as possible need to be built into relief responses. All these arguments suggest the need for a single unified strategy. Neither NGOs nor UN agencies are in a position to impose this sort of discipline. DHA, which might logically be charged with such a mission, has neither the political clout nor the resources to inject some discipline into this unruly, feudal response system.

While the UN system and particularly DHA will argue that their coordination work in complex emergencies amounts to a strategic plan, few of the actors—UN organisations or NGOs—wish to be coordinated, much less conform to a single strategy. Coordination has many meanings in management theory. In the present context of complex emergencies, it has become a mechanism for combining the wish lists of the UN and NGO relief agencies, even if the programmes have little chance of being funded, or even contradict each other. It can become a lowest common denominator rather than a higher standard of policy or performance. Coordination in this context is not particularly helpful. It certainly does not solve the strategy problem.

Even if all actors in the response system agreed that some unified strategy were essential, one serious impediment remains. The highly decentralised, feudal nature of the response system itself is made up of the UN system, with three central headquarters staff directorates in the secretariat (humanitarian affairs, peacekeeping operations and political affairs); the big four UN organisations (UNDP, UNICEF, WFP and UNHCR); 40 major relief NGOs; the ICRC (and the Red Cross Movement, which is an organisationally discrete entity); the military units making up international forces (all of which report back operationally to their military command structures in their home countries rather than to the UN force commander in the field); the US State Department and foreign ministries of other interested countries; and the foreign disaster response offices of donor countries (OFDA and ECHO). If one were present at the creation of this Byzantine system, one could not have created a more complex and convoluted structure.

Wildavsky and Pressman argue persuasively that the more organisational entities involved in a decision-making process, the greater the opportunity for delay, if not paralysis.[12] They point out that the mathematical probability of reaching a decision on a public policy issue is quite low when dozens of organisations have veto power or the power to delay a decision. Maximum feasible participation in decision making, given the lengthy list of actors, equates to operational chaos, deadly delay and inevitable failure in disaster response. It is noteworthy that the most successful humanitarian response effort in the post–Cold War era—Kurdistan in 1991—initially involved no UN organisations or UN peacekeeping forces but rather three military commands that had just fought in the Gulf War together, one donor country response office and no more than half a dozen NGOs. Limited organisational participation in this context translated into operational success.

Absent is a complete reorganisation of the relief response structure, which is politically and administratively infeasible and perhaps even undesirable from a policy perspective, but we must focus on incremental reform of the existing humanitarian order. The most feasible and salutary changes that might now be made would be to aggregate relief actors within each organisational sector. The United Nations would centralise authority for the formulation of a single UN strategy in one entity, which after all was the original concept behind DHA. NGOs would similarly organise themselves through InterAction and ICVA. Donor disaster response offices would do the same. Then a small group of representatives, one for each set of actors (UN, NGO, ICRC, military representatives if peacekeeping troops were involved and donor aid agencies), could meet and design a strategy. This ultimately would involve a workable entity of no more than half a dozen people. Any serious attempt at aggregation would require a commitment by the actors to cede much organisational autonomy, something that is now jealously guarded. Such structural reform would require a high degree of organisational discipline and perhaps even some sanctions for organisations which refuse to participate in good faith. This reform stretches even the most expansive definition of coordination, perhaps the most abused and ill-defined word in the disaster response vocabulary. It is perhaps the best we can do under the circumstances.

The response system cannot continue to function as it does now; it is on the verge of breakdown. With the exception of military forces, all the organisations are seriously overcommitted in coping with the demands being placed on them. The rolling tide of complex emergencies is moving so rapidly that organisations have been drawn into each new major crisis before completing work on the last. The emotional toll that these emergencies are taking on relief staff cannot be calculated quantitatively, but it is significant. What is the psychological toll on staff watching the genocide in Rwanda or the atrocities in Bosnia? This has meant that NGOs and UN organisations are increasingly sending inexperienced staff to the field to run massive operations that even seasoned managers would find intimidating. This work is not a nine-to-five, Monday to Friday job. A rationalisation of the existing response system would progress some way towards relieving at least some of the organisational stress at a time when institutions are at a breaking point. More importantly, these reforms would increase, but not guarantee, the chances for designing successful strategies for managing and perhaps resolving these crises.

The marriage of convenience between NGOs and the UN system in relief responses over time may become comfortable enough that *ad hoc* arrangements will work, even if a passionate love affair never occurs. For most NGOs and most UN organisations, the marriage is a recent affair, beginning sometime over the last half decade. The organisational cultures are understanding each other better, perhaps at times even respecting each other. Given the horrific circumstances in the field in which this marriage of convenience has been consummated, problems are hardly surprising. Both sets of actors need each other, and that organisational need may be the key to the success of the relationship. The rationalisation of the design and execution of a unified strategy will increase the chances for success of the responses to complex emergencies. Nothing works better than success—however it is defined—to cement a partnership. There have been precious few successes, which has resulted in name-calling and finger-pointing among the actors. Success encourages collaboration and cooperation, failure discourages it. As the system matures, the marriage of convenience may ultimately work, but it will take time and patience.

Notes

1. See Johathan Benthall, *Disasters, Relief and the Meida,* London: Tauris, 1993; and Andrew Natsios, 'International Humanitarian Response System', *Parameters,* Spring 1995, pp. 68–81.

2. See *Office of Foreign Disaster Assistance Annual Report, FY 1991,* Washington, DC: Government Printing Office, 1991, pp. 8–9. However, little of this increased funding was initiated by the Bush administration, with the exception of the Kurdish emergency, where a special appropriation was requested. Congress offered the increased funding in the face of escalating disasters frequently in special appropriations outside the budget cycle. Without this rising tide of emergencies, appropriations for development assistance would have been no higher. Development assistance has never been a particularly popular programme in the US Congress, but disaster relief (cash and food) continues to enjoy broad congressional and pub-

lic support across party and ideological divides. In the case of food assistance for relief, much of the additional resources for complex emergencies has come from the Section 416 programme of the US Department of Agriculture, food aid which would probably not have been programmed for development purposes. With the depletion of Section 416, surplus stocks in FY 1993 and changes in the agricultural price supports that ensure that this depletion will not be restocked, increased food aid for emergencies will undoubtedly come at the expense of food for development under Title II of the Office of Food for Peace. The World Food Programme's (WFP) relief and development programmes have traditionally received equal shares of resources until the late 1980s when an appreciable shift began. At present, relief receives two-thirds of total resources, while the rest is programmed to development. This increased food aid for relief has not resulted in an actual decline in food aid for development; relief sources pledged by donor governments have increased markedly.

3. See Department of Humanitarian Affairs rankings of ODC countries' response to consolidated humanitarian appeals.

4. See AID 1994 Annual Report, entitled *Voluntary Foreign Aid Programs, Bureau for Humanitarian Response,* Washington, DC: Government Printing Office, 1994, pp. 70–97.

5. I visited the UNHCR headquarters at Goma in November 1994 and counted the mailboxes.

6. This figure is an estimate based on the grant-making experience of OFDA and the Office of Food for Peace. Four NGOs (CARE, Catholic Relief Services, World Vision and the Adventist Development and Relief Agency) received 87% of all NGO food aid grants for relief and development under Title II of P.L. 480. See Office of Foreign Disaster Assistance rankings of cash grants to NGOs for FY 1993.

7. See Mary Anderson & Peter Woodrow, *Rising From the Ashes: Disaster Response to Development,* Boulder, CO: Westview Press, 1989.

8. See Refugee Policy Group, *Humanitarian Aid in Somalia: The Role of the Office of US Foreign Disaster Assistance (OFDA) 1990–1994,* Washington, DC: Refugee Policy Group, November 1994, p. 27.

9. *Voluntary Foreign Aid Programs,* pp. 70–97.

10. UN High Commissioner for Refugees, *Refugees,* 97, 1994, p. 8. This issue is devoted to NGOs and UNHCR, with particular emphasis on PARinAC.

11. See International Committee of the Red Cross, *ICRC 1993 Annual Report,* Geneva; ICRC, 1993, pp. 273, 277.

12. Aaron Wildavsky & Jeffrey Pressman, *Implementation,* Berkeley, CA: University of California Press, 1979, pp. 105–108, 147.

17

Strengthening Compliance with International Environmental Accords

Harold K. Jacobson & Edith Brown Weiss

I n June 1992, heads of government gathered in Rio de Janeiro at the United Nations Conference on Environment and Development (UNCED) to launch a major international effort to achieve environmentally sustainable development. International environmental accords or binding legal instruments are an important part of this strategy. Twenty years earlier, when the United Nations Conference on the Human Environment was held in Stockholm, there were only a few dozen multilateral treaties dealing with environmental issues. By 1992, there were more than nine hundred international legal instruments (mostly binding) that either were fully directed to environmental protection or had more than one important provision addressing the issue.[1] In the early 1990s, about a dozen important multilateral negotiations on new international legal instruments were occurring at more or less the same time, and several of those were concluded prior to or at the Rio conference. The United Nations Framework Convention on Climate Change and the Convention on Biological Diversity were signed at Rio, as was Agenda 21—an approximately 850-page text that sets forth strategies for the many complex issues involved in integrating environmental protection and economic development. Yet we know very little about national implementation and compliance with the treaties and other international legal instruments that have been negotiated, despite their importance and growing number.

In 1990, working within the framework of the Social Science Research Council's Committee on Research on the Human Dimensions of Global Environmental Change, we launched a research consortium to explore how and the extent to which countries implement and comply with

Reprinted from *Global Governance: A Review of Multilateralism and International Organizations,* Vol. 1, No. 2 (May–August 1995), pp. 119–148. Copyright © 1995 by Lynne Rienner Publishers, Inc. Used with permission of the publisher.

international environmental treaties.[2] This article presents preliminary observations derived from a project that is very much in midstream. Nevertheless, the quantitative data and written material that are now available through the project and the discussions in the project workshops provide a basis for some tentative generalizations and conclusions.

Why Study Implementation of and Compliance with International Environmental Accords?

International environmental accords—treaties and other international legally binding instruments—have the potential to transform the ways in which humanity uses the planet, the quality of lives all over the world, relations among states, the global economic system, the development paths of advanced and industrializing countries alike, and the differences between North and South. Some speculate that these accords could create international authorities with unprecedented scope and power, predicated on the economic leverage of only a few countries. These accords might impose stringent sanctions on violators or use rewards to induce countries to conform. Conforming could, moreover, reshape a country's energy production, transportation, industrial processes, agriculture, animal husbandry, settlement patterns and migration, and population-growth patterns.

Countries have already negotiated many international treaties and other agreements to protect the environment and to conserve natural resources. While some of these accords existed before the 1972 Stockholm conference, most have been negotiated since then. The rate at which important accords have been proposed and concluded is increasing. The substantive and procedural duties contained in the accords have become more stringent and comprehensive, and the range of issues subject to such accords has expanded. Calls for international treaties and other international legal instruments to protect the global environment will continue and likely accelerate. Indeed, several efforts are in progress. But even if no more accords were negotiated, it would be essential to make those that are in force work effectively.

International accords are only as effective as the respective parties make them. Effectiveness is the result not only of how governments implement accords (the formal legislation or regulations that countries adopt to comply with the accord) but also of how they comply with them (the observance of those regulations and the commitments contained in the international accord). Weak legislation can produce weak compliance, but unenforced strong legislation can have the same effect. One cannot simply read domestic legislation to determine whether countries are complying. While some claim that most states comply with most international treaties most of the time, there are reasons to believe that national implementation of and compliance with international accords are not only imperfect, but often inadequate, and that such implementation as takes place varies significantly among countries. It is not known to what extent environmental accords have or have not evoked compliance or whether the same factors that presumably motivate compliance with arms control, trade, or human rights agreements will motivate compliance with environmental accords.

There is a literature regarding compliance with international accords concerning arms control, trade, and human rights, and some of the findings in this literature may be applicable to environmental accords. In addition, a general literature exists on enforcement of international treaties and on enforcement of national environmental laws and regulations.[3] There is also a broad literature on the impact of international institutions.[4] Studies of the management of common resources offer additional valuable insights.[5]

Yet there are very few studies of the implementation of and compliance with international environmental accords. The limited studies that do exist include a notable one by the U.S. General Accounting Office that looks broadly at compliance of governments with eight international environmental accords and concludes that compliance has been low;[6] a survey of international environmental treaties and instruments prepared by the secretary-general of UNCED, which includes a brief description of accord implementation;[7] a monograph by Peter Sand on global environmental governance that focuses on the institutional design of international accords to encourage compliance;[8] and an article by Jesse H. Ausubel and David G. Victor[9] and a study by David Feldman on the characteristics of international environmental accords that facilitate implementation.[10] None of these studies focuses on factors at the national level that affect compliance, which is the focus of our study.

There has never been a systematic study of factors affecting compliance at the national level of the international environmental accords into which countries have *already* entered. Our study takes a first—but we hope large—step toward drawing from the experience of existing international environmental law those lessons that might instruct us how better to proceed in the future.

Without better knowledge about the implementation of and compliance with international accords, it is impossible to assess their effectiveness in protecting the global environment or to evaluate the merits of proposed accords. Formally binding international treaties or agreements are only one of the available instruments for dealing with global environmental issues. One cannot appropriately weigh the advantages of negotiating a treaty to obtain global environmental goals as opposed to relying on market forces or education without knowing more about what states tend to do to give effect to the provisions of treaties. Nor is it possible to make sensible suggestions about measures that might be taken to improve the implementation of and compliance with existing and proposed accords. If we understood these processes better, we should be able to design better international accords that would enhance the chances of national compliance.

The Stylized View of Compliance and Reality

A traditional, stylized view of international law might maintain that (1) countries accept treaties only when their governments have concluded that they are in their interest; (2) because of that, countries generally comply with treaties; and (3) when countries do not comply with treaties, sanctions are employed both to punish offenders and to serve as deterrents designed to encourage first-order compliance. Reality with respect to many types of treaties, particularly environmental accords, is quite different. While countries might join only treaties that they regard as in their self-interest, there are a variety of reasons countries find them in their interest, and those reasons affect their willingness and ability to comply with them. Governments may choose to accept a treaty because of a desire to jump on an international bandwagon or because of pressures from other governments with leverage over them. Or there may be domestic interests that force the issue. In some cases, countries may enter treaties without intending to modify their behavior significantly so as to comply fully. Even if they intend to comply, some countries may find it difficult or impossible, because they lack the local capacity to do so. Scattered evidence suggests that implementation of and compliance with international environmental accords are often haphazard and ragged. Parties rarely resort to adjudication of violations or employ significant sanctions against noncomplying parties. While blandishments may be used to encourage compliance, these are rarely of major proportions.

Nevertheless, as the experience with human rights treaties so vividly illustrates, over time many countries have gradually begun to do more to implement treaties and improve compliance. The force of environmental accords probably comes not from the possibility of sanctions but from the felt need to coordinate activities affecting the environment and to ensure stable and predictive patterns of behavior that will sustain the commonly held environment.

This less elegant reality of imperfect, varied, and changing implementation and compliance is the starting point for this study. The purpose of the analysis is to discover factors that lead to improved implementation and compliance with treaties that cover environmental issues. We assume that cost-benefit calculations are murky, military sanctions are out of the question, and economic sanctions are exceptional and may violate international trading arrangements. Because of those assumptions, the applicability of the literature with respect to arms control and trade is limited. That with respect to human rights is more relevant. Public goods theory may be more appropriate than game theory for the type of treaties that concerns us. We assume that the propensity of various countries to comply with different treaties will vary and change over time. Our task is to understand the factors that shape that variation and propel the change.

Assessing Implementation, Compliance, and Effectiveness

An essential first step is to have clear definitions of implementation and compliance. *Implementation* refers to measures that states take to make international accords effective in their domestic law. Some accords are self-executing; that is, they do not require national legislation to become effective. But many international accords require national legislation or regulations to become effective. Countries adopt different approaches, ranging from accounting procedures, to incentives to induce compliance, to taxation, to sanctions for noncompliance. This study seeks to identify systematically the various methods that are employed for implementing international accords and to analyze which are used with what effectiveness. In examining steps that have been taken to implement treaties, several questions arise. How comprehensive is the legislation that has been adopted? How much time elapsed before implementing legislation and regulations were adopted? Has the stringency of the legislation changed over time? What factors have affected this change? In many countries, complicated issues of federalism are raised by the implementation of international accords. In those cases, provincial and local-level legislation is also essential.

Compliance goes beyond implementation. *Compliance* refers to whether countries in fact adhere to the provisions of the accord and to the implementing measures that they have instituted. The answer cannot be taken as given, even if laws and regulations are in place. Measuring compliance is more difficult than measuring implementation. It involves assessing the extent to which governments follow through on the steps they have taken to implement international accords. Some measurable factors, such as the staffing and budget of bureaucracies charged with ensuring compliance, the quantity and quality of data that are kept, and the extent to which incentives and sanctions are actually used and imposed, give indications of efforts toward compliance. In the end, however, assessing the extent of compliance is a matter of judgment.

Compliance has several dimensions. Treaties contain specific obligations, some of which are procedural, such as the requirement to report, and others of which are substantive, such as the obligation to cease or control an activity. In addition, preambles or initial articles in treaties place those specific obligations in a broad normative framework, which we refer to as the spirit of the treaty.

Compliance is probably never perfect; substantial compliance is what is sought by those who advocate treaties and agreements. We seek to assess the extent to which substantial compliance is achieved with the procedural and substantive obligations contained in treaties and also with the spirit, or broad norm, involved in the treaty, and to compare the extent of success within and among political units and over time.

Compliance is related but not identical to effectiveness. Countries may be in compliance with a treaty, but the treaty may nevertheless be ineffective in attaining its objectives. And even treaties that are effective in attaining their stated objectives may not be effective in addressing the problems they were intended to address. To illustrate the latter point, compliance with a treaty may result in the cessation of an activity that contributed to pollution, but it might lead to an overall increase of pollution by encouraging other activities as substitutes whose consequences are even worse; or a treaty prohibiting international trade in elephant tusks could effectively stop the trade but have little impact on the decimation of the elephant population.

Table 17.1 shows the several dimensions of implementation, compliance, and effectiveness. Our project is particularly concerned with assessing implementation and compliance. Effectiveness is very important, but until implementation and compliance are better understood, the contribution of treaties to solving international environmental problems cannot be known. Learning about implementation and compliance is an essential first step to learning about effectiveness.

Factors that Affect Implementation and Compliance

Many factors may affect a country's implementation of and compliance with international accords. We are interested in how several interrelated factors affect the extent to which and the way in which countries have met their commitments. These factors include the character of the activity, the character of the accord, country characteristics, policy history, leadership, information, the role of nongovernmental organizations (NGOs), actions of other states, and the role of international governmental organizations (IGOs).

Character of the activity. Environmental accords are about human activities—activities that extract resources, produce pollutants or other emissions, change ecosystems, or reduce biodiversity. Some substances or activities have little economic importance, whereas controlling others has consequences for entire economies. Some also have little intrinsic economic value, but the process of compliance can disrupt economic activities in lots of other areas. Some are easy to monitor, while others can be

Table 17.1   International Environmental Accords: Implementation, Compliance, and Effectiveness

I. Implementation

II. Compliance

    A. Compliance with the specific obligations of the treaty
      1. Procedural obligations
      2. Substantive obligations

    B. Compliance with the spirit of the treaty

III. Effectiveness

    A. In achieving the stated objectives of the treaty

    B. In addressing the problems that led to the treaty

detected only through very intrusive measures. The costs and benefits of regulating substances and activities and their distribution among various social classes and geographical regions can also be important.

The accord itself.   The characteristics of the treaty or agreement itself are an important factor. Some issues relate to the process by which the accord was negotiated. By whom and how was the process initiated? What form did the negotiations take? Were issues settled consensually or by majority vote? What was the extent and depth of agreement? The substantive characteristics of the accord also raise important issues. What is the nature of the obligations contained in the accord? Are the duties general or precise? Are they binding or hortatory? What compliance mechanisms are contained in the accords? How does the agreement treat countries that do not join? The Montreal Protocol on Substances That Deplete the Ozone Layer and the Convention on International Trade in Endangered Species obligate parties not to trade controlled substances with countries that are not parties to the agreement. How effective is this provision in inducing compliance? What benefits accrue to signatory countries? What special dilemmas does the accord produce, such as the problem of how an item once placed on the World Heritage Convention's list of protected things ever gets taken off that list?

Country characteristics.   The social, cultural, political, and economic characteristics of the countries clearly influence implementation and compliance. We assess the relative importance in shaping a country's actions of its broad political culture, the level of its economic development, and the trajectory and pace of its economic growth. Are there cultural traditions that influence how a country complies? What difference does it make whether the country has a market or a planned economy, or if it is mixed?

Does it make a difference in which sector the substance or activity is included? What are the effects of the characteristics of the political system? How strong and effective is the bureaucracy, and what difference does that make? What is the strength of nongovernmental groups, including those engaged in lobbying and domestic and international agenda setting? What is the nature of the legal system? What procedures are required to adopt the regulations or other strategies necessary to implement the agreement?

Policy history. A country's policy history regarding the substance or activity being regulated is another basic factor. What was the country doing about the substance or activity before adhering to the international accord? Had the country already recognized the existence of an environmental problem? What role did the country play in the negotiation of the accord?

Leaders. People make a difference. Some leaders are more committed to and effective in promoting compliance with international environmental accords than others. Some countries have drawn leadership on an issue from the scientific community, while others have not had such communities from which to draw. What are the consequences of changes in and differences among leaders?

Information. It is broadly assumed that the more information there is about an environmental issue and the clearer the understanding of the issue, the more effective implementation and compliance will be. That assumption impels much of the work of international organizations. We want to assess how the availability of information about and the extent of understanding of the environmental issues covered in the treaties affect national implementation and compliance with them.

NGOs. What role do local, national, and international nongovernmental organizations have in determining the compliance of states with international accords? What role, in particular, do international nongovernmental organizations (INGOs) such as Greenpeace or the International Institute for Environment and Development play? What is the role of multinational corporations?

Actions of other states. The actions of other states in implementing and complying with the accord can also affect a state's compliance with an agreement. To what extent have other countries' noncompliance or compliance with the accords affected the willingness of countries to abide by these accords? How does the answer to that question vary with the subject and obligations of the international accord? To what extent can a state be a freeloader under the accord?

IGOs. Finally, international governmental organizations have important roles in promoting the implementation of and compliance with international accords. We investigate how countries relate to the IGOs that have responsibilities for these accords. What importance, if any, was attached to involvement by international organizations such as the United Nations?

These factors can be grouped into four broad headings: (1) characteristics of the activity that the accord deals with; (2) characteristics of the accord; (3) characteristics of the country, or political unit, that is a party to the accord; and (4) factors in the international environment. Figure 17.1 presents a graphic representation of the interaction of those factors with a state's implementation of and compliance with an accord and the effectiveness of the accord.

In examining these factors, we want to test certain hypotheses that are nested within the questions posed in the preceding paragraphs. Some of these hypotheses have been deduced from rational choice assumptions, others have been derived from the existing literature, and still others have been derived from preliminary analyses of empirical data that we have gathered. Some relationships seem obvious. Some have been identified in the assessments by the U.S. General Accounting Office and the secretary-general of UNCED.[11]

Given the realist and rational choice assumptions that undergird game theory, one would expect that the smaller the costs and the greater the benefits associated with the accord, however difficult they may be to calculate, the greater the probability of implementation and compliance. The likelihood of significant sanctions would be included in the prospective cost element of this hypothesis. Since implementation and compliance require monetary and bureaucratic resources, it would seem logical that the larger a country's gross national product and the higher its per capita GNP, the greater the probability of implementation and compliance. Because costly measures can be accommodated with minimal or no redistribution in a period of rapid economic growth, the higher the rate of a country's economic growth, the greater the probability of implementation and compliance. Since domestic group and mass public pressure comprises important mechanisms for promoting implementation and compliance with treaty obligations, several scholars and policymakers have assumed that the more a country adheres to democratic norms concerning political and civil rights and political participation, the greater the probability of implementation and compliance. Many have also assumed that decentralization would promote more effective compliance.

We expected those hypotheses to be confirmed. We expected them to bound other findings. We expected that the variables involved in those hypotheses would explain the largest share of the variance among countries

Figure 17.1 International Environmental Accords: Model of Factors That Affect Implementation, Compliance, and Effectiveness

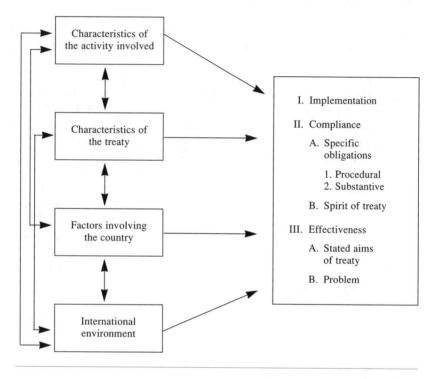

and treaties, but we also were very conscious that it would not be surprising or particularly helpful to those interested in improving compliance for us to discover that rich countries were more likely to comply with treaties than poor countries, or that countries were more likely to comply with those treaties that impose few burdens. Countries cannot be made rich overnight, nor can the burdens that compliance might entail always be eliminated.

Since administrative and bureaucratic capacity is obviously essential for implementing accords, we explore the extent to which such capacity has been and could be increased in ways independent from broader economic, political, and social development. Clearly, the greater the capacity of the political unit to implement the accord, the more likely it is that it will comply. Administrative and bureaucratic capacity depends on economic resources, but it also involves education, technical training and skills, and attitudes.

The relationships that hold greatest fascination for us are those involving international and domestic processes. Many of these have been identified by Abram Chayes and Antonia Handler Chayes, Roger Fisher, Peter M. Haas, Robert O. Keohane, and Elinor Ostrom.[12] Game theory and public goods theory provide the foundation for many of the suggestions of these scholars. Factors that one or more of them have stressed are: (1) international momentum toward compliance, which increases the benefits of compliance and the costs and consequences of noncompliance for any signatory state; (2) the amount, quality, and availability of information about the issues involved so that they can be understood; (3) the involvement and/or engagement of domestic officials and bureaucracies so that their personal interests and reputations become issues at stake; and (4) the creation and engagement of communities of interested parties, especially scientists and specialists in the topic, or what Haas has termed "epistemic communities."[13] The first factor involves international processes; the second, international and domestic processes; and the third and fourth, predominantly domestic processes. We are primarily interested in the consequences for implementation and compliance of processes that occur within the lower two boxes on the left-hand side of the diagram in Figure 17.1, those involving the characteristics of the country or political unit that is a party to the accord and those involving the international environment.

Hypotheses concerning those factors are straightforward. With respect to international momentum, the most direct hypothesis is: The greater the number of countries that have ratified an accord and the greater the extent of their implementation and compliance, the greater the probability of implementation and compliance by any individual signatory. Countries have a deep and abiding interest in creating and maintaining a relatively stable and predictable international environment. The more stable and predictable an environment, the higher the costs of disrupting it and, thus, the greater the probability of implementation and compliance. International momentum also has broader aspects, such as the extent to which international public opinion is committed to the issue. International nongovernmental organizations capture and articulate important sections of international public opinion; hence, the stronger and more active the INGOs are in the issue area of the treaty, the greater the probability of implementation and compliance.

With respect to information, the hypothesis is: The greater the flow of scientific and technical information about targeted activities in a form that is understood by governments and public pressure groups, the higher the likelihood of implementation and compliance. Particularly with environmental accords, these actors must rely on scientific and technical information flows to identify and assess risks, address targeted activities, and identify available technical options to enhance compliance.

Hypotheses concerning domestic processes are equally uncomplicated. Two are very important. Because repeated encounters and associations with counterparts as well as concern for reputations have a powerful impact on behavior, the more involved a country's domestic officials and bureaucracies are in the preparation, implementation, and oversight of an accord, the greater the probability of implementation and compliance. Since epistemic communities are deeply committed to the goals of particular accords because of their knowledge and professional interests, the greater the size, strength, and activism of epistemic communities, the greater the probability of implementation and compliance.

Our research efforts focus on these process factors because previous research indicates that they are important. The evidence for them, however, is largely anecdotal. We examine them empirically on a multicountry basis. Since the factors are subject to directed and purposeful modification, policies could be adopted that target them in order to increase implementation and compliance with international environmental accords.

We are also interested in other process factors, such as leadership and the extent of transparency surrounding the activity covered by the accord. Obviously, the more committed a country's leader is to the goals of an accord, the greater the probability of implementation and compliance. Leaders are chosen for many reasons. To some extent, in terms of the focus of this research, a country's choice of leaders is a stochastic process. We study how leaders, whatever their initial inclinations, become more engaged in ensuring compliance with the accord.

Transparency may promote compliance because it makes noncompliance more apparent and makes it easier for international and domestic actors to take actions to encourage and enforce accountability. Transparency is closely linked with the character of the issue covered by the treaty and democratic norms. Cultural factors may affect the acceptability of transparency internally and hence its effectiveness in inducing compliance. We test the hypothesis that transparency promotes implementation and compliance and seek to identify the conditions that bound the hypothesis. We also analyze the extent to which transparency can be promoted.

Stating the hypotheses that have guided our research in such a bald manner may make the project appear overly mechanistic. The project could not have been conducted in a mechanical and simplistic way. Context and institutions are terribly important. The hypotheses are important because they provide a framework that guides and directs the project, useful both as a way of structuring our analyses and guiding comparisons and as a way to link our study with others at a basic, practical level as well as at a theoretical one.

In varying degrees, the factors involved in the hypotheses that are of most concern to us are subject to deliberate manipulation by those who prepare accords and who are responsible for overseeing their implementation and compliance with them. The research seeks to develop a basis for reasoned speculation about how manipulation of these factors might improve implementation and compliance. For example, a broad issue to be investigated is whether the more a country has been involved in the negotiation of a treaty, the more likely it will be to implement and comply with the treaty. Or it is possible that a key step in obtaining compliance with environmental treaties from the countries of the South is to improve their indigenous scientific capability so that they can produce independent assessments of environmental problems and evaluate their options for dealing with them. Or a key step might be to control the behavior of multinational corporations, which would then exert influence on behalf of environmental goals in the countries where they operate. Moreover, as has become evident with respect to human rights treaties, compliance with international accords can change and improve over time, even if compliance was not actually intended by all signing governments at the time of agreement. The research seeks to understand how improvement might be induced and promoted.

The Research Design:
The Countries and the Treaties

To investigate these hypotheses and issues, we have chosen to focus on eight countries and the European Union (EU) and international treaties covering five broad areas of environmental concern. We have chosen the nine political units and the five areas in the hope that the study will yield knowledge that will have worldwide utility and pertain to most kinds of environmental accords that may be concluded in the future.

Political Units of Great Importance
and Widely Differing Character

The eight countries selected are Brazil, Cameroon, China, Hungary, India, Japan, Russia, and the United States. We also include one group of countries, the European Union. These countries have been chosen because they are very important to the effective implementation of broad international environmental accords. They include those that have contributed most to the anthropogenic effects that bring about global change (Japan, Russia, the United States, and the EU and its members) and others that have the potential of making major contributions to anthropogenic effects (Brazil, India, and China).

Cameroon and Hungary were included to illustrate the problems and processes of implementation and compliance in smaller countries—countries that although their total contribution to global environmental problems may be individually small, when considered as a group constitute by far the largest number of states in the global political system. This vantage point is necessary to draw inferences about collective action. The United States and other large countries can benefit directly by their actions regardless of others. But most countries, such as Hungary and Cameroon, cannot, even though collectively countries their size could be more important than the United States. So why do countries that will see the costs so much more clearly than the benefits, due to their relatively small size, become parties or comply?

The EU[14] has been chosen because it increasingly behaves as a state actor through directives and regulations that are applicable in all member states. It represents a new form of governmental organization, one that conceivably could be duplicated elsewhere, such as among the states that constituted the former Soviet Union. It merits study for that reason as well as for the reason that the EU will be a major political and economic actor in forthcoming negotiations. Although the EU is a party to only two of the treaties, most of its twelve member states are parties to all of them.

In the 1990s, those countries included in this study accounted for about three-fifths of the world's population, their GNP constituted about four-fifths of the world product, and they contributed more than two-thirds of the global greenhouse emissions.[15] Table 17.2 presents data that show the importance for environmental issues of the nine political units. They spanned the globe and encompassed a range of forms of political organization and culture. Furthermore, they included both developed and developing countries, some with mixed-market economies and others that were restructuring centrally planned economies. Finally, some of these countries could be particularly affected by global change.

Five International Environmental Treaties

The five international treaties were chosen to maximize the knowledge that could be gained about ways of managing global environmental change. We deliberately avoided the preconception that the only kind of international environmental agreement that can be entered into is one that regulates emissions; there is considerable variety among these treaties in terms of what they concern and how they deal with it. We have selected only treaties for which there is a significant number of signatories and for which there is already some experience with implementation and compliance. A study of proposed accords that have not yet been implemented would tell us little about what makes for crafting a successful agreement. The five treaties we have chosen include three that deal with the management of natural resources and two that are aimed at controlling pollution. They are:

1. United Nations Educational, Scientific and Cultural Organization (UNESCO) *Convention for the Protection of the World Cultural and Natural Heritage,* 16 November 1972, 27 U.S.T. 37, T.I.A.S. No. 8226 (referred to as the World Heritage Convention). Secretariat, United Nations Educational, Scientific and Cultural Organization, Paris.

Table 17.2 Study of Adherence to International Environmental Accords: The Political Units and Their Characteristics

Country	Population (millions)	GNP per capita (U.S. dollars 1990)	GNP per capita growth rate, 1965–90	CO_2 emissions per capita (tons of carbon)	CFC net use (thousands of metric tons)	Change in forest and woodland
Brazil	150	2,680	3.3	0.38	9	–0.4
Cameroon	12	960	3.0	0.14	0	–0.4
China	1,134	370	5.8	0.59	18	0.0
EU[a]	343	17,058	2.5	2.20	228	1.1[b]
Hungary	11	2,780	—	1.65	1	0.6
India	850	350	1.9	0.21	0	–0.2
Japan	124	25,430	4.1	2.31	58	0.0
Russia	148.7	3,220[c]	—	3.60	—	—
USA	250	21,790	1.7	5.37	197	–0.1
Average	—	8,293	2.8	1.8	63.88	0.08
World average	—	4,964	1.6	1.09	5.4	–0.13
Total	3,022.7	—	—	—	511	—
World total	5,222	—	—	—	659	—

Source: World Bank, *The Environment Data Book: A Guide to Statistics on the Environment and Development* (Washington, D.C.: World Bank, 1993), pp. 10–13.
[a]Not including Luxembourg
[b]Not including Belgium
[c]1991

2. *Washington Convention on International Trade in Endangered Species of Wild Fauna and Flora,* 3 March 1973, 27 U.S.T. 1087, T.I.A.S. No. 8249 (referred to as CITES). Secretariat, United Nations Environment Programme, Geneva, Switzerland.

3. *International Tropical Timber Agreement,* 18 November 1983, U.N. Doc. TD/Timber/11/Rev. 1 (1984) (referred to as the International Tropical Timber Agreement). Secretariat, International Tropical Timber Organization, Yokohama, Japan.

4. *International Maritime Convention on the Prevention of Marine Pollution by Dumping of Wastes and Other Matter,* 29 December 1972, 26 U.S.T. 2403, T.I.A.S. No. 8165 (referred to as the London Convention and formerly referred to as the London Ocean Dumping Convention). Secretariat, International Maritime Organization, London.

5. *Montreal Protocol on Substances That Deplete the Ozone Layer,* 6 September 1987, 26 I.L.M. 1550 (referred to as the Montreal Protocol), together with the *Vienna Convention for the Protection of the Ozone Layer,* 22 March 1985, 26 I.L.M. 1529 (referred to as the Vienna Convention). Secretariat, United Nations Environment Programme, Nairobi, Kenya; Secretariat, Montreal Protocol Fund,

Montreal, Quebec, Canada. The Vienna Convention is the framework treaty under which the Montreal Protocol was negotiated. We look at this treaty only insofar as it relates to the Montreal Protocol.

The *World Heritage Convention,* 1972, puts international constraints on the use of designated sites within a country.[16] It is a useful model for studying the increasingly common international legal instruments designed to affect a country's behavior toward its own natural and cultural resources. Under the convention, parties nominate sites within their countries for inclusion on the World Heritage List. A meeting of the parties determines whether to include the nominated sites on the list. Once the sites are included, parties are obligated to protect their integrity. If they are in need of financial or technical assistance in doing so, they may receive assistance from the World Heritage Fund, financed by contributions from the parties. A secretariat, which in May 1992 consolidated the separate offices for natural and cultural heritages, administers the convention. Parties vest authority in the elected World Heritage Committee of twenty-one member states, which meets annually and until recently has been primarily devoted to considering proposals to list sites on the World Heritage List. The convention relies on voluntary compliance by the parties. There are no sanctions other than publicity about acts of noncompliance.

The *Convention on International Trade in Endangered Species* (CITES), 1973, is designed to control international trade in endangered species of plants and animals.[17] It is a useful model for studying the technique of protecting the environment by controlling trade in an endangered natural resource or environmentally hazardous product. Under the CITES convention, species are classified into three categories and listed in appendixes: internationally endangered species in which trade is prohibited, species that may become endangered unless trade is controlled, and species not in those two classes but endangered in a particular country that wants the help of others to enforce its control of exports. Under the convention, exports and imports of live specimens listed in the appendixes and of parts and derivatives are to take place only with a permit.

A conference of parties to the treaty meets every two years to review the implementation of the convention and, as appropriate, to revise the categorization of endangered species. A secretariat services the conferences of the parties to the treaty and assists countries in meeting their obligations. It also assists in monitoring trade and helps parties comply with the convention. Inquiries may be conducted into allegations that a species is being adversely affected or that the provisions of the treaty are not being effectively implemented. The conference can review the results of such inquiries and make appropriate recommendations. Publicity is the principal sanction against failures to implement or comply with the treaty, although countries have threatened to invoke trade sanctions.

The *International Tropical Timber Agreement*, 1983, was negotiated to facilitate trade in timber from tropical forests.[18] It includes the major producing and consuming countries and is primarily a commodity agreement. Among its several objectives, however, is "the development of national policies aimed at sustainable utilization and conservation of tropical forests and their genetic resources, and at maintaining the ecological balance in the regions concerned."[19] This goal is to be accomplished by encouraging expansion and diversification of tropical timber trade, improved forest management and wood utilization, and reforestation. To this end, the convention provides for the creation of the International Tropical Timber Organization (ITTO), which functions through the International Tropical Timber Council. The ITTO is charged with monitoring market conditions, conducting studies, and providing technical assistance. The convention is designed to attain its objectives with respect to forest management through development of knowledge, exchange and dissemination of information, and technical assistance.

The ITTO issued on 21 May 1990 the "ITTO Guidelines for the Sustainable Management of Natural Tropical Forests," which are voluntary guidelines for the parties. In the environmental context, national implementation of the convention raises important problems of how to effect substantial changes in the practices of an industry that is central to the economy of countries with tropical forests. It also provides insights into the effectiveness of using information and voluntary measures to induce changes in behavior.

The International Tropical Timber Agreement was drafted to be in force only through March 1994. It has been extended by a resolution of the parties until the new successor agreement goes into effect.

The *London Convention*, 1972, is intended to protect the marine environment from the dumping of certain kinds of pollutants.[20] States are obligated to regulate (or prohibit) dumping of materials that are listed in two annexes and to enforce these measures against vessels or aircraft registered in their territory, flying their flag, or otherwise under their jurisdiction. There is a regular meeting of the parties to review implementation of the agreement and to develop measures with regard to liability, and there are several advisory groups of scientific experts that meet regularly on particular issues. The convention is interesting because it requires states to control the behavior of actors operating in a globally shared resource (the oceans) and to develop measures of accountability.

The *Montreal Protocol on Substances That Deplete the Ozone Layer*, 1987, imposes the most arduous obligations on parties of any of these conventions. It was negotiated within the broad terms of the Vienna Convention, 1985—a framework convention that commits parties generally to take actions to protect both human health and the environment from the adverse effects of activities that modify the stratospheric ozone layer. The Vienna Convention provides for monitoring, the dissemination of information, and research.

The Montreal Protocol requires states that are parties to reduce their consumption of chlorofluorocarbons and to freeze consumption levels of halons.[21] The convention provides target dates, allowing less stringent dates for the developing countries. It provides for regular meetings of the parties and for scientific assessments to be prepared in anticipation of these meetings. At the November 1992 meeting of the parties in Copenhagen, countries agreed to phase out chlorofluorocarbons completely by the year 1996, and halons (except for certain essential uses) by the year 1995, and to add new chemicals to the control list—going well beyond the initial terms of the protocol.

Countries are to report on measures they have taken to implement the protocol. The protocol obligates the parties to establish measures for determining noncompliance with its provisions and for treatment of parties that are found to be in noncompliance. It controls trade in the indicated substances with countries that are not parties to the protocol.

The protocol also recognizes the special needs of the developing countries in implementing the agreement. At the June 1990 meeting in London, the parties agreed to create a new mechanism to provide financial and technical cooperation, including the transfer of technologies, to assist these countries in complying with the control measures of the protocol; that mechanism was established as the Montreal Protocol.

The Montreal Protocol is particularly interesting because of the binding regime it has established for controlling production and consumption of ozone-depleting substances, and for the provision it has made to facilitate compliance by developing countries.

These treaties have been selected for a number of reasons. They involve several key environmental issues connected with global change. They contain a range of types of obligations, and various techniques regarding implementation and compliance. They address both pollution and natural resource problems. They involve issues that occur primarily within states' borders, those that cross borders, and those that are inherently global in nature. These treaties have been in effect a sufficient amount of time, so there is an adequate data base with which to analyze implementation and compliance. Finally, each of the selected states is a party to at least three of these accords, and a majority are parties to all of them. Table 17.3 shows which countries and groups of countries have acceded to which treaties.

Implementation and Compliance: Some Preliminary Observations

A secular trend toward improved implementation and compliance was visible by 1994. Not all nine political units were doing a better job of implementing and complying with all of the five treaties—indeed, several were

Table 17.3   Adherence of the Political Units to International Environmental Treaties as of 1 January 1994 (p = party to treaty)

Political Units	World Heritage	CITES	Tropical Timber	London Convention	Vienna Convention	Montreal Protocol
Brazil	p	p	p	p	p	p
Cameroon	p	p	p		p	p
China	p	p	p	p	p	p
European Union			p		p	p
Hungary	p	p		p	p	p
India	p	p	p		p	p
Japan	p	p	p	p	p	p
Russia	p	p	p	p	p	p
USA	p	p	p	p	p	p

not even parties to all of them—but the overall trend was positive. More and more actions have been taken to implement the treaties, and both procedural and substantive compliance have improved. The political units in general are increasingly acting in terms that accord with the spirit of the treaties.

Beyond this secular trend, the political units have also agreed to strengthened and improved treaties. This fact is evident both in the London and Copenhagen supplements to the Montreal Protocol and in the renegotiated International Tropical Timber Agreement.

Those broad points having been made, there are some important qualifications. The performance of some countries with respect to CITES has sharply declined since the mid-1980s. With respect to developing countries, the substantive obligations of the Montreal Protocol are not yet severe. Thus, it would be premature to be extremely optimistic about their performance. Many signs thus far have been positive, but they provide only a weak basis for projecting a positive trend.

Among the five treaties, implementation and compliance seem to be stronger with respect to the Montreal Protocol, the London Convention, and the World Heritage Convention than they are with respect to CITES and the Tropical Timber Agreement. Among the last two, CITES imposes the most stringent obligations of the five accords, and it is the one that has encountered the most serious difficulties in the late 1980s and early 1990s. The Tropical Timber Agreement, with its nonbinding, sustainable forest guidelines, has had the least environmental impact.

No political unit does a perfect job of implementing and complying with the treaties, but the EU, Japan, the United States, and to a lesser extent Russia have done more than the other units in our study. During the past decade, Cameroon has been having the greatest difficulty of the nine political units in implementing and complying with the treaties.

As noted above, even strong implementation and compliance with treaties do not ensure their effectiveness in terms either of meeting the objectives of the treaties or of dealing with the problems that led to the treaties in the first place. In the case of the five treaties that are included in our study, the record is mixed. The Montreal Protocol and the London Convention seem, respectively, to have contributed to a decline in the production and consumption of ozone-depleting substances and in the intentional dumping of wastes in the high seas. The World Heritage Convention appears to have contributed to the preservation of cultural and natural resources. The Tropical Timber Agreement has not yet resulted in the "sustainable utilization" of forest resources, and—unfortunately, despite CITES—there appears to have been, especially since the mid-1980s, an increase in the illicit trade in endangered species. Moreover, while some endangered species have become less critically endangered, others have become more so; but, arguably, the situation could have been even worse absent the treaty.

Revisiting the Model

With these rough assessments as benchmarks, what explains what has happened? The model presented in Table 17.2 grouped the variables we thought might be important into four broad categories: (1) characteristics of the activity involved, (2) characteristics of the treaty, (3) factors involving the country, and (4) the international environment. The model shows that all the factors interact to produce a combined effect on implementation, compliance, and effectiveness. In our discussion, however, for clarity and manageability, the factors must be treated individually. Thus, each of the statements in the following paragraphs requires the qualification "other things being constant."

With reference to the characteristics of the activity involved, our study confirms the conventional wisdom that the smaller the number of actors involved in the activity, the easier it is to regulate it. Because by early 1995 only a limited number of facilities have produced ozone-depleting substances, it has been relatively easy to control the production of those substances as the Montreal Protocol requires. The situation may become more difficult as more production facilities come on-line. The striking contrast between the limited number of facilities that have produced ozone-depleting substances and the millions of individuals who could engage in illicit trade in endangered species contributes to CITES being a much more difficult treaty to enforce than the Montreal Protocol.

Activities conducted by large multinational corporations are also easier to deal with than those conducted by smaller firms that are less visible internationally. Again, the production of ozone-depleting substances provides the example. The large multinational firms are much more subject to the pressure of public opinion and diverse consumers throughout the world than are the smaller, lesser-known firms that engage in much of the timber trade. Obviously, since the characteristics of activities that contribute to environmental degradation are more or less fixed, treaties must address activities whether or not their characteristics facilitate implementation and compliance. To the extent that treaties can decompose problems and define points of attack, these generalizations could be used to shape treaties.

Factors Involving the Treaties

The characteristics of treaties obviously do make a difference. The London Convention, CITES, and the Montreal Protocol impose relatively precise obligations. It is consequently relatively easy to judge whether or not states and other political units are fulfilling these obligations. The World Heritage Convention and the Tropical Timber Agreement are much vaguer; thus, assessing implementation and compliance becomes much more difficult.

Requiring the filing of regular reports is a standard feature that four of the treaties under consideration here, and most others, use to monitor implementation and compliance. Clearly, this is one of the few instruments that is available. Yet it is an instrument that is not well understood. The record of compliance with reporting requirements is spotty at best. Governments, particularly of smaller political units, are extremely overburdened; filing reports is yet one more burden. The locus of the responsibility for preparing the report may be uncertain—is it with foreign offices or with substantive ministries? What is clear is that international secretariats can use the reporting exercise to help them clarify for government officials what the obligations of treaties are and what techniques have been and might be used to fulfill them. Thus, reporting is probably best seen as an educational process rather than a rigorous process of monitoring, and as a tool that enables secretariats, other states that are parties to the treaty, and national and international nongovernmental organizations to intervene to encourage compliance.

It is also clear that even though they have no formal standing under the treaties we have considered, NGOs and multinational corporations can play an important role in providing information about activities that are addressed in international environmental treaties. The TRAFFIC reports on illicit trade in endangered species provide information that governments might find difficult to gather or publish. Greenpeace is an important source of information about ocean dumping. The knowledge that monitoring goes on outside of formal governmental and treaty channels is probably an important restraining factor on governmental actions. The multinational firms that produce ozone-depleting substances sometimes may have had better information than governments about their production. Also, since there are proprietary aspects to this information, these firms have access that governments might not be able to achieve easily. Clearly, the private sector must be engaged if monitoring is to prove effective.

Not surprisingly, for parties to implement and comply with treaties, they must feel that the obligations imposed are equitable. India and China would not become parties to the Montreal Protocol until the agreement about compensatory financing had been reached at the London meeting in 1990. Part of the difficulty with the Tropical Timber Agreement seems to be a sense that burdens are disproportionately imposed on the producer countries; the consumer countries' activities with respect to their forests are unregulated. The new agreement attempts to address this issue by having a separate formal statement regarding temperate forests accompany it.

Factors Involving the Country

The performance of the eight countries and the EU in implementing and complying with the five treaties examined in this study varies substantially across countries and time. The record, however, must be viewed in context. One very important factor shaping how well a country does is what it has traditionally done in the past with respect to the issue in question, including what legislation and regulation it already had in place at the time it became a party to the treaty. For instance, since Japan has had a long tradition of protecting its cultural heritage, becoming a party to the World Heritage Convention did not require vast changes in the way it treated its historical treasures. Its standards may previously have been even above those required by the treaty.

Beyond this, perhaps the most important factor contributing to the variance is administrative capacity. Countries that have stronger administrative capacities can do a better job. Administrative capacity is the result of several factors. Having educated and trained personnel is important. But such individuals usually must have financial support to be effective. For example, while the Indian administrative service is well staffed and well trained, its financial resources are extremely limited, and thus its effectiveness is restricted. Administrative capacity depends on having authority. Administrators whose mandate is narrower than their assigned responsibilities or who are subject to capricious interference cannot do as well as their training and skills would make possible.

Economic factors are important but rather indirectly. The political units in this study have widely varying GNPs per capita that have grown or declined at substantially different rates. Of course, the larger a country's GNP, the more likely it could have a strong administrative capacity; but changes in GNP or the rate of growth of GNP have had little discernible effect on implementation and compliance. Economic collapse and chaos, however, can have a profound effect. In Cameroon and Russia, compliance with CITES seems to have declined since the mid-1980s, and this phenomenon seems to be directly attributable to economic collapse and chaos. Limited government resources and rapid rates of inflation have had an impact on the incentive structure of the individuals who must enforce the provisions of CITES: the customs inspectors. In some instances they have not been paid. In others, they have seen the value of their salaries decline precipitously. Conversely, the value of illicit trade in endangered species has increased. Under the circumstances, the apparent increase in illicit trade in endangered species is perhaps understandable.

Political systems have an effect on implementation and compliance, but, again, the effect is mixed and complex. Large countries have a much more complex task of complying with the obligations of treaties than do smaller ones. There are several levels of political authority in Brazil, China, the EU, Russia, and the United States. In cases where activities that the treaty deals with are widely dispersed—as in CITES, the Tropical Timber Agreement, and the World Heritage Convention—these levels of political authority must be coordinated, which is not always an easy task. Sometimes the authority of the central government, which accepts international obligations, does not reach deeply into local areas. Moreover, these large countries contain within their borders widely different ecological regions, which require variation in the way administration is conducted.

As part of its reform, Russia has attempted to decentralize authority. In the process of decentralization, the authority of Moscow over localities has been weakened. This shift appears to have resulted in a decline in Russia's compliance with CITES. Whether this is the temporary result of an administrative restructuring or a longer-term change is yet to be determined.

Political stalemate and chaos can bring about a noticeable decline in implementation and compliance. These factors seem to have affected Brazil, Cameroon, and Russia.

There are many features of democratic governments that contribute to improved implementation and compliance. Democratic governments are normally more transparent than authoritarian governments, so interested citizens can more easily monitor what their governments are doing to implement and comply with treaties. In democratic governments, it is possible for citizens to bring pressure to bear for improved implementation and compliance. Also, NGOs generally have more freedom to operate in countries with democratic governments. At the same time, however, democratic governments are normally more responsive to public opinion than authoritarian governments. Public opinion is not always supportive of environmental concerns: indeed, the economy is usually the public's greatest concern. Democratic governments allow conflicts about environmental issues to flare. It is probably the case that because of the balance of factors mentioned in this paragraph, democratic governments are more likely to do a better job of implementing and complying with international environmental accords than nondemocratic governments; but this generalization does not always hold, and democratization does not necessarily lead automatically or quickly to improved compliance.

The importance of NGOs has already been mentioned. They play a crucial role in implementation and compliance. They mobilize public opinion and set political agendas. They make information about problems available, sometimes information that governments do not have or would prefer to keep confidential. Often the information they make available is essential to monitoring. They bring pressure on governments directly and indirectly. Because many local and national nongovernmental organizations have connections with NGOs in other countries and INGOs, they are a means of ensuring a uniformity of concern throughout the world. There are also significant transfers of funds among NGOs, so NGOs in poorer countries may have surprisingly extensive resources at their disposal. NGOs have become an instrument for universalizing concern.

Individuals make a crucial difference in the implementation and compliance with treaties. It matters who is the head of state. Brazilian president Fernando Collor took a special interest in the environment, played a major role in having Rio de Janeiro selected as the site for UNCED, and advanced environmental causes within his country. Brazil's compliance with the five treaties improved during his presidency. Russia's prime minister insisted on revealing the Soviet Union's past violations of the London Convention and sought to bring the Russian navy's activities into compliance with the terms of the treaty. Individuals in less exalted positions can also play important roles. Russell Train, as chairman of the U.S. Council on Environmental Quality and administrator of the Environmental Protection Agency, initiated actions within the United States and extended them abroad. He played a crucial role in starting the international momentum in the 1970s. Other individuals through their knowledge, skills, and persistence have played important roles in NGOs. The designation of some heritage sites should clearly be attributed to individuals. Individuals are important also as members of epistemic communities.

The International Environment

The international environment is undoubtedly the most important factor explaining the secular trend toward improved implementation and compliance. Since the Stockholm Conference in 1972, international momentum toward concern for the environment has increased, and it increased sharply starting in the mid-1980s with the publication of the report of the World Commission on Environment and Development, *Our Common Future,* in 1987, and the preparations for the 1992 UNCED meeting in Rio de Janeiro.

The Rio conference was a massive event. It was the largest gathering of leaders of countries in history. It brought together an unprecedented number of NGOs. Significantly, thanks to a decision taken in Working Group III of the Preparatory Commission for UNCED, improving implementation and compliance with international environmental accords was specifically addressed at the conference.[22]

Increased salience for environmental issues was one aspect of the international momentum that developed. The increased salience roused public opinion and mobilized both national and international nongovernmental organizations, and public opinion and NGOs put increased pressure on governments to deal with environmental issues, which enhanced implementation and compliance.

Another aspect of international momentum was that more and more treaties were signed and more and more countries became parties to these treaties. This increase had an effect on implementation and compliance. Governments did not want their countries to be seen as laggards. Moreover, there are practical economic consequences. Once it became apparent that the major countries would stop producing and consuming chlorofluorocarbons, other countries did not want to deal with outmoded technologies. Finally, in the case of a treaty like CITES, it is easier for a government to attempt to enforce its obligations if all of the neighboring countries are also parties.

Figure 17.2 attempts to portray this more nuanced picture of how factors within countries and the international environment affect implementation and compliance. A country's physical conditions, its history, and its culture establish basic parameters that affect implementation and compliance. The economy, political institutions, and public opinion have an effect, but it is generally indirect. These factors operate through proximate variables. In our view, the most important proximate variables are administrative capacity, leadership, NGOs, knowledge and information, and epistemic communities. All these factors, of course, are shaped by the country's preexisting traditions, legislation, and regulations in the area involved. Finally, the international environment, especially in the form of international momentum, is also a proximate variable. And it has been exceedingly important.

What prescriptions do these findings suggest? They underscore the importance of the underlying strength and health of national political-economic systems for efforts to protect the global environment. The strength and health of national political-economic systems are the most important factors; thus, long-term strategies must squarely focus on these issues, as indeed Agenda 21 does. In the shorter run, engaging national leaders in the effort to protect and improve the global environment will make a difference. Strengthening national bureaucracies charged with responsibilities for environmental management, supporting international and national nongovernmental organizations that focus on environmental issues, and building epistemic communities all will help. Maintaining and increasing the international momentum for the protection and improvement of the environment is crucial for both its own effects and the stimulus it provides for all the other factors that are important.

Figure 17.2   Factors That Contribute to Lessening or Improving National Compliance with International Environmental Accords

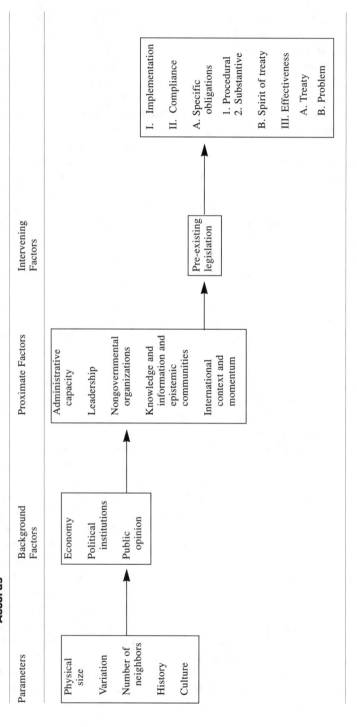

Notes

1. Edith Brown Weiss, Daniel B. Magraw, and Paul C. Szasz, *International Environmental Law: Basic Instruments and References* (New York: Transnational Publishers, 1992).

2. Although Harold K. Jacobson and Edith Brown Weiss are the authors of this article, it is very much the result of a collaborative project that has involved the entire research consortium that is responsible for the project and others. The article draws heavily on discussions we have had during the course of the project. It also draws on the various applications we submitted when seeking funding for the project. We particularly wish to acknowledge the rich contribution of Richard Rockwell, who played a major role in drafting the application to the Ford Foundation when he was a program officer at the Social Science Research Council. We also want to acknowledge the vital critical assistance of our research assistants, Cheryl Shanks and Gideon Rottem. The members of the research consortium are Danae Aitchison, Murillo Aragao, Anthony Balinga, Laszlo Bencze, Erach Bharucha, Piers Blaikie, Stephen Bunker, Abram Chayes, Antonia Handler Chayes, Jim Clem, Ellen Comisso, Liz Economy, Fang Xiaoming, James Vincent Feinerman, Koichiro Fujikura, Michael Glennon, Saul Halfon, Peter Hardi, Allison Hayward, Ronald Herring, Philipp Hildebrand, Takesada Iwahashi, Jasmin Jagada, Sheila Jasanoff, Tim Kessler, Ron Mitchell, Elena Nikitina, Kenneth da Nobrega, Michel Oksenberg, Jonathan Richards, Alberta Sbragia, Thomas Schelling, John A. Mope Simo, Alison Steward, David Vogel, Wu Zijin, Zhang Shuqing, Andrea Ziegler, and William Zimmerman. An earlier version of this article was presented as a paper at the Annual Meeting of the International Studies Association, Washington, D.C., March 1994.

3. Materials on the enforcement of domestic environmental law that are relevant include Keith Hawkins, *Environment and Enforcement* (Oxford: Clarendon Press; New York: Oxford University Press, 1984); and Clifford Russell, Winston Harrington, and William Vaughan, *Enforcing Pollution Control Laws* (Washington, D.C.: Resources for the Future, 1986).

4. See especially David A. Kay and Harold K. Jacobson, eds., *Environmental Protection: The International Dimension* (Totawa, N.J.: Allenheld, Osmun, 1983); Robert O. Keohane, *After Hegemony: Cooperation and Discord in the World Political Economy* (Princeton: Princeton University Press, 1984); Oran R. Young, *Resource Regimes: Natural Resources and Social Institutions* (Berkeley: University of California Press, 1982).

5. See Elinor Ostrom, *Governing the Commons: The Evolution of Institutions for Collective Action* (Cambridge: Cambridge University Press, 1990); and the special issue of *Evaluation Review* edited by Steven Rayner devoted to managing the commons, *Evaluation Review: A Journal of Applied Social Research* 15, no. 1 (February 1991).

6. U.S. Government Accounting Office, *International Environment: International Agreements Are Not Well Monitored,* GAO/RCED 92–43 (January 1992).

7. "Survey of Existing International Agreements and Instruments and Its Follow Up," report by the secretary-general of the United Nations Conference on Environment and Development, A/Conf. 151/PC/103 and Addendum 1 (1992). See also the follow-up, expanded version of the study, Peter H. Sand, ed., *The Effectiveness of International Environmental Agreements: A Survey of Existing Instruments* (Cambridge, England: Grotius, 1992).

8. Peter H. Sand, *Lessons Learned in Global Environmental Governance* (Washington, D.C.: World Resources Institute, 1990).

9. Jesse H. Ausubel and David G. Victor, "Verification of International Environmental Agreements," *Annual Review of Energy and the Environment* 17 (1992): 1–43.

10. David Lewis Feldman, "Institutions for Managing Global Climate Change," *Global Environmental Change* 2 (1992): 43–58. See also Peter M. Morisette, Joel Darmstadter, Andrew J. Plantinga, and Michael A. Toman, "Prospects for a Global Greenhouse Gas Accord," *Global Environmental Change* 1 (1991): 209–223. Although the article looks at the process of reaching the agreement, the process has implications for implementation.

11. U.S. Government Accounting Office, *International Environment;* and "Survey of Existing International Agreements."

12. See Abram Chayes and Antonia Handler Chayes, *The New Sovereignty: Compliance with International Regulatory Agreements* (Cambridge: Harvard University Press, forthcoming); Abram Chayes and Antonia H. Chayes, "On Compliance," *International Organization* 47, no. 2 (Spring 1993): 175–206; Roger Fisher, *Improving Compliance with International Law* (Charlottesville: University of Virginia Press, 1981); Peter M. Haas, *Saving the Mediterranean: The Politics of International Environmental Cooperation* (New York: Columbia University Press, 1990); Peter M. Haas, Robert O. Keohane, and Marc A. Levy, *Institutions for the Earth: Sources of Effective International Environmental Protection* (Cambridge: MIT Press, 1993); Keohane, *After Hegemony;* Robert O. Keohane, "Reciprocity, Reputation, and Compliance with International Commitments," paper delivered at the Annual Meeting of the American Political Science Association, Washington, D.C., 1–4 September 1988; and Ostrom, *Governing the Commons.*

13. See Haas, *Saving the Mediterranean.*

14. The members of the European Union are Belgium, Denmark, the Federal Republic of Germany, France, Greece, Ireland, Italy, Luxembourg, the Netherlands, Portugal, Spain, and the United Kingdom.

15. Allen L. Hammond, ed., *World Resources 1990–1991: Guide to the Global Environment: A Report by the World Resources Institute in Collaboration with the United Nations Environment Programme and the United Nations Development Programme* (New York: Oxford University Press, 1990): 244–245, 254–255, 348–349.

16. See Simon Lyster, *International Wildlife Law* (1985): 222–227 (description of implementation in Australia); Daniel B. Magraw, "International Law and Park Protection: A Global Responsibility," in David J. Simon, ed., *Our Common Land* (Washington, D.C.: Island Press, 1988) (brief discussion of implementation of the World Heritage Convention in the United States); Keith D. Suter, "The UNESCO World Heritage Convention," *Environmental Planning and Law Journal* 8 (1991): 4–15; Juliet Bedding, "Private Interests in World Heritage Properties: Peko-Wallsend Versus the Commonwealth," *University of Tasmania Law Review* 9 (1989): 316–324.

17. See Michael Glennon, "Has International Law Failed the Elephant?" *American Journal of International Law* 84 (1990): 1–43. Kathryn Fuller, Ginette Hemley, and Sarah Fitzgerald, "Wildlife Trade Law Implementation in Developing Countries: The Experience in Latin America," *Boston University International Law Journal* 5 (1987): 289–310; Laura Kosloff and Mark Trexler, "The Convention on International Trade in Endangered Species: Enforcement Theory and Practice in the United States," *Boston University International Law Journal* 5 (1987): 327–361; Eric McFadden, "Asian Compliance with CITES: Problems and Prospects," *Boston University International Law Journal* 5 (1987): 311–325; and Jorgen Thomsen and Amie Brautigam, "CITES in the European Economic Community: Who Benefits?"

Boston University International Law Journal 5 (1987): 269–287. See also Alan H. Schonfeld, "International Trade in Wildlife: How Effective Is the Endangered Species Treaty?" *California Western International Law Journal* 15 (1985): 111–160; and Gwyreth Stewart, "Enforcement Problems in CITES: Reservations Regarding the Reservations Clauses," *Cornell International Law Journal* 14 (1981): 429–455.

18. See Ursula Wasserman, UNCTAD: "International Tropical Timber Agreement," *Journal of World Trade Law* 18 (1984): 89–91 for brief discussion of the agreement.

19. International Tropical Timber Agreement, 1983, chap. 1, art. 1, par. h.

20. See Daniel Suman, "Regulation of Ocean Dumping by the European Economic Community," *Ecology Law Quarterly* 18 (1991): 559–618. Allan Bakalian, "Regulation and Control of United States Ocean Dumping: A Decade of Progress, an Appraisal for the Future," *Harvard Environmental Law Review* 8 (1984): 193–256; R. G. V. Boelens, "London Dumping Convention: Its Development and Significance to Marine Pollution Control," in *Canadian Conference on Marine Environmental Quality: Proceedings, February 29–March 3, 1988* (Halifax, Nova Scotia: International Institute for Transportation and Ocean Policy Studies, 1988) (issues of economic, social, and geographical differences among the member states); W. L. Lahey, "Ocean Dumping of Sewage Sludge: The Tide Turns from Protection to Management," *Harvard Environmental Law Review* 6 (1982): 395–437 (a study of regulation efforts by the U.S. Environmental Protection Agency); and Judith Spiller and Cynthia Hayden, "The Ocean Dumping Controversy: Social, Economic, Political, and Scientific Issues," *Ocean Development and International Law* 19 (1988): 345–366 (examination of initiatives by developing countries to amend the convention).

21. See Robert Hahn and Albert McGartland, "The Political Economy of Instrument Choice: An Examination of the U.S. Role in Implementing the Montreal Protocol," *Northwestern University Law Review* 83 (1989): 592–611; Orval Nangle, "Stratospheric Ozone: US Regulation of Chlorofluorocarbons," *British Columbia Environmental Law Review* 16 (1989): 531–580; Markus Jachtenfuchs, "The European Community and the Protection of the Ozone Layer," *Journal of Common Market Studies* 28 (1990): 261; Elizabeth P. Barratt-Brown, "Building and Monitoring a Compliance Regime Under the Montreal Protocol," *Yale Journal of International Law* 16 (Summer 1991): 519–570.

22. See "Survey of Existing International Agreements." See also *Effectiveness of International Environmental Agreements.*

18

The Global Women's Movement: Articulating a New Vision of Global Governance

Ellen Dorsey

The global women's movement is poised at the edge of the new millennium. We are witnessing today a dramatic proliferation of local movements and national and international organizations in a process that is both more coherently organized, more inclusive, and representative of the interests and needs of diverse communities of women. In their efforts to forge a global culture of women's rights, these organizations call for a revolutionary change in how societies should be organized, how institutions of global governance should be structured in equitable and just ways, and how the basic human rights and needs of all humanity can be met.

While that characterization may seem quite optimistic, paradoxically the broad picture depicting the current status of women's rights globally is quite bleak. In fact, it is those generally worsening conditions that have given rise to the concentrated efforts of women's organizations to forge transnational linkages of solidarity to exponentially increase the power they could harness in one particular national setting. As women's organizations around the world increasingly recognized that they were confronting transnational patterns of abuse, linked to failures in the global economy and international system to secure their rights and meet their needs, it was clear that a transnational response would be needed. And the call to define women's rights as human rights grew louder, evoking the legitimacy of international human rights norms while reflecting the disenfranchisement of women.[1] The confluence of opportunity and fear, expanding solidarity and intensifying challenges has been the underlying force behind the movement to redefine women rights as human rights, the newest hallmark of the rapidly expanding global women's movement.

The global women's movement is one of the most interesting and essential of transnational social movements for the analysis of global governance

Permission to use this original essay was granted directly from the author.

as 1) it offers a holistic *vision* of social transformation, articulating new norms, linking issues of development, the environment, and human rights with standards of participation, transparency, and accountability in decision-making into its agenda; 2) its *participation is inclusive* across communities, cultures, and states, and reflects both Northern and Southern world agendas; 3) its *strategy* is global targeting of formal political and economic institutions, as well as social practices; 4) and its *power* reflects the growing strength of global civil society. In many ways the global women's movement is the strongest, most inclusive, most dynamic, and viable of global movements operating in the world arena today. And its unique characteristics make it an important focus in the study of the new global actor that we have come to call a transnational social movement (TSM).[2]

The evolution of the global movement to define women's rights as human rights reflects the changes in focus of issues, the nature of organizing and strategies pursued, and greater attention than ever before to women's rights issues. It also reflects the experiences and growing sense of empowerment that women have had in joining forces in the past and witnessing the gains that their national and local organizations have made around the world in the last twenty years. With the Fourth World Conference on Women, Beijing, China, in September 1995, the last several years of the 20th century may prove to be critical to whether this emerging movement capitalizes upon its efforts towards greater coherence in advancing a global culture of women's human rights or breaks down on philosophical, organizational, or strategic lines.

To analyze both the potential for and the obstacles to attaining these new social, economic, and political relations embedded in the movement's vision for a truly new world order, it is important to examine first what underlies the foundation of the contemporary global women's movement. This paper will next address what conditions have precipitated the coming together of disparate movements and discreet organizations into a global formation. And then it will analyze what common strategies were adopted in the past that led to this current stage of redefining women's rights as human rights and human rights as women's rights. Finally, an analysis of the global women's movement as a model and vision of global governance will be offered.

A Global Movement Emerges

There are two essential factors that led to the transnationalization of disparate movements for women's rights into one global structure: a) recognition of shared and interlinked conditions of disempowerment which made a global response an imperative; b) transnational organization of networks that defined shared objectives and adopted *common, global* strategies.

Global Discrimination

Commonly cited statistics on the plight of women worldwide give a clear picture of the patterns of violence and poverty, of the denial of freedom to act, speak, make family and sexuality choices, and the failure to achieve economic autonomy and self-sufficiency that women have historically faced.

Women are one-half of the world's population, perform two-thirds of the world's work, and market over three-fifths of the world's food. Yet, women represent three-fifths of the world's illiterate, receive one-tenth of the world's income, and own less than one-hundredth of the world's property. Sex preferential practices in child birth and child care are endemic across the globe. In many parts of the world, girl children receive less education, less food, and less health care than boys. The World Health Organization estimates that one-sixth of all female infant deaths in India, Pakistan, and Bangladesh are due to neglect and discrimination. When women and girls represent three-fifths of the world's illiterate, yet women's education has been proven to lead to fewer births, fewer infant deaths, more women in the labor force, and greater economic growth—education is clearly a rights issue.

Women have begun to say sexism kills. A famous economist has noted that some 100 million Asian women are estimated to be missing—largely attributable to female infanticide and abortion of female fetuses. Discrimination starves. The plight of women in poverty is worsening, the number of rural women living in poverty has nearly doubled in the past 20 years. Today, women constitute at least 60% of the world's 1 billion rural poor.[3]

While the oppression of women has always been a global phenomenon, the globalization of economic forces has both had disproportionately harsh effects on women and has increasingly fallen outside of the control of any one state. While degrees of aggregate growth have certainly been achieved, the structural adjustment and economic stabilization policies of the International Monetary Fund and the macro development models of the World Bank have often been critiqued for their far reaching social and political costs. Women have increasingly begun to rally together to challenge the impact the restructuring of the global economy has had upon their daily lives.

More often than not, conditionality imposed on lending agreements has resulted in decreased public spending in the areas of health, education, and food subsidies. The burden of absorbing these shortfalls has fallen on women, who have to find alternative resources while facing diminishing employment prospects.[4] This created a need for organized resistance by women to simply achieve basic family security. But this resistance had to fit within the confines of women's everyday demands.

Consistent with other movements adopting a transformative agenda, women have increasingly called into question the capacity of their states to meet these basic human needs and to address the global challenges. Faced with transnational ecological degradation, subjugation to the dictates of investment capital and international lending practices, and confronted with a generalized downturn in the world economy, the national government no longer has the same capacity to fulfill its portion of the social contract. Coupled with greater corruption, authoritarianism, and clientalism, the states' ability to command authority also diminished. Again, women began to respond to the dramatic need for capacity building at the civic level to compensate for the inadequacies of national public policies.

The confluence of worsening economic conditions with expanding political opportunities acted as a gridlock on women's organizing. Women had to spend more time and energy filling the vacuums in their household economies—they had less time to be engaged politically. Thus traditional methods of participation found in party politics were increasingly rejected in favor of local organizing in the community where women worked, cared for their families, and sustained the local economy.[5] "New politics" were a natural outgrowth of concrete need and the failure of traditional methods of political participation appropriate to women's demands.

As women began to create new channels of political participation and develop new methods of development, their efforts were magnified by increasing communication and interaction across national boundaries. The self-conscious development of these linkages cross-nationally was seen as increasingly essential to success at the local level.

Development of Common Strategy, Forging Global Networks

While the history of women organizing for recognition of their rights, empowerment, and development is complex, rich, and diverse across the regions and localities of the world, currents of organizing in terms of methods, international forums, and common issues provided the foundation upon which women's groups began to develop bonds of solidarity and structured networks with shared goals. These currents have been typically classified under umbrella themes and often associated with the forums provided by United Nations conferences, as they brought women together in the first fully global setting and acted as on-going conduit of activity for the future.

In many ways, UN conferences came to frame symbolically the stages of the global women's movement. Generally, the evolution of the transnational women's movement can be characterized across decades into three central themes of development, substantive equality in the administration of justice, and, now, women's rights as human rights.

The 1970s and 1980s might most usefully be labeled the women's needs decades, where individuals concerned with the global plight of women focused on their concrete needs in conditions of poverty and oppression. In this period, the route to empowerment was development. It was increasingly believed that if women could gain control over their land, have equal access to property and decision making regarding its usage, then the structural features contributing to their subjugation and disproportionate share of the burden of poverty could be challenged on the ground, in the rural community and even through the family.

The first international conference on women was held in Mexico City, 1975, an event associated with the UN International Year of Women. Given the magnitude of the crises in women's status globally and the level of interest and participation by women from around the world, a Decade of Women was called to more fully address viable policy alternatives. The Decade stressed equality, development, and peace as its primary themes. Special attention was paid to problems in the areas of education, health, and employment. "The Declaration of Mexico," produced by an informal working group, was the first global statement that came from a representative group of women. It linked worldwide patterns of oppression to the inherent injustices in the global economy.

The Mexico conference served four important ends: 1) it launched development as a common strategy for the first time; 2) established new parameters for national policy debates and created norms of accountability by which policy could be evaluated; 3) national implementation mechanisms were initiated—no matter how ineffectual; and 4) the foundation was laid for cross-national networks. "With all of its apparent conflict, the meeting set in motion the most intricate network of women ever recorded. Women begun to realize that collective action was the key to their power and effectiveness. Solidarity links forged over the decade turned out to be stronger than ever imagined. They formed an unbreakable chain of women throughout the world dedicated to healing and liberating themselves, their children, and in turn, their men and their nations."[6]

In the 1980s women's organizations began to link the goal of development to the power of legal systems to inhibit women's growth. The link between development and the law reflected the perception that a new political space could be created if women were able to appropriate legal resources for enforcement of their development rights, while ensuring that control over the law did not render their development efforts moot. The law created and perpetuated the environment in which women's economic and social subordination occurred, by creating institutional constraints on the development of women, and by shaping the societal attitudes and values which upheld the institutions. Thus, the artificial and subordinating distinction between the public and private sphere of women's lives was reinforced through the law.[7]

Increasingly, as women began to challenge the laws governing access to social and economic resources the second stage of strategic organizing could be marked. In 1980, the Convention on the Elimination of All Forms of Discrimination Against Women (CEDAW), adopted by the UN, reflected both concern with control over legal processes and institutions and the introduction of efforts to utilize the legitimacy of international legal, human rights standards. CEDAW, in many ways, served as the bridge between the development emphasis and the adoption of a human rights methodology, foretelling the later redefinition of women's rights as human rights.

Often labeled the "International Bill of Rights" for women, CEDAW mandated that states meet minimum standards for achieving the equal rights of women. Signatories are required to submit progress reports on the degree to which their domestic laws conform to international standards. Patterns and incidence of discrimination that occurred in the public realm were to be sanctioned by national governments. In the private realm, national governments were to ensure that all institutions conform to domestic law in employment and other social sectors. As well, women were to be guaranteed the right to utilize the courts or legal tribunals to hear their claims. Perhaps most importantly, particularly in the latter period of global democratization trends, the Convention was to serve as the basis of constitutional development for all signatories.

While the Mexico conference was the critical consciousness-raising event that began the process of bringing women together into a loose global political formation, the 1985 Decade of the Women conference in Nairobi, Kenya, saw an explosion of activity essential for converting pre-existing connections into networks of women organizing across regions and by problem area. Fifteen thousand women representing broad constituencies from 150 different countries produced the Forward Looking Strategies for the Advancement of Women, documenting their common experiences, and advanced their political claims to be institutionalized internationally, nationally, and locally. In addition to outlining the platform of common claims brought to the world community, the Nairobi conference also acted as a catalyst for new transnational vehicles for organizing.[8]

Corresponding to the Nairobi conference and reflecting the new standards outlined in CEDAW, a movement was begun in the mid-1980s to equip women with a level of "legal literacy" to simultaneously question their rights under the law and whether they have the capacity to exercise them. This move reflected the frustrations that women were experiencing with the inadequacy of formal legal protections to overcome social and economic discrimination.

Legal literacy campaigns were increasingly a tactic used by grass roots women's organizations. Campaigns for legal literacy cannot simply be reduced to developing greater awareness of the impact of laws, but as a strategy for empowerment. Exploring the relevance of laws to the everyday lives of women helps build a perception of efficacy that women can transform those institutions which discriminate against them.

Providing women with forums in which they might learn about the law fed into defining women's rights as human rights. As women began to evaluate their place literally *under* the law, they not only questioned the failures of national legal protections but also questioned the inclusiveness of the international standards of rights to reflect their basic needs and political claims. Women increasingly began to document abuses and to demand accountability under the law, nationally legitimated and internationally sanctioned. The adoption of the human rights methodology was a logical outgrowth of the development and law nexus.[9]

As movements for rights under law expanded, evoking global standards, increased legitimation was brought to the demands of women's organizations. To bring pressure upon their governments to conform to international standards, they sought to use global pressure as leverage to heighten awareness about their plight under different regimes. Simultaneously, patterns of organizing around development, legal empowerment, equal access to political participation, against violence perpetrated by the state and increasingly within the family, were increasing throughout the 1970s and 1980s. Each pattern reflected a growth in the power that women experienced and the mutually reinforcing nature of their struggles. By 1985, when violence against women came to be a common theme across disparate communities of women, the clear relationship between development and rights had already been established.

CEDAW reflected that women's issues, organizing, and advancement of political claims would be greatly enhanced if there could be international legal codification of the common principles upon which the emerging movement was founded. The utility of such formal institutionalization, while limited as all international law is by the political will of states to uphold and enforce its tenets, was threefold. First, CEDAW codifies the standards upon which the movement was coalescing, symbolizing the elevation of these claims to the status of globally accepted norms. Similarly, the range of issues the new Convention incorporated reflected the composite activities of organizations with very different goals and memberships. In concrete terms, CEDAW not only reflected the common themes of the growing movement, but simultaneously served to foster a stronger shared identity among the participants.

Secondly, this codification could then in turn be used as a benchmark of state accountability, greatly empowering the work of organizations within the countries where abuses occur and for those operating to change conditions in that target state. Cross-national activism is then legitimated by global norms.

Thirdly, the failure of international organizations themselves to promote women's rights created a mandate for legal codification. How could the United Nations continue to relegate women's issues to a marginal status after the passage of an international covenant for the promotion of women's rights? And the establishment of the offices of a Commission for the Elimination of Discrimination of Women would optimally ensure that subsequent UN activity and programs would fully reflect the principles of the new law. But CEDAW was neither the reason that a human rights framework came to be integral to the movement, nor sufficient. Other factors were converging to frame the efforts to seek international legitimation in this particular way:

A. Gender-specific protections under international law, like those codified in CEDAW, ran the risk of being "ghettoized" in terms of apportionment of resources and human capital for their protection and enforcement. Also, the gender-specific rights currently codified in international law were not sufficiently inclusive to represent evolving rights claims, like reproductive rights or violence against women. CEDAW was only a first step. By claiming a new political space in the redefinition of women's rights as human rights, the whole conception of rights could be transformed more appropriately to deal with discriminatory norms that infuse social, economic, *and* political institutions and that have generalizable effects for all categories of the historically voiceless. While the passage of CEDAW was a critical step towards the protection of women's rights, it is only one mechanism to elevate the claims of women. In many ways, its limitations were the threshold for redefining all rights codification from a gender perspective.

B. A human rights orientation evolved naturally, although in the past women's organizations and movements had rejected the liberal bias of the HR approach. Pragmatically, the HR framework could encompass both the philosophical claims that individual rights transcended state control and were similarly integral to the public domain. The personal was political at the global level and the HR philosophy and methodology was clearly an appropriate one to encapsulate the demands by women's organizations that public accountability had to be established.

C. Much of the activism around women's rights issues throughout the world was often preceded by human rights activism more broadly defined. As such, women participating in these movements, often leading these movements, saw the more traditional human rights activism as a natural segue to globalizing the activities of the women's movement—both in terms of opportunity and in terms of their own efficacy to challenge those legal and social structures controlling them.

So the power of the global connection was increasingly recognized. But also out of the organizing around human rights issues more broadly defined, women started to question the place of their issues in those standards. Their gender-specific concerns were omitted from the human rights language, institutions, and laws. With growing recognition of the inherent weaknesses of the human rights prism to defend those issues most salient to their very survival coupled with the expanded sense of efficacy that women could challenge centuries-old patterns of domination, women began to use the language of the human rights movement to call attention to issues of economic security and structural patterns of violence.

D. The language of the indivisibility of human rights also linked issues of enhanced development to increased political participation and freedom from violence for women. Global human rights standards have always formally symbolized a package of rights issues ranging from protecting the freedom of association to the physical integrity and social dignity of the individual. But Cold War politicization broke concerns for political rights and those of human needs into competitive sets of political claims.

The global women's movement has consistently linked all categories of rights to the structural conditions that discriminate against women and produce profound patterns of inequality and violence. By utilizing the broad conception of an inclusive, universal, and indivisible notion of rights formally codified in the Universal Declaration of Human Rights, the notion of "Women's Human Rights" stakes a claim to the Declaration's universality.

Women Organizing at the United Nations World Conferences: Building a Women's Rights as Human Rights Strategy

Throughout the world, women's organizations had begun to develop a strategy for the World Conference on Human Rights to be held in Vienna in June of 1993 and for the sequence of summits in 1994 and 1995 (Population, Social, and Women's). But the global attention to the rape issue in the Bosnian war, magnified by the media and catapulted into homes throughout the world, provided an opening political space upon which the debates and activism around rape and all forms of violence against women in the Western and Southern worlds could coalesce and be used as political capital at the World Conference.

The Vienna Conference on Human Rights was a critical opportunity to give full legitimation to the claim that Women's Rights are Human Rights. It was also the vehicle to seek new institutional mechanisms to promote and enforce those rights with equal status to the entire package of universal human rights. One central rallying point and strategic goal of women's organizations was to establish a war crimes tribunal where rape would be incorporated as a crime against humanity. A global tribunal of violations of women's rights drew more than a thousand people into a packed auditorium. Women from over 25 countries testified to abuses that they suffered under existing human rights laws.[10]

Vienna was both a platform and a visible symbol of the growing strength of the transnational women's movement. With the broader human rights movement plagued by divisiveness, it was clear that the most coherent force at the Conference was the women's groups organized across the world. No other group or set of organizations were as effectively organized, large in numbers, dynamic in presence, or clear in articulated message. In addition to the establishment of the War Crimes Tribunal with rape recognized as a crime against humanity, their immediate goals included the appointment of a Special Rapporteur on Violence Against Women, and the demand that a gender perspective be integrated into all aspects of the UN human rights machinery. But in the process, the movement also simultaneously reaffirmed the universality and indivisibility of human rights, while expanding the scope of accountability for all rights violations affecting women to include social, economic, and cultural practices. This latter innovation served as the springboard from Vienna to the Fourth World Conference on Women in Beijing, China, 1995.

Building a Comprehensive Agenda:
From Cairo to Copenhagen to Beijing

A rapid-fire succession of meetings in late 1994 and through 1995 followed the Vienna Conference of 1993. Women's organizations from around the world, in wake of successes at Vienna, began to build a common strategy to move through the preparatory and final meetings for the International Conference on Population and Development in Cairo, Egypt, in September 1994 to the World Summit on Social Development in Copenhagen in March 1995 to the Beijing conference.

Given the high-profile media coverage throughout the world, the Cairo conference was, in many ways, a watershed event. The conference represented a paradigmatic shift in the recognition that women's empowerment and access to reproductive health were central to demographic control and development. The final 20-year Programme of Action commits governments to expand resource commitments to women's reproductive health, both in providing family planning services and fighting sexually transmitted diseases. It also demands that governments provide primary education for all children and enhance commitment to secondary education for girls.

A dramatic shift in the population debate took place at Cairo, away from seeing women as targets of restrictive reproductive control programs to agents of a social transformation that will have a marked effect on both demographic patterns and social development. The conference also served to forge an immediate link to preparations for the Social Summit. While celebrating victories that were achieved at Cairo, particularly in fighting a sophisticated strategy by the Vatican and fundamentalist religious organizations around the world to restrict women's access to family planning choices, women's organizations immediately highlighted the relatively weak priority assigned by governments to the development component of the conference.[11]

Three strategic foci emerged from the Cairo conference leading to the Copenhagen meeting: 1) a call for the redistribution of development assistance along a 20:20 formula, where 20% of donor country funds and 20% of recipient country investments are earmarked for the social sector and women's empowerment, 2) greater transparency and accountability by international financial institutions for the social and economic impact of their mandated investment strategies, and 3) greater participation of women and NGOs in formal governmental and inter-governmental economic and political decision making.

The strength of women's organizations at the Copenhagen non-governmental meeting created the parameters of policy debate for the meeting of government delegates. Organized around the themes of alleviating poverty, creating jobs, and fostering social integration the Social Summit became, in many ways, the key linchpin in the series of world conferences. It went right to the center of the development debate and the feminization of poverty. Women's organizations changed the terms of the debate away from looking at the impact of international assistance and financial practices upon women's lives to the inequity and injustice inherently embedded in contemporary development models and trade practices. Women argued that they are no longer simply the victims of these practices, but the agents of change and models of humane growth.

The shift from raising consciousness about the oppression of women to implementation of plans for women's empowerment is clearly reflected in the consensus women had at Copenhagen in the NGOs forums, caucuses, and during the intergovernmental meeting itself. In addition to intensifying the demand for a 20:20 proposal, a major campaign was developed to pressure for the diversion of military expenditures to civil and socially productive investment. As well, women's organizations built upon demands for financial accountability established in Cairo to call for specific, measurable time-bound commitments to reduce poverty, increase access to financial services and shelter, generate new resources for social development through taxes on international financial transactions and investments of TNCs, and the imposition of new, global codes of conduct for corporate practices in Southern and Northern countries.[12] While the feasibility of government enforcement of these programs is highly questionable in the near term, even the most cynical of participants at the Copenhagen conference maintained that the proposals were real innovations and given serious consideration. Several key Western governments endorsed new regulatory taxes with revenues diverted to social development programs.

Demanding commitment to implementation and a measure of accountability was the key link between the strategies for the Copenhagen and the subsequent Beijing meetings. Designed to assess change in women's lives in the ten years since the end of the UN Decade of Women and implementation of the Forward Looking Strategies that emerged from the Nairobi conference in 1985, the Fourth World Conference on Women had as its center the notions of accountability.

Beijing: A Conference of Commitments

Preparations for the Beijing conference among women's groups from around the world were unprecedented in scope and depth. Over 35,000 women and men registered to participate. This made the Fourth World Women's Conference the largest international conference to date. Beijing is expected to mark a shift from raising global awareness and attention about the oppression of women to the implementation of plans for women's empowerment. To this end, in preparation for the meeting, women's organizations demanded that governments sign a pledge for gender justice and subscribe to an implementation plan that would include:

- a commitment to funding one major project at the meeting itself
- planning a follow-up meeting to draft a schedule for implementation to be held with key individuals from relevant government agencies (health, justice, defense, state, education) and with representatives of NGOs that participated in the preparation process for Beijing
- agreement to fulfill commitments made in the Platform of Action by the year 2000

Following great controversy regarding China's handling of the conference (FWCW), the formal inter-governmental meeting at the FWCW proved to be a dynamic and often acrimonious affair. Debate and intensive NGO lobbying on issues of sexual freedom, parental rights, recognition of women's unpaid work, and cultural relativity of rights standards ultimately gave way to a document representing both compromise and real advances for women's empowerment. The 189 country delegations agreed to adopt the Platform of Action for the 12 thematic goals of the conference. Immediately after the formal signing, 40 countries rose to announce reservations to certain portions of the document.

Notwithstanding, governments and NGOs alike now view the document as a mandate for action. And NGOs played a more fundamentally unique role than in any formal UN conferences that preceded it. They moved in and out of their traditional role of lobbying governmental delegates to working closely with them to craft language, provide information, and develop strategies. For many governments, representatives of women's organizations were appointed as official government delegates.

Violence against women, not even mentioned in the Nairobi Forward Looking Strategies, was a central concern of NGOs and governments around the world. The language incorporated in the Platform goes beyond rhetorical statements assessing the need to study and act, but outlines specific actions for government implementation. In addition to the issue of violence, "the Platform of Action is noteworthy for advancing several concepts in provisions such as those that promote sexual rights, the valuation of women's unpaid work, the equal right of women to inheritance, the concept that women's rights are human rights. . . "[13]

With only a few months into the post-conference period, some tentative assessment of implementation of the Beijing document can be made. It is important to look at the path taken by national governments, international institutions, and NGOs towards implementation.

Governments. In preparation for the Beijing conference, the Australian government called upon all governments to make the meeting a "conference of commitments." While not accepted as part of the formal proceedings or obligations under the Platform, slightly less than half of the governments announced a set of commitments at the conference itself. Reinforced by the NGO call for governments to adopt the pledge for gender justice and a highly visible "Scorecard of Commitments" hung by women's organizations at the UN conference center, great pressure was exerted upon governments to take formal policy action to advance the goals of the movement. Daily briefings hosted by the NGOs centered around the Scorecard, with NGOs from different countries rating the performance of various governments.

Also, it was recommended in the Platform that governments set up national bodies charged with oversight of implementation. Those mechanisms, many of which were created out of the Nairobi process, are charged with designing strategies and overseeing the infusion of the Platform themes into government agencies and public policy initiatives. Different governments have already begun to develop national implementation mechanisms in the wake of the conference.

Some of the commitments made at Beijing and subsequently developed reflect significant policy shifts and innovations in both domestic and foreign affairs. In other cases, governments made rather hollow commitments, unlikely to be enforced or merely reflecting existing policies repackaged in the language of women's empowerment.

On domestic policies, the United States committed to action in seven areas at Beijing, with an additional commitment made in the area of education once government delegates returned. While most of the commitments reflect little more than existing programs or their enhancement, the most innovative and important of commitments was the establishment of a national implementation mechanism, albeit an ad hoc one. An interagency council was created, with a one year mandate, to coordinate policies undertaken by separate government agencies and to provide a vehicle for NGO and citizen input into the planning process. An official statement by the Interagency Council on Women read, "This intergovernmental body is charged with coordinating the federal implementation of the Platform of Action adopted at Beijing, including the US commitments announced at the conference. The Council will also develop related initiatives to further women's progress and engage in outreach and public education to support the successful implementation of the conference agreements. The Council will hold monthly public meetings to discuss its work." NGOs in the United States immediately began to lobby for a more effective and substantive integration of NGOs into the policy planning process. Many NGOs came together to demand a long-term mandate for the council be established and a full national plan referenced to the twelve areas of concern in the Beijing agenda be developed.

An example in the area of foreign policy, the German government was the first to announce specific financial commitments to overseas development assistance. Germany's senior delegate to the FWCW, Michael Bohnet, announced that his country would increase its overall foreign development aid in 1996 by 1.7% to $5.5 billion. At Cairo, Germany had committed $2 billion in population projects for developing countries with a primary emphasis upon family planning programs, health education, and women's employment. As a follow-on initiative at Beijing, Germany committed $40 million over the next five years for legal counseling programs in Southern world countries with particular emphasis upon the needs and interests of women. And it has increased its development assistance expenditures for social welfare programs in accordance with the 20:20 principle advanced at the social summit. As Bohnet noted, "So you see, this UN conference has a concrete impact on decision making structures of an individual country."[14]

World Bank. James Wolfenson, the new president of the World Bank, announced at the FWCW a commitment to prioritizing girls education as the "single most important contribution" the Bank could make to the goals of the conference. "He said the Bank plans to commit $900 million to girls education over the next five years. Wolfenson listed participation of women in designing economic reforms, access to primary health care and access to credit as areas where progress is most needed."[15] Upon returning from Beijing, Wolfenson asked the Bank's gender unit to put together an NGO advisory team to shape implementation of commitments made at Beijing. Heralded as minimal at best, the long-standing critique of the link between structural adjustment programs and increasing Southern poverty ensures that the Bank's commitments will be the focus of NGO monitoring.

United Nations.   In November, 1995, many discussions in the General Assembly of the UN focused on effective implementation of the Beijing Platform and mechanisms for infusing gender concerns into all UN specialized agencies. The Secretary General issued a report in which he rejected the Platform recommendation that a coordinating agency be spearheaded by a new high-level official. He has, instead, decided to integrate implementation responsibilities into the portfolio of one of his senior officials. "He also proposed the establishment of a high level board on the Advancement of Women, which would help strengthen the partnership between the UN and civil society."[16] Given the range of financial, bureaucratic, and leadership crises that the United Nations faces, the GWM has attached guarded importance to ensuring that it enforces its commitments. Greater attention is being paid to the development of gender-sensitive programs initiated by UN specialized agencies.

NGO enforcement.   These commitments made at the national and international levels fall far short of what the GWM and NGOs have been lobbying through the UN conference process. But with the imperative for action created when governments signed the Beijing document, these policy initiatives frame the basis of NGO leverage and create new standards of accountability.

Following the Beijing conference, actions taken by women's organizations at the local, national, and international levels can be categorized in five ways: 1) determining strategic priorities for action from the rich agenda developed at Beijing, 2) expanding the base of the movement by building new coalitions and raising public consciousness, to develop new constituencies for policy work and advocacy at the national level, 3) monitoring the enforcement of commitments made by governments and international institutions alike, 4) pressuring for NGO involvement in the design of these implementation strategies, and 5) developing popular education materials on the Beijing principles to shape societal values and reinforce the work of women's organizations in local communities, religious and social institutions, and in the family.

In terms of measuring the real impact of the NGOs and the strength of the GWM in the wake of Beijing organizing, the third function of monitoring compliance by governments and international institutions warrants closer examination. Women's organizations realize that real commitment extends beyond wrapping existing policies in the language of the FWCW, to ensure that the spirit of the Beijing agenda infuses action and policies developed in an on-going way. As well, there is universal agreement by NGOs that implementation by governments and international institutions must be tied to the Platform itself and not the inadequate commitments they might have made at Beijing.

Immediately after Beijing, a campaign was launched by the Women's Environment and Development Organization and the International Women's Tribune Center to coordinate accountability initiatives by NGOs from around the world. "Developing a commitments campaign is intended to catalyze the process of getting groups engaged with governments to advocate for longer term implementation of the entire Platform of Action."[17]

In addition to broad global campaigns for implementation, sectoral-specific initiatives have also been launched. Women's Eyes on the Bank Campaign links NGOs globally, with different national groups focusing on specific aspects of the Bank's lending practices. The U.S.-based group will focus on monitoring and influencing country departments to oversee the effectiveness of the Bank's incorporation of gender analysis into their poverty assessments and country assistance strategies. Following Women Watching the ICPD (Cairo conference), Family Care International has produced a summary report regarding government commitments made at Beijing. Titled, "Commitments to Sexual and Reproductive Health and Rights: A Framework for Action," the document will serve as a tool for cross-national advocacy to pressure governments and international institutions to uphold the terms of the Platform.

These are just a few samples of the types of projects, campaigns, and programs established to move the Beijing agenda from symbol to action. In the few months following the conference, it is far too early to attempt to assess the long-term implications of the conference itself. That there has been an explosion of activity, linking NGOs, constituencies, and public officials, at the local, national, and international levels cannot be questioned. Scholars, activists, and government officials must begin now to examine, chart, and analyze the real impact of the conference process as one measure of the strength of the women's movement.

Implementation as a Measure of the Power of the Movement

In many ways, implementation of the Beijing process will be the key measure of the power of the movement itself. The ways in which the power of the global women's movement can be measured are numerous and challenging. Very little analysis has been done evaluating the power and impact of social movements, let alone transnational social movements. The platform of action outlined at Beijing provides a ready benchmark by which the success of the organizing strategies of the global women's movements can be assessed. Securing the commitment of governments and international institutions to specific plans of action and monitoring their enforcement and implementation is the test of political and social leverage.

Beijing is about power. It is about demanding accountability for the advancement of new norms, challenging existing social structures that oppress, and challenging the power invested in national governments, international organizations, and financial institutions. It is about amplifying the shift in power from those states that purport to speak on behalf of citizens to the social movements. These movements are merging out of the grass roots and are linked to a global network of NGOs demanding to voice and define their rights and needs. And it is about optimizing power, harnessing the power of the global movement, to target abuses cross-nationally.

While each international conference has produced its own sets of agendas, the strength of the movement had to grow and the momentum of organizing had to build before women had the power to demand the transformation of social, economic, cultural, religious, and political practices. The Decade launched in the 1970s was that of global consciousness-raising of women's common problems and shared demands. In the 1980s women translated their decade of building networks and expanding their movements into the stage of formulating common principles and a shared agenda for the global women's movements, as embodied in the Forward Looking Strategies.

Outlining these goals and basic demands was not enough. The last decade has witnessed the failure of the movement to pressure governments and international organizations to implement the commitments they made in Nairobi and, in some cases, even to set up the most preliminary of action plans. The plans were too big, the problems too complex, governments too unconcerned, and the movement was insufficiently mobilized to secure real change. Not only were women's organizations unable to secure implementation in their own national contexts, but they were not able to harness the global leverage to externally pressure the government that most egregiously violates their women's rights—which is the real premise upon which the power of a transnational movement rests.

The global women's movement has entered the next phase in organizing and strategy development at the international level. Reflecting sophistication in utilizing the UN system, great attention has been paid to ensuring that the language of government implementation has been incorporated into the Beijing documents and that the gains of each separate issue conference are not set back. But in organizing the movement's presence and leverage at these meetings, coupled with the energy consumed in the preparatory process for Beijing, little attention has been devoted to building the political leverage and policy-specific focus for post-Beijing implementation at the national level. In the United States, for example, key women's organizations were only beginning to strategize about enforcing the government's commitments in the last weeks before Beijing. Nonetheless, a flurry of activity followed the conference and creative plans have been laid for on-going monitoring and advocacy of government implementation.

Global conferencing: Elite party or vehicle for change? The concern with implementation is not unique to the Beijing conference or to the concerns of the global women's movement. Often, the world conference process has been critiqued as gatherings of elite activists, issue specialists, and government agents charged with the oversight of the specific problem areas at stake. Irrespective of the degree of grass roots organizing and participation that precedes it, governments will still elaborate complex and inclusive agendas.

The conference documents represent new visions of transforming global conditions, typically without elaborating how these visions can be achieved, financed, or enforced. The Rio Earth Summit is a case in point. Agenda 21, the guide for action that came out of the meeting, is a profound and transformative vision of cooperation between governments, global civil society, international institutions, and financial and economic powers. Billions of dollars were both assessed and rhetorically committed to its implementation, without which no real progress on sustainable development is likely to be made. To date, much of those resources to implement Agenda 21 have not materialized. Some dialogue among new sets of political actors has been initiated.

The documents that have been prepared at the intergovernmental level specify that the primary responsibility of implementation lies with governments. There are provisions for monitoring compliance written into the documents, but they are weak, limited, and lack real enforcement capacity. Many of the world's governments have fought each step of the way to dilute the language of international covenants and many of the preparatory documents for Beijing. Moreover, governments have failed to address deepening patterns of poverty and violence against women. There is little expectation that governments will craft their own plans to implement Beijing. If they do so, it is not a process that women's organizations would be likely to see as perfectly congruent with their agendas.

Therefore, the process of implementation alone is not an adequate measure of the strength and power of the global women's movement, but it is the degree of control over the nature and terms of the process of implementation that is essential. Women's organizations, to be successful in achieving their objectives, must exert sufficient leverage to affect government policies. And they must monitor how those programs are distributed across diverse populations of women. The old model of state power is "who gets what, where, when, and how." A new formula must be devised to assess the power of the social movement to determine which women get what, when, where, and how and the degree of participation women play in making those decisions.

Towards a Global Culture of Women's Human Rights and a New System of Global Governance

The goals of the movement are lofty—not simply to build a global culture of women's rights but to redefine the roles of governments and international institutions in promoting those rights, in meeting basic standards of human needs, and including representatives of civil society in making the decisions that affect women's daily lives. The challenge of establishing new standards of accountability for states, the institutions of the global market economy, and social and religious forces crossing borders with unprecedented speed is daunting.

Is a global women's rights culture likely to emerge? Historical patterns of patriarchy are too deep, the supporting structures too extensive and all encompassing to think that it is likely to emerge in the near future. But the mere focus on the goal and the articulation of the standards that women are grappling with today are critical foundations for the ultimate achievement of a women's rights culture. If the movement does not factionalize too deeply on philosophical or strategic grounds, if the forces of fundamentalism and ethnic identity are not too strong, if the intensification of global poverty does not completely decimate the opportunities for women to secure their very survival, then real gains may be evidenced. Obviously, these are huge barriers with profound implications.[18]

Obstacles

Philosophical Tensions

Any movement organizing across communities with different national, ethnic, and religious identities *and* socio-economic, political, and historical backgrounds faces great potential for fracturing along philosophical principles and common goals. While many social movements share some degree of commonality in backgrounds, demographics, or identities of participants, the linkage in the global women's movement is solely gender based—a link that is simultaneously more inclusive of experience than sheer numbers would imply, yet representative of extreme diversity. In the case of the women's movement, philosophical fault lines can be precipitated by differences in attitudes about relationships to the family, men, responsibilities to the community, prioritization in the hierarchy of goals. Or they might stem from differences in characteristics ranging from the degree of collective action pursued by the community, levels of education, exposure to different opportunities, and, most importantly, the degree of efficacy perceived by the differing communities of women for transforming their particular conditions of discrimination.

Potential tensions would most likely translate into disagreement over commonality in principles, goals, strategic agendas, and tactical plans. In their nascent stage, other movements have teetered at the brink of dissolution on many of these issues, the management of which will determine the capacity to incorporate difference and change in the future. As the global women's movement has followed a path of preceding first with coalition building and development of common goals from shared issue orientation, some philosophical conflicts have been averted. The potential for breakdown is no less great as the harder, perennial questions of how a vision for a women's rights culture can transform society are operationalized, when the very real challenge of control of capital is at the core of social, economic, and political rights issues.

Competing Strategies

Another potential challenge to the movement in crafting a viable common strategy is another pattern that has plagued all social movements, domestic or transnational. Increasing sophistication in the movement's operations and the proliferation of organizations associated with the movement represent success in organizing and an increase in the potential power that can be wielded. Yet it also creates an imperative for professionalization and organizational vested interests that can manifest themselves in competition over resources and a battle for legitimacy to speak with representative voice for the movement as a whole.

Preparations for the Beijing conference surfaced tensions simmering beneath the GWM. Many activists have questioned the strategy of working through the UN conference process to advance women's rights. There is real concern that participating to impact pre-set agendas and working to impact inter-governmental documents threatens to mainstream and to co-opt. Many argue that close working partnerships with governments and UN agencies to pass official documents and resolutions gives legitimacy to frameworks being proffered by governments and international institutions that do not typically represent women's interests. In addition, the nature and efficacy of the relationship of grass roots struggles to the GWM and their impact on each other is open to question. The movement is in the process of debating the limits of working through the conference process and forging partnerships with national governments for implementation.

Preventing Demobilization

Sustaining a mass mobilization actively engaged in pressing the goals of the women's movement will become more difficult over time without the benefit of critical and transformative events like the Population Conference, Beijing, etc. While the social movement formation allows great flexibility and power appropriate to the goals and status of its participants, it is not aided by the organizational logic of a political party or national electoral process that provides both legitimacy and accountability. While major mobilization events like the UN forums allow great opportunity and creativity for participatory input, developing on-going mechanisms is a much more difficult task.

Those that speak and organize in the name of the global movement at world forums, in the halls of the UN and corridors of power in the economic and political capitals of the world, must consciously feed the activities and concerns of the disparate local patterns of organizing. They must do this not simply to reflect the movement's needs, but to guarantee its continued mobilization along a global formation. The failure to engage the diversity of issues and patterns of organizing locally into global goals and political campaigns will have the slow effect of eroding the mass constituency of the movement. There will not always be global events to organize around, nor will women have the on-going capacity to work for those events without great cost to their particular interests and needs locally. It will therefore fall on those organizations and critical thinkers that speak in the name of the global movement to carefully tred the line between building common strategies and reflecting the actual concerns and dynamism of the movement on the ground.

There is a very real potential for strategic breakdown, either out of competitive conceptions of feasible goals, competition over resources precluding effective coordination of strategies, or the inability to adapt to changed conditions and management of success. They all have implications for continued and effective mobilization of the grass roots constituency upon which all movements derive their leverage and legitimacy.

Articulating a Vision of a New System of Global Governance

In many ways, the global women's movement is a unique actor in the emerging system of global governance. It is so inclusive in participants and so broad in its transformative agenda, that its potential for demobilization, factionalization, or failed expectations is great. If the movement's success were to be measured by whether the broad vision that women's organizations are articulating for a new global order is achieved, many will likely claim it is an abject failure. But, if we think in terms of the process forged for articulating a new vision, organizing communities of disparate people to fight for that vision, and the advancement of new norms around which the practices of international institutions, social and economic forces, and government policies are increasingly held accountable—the successes have already been overwhelming.

The mere language of women's human rights and empowerment evoked by the United Nations, international financial institutions, governments, and religious institutions marks the successful globalization of the strategy of the women's movement. Today, the dominant language is of women's empowerment, whether legitimately upheld or not. As a product, new barometers of legitimacy and success in governance have been established.

Additionally, few movements have ever had such success in using the resources, forums, legitimacy, and agencies of the United Nations to advance their strategies.[19] By generating an explosion of activity in the non-governmental forums that correspond to the inter-governmental meetings, women's organizations are profoundly transforming the inter-governmental decision-making process. Roundly recognized as the strongest force in the NGO forums of all of the recent world conferences and summits, the women's caucuses became a point of access for the historically marginalized and powerless, amplify a common agenda on specific policy issues being debated in the inter-governmental meetings, and became a vehicle for oversight of government commitments.

As such, the global women's movement has adopted a truly global strategy in its efforts to shape government agendas in international forums and in using global pressure to shape international institutions and national commitment to implementation. The global forums are a mechanism to amplify the work and the demands from the localities at the global level and to, in turn, harness the leverage created in the global context to deepen the power base of activities on the ground. In a classic sense, the movement is working above and below the state. The greatest success of the movement may be the most intangible—an expanded sense of efficacy by women's activists around the world. The belief in the capacity to transform institutions that oppress, the solidarity in action, and erosion of walls of disaffection are more powerful than the passage of new legislation, the funding of a new project, and the election of a few to positions of power. The sense of efficacy comes from all of these victories and, through the power of the global movement, is magnified throughout the networks of women's organizations. The shared sense of struggle and the shared sense of victory is revitalizing, provides courage, and brings hope.

Notes

1. The human rights framework is one predicated on the principle that transnational linkages and global norms are essential for the protection of all human rights and could readily serve as an organizing principle upon which women's political claims could be advanced globally.

2. For further exploration of this notion of a transnational social movement, see Dorsey, 1992.

3. "Women: Conference to Set Women's Agenda into Next Century," Background Information notes, United Nations Department of Information, DPI/1424. Rev. 1. October 1994.

4. Nelson, 1994, p. 5.

5. Nelson, 1994.

6. Wetzel, 1993, p. 3.

7. Schuler, Kadirgamar-Rajasingham illustrate the growing recognition of the centrality of law to women's empowerment: "Since law can and does reflect the contradictions that exist among visions of the 'ideal' society, it represents a 'work in progress' as society struggles to define itself. Perceiving the law in monolithic terms is a way of empowering the law in a negative sense. Regarding it as sacrosanct and unapproachable is to imbue it with extraordinary and undeserved power and fail to recognize that in fact, the law is not a finished product, but it is the product of historical social processes.

"Recognizing the law as a project of social endeavor is to perceive law making and adjudication in political terms, and to recognize that law can be both an instrument of social change and an obstacle to it. Understanding these dynamics led the women's movement to perceive the potential in using the law for creating new norms reflecting new values." 1992.

8. One such forum was the Third World Forum on Women, Law and Development. Initiated by a project begun several years earlier by OEF International to link women in Africa, Asia, and Latin America working in the intersection of concerns with development and its place within the legal framework and to develop strategies for improving women's legal status to increase their participation in development efforts. As an organizing mechanism, the Forum produced quite productive results—establishing regional committees and an international coordinating mechanism that became a central integrating force in the globalization of the women's movement. The committees are both a vehicle for participation and a forum for sharing research, methods of advocacy, and initiating dialogue about emerging coordinated strategies (Shuler, 1990). Subsequently, the Forum laid a new layer to existing global networks, upon which preparations for the UN Fourth World Conference on Women would proceed.

9. Dorothy Thomas, "Holding Governments Accountable by Public Pressure," in *Ours by Right: Women's Rights as Human Rights,* The North-South Institute, 1993, p. 82.

10. The planning for the Tribunal reflected the broader efforts and planning of the Global Campaign for Women's Rights initiated by the Center for Women's Global Leadership at Rutgers University and the work of the International Women's Tribune Center. At a leadership institute in June of 1991, activists from around the world discussed ways to promote a world dialogue between women's and human rights groups. As well, they discussed how to focus world attention on the commonality in patterns of violence against women and as a violation of human rights. The kick-off initiative (which is now an annual event) was 16 days of Activism Against Gender Violence from November 25, International Day Against Violence Against Women to December 10, International Human Rights

Day. The first event launched a global petition drive for the UN to recognize Women's Human Rights at the 1993 World Conference on Human Rights. As it was initially co-sponsored by the International Women's Tribune Center, the petition was then translated into 21 different languages and sponsored by over 900 women's organizations globally. Eventually almost 500,000 women in 124 countries signed the document.

11. *WEDO News and Views,* vol. 7, #3, December 1994/January 1995.

12. Highlights of Working Groups Reports from Women's Global Strategies Meeting, op. cit. #1.

13. *Earth Times,* September 16, 1995.

14. Ibid.

15. Ibid.

16. Monthly Meeting Notes, InterAction Commission on the Advancement of Women, December 12, 1995. It goes on to elaborate the Secretary General's initiative: "The UN Administrative Committee on Coordination (ACC) has established four high level inter-agency task forces to coordinate their activities and to help individual countries devise strategies for follow-up on all recent UN conferences. They will be divided into four areas of responsibility: availability of basic social services, employment and income generating activities, enabling the environment for sustainable development, and the advancement of women."

17. Ibid.

18. There are a variety of different ways that the potential contributions of the global women's movement can be assessed. One could evaluate whether the goals that organizations speaking on behalf of the movement have set have been achieved, such as the establishment of the office for a High Commissioner for Human Rights and a Special Rapporteur for Violence Against Women. Or they could look to the concrete influence that the women's movement has recently exerted in global forums, such as the environmental conference in Rio, the human rights conference in Vienna, etc. And, ultimately, measures could be crafted to evaluate the transformation of the impact that institutions of global governance have had on the daily lives of women. But beyond such concrete evaluations, the opportunities the movement presents for social transformation must also be examined. The potential is far reaching for the transformation of social practices, economic justice, and the advancement of rights and democratic norms.

19. While the United Nations was essential to the strength, strategies, and effectiveness of the Transnational Anti-Apartheid Movement to raise consciousness and impose sanctions against the apartheid regime in South Africa, the global women's movement has utilized the forums of the UN in an unprecedented way.

References

Bunch, Charlotte. "Women's Rights as Human Rights: Toward a Re-vision of Human Rights" in *Human Rights Quarterly* 12 (1990) 486–498.

Bunch, Charlotte. *Bringing the Global Home,* Antelope Publications. 1985.

Bystydzienski, Jill M. *Women Transforming Politics: Worldwide Strategies for Empowerment,* Indiana University Press. 1992.

Center for Women's Global Leadership. *Women, Violence and Human Rights, Women's Leadership Institute Report.* 1991.

Freeman, Martha and Arvonne Fraser. "Women's Human Rights: Making the Theory a Reality" in *Human Rights: An Agenda for the Next Century,* Louis Henkin and J. Lawrence Hargrove, American Society for International Law. 1994.

Funk, Nanette and Magda Mueller. *Gender Politics and Post-Communism: Reflections from Eastern Europe and the Former Soviet Union*, Routledge. 1993.

Mohanty, Chandra Talpade, and Russon and Lourdes Torres. *Third World Women and the Politics of Feminism*, Indiana University Press. 1991.

Nelson, Barbara J. and Najma Chowdhury. *Women and Politics Worldwide*, Yale University Press. 1994.

Phillips, Anne. *Engendering Democracy*, Pennsylvania State University Press. 1991.

Schuler, Margaret, ed. *Claiming Our Place: Working the Human Rights System to Women's Advantage*. 1993.

Schuler, Margaret, ed. *Women, Law, and Development—Action for Change*, OEF International. 1990.

Schuler, Margaret and Sakauntala Kadirgamar-Rajasingham. *Legal Literacy: A Tool for Women's Empowerment*, UNIFEM. 1992

Sklair, Leslie. *Sociology of the Global System*, Johns Hopkins University Press. 1991.

Thomas, Dorothy Q. and Michele Beasley, Esq. "Domestic Violence as a Human Rights Issue," *Human Rights Quarterly* 15 (1993) 36–62.

Thomas, Dorothy Q. "Full Integration of Women's Human Rights into U.S. Foreign Policy: Recommendations to the U.S. Department of State." Report prepared by *Human Rights Watch*, October 1993.

Tomasevski, Katarina. *Women and Human Rights*, Women and World Development Series, Zed Books, Ltd. 1993.

Wetzel, Janice Wood. *The World of Women: In Pursuit of Human Rights*, MacMillan. 1993

Yuval-Davis, Nira and Floya Anthias. *Women-Nation-State*, St. Martin's Press. 1989.

Part 7

INTERNATIONAL ORGANIZATIONS AND THE FUTURE

WE began this book by noting the polar views of international organizations held by the general public. In the preceding articles, there seemed to be some evidence to support, in part, both the cynical and the idealist viewpoints. As a conclusion to the book, we present divergent views on the future potential of international organizations in global governance; the views expressed by the two authors in Part 7 perhaps are not at the extremes that characterize the cynical and idealist perspectives, but they do present fundamentally different assumptions and approaches to the roles that international organizations can effectively perform. The debate on the utility of international organizations is similar to national debates in the United States and elsewhere about the proper size and functions of government; this often includes a juxtaposition of government solutions against a reliance on other mechanisms such as the free market.

Not surprisingly, UN Secretary-General Boutros Boutros-Ghali sees great potential for the United Nations in addressing the world's problems. He calls for strengthening efforts in the security and economic areas and makes a familiar plea for greater financial resources and stability. Yet Boutros-Ghali implicitly acknowledges the validity of the claims made by many UN critics when he also supports administrative reform within the organization. Still, he presents an optimistic assessment of the things that the United Nations can accomplish. In contrast, Giulio Gallarotti argues not merely that international organizations have stumbled in many of their tasks, but that in many cases they are inherently incapable of dealing with global problems. Indeed, there may be too much international organization activity in some areas. The author is able to draw upon a variety of examples from many international organization critics to make his case. He concludes that more limited roles for international organizations may be desirable, or at least that common or cross-national problems should not necessarily prompt the creation of international structures to deal with them.

19

Empowering the United Nations

Boutros Boutros-Ghali

A new chapter in the history of the United Nations has begun. With newfound appeal the world organization is being utilized with greater frequency and growing urgency. The machinery of the United Nations, which had often been rendered inoperative by the dynamics of the Cold War, is suddenly at the center of international efforts to deal with unresolved problems of the past decades as well as an emerging array of present and future issues.

The new era has brought new credibility to the United Nations. Along with it have come rising expectations that the United Nations will take on larger responsibilities and a greater role in overcoming pervasive and interrelated obstacles to peace and development. Together the international community and the U.N. Secretariat need to seize this extraordinary opportunity to expand, adapt and reinvigorate the work of the United Nations so that the lofty goals as originally envisioned by the charter can begin to be realized.

Peacekeeping Is a Growth Industry

Peacekeeping is the most prominent U.N. activity. The "blue helmets" on the front lines of conflict on four continents are a symbol of the United Nations' commitment to international peace and security. They come from some 65 countries, representing more than 35 percent of the membership.

Peacekeeping is a U.N. invention. It was not specifically defined in the charter but evolved as a noncoercive instrument of conflict control at a time when Cold War constraints prevented the Security Council from tak-

Reprinted by permission of *Foreign Affairs* (Winter 1992–93), copyright © 1992 by the Council on Foreign Relations, Inc.

ing the more forceful steps permitted by the charter. Thirteen peacekeeping operations were established belrueen 1948 and 1978. Five of them remain in existence, and are between 14 and 44 years old. Peacekeeping has sometimes proved easier than the complementary function of peacemaking. This shows that peacekeeping, by itself, cannot provide the permanent solution to a conflict. Only political negotiation can do that.

During the Cold War years the basic principles of peacekeeping were gradually established and gained acceptance: the consent of the parties; troops provided by member states serving under the command of the secretary general; minimum use of force; collective financing. It was also learned, often the hard way, that peacekeeping success requires the cooperation of the parties, a clear and practicable mandate, the continuing support of the Security Council and adequate financial arrangements.

The end of the Cold War has led to a dramatic expansion in demand for the United Nations' peacekeeping services. Since 1988 14 new operations have been established, five of which have already completed their mandates and been disbanded. In the first half of 1992 the number of U.N. soldiers and police officers increased fourfold; by the end of the year they [exceeded] 50,000.

Some of these new operations have been of the traditional, largely military type, deployed to control unresolved conflicts between states. Examples are the military observers who monitored the ceasefire between Iran and Iraq from 1988 to 1991 and those who currently patrol the demilitarized zone between Iraq and Kuwait.

But most of the new operations have been set up to help implement negotiated settlements of long-standing conflicts, as in Namibia, Angola, Cambodia, El Salvador and Mozambique. Namibia was a colonial situation but each of the other four has been an internal conflict, albeit with significant external dimensions, within a sovereign member state of the United Nations.

There is another aspect to the end of the Cold War. The thawing of its frozen political geography has led to the eruption of savage conflicts in, and sometimes between, newly emerging independent states. The former Yugoslavia has become the United Nations' largest peacekeeping commitment ever. Ethnic conflict across political borders and the brutal killing of civilians there are reminiscent of the ordeal that U.N. peacekeeping forces faced in the 1960s in the then Congo. U.N. forces again are taking an unacceptable level of casualties. It is difficult to avoid wondering whether the conditions yet exist for successful peacekeeping in what was Yugoslavia.

The 1990s have given peacekeeping another new task: the protection of the delivery of humanitarian supplies to civilians caught up in a continuing conflict. This is underway in Bosnia-Herzegovina and Somalia, member states whose institutions have been largely destroyed in a confused and cruel web of civil conflicts. This task tests the established practices of peacekeeping, especially the circumstances in which U.N. soldiers may open fire. Existing rules of engagement allow them to do so if armed persons attempt by force to prevent them from carrying out their orders. This license, used sparingly in the past, may be resorted to more frequency if the United Nations is to assert the Security Council's authority over those who, for personal gain or war objectives, try to rob or destroy humanitarian supplies destined for suffering civilian populations.

Beyond Peacekeeping

All these new modes of peacekeeping have had far-reaching implications for the way in which U.N. operations are organized and conducted.

In internal conflicts, or indeed in interstate conflicts where one or other of the governments is not in a position to exercise full authority over territory nominally under its control, not all the parties are governments. As a result the peacekeepers have had to learn how to deal with a multiplicity of "authorities." The leaders of such groups are often inaccessible and their identity even unknown; chains of command are shadowy; armed persons who offend against agreements signed by their supposed leaders are disowned; discipline is nonexistent or brutal. And everywhere there is an evil and uncontrolled proliferation of arms.

Peacekeeping operations still invariably include military personnel. But now the civilian elements often have an even more important role. This is especially true when the task is to help implement comprehensive and complex settlements, as was or is the case in Namibia, El Salvador, Cambodia and Mozambique. Political action is required to resolve disputes between the parries and persuade them to implement the agreed arrangements. Information programs must explain the United Nations' role and advise the people of the opportunities the settlement gives them. Refugees must be brought home and resettled. Elections must be observed and verified or even, in Cambodia, organized and conducted by the United Nations.

Local police must be monitored to ensure that they carry out their duties in the spirit of the new order and not the old. Respect for human rights must be verified, an especially important task in El Salvador and Cambodia. In the latter country the United Nations also has responsibility for controlling the key parts of the existing administrative structures.

All of these tasks, some of them very intrusive, must be carried out with complete impartiality by civilian peacekeepers. Staff members of the U.N. system, with policy and election observers made available by member states, have risen to these new civilian challenges.

The involvement of such a variety of civilian personnel, alongside their military colleagues, creates a need for tight coordination of all aspects of an operation. As a result it has become normal for the overall direction of a multifaceted peacekeeping operation to be entrusted to a senior civilian official as special representative of the secretary general, to whom the force commander, the police commissioner, the director of elections and other directors report.

Responses Must Be Quick

One of the lessons learned during the recent headlong expansion of U.N. peacekeeping is the need to accelerate the deployment of new operations. Under current procedures three or four months can elapse between the Security Council's authorization of a mission and its becoming operational in the field. Action is required on three fronts: finance, personnel and equipment.

On finance, the member states should provide the secretary general with a working capital fund for the start-up of new operations, so that cash is immediately available. They should also revise existing financial procedures so that the secretary general has authority to spend that cash, within reasonable limits, as soon as the new operation is authorized.

The question of personnel is more complicated. Procedures for the transfer of U.N. staff to new operations in the field are being simplified for more rapid reaction. But most peacekeeping personnel (troops, police, election observers) are made available by governments. The answer is not to create a U.N. standing force, which would be impractical and inappropriate, but to extend and make more systematic standby arrangements by which governments commit themselves to hold ready, at an agreed period of notice, specially trained units for peacekeeping service.

A handful of governments already do this. A recent invitation to all member states to volunteer information about what personnel and equipment they would in principle be ready to contribute, if asked, produced disappointing results. I have now decided to take the initiative and put specific proposals to governments, in order to identify with reasonable certainty sources of military and police personnel and equipment that governments would undertake to make available at very short notice. These commitments would constitute building blocks that could be used, when the moment came, to construct peacekeeping operations in various sizes and configurations, ranging from a small group of military observers to a full division, as required.

Allied with this effort will be the provision of more extensive guidance to governments on training troops and police who they may contribute to the United Nations for peacekeeping duties.

Equipment can cause even greater bottlenecks than personnel. There are two complementary ways in which this problem can be eased. First, member states should make it possible for the United Nations to establish a reserve stock of basic items (vehicles, radios, generators, prefabricated buildings) that are always required for a new peacekeeping operation. Second, member states could agree to hold ready, at various locations around the world, reserves of such equipment. These would remain their property but could be made immediately available to the United Nations when the need arose.

An even more radical development can now be envisaged. It happens all too often that the parties to a conflict sign a ceasefire agreement but then fail to respect it. In such situations it is felt that the United Nations should "do something." This is a reasonable expectation if the United Nations is to be an effective system of collective security. The purpose of peace enforcement units (perhaps they should be called "ceasefire enforcement units") would be to enable the United Nations to deploy troops quickly to enforce a ceasefire by taking coercive action against either party, or both, if they violate it.

This concept retains many of the features of peacekeeping: the operation would be authorized by the Security Council; the troops would be provided voluntarily by member states; they would be under the command of the secretary general; and they would be impartial between the two sides, taking action only if one or other of them violated the agreed ceasefire. But the concept goes beyond peacekeeping to the extent that the operation would be deployed without the express consent of the two parties (though its basis would be a ceasefire agreement previously reached between them). U.N. troops would be authorized to use force to ensure respect for the ceasefire. They would be trained, armed and equipped accordingly; a very rapid response would be essential.

This is a novel idea that involves some obvious difficulties. But it should be carefully considered by the international community as the next step in the development of the United Nations' capability to take effective action on the ground to maintain international peace and security.

Unpaid Bills

There have been prolonged delays by member states in meeting their financial obligations regarding peacekeeping operations. For instance, four months into one of the largest and most complex U.N. operations ever, only nine member states had fully paid their obligations to the U.N. Transitional Authority in Cambodia. Delays in payment add to the fragility of an already delicate mission by hampering the United Nations' capacity to deploy and causing delays in the schedule. These in turn threaten the agreed timetable and jeopardize the entire peace process. At a time when the United Nations is being asked to do more than ever, it is being shortchanged by the member states who have breached their legal obligations and deprived the United Nations of necessary resources.

These difficulties occur against a background of dramatically increasing costs for establishing and maintaining peacekeeping operations. During the first half of 1992 there was a fourfold increase in peacekeeping costs—from some $700 million to about $2.8 billion. Expenses are likely to rise even higher with new and expanded operations. Meanwhile the continued failure of most member states to meet their financial commitments to peacekeeping operations and to the United Nations in general is a most serious problem. The continued viability of these missions, as well as the credibility of the United Nations itself, is threatened.

Mounting Development Needs

Political stability is not an end in itself; it is a condition of durable economic and social development and the fulfillment of the human potential. At the same time inseparable links between peace and development need to be acknowledged and understood. The world has seen the deterioration of economic and social conditions give rise to political strife and military conflict. The activities of the United Nations for peace and security should not be carried out at the expense of its responsibilities for development. It is essential that peace and development be pursued in an integrated, mutually supporting way.

One can point to a number of situations where the United Nations has kept the peace, or at least prevented conflicts from escalating, but the balance sheet on the development side is less than encouraging. A billion people live on less than one dollar a day; children in many parts of the world are dying unnecessarily of diseases that could easily be cured; women are striving to be both breadwinners and homemakers in situations of intolerable strain; and there are too few jobs. The crisis is deeper than merely another manifestation of the familiar disparity between the developed nations of the North and the developing South.

No such clear-cut pattern offers itself to our eyes today. East European countries and the former Soviet Union are struggling in their transition toward democracy and market-based economies. Even the nations of the Organization for Economic Cooperation and Development are not immune to economic and social ills. Poverty, unemployment, inequity and growing insecurity exist in virtually every part of the globe. Even rich nations are tempted to turn inward to attend to their own agendas. But today there is no longer any such thing as "someone else's problem"; the globalization of economies and communications deepens our interdependence.

The responsibilities of the United Nations in the field of social and economic development are central to the purposes and principles of the charter: first, because the maintenance of international peace and security is inextricably entwined with economic and social progress and stability;

and second, because the promotion of social and economic progress is a specific task given to the United Nations by the charter.

Development policy was significantly shaped by the Cold War and the process of decolonization. When the charter was being framed at San Francisco in 1945, and when most of our current world economic institutions were being created, most of today's states were either colonies, semi-colonies or parts of extensive empires. The notion of "development" was unformed; the concept of the "Third World" had not emerged. The idea that the United Nations should be concerned with economic and social issues sprang from what has been called "welfare internationalism," which evolved in wartime planning for the peace and was a formative influence on the Bretton Woods institutions dating from that period.

As demands for independence gathered momentum in African and Asian lands, programs of assistance and economic cooperation were initiated by former colonial powers. These were joined by assistance programs established by states with no recent colonial past, such as the Nordic countries. Meanwhile the World Bank was becoming the lead institution in the channeling of multilateral development finance to developing countries.

Provision of development assistance to newly independent nations became part of the foreign policies of the industrialized countries, intricately bound up with the global contest for power and influence. The United States, through its Agency for International Development, became a major provider of development finance and technical assistance in Africa, Asia and Latin America. The Soviet Union was deeply involved with a relatively small number of states considered potentially significant in its ideological sphere, and provided substantial technical support for them. In both cases development assistance was often interwoven with military aid.

Just as the Cold War distorted the vision of collective security set forth in the U.N. charter, it also impaired cooperation for development. Bilateral foreign aid programs were often an instrument of the Cold War, and remain deeply affected by considerations of political power and national policy. Multilateral development programs, even when managed well and with admirable ethical purpose, derived from ideas and ideologies that proved inadequate at best and in some cases ruinous.

At this time of change in world affairs, when restructuring the institutions of international relations is high on the agenda, there are increasing demands for action in the field of economic and social development. The call for a new unity and clarity of purpose from the United Nations in the field of development—which is now commonly understood to include social and economic development and environmental protection as well—has come from developing and developed countries alike.

Traditionally U.N. social development activities have concentrated on the most vulnerable groups of populations. Increasingly in developing countries efforts at modernization tug at institutions that hold the social fabric together. Declining social cohesion, in turn, can undermine economic progress. The organization is beginning to take a closer look at specific phenomena affecting social cohesion and to view the social and economic dimensions of development in a more integrated way. Issues of demography and cultural, religious, ethnic and linguistic diversity are so closely related today to prospects for political stability and economic advancement that the involvement of the United Nations in issues of social development is acquiring a qualitatively different nature.

If the process of decolonization is over and the Cold War has ended, and now that there is no "struggle" or bipolar competition to dramatize and distract development efforts, how can the United Nations seek consensus on the need for a fairer, more just, world and focus on the long-standing needs of the poor?

Today a consensus is emerging around a fundamental perception that the unfettered talents of individual human beings are the greatest resource a society can bring to bear on the task of national development. But the troubled state of the global economy indicates that we are still far from achieving universal economic prosperity, social justice and environmental balance. Cooperation for development will require the greatest intellectual effort in the period ahead because, as understood and applied until now, it has not resolved the urgent problem of the development of the planet. The need is comprehensive. Issues once approached separately, or sequentially, now may be seen as essentially indivisible.

Changed View of Sovereignty

The transition from one international era to another is symbolized today, as it has been at earlier turning points in the history of the United Nations, by a new group of member states taking their seats in the General Assembly. (Armenia, Azerbaijan, Bosnia-Herzegovina, Croatia, Georgia, Kazakhstan, Kyrgyzstan, Moldova, San Marino, Slovenia, Tajikistan, Turkmenistan and Uzbekistan all joined in 1992.) Their entrance reaffirms the concept of the state as the basic entity of international relations and the means by which peoples find a unity and a voice in the world community.

While respect for the fundamental sovereignty and integrity of the state remains central, it is undeniable that the centuries-old doctrine of absolute and exclusive sovereignty no longer stands, and was in fact never so absolute as it was conceived to be in theory. A major intellectual requirement of our time is to rethink the question of sovereignty—not to weaken its essence, which is crucial to international security and cooperation, but to recognize that it may take more than one form and perform more than one function. This perception could help solve problems both within and among states. And underlying the rights of the individual and the rights of peoples is a dimension of universal sovereignty that resides in all humanity and provides all peoples with legitimate involvement in issues affecting the world as a whole. It is a sense that increasingly finds expression in the gradual expansion of international law.

Related to this is the widening recognition that states and their governments cannot face or solve today's problems alone. International cooperation is unavoidable and indispensable. The quality, extent and timeliness of such cooperation will make the difference between advancement or frustration and despair. In this setting the significance of the United Nations should be evident and accepted. Nothing can match the United Nations' global network of information-gathering and constructive activity, which reaches from modern world centers of power down to the villages and families where people carry out the irreducible responsibilities of their lives.

At the other end of the scale only the United Nations can convene global-scale meetings of ministers and heads of states or governments to examine complex issues and propose integrated approaches. Such gatherings can have enormous implications for the world's good. At the Conference on Environment and Development in Rio de Janeiro in June 1992, for example, states obligated themselves to take global consequences into consideration in their domestic decisions. This is a fundamental philosophic undertaking by the world's nations, adding one more pillar to the gradually growing array of internationally accepted principles of national conduct.

Reforming the U.N.

Renewing the promise of an effective and cooperative United Nations means, in the first instance, reform of the organization and the broader system of specialized agencies from within. There is much that can be done now, but it must be understood that this will be an evolutionary process. The world is still in some ways in its "Middle Ages" when it comes to international organizations and cooperation. Centuries were required before the struggle among monarchical and baronial forces was transformed into states capable of carrying out responsibilities in the fields of security, economy and justice. There is no doubt that the institutions of the U.N. system must travel such a path if chaos is to be avoided.

Given firm leadership and a common resolve by member states I am confident that major achievements can be made by the end of this century.

To initiate reform from within I launched a process of restructuring the U.N. Secretariat. My first short-term aim was to eliminate duplication, redundancy and excessive layering of offices and duties at headquarters. This process has brought some results and must continue toward a coherent institutional strategy.

The Administrative Committee on Coordination is the highest body bringing together the executive heads of all the specialized agencies and organizations of the U.N. system. This committee must act more definitively to guide and harness the work of the various organizations of the system.

Similarly, the Economic and Social Council, despite its preeminence in the charter, has proved too weak to provide coherence and form to the work of the specialized agencies, the Bretton Woods institutions, the regional economic commissions and the array of U.N. programs. Duplication is widespread; coordination is often nominal; bureaucratic battles aimed at monopolizing a particular subject are rife, and organizational objectives are sometimes in conflict.

The proliferation of institutions that characterize U.N. work in the economic, social and environment fields has been another product of previous decades. Member states often pressed for measures on a piecemeal basis. Bureaucracies were sometimes set up as substitutes for problem-solving and served, in some cases, to camouflage problems rather than expose them to serious attention.

I have recommended the introduction of a flexible high-level inter-sessional mechanism to enable the council to respond in a continuous and timely way to new developments in the economic and social sphere. It should possess an early-warning function encompassing threats to security and well-being: from energy crisis to the burden of debt, from the risk of famine to the spread of disease. As the Security Council can envision new possibilities in the cause of peace, so the Economic and Social Council's role can be significantly strengthened. At this time when old conceptions of development are fading and new departures are required, each element of the U.N. system will need to reexamine and justify anew its mission and the human and financial resources it employs.

The Interaction of Peoples

New possibilities exist for shared, delegated and interactive contributions to the world organization from the burgeoning number of regional associations and agencies and the huge network of nongovernmental organizations that in the past largely operated from North America and Europe but increasingly are a feature in countries all over the world. More than a thousand NGOs are active in the United Nations, working through and with people everywhere.

There is an even deeper level to this trend: relationships among nations are increasingly shaped by continuous interaction among entire bodies politic and economic. Such activity almost resembles a force of nature, and indeed may be just that. Political borders and geographic boundaries pose slight barriers to this process. Governments increasingly prove ineffective in efforts to guide or even keep track of these flows of ideas, influences and transactions. The challenge for the foreseeable future will be to make sense of these evolving relationships between and among peoples.

As one area for such efforts, I have put forward the concept of "post-conflict peace-building." In the aftermath of warfare, concrete cooperative projects that link two or more countries and peoples in a mutually beneficial undertaking can not only contribute to economic and social development but also enhance the confidence that is so essential to peace. Freer travel, cultural exchanges, youth projects and changes in educational practices all could serve to forestall a reemergence of cultural and national tensions that could spark renewed hostilities. Post-conflict peace-building will be needed not only in cases of international conflict, but also for the increasing number of intrastate, internal conflicts arising today.

Changing U.N. Culture

The spirit of the U.N. Charter was kept alive for decades under very difficult circumstances. Hope has been crucial; achievement is now required. Beyond declarations, beyond position-taking, the time is here to look at ideas as plans for action. Beyond restructuring, the culture of the United Nations must undergo a transformation.

The bipolar contest relegated the United Nations to a status far removed from its original design. A propensity to rhetoric, to protocol and a delight in maneuvering for marginal advantage or national prestige came to characterize many delegations' activities. Committees and commissions have been assigned important duties only to find governments participating through assignment of lower level officials, unauthorized to engage seriously. Time is too precious and the tasks too urgent today to permit these indulgences.

In the Cold War era a fundamental split was taken for granted on virtually every issue. We have been relieved of that burden. But we cannot expect to be free of controversy, dispute or debate. The problems before us are complex and the solutions not at all obvious. If we work seriously on them, we must expect serious differences of opinion. Rather than be deterred by this we should be grateful and eager to engage in the intellectual struggle that is needed. Sharp differences are inevitable, but consensus is possible. I am committed to a broad dialogue between the member states and the secretary general. Preserving the authority of the United Nations requires the fullest consultation, participation and engagement of all states, large and small. This in turn requires the empowerment of people in civil society and a hearing for their voices at all levels of international society and institutions.

20

The Limits of International Organization: Systematic Failure in the Management of International Relations

Giulio M. Gallarotti

"**N**othing in excess" is the warning inscribed on the Temple of Apollo at Delphi and echoed in the literature and mythology of ancient Greece. According to the logic of excesses, too much of anything—even a "good" thing—can be detrimental. This lesson appears to be as relevant for international organization (IO) as it is for other social contexts.[1] Just as poorly managed or "bad" IO can be harmful, "good" IO in excess can have adverse effects.

On the one hand, IO can be counterproductive when management is of the wrong kind or is executed poorly. Critics of the Food and Agriculture Organization, for example, argue that the institution's administration supports a model of agricultural development that is antithetical to private sector growth and therefore inhibits general economic development in Third World countries.[2] On the other hand, excessive IO can be bad even when the management is apparently good. Some have argued, for example, that the provision of abundant liquidity to debt-ridden nations creates a moral hazard in that it gives debtors fewer incentives to promote the economic changes that would make them less dependent on foreign lending.[3] In this case, as with the recent case of savings and loans bailouts in the United States, it appears that safety has it price. Similarly, food aid, as traditionally practiced with respect to less developed countries (LDCs), has often served to compound problems of hunger and food dependence because of its "disincentive effects" on domestic food production.[4] And, finally, too much IO may be undesirable if it is costly and has no appreciable effect on international relations.

Reprinted from *International Organization,* Vol. 45, No. 2, Spring 1991, Giulio Gallarotti, "The Limits of International Organization: Systematic Failure in the Management of International Relations," by permission of MIT Press. © 1991 by the World Peace Foundation and the Massachusetts Institute of Technology.

While IO can be said to "fail" in any of these ways, it is most antithetical to orderly international relations when its failures make international problems worse or generate new problems—that is, when IO itself is a destabilizing force in world politics. In his first annual report on the work of the United Nations (UN), Secretary-General Javier Pérez de Cuéllar sensitized the international community to such destabilizing failings in the multilateral management of interdependence by citing the adverse effects that UN resolutions can have on international security and by admitting that the misuse of the UN has contributed to the global problems facing the organization.[5] In light of the failures of IO, bureaucrats and scholars alike need to reassess the role of multilateral management and its effects on international relations within and across issue-areas. Or, more formally, they need to take into account the limitations of IO when considering the optimal scope and level of multilateral management.[6]

As Friedrich Kratochwil, John Ruggie, and J. Martin Rochester have argued, recent scholarship has increasingly strayed from the study of IO as distinct from world politics and has relinquished much in terms of the normative foundations of the traditional literature on IO. A result is that the processes of IO and international relations have been conflated in a way that makes the specific assessment of managerial processes and institutions more difficult. Furthermore, the analytic modes and conclusions generated by recent work have insufficiently addressed issues that contribute to social engineering at the level of multilateral management; that is, they have provided little food for consumption on the part of international bureaucrats and national policymakers.[7] Historically, the study of IO has to a large extent been coterminous with the study of the structures, roles, and goals of international institutions. The traditional literature has placed much emphasis on institutional origins and developments in the frameworks and objectives of specific organizations and has paid considerably less attention to the effects of these organizations on international relations. Moreover, when scholars have assessed the effects, they have tended to offer a rather benign vision in which the process of multilateral management in characterized as invariably contributing to the stabilization of relations among nations and in which the limitations of management are ignored or downplayed. Thus, traditional contributions to the IO literature have been heavy on the positive side (the stabilizing outcomes of management) and light on the negative side (the failures of management), whereas the recent contributions have been instrumental in addressing the negative side but have taken a somewhat restricted approach to organizational failure. To use Kratochwil and Ruggie's analogy, while the doctor has more recently stopped visiting the patient altogether, the doctor has traditionally visited the patient without systematically diagnosing illness.[8]

In addressing these limitations in the IO literature, this article presents a typology of the systematic (inherent rather than mistake-related) failures of IO. In doing so, it brings the processes and institutions of multilateral management back into focus as phenomena that are sui generis and therefore distinct from the underlying relations they oversee. While its conclusions about the nature of overmanaged relations and the partial solutions that it offers are intended to serve as potential normative guidelines, its focus on the effects of IO is intended to complement the traditional focus on the roles, goals, and structures of international institutions. Thus, by emphasizing the destabilizing effects of IO and presenting a less benign view of the management of international relations, the article makes a contribution toward filling in the negative side of the managerial ledger. In Kratochwil and Ruggie's terms, the present enterprise once more attends to the patient, but with an emphasis on diagnosing illness.

The article begins with a discussion of the managerial approach to IO and the recent revisionist scholarship. It then confronts the managerial vision of IO by offering a more general theoretical approach to understanding the destabilizing effects of multilateral management than has commonly been taken in the critical IO literature. In presenting a typology of systematic failures, it seeks to bridge the gaps in our understanding of why many different institutions and managerial schemes fail. That IO has virtues and can have a positive impact on international relations is not denied. Nevertheless, the article concludes that it is often in the best interest of stable international relations in and across issue-areas to be regulated by IOs that are limited in their scope or level of management. In addressing the general issue of IO failure, rather than addressing why a particular institution or managerial scheme fails, the analysis is thus intended to serve both as a focal point for understanding critical approaches to the study of IO and as an alternative rationale for eliminating the excesses of multilateral management.[9]

The Managerial Approach
to International Organization

Traditional IO scholars have tended to take a rather benign view of the process of multilateral management.[10] For these scholars, IO at best provides the necessary management dictated by the growing complexity of interdependence within and between issue-areas. At worst, this management appears as a benign redundancy in functions insofar as it is targeted to bring about order that is already existent in some set of relations. The tone of the literature has for the most part been uncritical both on a systematic and a general level,[11] and any explicit or implicit critiques that have been offered have tended to be issue- or case-specific.[12]

According to the functionalists, the growth of technology, the awareness of its possible adverse and positive effects, and the spread and intensification of demands for higher material welfare place increasing pressure on nations to seek what Ernst Haas calls "managerial leadership" at the multilateral level.[13] The growth of "common activities and interests across nations," argues David Mitrany, requires a concomitant growth in the "common administrative agencies" that manage interdependence. International government must grow so that it remains "co-extensive with international activities." Hence, like the activities it must oversee, international management must itself become "all-embracing and all-pervasive."[14] In this sense, the growth of IO is consistent with the ongoing evolution and greater centralization of functions in human society. For a working peace system, notes Mitrany, nations must collectively "take over and coordinate activities hitherto controlled by the nation state, just as the state increasingly has to take over activities which until now have been carried on by local bodies."[15] Thus, the goal of global security is reached through a process involving "a sufficient addition" of managerial functions, which together "would create increasingly deep and wide strata of peace."[16]

For neofunctionalists, the causal link between technological and welfare problems on the one hand and international management on the other is mediated by interest groups and elites, but the vision of IO is quite similar. For them, the process of spillover is the forcing variable.[17] As the pressures for integration spread laterally and vertically, the level and scope of international management must be expanded. According to Haas, the problems of international security, economic development, and technological and scientific interdependence require an "upgrading of common interests" among nations, which is only realizable within "the framework of supranational institutions." The intensification of this "upgrading" in turn requires "continuing supranational activity."[18] For Ruggie, the impact of scientific and technological interdependence on international relations necessitates a "collective response" based on "mutual accountability."[19] The collective response will be manifest in "greater amounts of joint services and joint production, and a greater degree of joint regulation of national activities."[20] For Eugene Skolnikoff, this interdependence requires that nation-states "accept a degree of international regulation and control over their nominally domestic activities that goes well beyond the situation today."[21]

Traditional scholarship in the field of modernization and interdependence has similarly argued that the greater interpenetration of the social and economic spheres that occurs with industrialization necessitates a collective approach to the specific needs of nations. Edward Morse, for example, indicates that "modernization is accompanied by increased levels and types of interdependencies among societies, which require . . . a high level of cooperation."[22] This interdependence, adds Morse, makes "international coordination of policies highly desirable" because the "attainment of basic domestic policy goals" can no longer be realized through independent actions.[23]

These managerialist strands in the traditional literature on IO and interdependence have numerous counterparts in the general literature on international relations. For example, Seyom Brown and Larry Fabian would address the problem of the global commons with a comprehensive oceans authority, an international scientific commission on global resources and ecologies, a global weather and climate organization, and an outer space project agency.[24] Stanley Hoffmann, in mainstream fashion, argues that the future of the world order will depend on the growth of IO as a means of integrating inherently conflictual interests and realizing joint gains both in a political and an economic context.[25] In explicating the assumptions underlying Hoffmann's vision, Richard Cooper states that "where trust is not complete, some form of international organization may be helpful to police the rules and supervise the imposition of penalties for violations of the rules."[26] Regarding the international political economy, the exhortations of Fred Block and Robert Solomon are characteristic. According to Block, "If our goal is the improvement of human welfare, this requires subordinating market forces to conscious human will."[27] Similarly, Solomon argues, "Cooperation and joint management are still necessary. . . . The international system has tended to follow the evolution that has occurred within individual countries. One of the major lessons learned in the thirties . . . is that the pursuit of self-interest by individual entities in an economy does not necessarily bring about optimal results for the economy as a whole."[28] The high point of this managerialism in international economic relations is embodied in Irving Friedman's call for a "new Bretton Woods."[29]

More recently, scholars have taken a much more systematically critical approach to IO and have qualified the traditional arguments about the need for extensive supranational government. IO has been attacked both from the right and the left and both in theoretical and nontheoretical treatises. On the right, the ongoing studies of the Heritage Foundation have expounded a vision of IO, especially as manifest in the UN, as a destabilizing force in international politics because of the inflammatory way it mediates disputes (for example, supporting the positions of guerrilla groups) and the way it generates other managerial failures.[30] A frequent critique of the UN is that it perpetuates underdevelopment because its approach is biased against market solutions. In exploring the ways in which UN management in and across issue-areas makes the world a more "dangerous place," Abraham Yeselson and Anthony Gaglione have adopted the same destabilizing view of the UN.[31] Others have underscored that deficiencies in the managerial structures of the UN are the sources of its failure and inefficiencies.[32]

The leftist literature on IO has tended to take the same pejorative view of supranational structures of governance that leftists normally take of domestic structures of governance: both types institutionalize class hegemony. In the case of supranational government, leftists speak of economic (capitalist) classes of nations as well as social classes. Most of their studies are targeted at specific organizations, while some contributions exhibit a general orientation.[33]

On a more theoretical level, proponents of rational choice and public choice approaches to IO have argued that supranational management is either redundant or the source of inefficiencies in the relations between nations. John Conybeare argues that the market can sufficiently allocate goods and address international problems in relations that do not exhibit high levels of publicness and that supranational management in these relations is unnecessary and would only replicate the outcomes generated by less centralized schemes.[34] John Ruggie and Per Magnus Wijkman marshal similar, albeit more restrictive, arguments.[35] Roland Vaubel sees the collusive and redistributive nature of international collaboration as inherently imposing welfare losses on the international system in general as well as on specific subnational groups.[36]

At the same time that scholars have taken a more critical approach to IO, they have also taken a more decentralized approach to the possibilities for order and cooperation in international politics. This trend is particularly evident in the regime and neoliberal institutionalist contributions to the international relations literature. According to proponents of the decentralized approach, institutions serve as facilitators of cooperation. This suggests positive, rather than critical, sentiments about the role of IO. Where they depart from traditional managerial approaches, however, is in their sensitivity to the conditionality of management. Since relations in and across issue-areas are seen as heterogeneous, rather than homogeneous, the requirements for regulation will vary in scope and level. Some constellations of relations (particularly those with preexisting norms about appropriate policies) will require institutions only to reduce the organization or transaction costs of cooperation, while others will require more careful and extensive regulation.[37]

Although the revisionist literature on IO offers a valuable counterbalance to the traditional managerial view, it nevertheless exhibits limitations in its identification and analysis of organizational failure. The existing critical literature, for example, tends to be disproportionately specific in its targets and orientation. While the work of Yeselson and Gaglione, the studies from the Heritage Foundation, and the literature on bureaucratic failure are specifically targeted toward the UN, the leftist literature has commonly focused on the World Bank, International Monetary Fund, and the UN. Even the work that appears to be of a more general orientation is still quite restricted and sometimes insufficiently systematic in its identification of IO failure. General leftist critiques, such as those of Robert Cox and Teresa Hayter,[38] are fundamentally restricted to the adverse distributional effects of the institutionalization of First World hegemony and are much less concerned with instabilities within classes of nations. Cony-beare, Wijkman, and Ruggie are more concerned with why IO might be unnecessary than with how and why IO fails. Although Vaubel is both general and systematic in the identification of IO failure, he is more concerned with the inefficiencies than with the destabilizing effects of IO, and his analysis of inefficiencies is restricted to those generated by the collusive and redistributional nature of IO.

In contrast to the revisionist literature, which offers a restricted critique of how IO can fail *within* specific issues and institutions, the following general critique of managerialism offers a typology of systematic organizational failure and suggests how IO can fail *across* issues and institutions.

Critique of Managerialism: The Systematic Failure of International Organization

The failures of IO, defined here as the negative or destabilizing effects of IO on international relations, can generally be classified as either unsystematic or systematic. While unsystematic failures are related to mistakes or malfunctions in the management of international problems, systematic failures are considered inherent in or endemic to IO.[39] There is no systematic reason, for example, why one supranational organization would make the mistake of overmanaging relations while another would not; why one would be too extreme in demanding adherence to its rules while another would not; or, more generally, why one institution or managerial scheme would be characterized by or result in poor management. While unsystematic failures are stochastic and have a chaotic distribution, systematic failures are determined by bias (by the roles, functions, and goals of IO, which naturally encourage failure) and have an identifiable pattern in their distribution. IO can fail systematically in four general ways that will be summarized briefly here and discussed in detail below.

First, IO can be destabilizing when it attempts to manage complex, tightly coupled systems. Because management of complex relations and issues is one of the goals of IO and because these complex systems are difficult to understand and therefore manage successfully, there are inherent possibilities for destabilizing management.[40]

Second, IO can be destabilizing when its solutions discourage nations from pursuing more substantive or long-term resolutions to international problems, including disputes, or when it serves as a substitute for responsible domestic or foreign policy. It is in the nature of supranational management to generate solutions and resolutions (output) that address international problems, and to the extent that it does so, it reduces the incentives of nations to come up with better alternatives.

Third, IO can actually intensify international disputes under several circumstances: when it is used as a weapon of confrontational statecraft, when it encourages confrontational solutions to problems, when it creates roadblocks to the resolution of disputes, when it is a source of destabilizing linkages, when it is a source of predatory or confrontational collusion, and when it takes sides in international disputes. In the case of international disputes, IO is by nature prone to confer greater legitimacy to one of the competing factions and thereby shift the moral balance of power. Like other instruments of international competition, then, IO support can be an important instrument of statecraft. This was evident, for example, in President Kennedy's desire to have the approval of the Organization of American States before confronting the Soviets on the issue of Cuban missiles.

Fourth, IO can have destabilizing effects when it is a source of moral hazard. Supranational management is fundamentally based on the desire to prevent crises or provide insurance against the untoward effects of potential crises that emanate from a state's irresponsible behavior. In mitigating the adverse consequences of this behavior, IO reduces the incentives for the state to eliminate the underlying problem, which is the behavior itself.

The principal element of failure in the first category—the management of complex, tightly coupled systems—is essentially a technical one: cooperation yields inferior outcomes because of the technical difficulty of managing systems of relations and issues. The principal element of failure in the other three categories—which we can label adverse substitution, dispute intensification, and moral hazard—is not technical: a technical basis for cooperation does exist, but the political systems act in ways that can make cooperation destabilizing.

Managing Complex, Tightly Coupled Systems

Organizations often attempt to manage systems whose problems emanate from what Charles Perrow would refer to as the "complex, tightly coupled" nature of international relations.[41] As with any cybernetic system, the feedback effects of the systems of relations and issues are complicated and frequently unpredictable. And as with any complex chaotic system, these systems commonly exhibit what the chaos literature refers to as a sensitivity to initial conditions, or a macrosensitivity to developments in microconditions. Their complexity and unpredictability are thus a function of the numerous and highly conditional connections between the many variables that contribute to systemic outcomes. As Perrow argues, the complexity of tightly coupled systems makes it impossible to manage them in a way that avoids periodic crises; in other words, catastrophes and accidents are "normal" and are the rule rather than the exception.[42] Not only is IO incapable of avoiding crises, but IO often causes or exacerbates problems by offering solutions that have unpredictable and destabilizing effects.[43]

Contributors to the literature on interdependence, most notably Robert Keohane, Joseph Nye, Richard Cooper, and James Rosenau, have essentially viewed the international political economy as a system with the characteristics noted above and have emphasized the complexity of interdependence emanating from process and issue density (the tight linkage of different economic processes and international issues).[44] The literature has also highlighted the similarities between international political economic relations and the processes of systems theory and chaotic systems: feedback processes are numerous and not fully understood; knowledge about principal relationships is often indirect and inferred; there are strong systemic sensitivities to small changes in underlying conditions; policies and actions are connected in complicated constellations of relations; and simple policy initiatives often generate unintended systemic outcomes.[45]

The period from the mid-1940s to the present, for example, has been one in which international monetary schemes have been aimed at instituting and managing equilibrium exchange rates while economists have continually argued that we do not know what equilibrium rates are *ex ante* and can only know what they are *ex post*. Gottfried Haberler's statement on the equilibrium value of the dollar is representative: "With all due respect, it must be said that we, economists as well as ministers and other officials, simply do now know enough to say what the equilibrium exchange rate is."[46] More generally, William Branson argues that the management of exchange rates is well beyond our state-of-the-art methods of rational organization: "With this range of disagreement on [the] economic analysis [of exchange rate equilibration], how are negotiators to reach agreement? The topic is one for the National Science Foundation, not a new Bretton Woods."[47]

There is significant disagreement on a plethora of issues, not the least of which is what economic indicators are a valid reflection of equilibrium. It has been commonly thought that equilibrium is determined on the real side: the exchange rate at which trade balance is encouraged. But even this long-honored wisdom has been called to task both on the empirical and the theoretical side. The U.S. deficit with Japan budged only hesitantly from 1985 to 1987, while the dollar lost 50 percent of its value vis-à-vis the yen during this period. Japanese retail pricing trends showed that the yen-denominated prices of American goods in Japan had remained almost unchanged. Evidently, Japanese importers enjoyed the greater purchasing power of the yen but did not pass the savings on to the Japanese consumer. Hence, the decline of the dollar vis-à-vis the yen effected a redistribution from American exporters and Japanese consumers to Japanese middlemen, rather than eradicating the bilateral trade imbalance. Outcomes such as this have led some economists, Jagdish Bhagwati and Robert Mundell included, to question whether any continued change in the dollar will significantly dent the trade deficit. They argue that because competition in industrial markets is imperfect and because nations can counteract an appreciating currency with more protectionism so as to maintain a trade balance, exchange rates are rendered less effective in adjusting trade flows.[48]

Attempts at managing the complex, tightly coupled system of political economic relations have created a trail of international events that leads to the graveyard of misguided social engineering. The Louvre Accord of February 1987, for example, was negotiated and adopted by the G-7 for the purpose of strengthening the dollar following its sharp two-year decline. It ended up having just the opposite effect in the short run because it was perceived by the market as a signal of the dollar's weakness rather than its strength, and the resulting run against the dollar brought it well below the Louvre target. The G-7 did not anticipate this negative feedback. As it turned out, the intervention scheme initiated a destabilizing self-fulfilling prophecy: investors, thinking that the fall of the dollar was not yet over, took actions that brought such an outcome about. If the accord had not been concluded, the market might have been prepared to accept the Louvre target. In other words, less management might have brought about a better outcome.[49]

Unfortunately, the Louvre story does not end there. U.S. authorities tried to counteract the destabilizing speculation by raising interest rates and demanding specific macroeconomic policies from other G-7 nations. These actions destabilized financial markets during the period in which the Dow speculative balloon was most inflated. The October crash followed. Haberler bluntly called the Louvre Accord "a striking example of how *not* to fix exchange rates."[50] Pointing out the dangers involved when less than well conceived and organized schemes are used in an attempt to manage complex systems, he argued that "the foreign exchange market, like the stock market, is a very delicate and sensitive mechanism that does not lend itself to continued manipulation by a loosely organized group of nations."[51] In this case, the solution made the problem worse because the approach in counteracting the adverse effects of the initial managerial miscalculation was essentially a linear solution to a tightly coupled problem. Decision makers proceeded as if moods in domestic financial markets were isolated from international policy initiatives. They erroneously assumed that policies geared toward the defense of the dollar in international forums would not feed back adversely onto perceptions of prevailing trends in domestic financial markets.[52]

The Louvre Accord was presented to the public in a way that reduced rather than increased confidence. "The accord," noted one journalist, "focused attention on the weakest elements of cooperation. Every time [James] Baker spoke he offered a new version of what the accord was expected to achieve, and of the roles of the various partner countries' policies. . . . Each new disagreement with West Germany . . . made the Louvre agreement seem hollower than it really was."[53] The April 1987 communiqué of the G-7 on the state of monetary relations was an especially glaring failure. Baker called the April meeting of the G-7 "quite successful," but the communiqué failed to make mention of any specific intentions to support the dollar. A strong-dollar statement was necessary to get the dollar out of its bearish state, given that trade figures for February were announced in mid-April and were dismal, causing dismay among dollar holders. James Vick of Manufacturers Hanover Trust reflected how the market in general perceived this omission and what it indicated about G-7 intentions when he commented that the G-7 "seemed to be accepting the current level of the dollar and the downward direction."[54] This perception was reinforced by the G-7's approval of the new rate around "the most current levels."[55] These outcomes were further manifestations of the strong sensitivity of macroproperties to apparently small developments in international markets.

The managerial pattern continued under James Brady. In November 1988, following the election of Bush, the dollar declined sharply. This was met with intervention both by the Federal Reserve Bank and by several European central banks to keep the dollar from declining to a new low against the yen. On the second day of this intervention, Brady made the following statement: "Markets go up and down. I really don't worry about it very much."[56] The statement was perceived as signaling that the commitment of the G-7 was not strong and that the dollar might fall even more. This led to foreign exchange trading that ran counter to the intervention of the central banks (and, of course, imposed losses on the banks that had purchased depreciating dollars). One New York banker said, "We've had Brady make several statements early on that have not given the indication that he recognizes or has the judgment to understand that he has a profound impact on the marketplace."[57]

In the cases of both the Louvre Accord and the Plaza Accord that preceded it, policymakers failed to accept a fundamental lesson: exchange rate are not imposed upon markets; they are determined by markets.[58] In 1987, after Louvre ranges were established and defended, Baker and the G-7 kept talking (telling the market what equilibrium rates were), but the market failed to listen.[59] In both cases, agreements were ill-conceived because they were attempting to coordinate unstable policy preferences.[60] The outcome was that the nations violated both the letter and the spirit of the agreements, thereby producing bad relations among the participants.[61] These events served to further destabilize financial markets. Investors perceived that the G-7 was unable to impose order on the international monetary system, and this in turn fed back domestically and internationally to create pessimistic investment moods.[62] Decision makers continued to remain out of touch with the complete range of reactions to the nature and effectiveness of their multilateral policy initiatives. And these reactions continued to be principal sources of instability in financial and exchange markets.[63] In sum, for reasons relating to the limitations of regulating complex economic systems, the Louvre and Plaza schemes produced some cures that ended up being worse than the diseases.

The outcomes of policy coordination in recent years are quite consistent with recent theoretical findings regarding the pursuit of collective macroeconomic management in the face of disagreements on the fundamental workings of national and international economies and in the face of limited information. Jeffrey Frankel and Katherine Rockett, for example, have shown that in cases in which nations disagree on the macroeconomic models (an expected situation, since macroeconomies themselves constitute complex, tightly coupled systems) and in which the effects of economic policy are not perfectly predictable because of the complexity and tightly coupled nature of causal relations in economic markets, macroeconomic policy coordination can almost as likely be bad for nations in terms of welfare as it can be good. In some instances, constellations of uncoordinated unilateral actions would be preferable to cooperation, especially the type of cooperation founded on linear approaches to market interventions.[64]

These findings point to a common failure for any organization solving problems in complex, tightly coupled systems. There are side effects, many of which are unforeseeable. With respect to the problem of economic development, Paul Streeten notes that "scientists may have a solution to every problem, but development has a problem for every solution."[65] Such conditions put a premium on nonlinear solutions to the problem of poverty. "Single actions which look technically correct," he emphasizes, "can be worse than useless if they are not accompanied by supplementary actions."[66] This is especially true about managing nations toward higher levels of economic development. According to Streeten, "Development is . . . like a jigsaw puzzle. To be effective, several actions must be taken together, in the right order; rural education has to be combined with the improvement of rural amenities or the educated will leave the countryside. The new seeds have to be applied with fertilizers and water at the right time; there must be extension services and roads to get the food to the markets."[67]

Adverse Substitution

Nations are continually faced with difficult domestic and international problems whose resolution entails political, economic, or social costs. Although IO can alleviate short-run pressures and provide nations with an "out" from more costly solutions, doing so can be counterproductive in that it discourages nations from seeking more substantive and longer-term resolutions to their problems. To the extent that time horizons are short (which is certainly the case in domestic political systems where political survival is predicated on short-run imperatives) and national leaders are sensitive to differing domestic costs of competing solutions to domestic and international problems (which also appears to be the case), nations will be encouraged to substitute less costly and less viable multilateral schemes for more costly and substantive solutions.[68] The problem of substitution is systematic because it is in the nature of IO to solve international and domestic problems. But because of jurisdictional limitations and the bargaining process, the solutions offered by IO are often not substantive.

Secretary-General Pérez de Cuéllar pointed to one of the largest and most prevalent drawbacks of IO substitution in his first annual report on the work of the UN: "There is a tendency in the United Nations for governments to act as though the passage of a resolution absolved them from further responsibility for the subject in question."[69] Particularly in the case of dispute resolution, the tendency has been to offer flimsy "patch job" solutions that reduce the incentives for disputants to find a better way of resolving their differences. This point was emphasized by James Stegenga in his 1968 assessment of the effects of UN efforts in Cyprus: "UNFICYP [the UN Peacekeeping Force in Cyprus] is vulnerable to the charge that it may very well be inhibiting settlement. By helping to protect and thus consolidate the abnormal status quo and by reducing the sense of urgency felt by both sides, the Force may actually be making a negative contribution to what in the long run is the most important requirement, a viable political order."[70] Yeselson and Gaglione have questioned whether the UN Emergency Force (UNEF) efforts in the Middle East have had the same negative effect by providing an inferior substitute for a viable resolution in the region.[71]

Patrick Garrity has recently argued that UN peacekeeping efforts have allowed U.S. policymakers to postpone crucial security decisions that eventually must be made.[72] In this regard, we must question the effects of the UN in general and its solutions in particular on the relations between the superpowers. In the UN General Assembly, majorities have always favored one superpower over the other, offering more support to the United States in the early decades and more to the Soviet Union in later decades. Historically, the UN has provided a rational incentive for one of the superpowers to try to marshall collective support for a UN resolution against the other and thereby extract some desired action or policy through collective confrontation rather than through direct negotiations that would involve some form of concessions or quid pro quos. In short, given the tendency of UN members to automatically side with the appropriate superpower, collective confrontation via the UN has provided the superpowers with a relatively costless substitute for more costly direct bargaining. As Yeselson and Gaglione have observed, "Victories at the [UN] were cheap. They involved no cost in blood and very little in treasure, and they lent an aura of righteousness to . . . foreign policy."[73]

For the same or similar reasons, the diversion of important issues or controversies into IOs that are mainly ceremonial forums (which many are) is often counterproductive. Nations may perceive negotiations in international forums either as viable substitutes for more fruitful negotiations at the bilateral or multilateral level or as viable substitutes for real cooperation.[74] The result, as Robert Rothstein pointed out in his study of the UN Conference on Trade and Development (UNCTAD) is that "the situation may get worse simply because living with an increasingly ceremonial process is much easier than trying to reform it. . . . And, of course, the most obvious consequences ought to be reemphasized: problems get worse, time is lost, and resources are expended."[75]

Critics of IO-orchestrated development schemes argue that the public funds of IOs are inferior substitutes for private investments in the Third World and tend to generate negative externalities. IO funds are often tied to government planning that is antithetical to market processes. Because regulated economies are less attractive to international investors, this has the effect of driving out private investment, which is especially bad given the link between economic development and the growth of the private sector in underdeveloped nations.[76] Roger Brooks makes a related point with respect to agricultural development in Africa.[77]

Food aid, as commonly practiced before the 1970s, has encouraged LDCs to substitute food transfers for domestic agricultural production. This has served to reduce agricultural self-sufficiency in the long run through disincentive effects on local food production, thus compounding the problems of hunger and food dependence in underdeveloped nations. Moreover, food transfers have disrupted local systems of food production and distribution, generated extremely expensive subsidy programs, created administrative nightmares, and encouraged corruption.[78]

It is interesting, Inis Claude notes, that some of the fiercest enemies of IO have been strong proponents of world government (federalists).[79] This animosity is not surprising, however, according to the federalist logic. As an unsatisfactory substitute for more comprehensive managerial arrangements, IO serves as a "palliative" that reduces the fervor for real world government. In this sense, IO is more antithetical to international government than anarchy is. Agreeing with this assessment, Claude has argued that world government requires an existing community. IO can delay or prevent that community from arising because it reduces the sense of urgency for real and substantive community building.[80] Consistent with this same line of argument, Adam Roberts and Benedict Kingsbury have argued that the UN has actually worked against international security in its function as a perceived potential substitute for arms control. "By presenting a mythological alternative to armaments," they argue, "it may distract attention from other possibly more fruitful approaches to the urgent problem of controlling and limiting military force."[81]

IO sometimes functions as another kind of substitute: a substitute for responsible domestic policies. In this function, IO can be destabilizing in the long run not only at the national level but also at the international level if domestic disorder spills over into international relations. In the case of the Plaza Accord, for example, the United States was given a way of escaping necessary and costly adjustments in government spending: bringing down the dollar through intervention was preferred to bringing down the dollar by cutting the budget, which would have brought interest rates down.[82] Defenders of the conditionality policies of multilateral lending institutions have used the substitution logic to justify their argument that unconditional lending would only make loans a substitute for responsible macroeconomic and foreign economic policy management.[83] In the case of the Bretton Woods system, liquidity became a substitute for adjustment. External adjustment was constrained by means of fixed exchange rates and rules governing trade policy, while internal adjustment was no longer accepted as a viable means of eradicating external payments imbalances.[84] In another context of adverse substitution, Vaubel argues that as a forum for collusion, IO can make it easier for governments to pursue unstable economic policies. Monetary collaboration, for example, can shield policymakers from criticism over high inflation by bringing inflation rates into conformity.[85]

Jan Tumlir and others have argued that it should be a principal goal of IO to limit this substitution and enhance responsible policies at home. According to Tumlir, IO should "help national governments . . . discharge those basic domestic functions on which the economic stability of their societies depends in the long run."[86] If nations would all follow responsible policies at home, then IO would be less necessary. Certainly this argument is common in the context of international economic relations. As a recent article in the *Economist* noted, economic ministers could "think of cooperation as a boring means to an end, not as a glorious goal in its own right. Because if they all stayed home and adopted sensible domestic policies there would be precious little need for cooperation on trade or exchange rates."[87] A similar view was offered by Max Corden: "It can be argued that if countries make adequate use of the policy instruments available to them, there is no need for coordination of policies. . . . One can thus imagine countries reacting quickly and atomistically to the events from outside them, including the consequences of other countries' stabilization policies. And if their policies are intelligent and speedy, they will achieve whatever stabilization they wish to achieve."[88]

The argument for responsible domestic policies reflects the belief that domestic problems have a tendency to spill over and become international problems. In the economic realm, excessive internal deficits and inflation alter exchange rates, and this in turn influences external positions. Differential rates of inflation in a fixed exchange rate system redistribute trade surpluses to nations with low inflation. While these effects are unintentional (externalities), there are also international actions (policies) that are instituted to redistribute external surpluses—for example, tariff barriers and exchange controls keep imports down and capital in. Both externalities and policies can therefore be quite destabilizing internationally.[89] Similarly, in the political realm, domestic problems can become international problems. For example, oppressive authoritarian regimes may find foreign adventurism a necessary remedy to quell domestic unrest.

Dispute Intensification

IO can be a destabilizing force when it intensifies disputes. Because IO can lend moral force to the foreign policy positions of nations, it has the tendency to be used by them as a means of statecraft to further their global interests. To the extent that these interests create confrontational behavior, IO generates utility not only as a forum in which accusations are made and brinkmanship is practiced in front of the community of states but also as a vehicle through which collusion and alliance building are effected.

In general, scholars have tended to underplay these and other negative uses of IO that interfere with negotiations and make agreements difficult to achieve. Rather than serving as vehicles to resolve conflict, IOs are often used to promote or magnify conflict. As Claude has noted, they frequently function as arenas "for the conduct of international political warfare."[90] The UN, for example, has historically served as a forum to embarrass nations. In 1956, Western nations brought up the Hungarian issue for the purpose of embarrassing the Soviet Union. The Soviets vindicated themselves in 1965 when they brought up the Dominican Republic issue to embarrass the United States. As Yeselson and Gaglione have pointed out, "Real negotiations require that the parties define differences as narrowly as possible, avoid recrimination, and exclude extremists from discussions. At the UN, issues are widened, insults are common, and the most violent spokesmen frequently dominate the debate. The effects of such deliberately provocative discussions is to contaminate efforts to achieve peaceful settlements."[91]

The "safety valve" rationale for IO, which reflects the famous Churchill quote "better to jaw, jaw than war, war,"[92] is based on the erroneous assumption that battle among diplomats is a perfect substitute for battle in the fields. In fact, however, "war jaw" in the UN merely compounds conflicts, as Maurice Tugwell has pointed out.[93] For example, the verbal aggression traditionally marshaled toward the United States by the Soviet Union and involving the use of terminology such as "racist," "imperialist," "antipeace," and "neocolonial" served to compound confrontations outside of the UN both directly and indirectly, since it prompted as well as justified the arms buildups and supported the extremist views of Cold Warriors in domestic debates over foreign policy. In this respect, Jeane Kirkpatrick, former U.S. Ambassador to the UN, was probably justified in saying that she has "never believed that the release of aggression is healthy or therapeutic" and that "it is a sorry state of affairs when the United Nations, which was conceived as an instrument for the building of peace, is now justified as an instrument for the release of aggression."[94] She was also at least partially correct in calling the UN a "dangerous place."[95]

The UN was historically used as an instrument of Cold War competition, with each superpower marshaling voting alliances against the other. Claude underscored the point that the superpowers competed for control of the organization and viewed it as the ultimate ally in the Cold War, while Ruggie added that the Soviets considered it "a vehicle to delegitimize the postwar international order constructed by the capitalist nations."[96] Yeselson and Gaglione have noted that what many have seen as UN failures in cooperation are in fact successful instances of the organization's use as a weapon to embarrass nations.[97] According to them, much can be understood about the UN if it is seen as a tool of statecraft in the Cold War. To say that this use has substituted for more direct confrontation assumes that the marshaling of alliances which occurred earlier outside the UN was subsequently replaced by the formation of voting blocs within the UN forum. This is not the case, however, since confrontations within the UN were merely added to confrontations outside it. In this sense, according to Tugwell, instead of acting as a "safety valve," the UN became "a threat to peace."[98] This is also evident in the fact that the organization has actively taken part in conflicts and either escalated them, as in the Korean War, or intervened to suppress them, as in the siding with Kasavubu in the Katangan revolt led by Tsombe. In the latter case, Belgian Prime Minister Paul Henry Spaak cited the intervention in the Congo affairs as a "UN war operation."[99]

In addition to these direct effects, IO has had indirect international and domestic effects that run counter to the ideals of multilateral cooperation. The constant attacks of the UN on Israel, South Africa, and Rhodesia, for example, have had the unfortunate effects of strengthening the political position of "hawks" in Israel and of providing racial extremists in the African nations with a weapon to use against moderates.[100] For this reason, nations have become reluctant to bring disputes or problems to IOs that have historically been mobilized against them. Israel, a victim of Egyptian and Syrian attack in 1973, chose not to bring the problem to the UN Security Council because of the anti-Israeli sentiment there. The Soviets bypassed the UN often during the earlier period in which the Western coalition dominated the organization, and the United States has done so following the organization's shift to Soviet and Third World domination.

Claude underscored this point with respect to the earlier period: "To the degree that the United States succeeded in using the [UN] as a pro-Western device, it reduced the utility of the organization as an agency of conciliation and stabilization in the Cold War."[101]

In resolving smaller controversies or contentious issues, IO has often created roadblocks to the resolution of more important issues. For example, the 1948 Security Council resolution endorsing self-determination in Kashmir drove a major wedge into Indian-Pakistani relations, while resolutions favoring South Korea fueled bad North–South Korean sentiment. The result was that substantive relation improvements were impeded. In the greater scheme of international relations, it may have been better for the resolutions not to have been made, regardless of their short-run successes in addressing injustices.[102]

Furthermore, as a facilitator of issue linkage, IO has often had negative rather than positive effects. Scholars have argued that linkage leads to greater possibilities for exchange and bargaining and thus enhances the potential for substantive agreements. "Clustering of issues," according to Keohane, "facilitates side-payments among these issues: more potential *quids* are available for the *quo*."[103] Although linkage can be stabilizing if it encourages cooperation, it can have destabilizing effects if it instead fuels conflict. In 1974, the Arab states traded votes with the Black African nations in the UN: the former pledged their vote to silence the South African delegation in exchange for the latter's vote in support of the Palestine Liberation Organization (PLO). This not only intensified old disputes but also brought new participants into the disputes. In IOs, voting alliances whose purposes revolve principally around confrontation are quite the rule rather than the exception.[104]

Along this line of logic, it is not the case that IO always enhances the conditions favorable to cooperation or dispute resolution. In the case of dispute mediation, IO may restrict, rather than expand, the number of mediators. The restriction occurs as a result of nations being identified as biased either because they took a particular position on an issue in IO debates or because they failed to take sides. For example, India's abstinence on a UN vote regarding Soviet intervention in Hungary discredited India as a Cold War mediator in the eyes of the United States. The potential for such outcomes is high, given that IO normally puts nations in a position of appearing to choose sides on divisive issues whether they elect to vote or not. This destabilizing transitivity can manifest itself also in terms of the effects of inner-IO confrontations on outer-IO negotiations. In 1973, for example, Americans were quite apprehensive about Chinese–South Korean interaction in the UN, given its potential effects on Chinese-U.S. rapprochement.

This tendency of "leaning" international support to one side or another is not peculiar to IO but is a characteristic of such social functions in general. When IO takes sides, however, it can have adverse effects on both the longevity and the intensity of a dispute. As Yeselson and Gaglione have observed, "Victorious states are emboldened by the vindication of their policies, and losers are embittered by injustice."[105] Taking sides without regard to consequences—even in the form of condemning what is considered an illegitimate use of force, as in the cases of the Israeli occupation of Arab territories in 1967, the Falklands invasion of 1982, and Soviet intervention in Afghanistan in 1979—encourages the use of counterforce.[106] Critics have often lamented the overt UN support of groups such as the PLO, the Southwest African People's Organization (SWAPO), the African National Congress (ANC), and the Pan-African Congress (PAC) and have argued that these groups use UN support as a legitimization of violent methods.[107] The following statement by PLO spokesman Massur on the murder of two Israelis by a PLO terrorist group in 1975 is revealing: "We sponsored the operation because it is our right to fight for our rights, and the whole world sponsored it . . . because the [UN] General Assembly has approved the right of the Palestinians to pursue their struggle *with all means* to gain usurped rights."[108] In the Falklands case, it is difficult to separate the aggressive Argentine foreign policy of the late 1960s and the 1970s from the fact that the Falklands problem had been linked to decolonization by the UN after 1965. Great Britain asserted its sovereignty over the islands throughout the century, but it was not until after 1965 that Argentine terrorism and militarism became pronounced.[109] The problem was probably compounded when the General Assembly passed a resolution in December 1976 praising the Argentine government for "facilitat[ing] the process of decolonization" and thus legitimized its confrontational methods of using verbal and military aggression in resolving the problem.[110]

Finally, and most obviously, IO can be destabilizing by stimulating cooperation in the negative form of predatory collusion. When nations collude for the purpose of exploitation, redistribution, or aggression, collective action is bad, just as it is bad for economic efficiency when firms with market power collude to restrict output. Nations perceive confrontational alliances as bad, just as consumer nations perceive international commodity cartels as bad. Depending on the goals of cooperation, it is sometimes in the interest of peaceful international relations for collective action and prisoners' dilemma problems to exist.

Moral Hazard

Situations involving moral hazard are those in which a nation is relieved of the obligation of incurring the full costs of its social, economic, or political actions because some protective scheme allows it to impose those costs onto other nations through risk sharing. The problem of generating moral hazard has been most extensively discussed in the context of the social inefficiencies of insurance. An inherent problem of insurance is that it encourages individuals to be more reckless in the management of their possessions and consequently raises the risk of losses, which in turn imposes greater costs on society. Similarly, an inherent problem of IO is that by helping to ward off catastrophes or by insuring nations against them, it discourages individually responsible behavior on their part.

There are numerous examples in which IOs have functioned as providers of insurance. The International Energy Agency (IEA) has traditionally insured against energy shortages through resource-sharing schemes. The escape clauses of the General Agreement on Tariffs and Trade (GATT) have provided partial insurance to domestic industries in distress and alleviated balance-of-payments difficulties. The Financial Support Fund, agreed to by members of the Organization for Economic Cooperation and Development (OECD) but never instituted, was meant to serve as a lender of last resort that would spread the risk of loans given to nations in economic difficulty. The compensatory and contingency finance facilities of the International Monetary Fund (IMF) were instituted specifically as insurance against sudden economic disruptions that negatively affect the balance of payments. And the Lomé Convention's Compensatory Finance Scheme for Exports (STABEX) was instituted as insurance against a sudden decline in the key exports of the African, Caribbean, and Pacific nations.

In their various protective or safeguard functions, these and other IOs have frequently generated adverse effects in encouraging nations to be reckless in the management of their domestic economies. As Charles Kindleberger has argued with respect to the debt problem, last-resort and crisis lenders reduce the incentives of nations to make the internal economic adjustments necessary for long-term domestic stability. The fact that trade deficits can be financed through external funds allows nations to overinflate without worrying about the adverse effects of high prices on their trade balances. The guarantee of external sources of liquidity also allows nations to increase government spending, to prolong or expand their budget deficits, to smooth over exchange rate mismanagement, and, worst of all, to compound their foreign debt.[111] These domestic problems, spread over many nations, have the capacity to spill over and become international problems. For optimal stability in the international economic system, Kindleberger thus prescribes a lender whose commitment is uncertain: "Because of moral hazard, there should be some ambiguity about whether there will or will not be a lender of last resort."[112] Shrinking the safety net would encourage nations to manage their external accounts and macroeconomies in a manner that makes them more self-sufficient in the long run and is conducive to both domestic and international stability.

The logic of moral hazard suggests that managerial schemes can create conditions that cut against the spirit of their original purposes. In the case of the Plaza Accord, for example, cooperation provided a multilateral substitute for addressing U.S. economic problems. Instead of encouraging U.S. policymakers to bring interest rates down by instituting domestic measures to reduce their budget deficit, the G-7 stepped in to manage the dollar. In the short run, this redistributed some of the costs of the large U.S. deficit to the community of industrialized nations. But because it also reduced the incentives for the U.S. government to manage its deficit more cautiously, the deficit worsened and has become a significant potential source of international economic instability.

A Better Approach:
Limited International Organization

Managerial prescriptions for IO and proscriptions against deregulating relations have led to a predilection for big supranational government. However, as Keohane and Nye have pointed out, supranational institutions "are not desirable for their own sake."[113] Nor does a high level or large scope of international management ensure optimal results. More limited forms of IO are in fact preferable in many cases, particularly those in which IO is prone to managerial failures of the types noted above and those in which the interactive patterns among nations are less conflictual and thus more representative of coordination games than of stag hunt or prisoners' dilemma. Contributors to the revisionist literature on IO and the literature on cooperation have recognized the negative effects and conditionality of management and have provided a partial solution to these problems by recommending more limited managerial functions for IOs.

In determining the proper level and scope of IO, we should begin by questioning to what extent stable international relations in the past have been the result of extensive management. Contrary to common assumptions, history shows that extensive management of international relations in both orderly and disorderly periods has been more the exception than the rule. IOs have rarely been constructed to manage any issue-area extensively or even effectively. The constitutions of IOs, like most other constitutions, have commonly been so vague as to tolerate a wide range of behavior on the part of actors both close to and far from implicit principles. Rule breaking has been tolerated, escape mechanisms have always been pervasive, and the problems of compliance have been compounded by the lack or general underdevelopment of enforcement instruments.[114]

The calls for an escape from the present "nonsystem" (nonmanagement) of monetary relations and an adoption of a new Bretton Woods system on the part of managerialists such as Irving Friedman are rather curious considering that some have questioned whether management under the old Bretton Woods plan was extensive or strong.[115] Robert Solomon has observed that under the old Bretton Woods system there were no accepted rules to govern changes in par values, yet such changes were necessary as economic policies and conditions diverged among nations. Furthermore, there was no systematic means for increasing countries' reserves in a growing world economy. The growth of reserves was the haphazard result of the outcome of the U.S. balance of payments, which then, as now, depended on developments in other countries as well as in the United States. For these two reasons alone, it may be concluded that the nostalgic desire to get away from the present "non-system" is a product of emotion rather than careful analysis.[116]

Furthermore, those who unequivocally profess the evils of decentralization and the superiority of extensive regulation ("bigger government is better") are sometimes guilty of overestimating the destabilizing elements in international relations and their effects on international politics, underestimating those forces which naturally inhibit nations from behaving predatorially in anarchic environments, and overestimating the capacity of IO to solve problems. Common rationales for extensive supranational management have centered around the conviction that international relations are permeated by prisoners' dilemmas, stag hunts, security dilemmas, and public goods problems. Under such conditions, even the least expansionist and aggressive nations would be rationally driven to participate in destabilizing behavior such as arms races, trade wars, and competitive depreciation. The result of the "pursuit of self-interest by each," Keohane and Nye have argued, would thus be a "disaster for all."[117] But as the growing literature on cooperation suggests, the incidence and the adverse effects of predatory games have been overstated. The games that nations play are much more varied than the traditional literature on international relations has suggested, and the effects of conflictual games can vary in their level of adversity. Moreover, even under conditions that are potentially destabilizing, such as relative gains maximization, cooperative outcomes are still possible. Interactional patterns, according to this literature, are not so inherently unstable that they cannot often converge toward orderly equilibria under more limited international management. As Keohane and Nye note, "Issues lacking conflicts of interests may need very little institutional structure."[118]

The fears of less centralized management, which are frequently founded on the misconception that prisoners' dilemmas and stag hunts are ubiquitous in international relations, systematically discount the costs of predation. Imposing suckers' payoffs onto other nations incurs significant costs that are independent of those costs incurred as a result of retaliation. This is not to say that exploitation does not pay; rather, the point is that it does not pay as much as many believe and that, moreover, managerialists tend to mistake other games for prisoners' dilemma and stag hunt. With tariffs, for instance, there are obvious deadweight losses with respect to social welfare. Tariffs are conducive to inflation, which bears high economic and political costs. They raise the cost of domestic production as well as reduce the efficiency of a nation's capital stock in the long run by shielding domestic industries from competition and making it difficult to import foreign capital and inputs. Declining capital efficiency will also have adverse effects on wages in the long run. Finally, tariffs can adversely affect a nation's capital balance if investors perceive them as a sign of external difficulties or mercantilistic policy styles.[119] Competitive depreciation causes not only inflation but capital flight. Depreciation can also adversely affect current balances if a nation's demand for imports and others' demand for its exports are inelastic.[120] Brinkmanship and wars can incur preponderant political as well as economic costs, as the Cuban crisis, the Vietnam War, and the Falklands War have demonstrated. The more prolonged and unsuccessful the adventurism, the greater are the costs.

The fears of decentralization are also fueled by a propensity to see disorder where it may not exist. For example, external imbalances are not in themselves a sign of economic disorder, any more than traders exchanging resources are a sign of market disorder. Much depends on the structure of the imbalances. In the present external imbalance between the United States and Japan, the former is running a current deficit against the latter, and the latter is running a capital deficit against the former. There are some important gains from trade in this reciprocal imbalance: Japan is helping finance the U.S. budget deficit in exchange for the exportation of goods.[121]

Various forms of limited IO have been suggested in the recent literature on cooperation and the critical literature on IO as a partial solution to the problems of managerial failure and the conditionality of international management.[122] The transaction costs approach to IO, for example, has modest aspirations for the functions of institutions. Keohane and Nye specifically cite them as facilitators "of bargaining among member states that leads to mutually beneficial cooperation."[123] In this sense, order is institutionally assisted rather than managed. Institutions, they argue, can "set the international agenda and act as catalysts for coalition formation and as arenas for political initiatives and linkage by weak states."[124] The principal function of IOs in this case would be the reduction of organization costs, such as those deriving from asymmetric information, deception, irresponsibility, uncertainty, risk, and unstable expectations, all of which are potential impediments to stable relations and exchange patterns. Cost reduction can be effected through limited functions relevant to the roles of gathering and disseminating data and information about the preferences of nations, facilitating side-payments and communication, and reducing the costs of decision making. In general, in cases in which the construction of extensive managerial schemes (what Keohane refers to as "control" schemes) is fraught with problems or is unnecessary, less ambitious schemes become desirable.[125]

The literature on regimes has also suggested substitutes for control schemes. According to this literature, preexisting norms and principles can reduce the need for extensive management in several ways.[126] First, they can render strategic international patterns less conflictual by altering payoffs. For example, they can make defection more costly. Second, they can facilitate intertemporal cooperation by generating expectations of reciprocity or, in more static games, by enhancing expectations of "nice" moves. And, third, in specific issue-areas where coordination games predominate, as described by Arthur Stein, or where spontaneous regimes exist, as described by Oran Young, the preexisting norms and principles either obviate the need for extensive regulation or eliminate the need for formal institution building.[127] The stable patterns of interaction in specific issue-areas, Duncan Snidal has argued, can be maintained through more modest functions concerned with "codification and elaboration of an existing or latent convention" and with "providing information and communication to facilitate the smooth operation of the convention."[128] In other words, by performing limited functions with regard to preexisting focal points, management can facilitate the convergence of expectations about international behavior.[129]

Ruggie has noted that epistemic communities can be viable substitutes for extensive control schemes.[130] They are capable, for instance, of generating stable structures of expectations that are conducive to nonconflictual relations. Some of the limited management functions in the case of communities concerned with technology, for example, relate to facilitating efficient exchange through consensus about how and under which conditions transactions can be effected.

As Keohane and Nye have pointed out and as the public choice literature on IO has demonstrated, in cases in which nations can agree upon reasonable entitlement rules, an institutionally assisted market solution is superior to an extensive managerial scheme.[131] The conventional minimum-support functions in these cases are the definition, adjudication, and enforcement of property rights; the dissemination of information about preferences; and other functions related to the elimination of market distortions such as externalities. Conybeare has noted that in international environmental law, for example, there has been an impressive evolution that "illustrates the ability of states operating in a market exchange environment to develop a system of property rights and liability rules consistent with global welfare, in the absence of any overarching supranational IO directly intervening to force states to internalize the effects of externalities."[132] Wijkman, who notes that environmental problems have historically been dealt with through the market approach of subdividing internationally shared resources into "national inheritances," has argued that this approach would be viable with regard to the deep seabed and the continental margin (which are less costly to subdivide than other environments) and possibly with regard to the orbital spectrum as well.[133]

Even the traditional literature on IO, which has a strong managerial orientation, exhibits strands of logic that attest to the utility of limited IO. The functionalist concept of "technical self-determination" suggests that the nature of technological problems will dictate the scope and level of supranational regulation. Although the mainstream vision of functional interdependence foresees a growing need for the integration and management of technical issues, there is nothing in the logic to suggest that decentralized solutions in which each nation addresses a problem independently of other nations cannot sometimes be viable. If autarkic solutions to technical and welfare problems do not suffice, IO can serve minor functions in facilitating stable relations. Moreover, limited technical integration need not spill over into greater political integration.[134] Neofunctionalists acknowledge that IO is sometimes ineffective in achieving specified goals.[135] If this is because the goals are set too high, as in the case of grand collaborative schemes, it may be preferable to moderate the targeted level of cooperation, since failure may serve to delegitimize cooperation not only in the short run but also in the long run.[136] Edward Morse has argued that in some ways modernization breeds conditions that abate conflict and tension in international politics, thereby reducing the need for international management. In bringing low politics to the fore (for example, making issues relating to welfare and technology as important as those relating to power and status), the content of foreign policies becomes less threatening because conflicts are diverted into the positive-sum contexts of economics and technology.[137]

The literature on collective action suggests another reason that limited IO can be viable. Russell Hardin, for example, has argued that it is easier to eradicate public "bads" than to procure or create public goods, since the goal of collective action in the former is more focused and since nations are likely to experience more "disutility" from bads than utility from goods.[138] In cases in which the elimination of bads is the primary goal, limited IO can be effective. Moreover, the classic Olsonian treatment of collective action suggests that IOs with limited membership are more effective than large IOs in both eliminating bads and procuring goods.[139] Historically, however, the target of IO has tended to be the management of goods with little publicness. As Ruggie has pointed out, it has been "the production of [private] goods and services which accounts for most of the activities of international organization."[140] This essentially means that IO has historically been redundant in its managerial functions and has expended more managerial capital than is necessary, since relations involving private goods require the least supranational regulation.[141]

That limited IO can be effective, however, does not mean that it will be. For IO to be a viable means of contributing to order in international relations, the environment in which it functions must be conducive to the effectiveness of supranational management in general. It appears from the logic in this article that IO will be more effective in the management of relatively simple constellations of intra- or inter-issue relations than in the management of complex chaotic systems in which relations between relevant variables are difficult to understand and forecast. With respect to the complexity of the two major issue-areas of international economic and security relations, it is interesting to note that management will most likely be effective where it is least likely to emerge. The processes involved in economic cooperation are much more complex according to Perrow's definition than those involved in security cooperation, but cooperation in security relations has historically been much less visible than that in economic relations.[142]

Moreover, IO will be more effective when it facilitates or encourages substantive and long-term solutions to problems than when it offers short-run and ad hoc approaches to them. UN peacekeeping functions, for example, have historically specialized in the latter approaches to abating conflict.[143] As valuable as these may be in insulating and desensitizing conflict, they need to be bolstered by viable schemes that raise and maintain the incentives for nations to continue pursuing substantive and lasting settlements to their foreign relations problems.[144] Economic cooperation among the G-7 has also had a history of ineffectiveness because it has remained open to and often encouraged domestic and foreign policies that are inconsistent with the intentions and spirit of substantive economic policy coordination. Economic summitry has exhibited a tendency to be a legitimator of national economic policies as well as an instrument of domestic politics, rather than serving exclusively as a forum for substantive negotiations.[145] While the United States was able to use macroeconomic coordination in the 1980s as a means of escaping tough but necessary adjustments in spending,[146] future effectiveness in coordination will depend on the revolve of nations to limit such domestic policy responses. Similarly, with regard to the debt problem, strengthening conditionality will make international monetary management more effective in the long run. Greater conditionality can be even more effective if accompanied by some uncertainties regarding the provision of crisis liquidity in the international system, as suggested by Kindleberger. Absolute guarantees not only generate excessive moral hazard in the management of debt but also make conditionality more difficult to maintain.

Finally, IO is more likely to be effective when it does not put itself in a position to be a vehicle of international competition. In managing international conflicts and disputes, the UN has had mixed results. Notwithstanding its value as a forum for positive interactions, it has (even when siding with a position that seems morally correct) added fuel to international fires by intentionally or unintentionally producing instruments of confrontation and competition. By discouraging confrontational rhetoric and debate and making other adjustments in style or function, the UN might be more effective in reducing international tensions. The argument that a world with an imperfect UN is preferred to a world without a UN does not sufficiently justify the continuation of a style of dispute settlement that exhibits destabilizing characteristics.

Conclusions

Contributors to the IO literature have traditionally been overly optimistic about the ability of multilateral management to stabilize international relations and have generally ignored the fact that IO can be a source of, rather than a remedy for, disorder in and across issue-areas. Although recent revisionist scholars have recognized the destabilizing effects of IO, they have taken a somewhat restrictive view of organizational failure. In addressing the general issue of the ways in which IO can fail and outlining the conditions under which more limited and less centralized modes of regulation are preferable, this article has sought to develop a set of guidelines that are pertinent to decision making and serve as a rationale for eliminating the excesses of IO. The findings of the article have implications not only for policymaking but also for theory and research in the field of international relations.

According to conventional theories of cooperation and conflict, the sources of international disorder are the underlying strategic structures of relations between nations. However, the findings presented here suggest that disorder springs from more heterogeneous sources. Important sources of disorder—sources that are seemingly unlikely and have thus tended to be overlooked—are the solutions proffered by IOs. While these solutions are intended to moderate or eliminate the disorder created by strategic structure, they often have the opposite effect of exacerbating existing problems or creating new ones. Theories thus need to endogenize these origins of disorder. They also need to expand their menu of dependent variables, which has traditionally been limited to the roles, goals, and functions of IOs. Far more attention needs to be paid to the effects (impact) of management in shaping international outcomes. The finding emphasized here with regard to impact is that IO has the potential for negative as well as positive results, a finding that supports the view that conflict and cooperation coexist in close proximity and even overlap in international relations.[147]

Recent research has tended to blur the distinction between international relations on the one hand and the schemes and institutions that are created to manage these relations on the other hand. In other words, it has failed to distinguish the forest from the trees. By focusing on the processes of IO, this article has attempted to avoid this pitfall. More work in this direction is needed, however, particularly with regard to better differentiating the impact as well as the roles, goals, and functions of IO.[148] Which specific IOs are more likely to generate moral hazard?[149] Which are more likely to generate inferior substitutes? Questions such as these only partially reflect the theoretical and empirical issues that need to be addressed.

Finally, international bureaucrats and national policymakers, like scholars, need to be more sensitized to the complexity of the effects of IO when considering optimal responses to international problems. The problems themselves should not comprise the sole criteria according to which managerial schemes are constructed but must instead be carefully considered in conjunction with the likely effects generated by these schemes. In other words, the specific roles, functions, and goals of IO should be dictated both by the nature or underlying strategic structures of the international problems and by the potential positive and negative effects of possible managed solutions. Such a "conditional orientation" toward organizational design seems best adapted to the realities of IO failure and the underlying relations among nations.

Notes

1. Throughout this article, I refer to international organization (IO) and international organizations (IOs) in keeping with the following distinction made in the mainstream IO literature: the term "IO" refers to both the formal (institutionalized) and informal (noninstitutionalized) processes of management, while the term "IOs" refers to the institutions engaged in the formal processes of management. IOs are thus a subset of IO. See J. Martin Rochester, "The Rise and Fall of International Organization as a Field of Study," *International Organization* 40 (Autumn 1986), pp. 753–75; Friedrich Kratochwil and John Gerard Ruggie, "International Organization: A State of the Art on an Art of the State," *International Organization* 40 (Autumn 1986), pp. 777–813; and Inis Claude, *Swords into Plowshares,* 4th ed. (Random House: New York, 1984).

2. See Roger Brooks, "Africa Is Starving and the United Nations Shares the Blame," *Backgrounder* 480, Heritage Foundation, January 1986.

3. General arguments on moral hazard in the international monetary system have most recently been made by Charles Kindleberger in *The International Economic Order* (Cambridge Mass.: MIT Press, 1988).

4. See Raymond Hopkins, "Reform in the International Food Aid Regime: The Role of Consensual Knowledge," *International Organization* (forthcoming).

5. Javier Pérez de Cuéllar, *Report of the Secretary-General on the Work of the Organization,* no. A/37/1 (New York: United Nations, 1982).

6. The scope of IO is defined by neofunctionalists as the range of issue-specific tasks involved in a managerial scheme, while the level is defined as the "central institutional capacity to handle a particular [issue-specific] task." See Joseph Nye, "Comparing Common Markets: A Revised Neo-Functionalist Model," in Leon Lindberg and Stuart Scheingold, eds., *Regional Integration* (Cambridge, Mass.: Harvard University Press, 1971), p. 201; and Philippe Schmitter, "Three

Neo-Functional Hypotheses About Integration," *International Organization* 13 (Winter 1969), p. 162.

7. See Kratochwil and Ruggie, "International Organization"; and Rochester, "The Rise and Fall of International Organization as a Field of Study." Regarding the normative rationale for the study of IO, see also John Gerard Ruggie, "The United States and the United Nations: Toward a New Realism," *International Organization* 39 (Spring 1985), p. 345.

8. Kratochwil and Ruggie, "International Organization."

9. Regime analysts and neoliberal institutionalists have argued that big government can be redundant and is unnecessary when limited forms of management are sufficient. But the viability of smaller government is all the more compelling when big government is subject to organizational failure.

10. As Conybeare notes, "Federalists, functionalists, neofunctionalists, and pluralists all agree as to the inherent desirability of world government. . . . It would not be a caricature to infer from the modern IO literature that the world needs more supranational authority to manage interdependence, public goods, and externalities in general." See John Conybeare, "International Organization and the Theory of Property Rights," *International Organization* 34 (Summer 1980), pp. 307–8. The critical focus of my article, however, is not the modern IO literature per se but, rather, those strands in the IO and international relations literature that uncritically profess the need for the extensive multilateral management of international relations and support the benign view of IO from which this prescription stems. Some strands are not overtly managerial in orientation. And in many cases, as pointed out in my article, the logics of their arguments are not antithetical to the usefulness and importance of limited forms of IO.

11. Critiques of domestic government have been far more prevalent and systematic than have general critiques of IO. For a typical example of the former, see Richard Rose, "What If Anything Is Wrong with Big Government?" *Journal of Public Policy* 1 (February 1981), pp. 5–36. An inquiry into the reasons for this neglect would be speculative. Perhaps it is simply a matter of specialization, with IO failing to attract the attention of erstwhile critics of big domestic government who are specialized in domestic political issues. Or perhaps the unpleasant effects of IO are not felt on an individual level to the same extent as the unpleasant effects of domestic government are. IOs do not conscript or tax individuals, for example. Their dues come from nations rather than individuals; their laws do not affect individuals directly; and there is no authoritarian appropriation of human capital and resources. Quite simply, there are fewer reasons for individuals to be angry with IO.

12. There are, of course, exceptions to this trend, notably in the classic literature on integration and interdependence. But even these show limitations. Early neofunctionalists argued that IO can have adverse effects on specific interest groups and elites within nations but have said much less about the adverse impact on international order and relations between nations. Haas noted that organizations can sometimes fail to achieve their goals, but he did not go on to explore the possible negative consequences of this failure. Morse noted that IO can adversely affect nations by limiting their autonomy, but he did not pursue the manifold consequences of this constraint. See Ernst Haas, *The Uniting of Europe* (Stanford, Calif.: Stanford University Press, 1958), pp. 288–89; Ernst Haas, *Beyond the Nation-State* (Stanford, Calif.: Stanford University Press, 1964), p. 126; and Edward Morse, *Modernization and the Transformation of International Relations* (New York: Free Press, 1966), p. 100.

13. Haas, *Beyond the Nation-State,* p. 31.

14. David Mitrany, *A Working Peace System* (Chicago: Quadrangle, 1966), pp. 52, 63, and 97.

15. Ibid., p. 37.

16. Ibid., p. 98.

17. Of course, even for neofunctionalists, spillover is not a given. Integration has been conceptualized as positive, stagnant, and negative.

18. See Haas, *Beyond the Nation-State,* p. 459; and Haas, *The Uniting of Europe,* p. 287.

19. John Gerard Ruggie, "International Responses to Technology: Concepts and Trends," *International Organization* 29 (Summer 1975), pp. 557–83.

20. John Gerard Ruggie, "Collective Goods and Future International Collaboration," *American Political Science Review* 66 (September 1972), p. 875.

21. Eugene Skolnikoff, *The International Imperatives of Technology* (Berkeley, Calif.: Institute of International Studies, 1972), p. 153.

22. Morse, *Modernization and the Transformation of International Relations,* p. 80.

23. Ibid., pp. 85 and 93.

24. Seyom Brown and Larry L. Fabian, "Toward Mutual Accountability in Nonterrestrial Realms," *International Organization* 29 (Summer 1975), pp. 887–92.

25. Stanley Hoffmann, "International Organization and the International System," in Leland Goodrich and David Kay, eds., *International Organization: Politics and Process* (Madison: University of Wisconsin Press, 1973).

26. Richard Cooper, "Prolegomena to the Choice of an International Monetary System," in C. Fred Bergsten and Lawrence Krause, eds., *World Politics and International Economics* (Washington, D.C.: Brookings Institution, 1975), p. 83.

27. Fred Block, *The Origins of International Economic Disorder* (Berkeley: University of California Press, 1977), p. 225.

28. Robert Solomon, *The International Monetary System, 1945–1981* (New York: Harper & Row, 1982), p. 379.

29. See Irving Friedman, *Toward World Prosperity: Reshaping the World Money System* (Lexington, Mass.: Lexington Books, 1987), p. 273. More specifically, Friedman calls for a resuscitation of the managerial instruments of the Bretton Woods system, which he and many others believed were strong. Actually, the system reflected rather weak management in configuring monetary relations. Relations carried on in a rather haphazard way with occasional multilateral (G-10) and unilateral (U.S.) management.

30. In its journal, *Backgrounder,* the Heritage Foundation has published numerous studies that take a critical view of UN operations. See especially Juliana Geran Pilon, "The Center on Transnational Corporations: How the UN Injures Poor nations," *Backgrounder* 608, October 1987; Thomas Gulick, "How the U.N. Aids Marxist Guerrilla Groups," *Backgrounder* 177, April 1982; and Brooks, "Africa Is Starving and the United Nations Shares the Blame." See also Charles Lichenstein et al., *The United Nations: Its Problems and What to Do About Them* (Washington, D.C.: Heritage Foundation, 1986); and Burton Yale Pines, ed., *A World Without a U.N.* (Washington, D.C.: Heritage Foundation, 1984).

31. See the following works by Abraham Yeselson and Anthony Gaglione: "The Use of the United Nations in World Politics," in Steven Spiegel, ed., *At Issue: Politics in the World Arena* (New York: St. Martin's Press, 1981), pp. 392–99; and *A Dangerous Place* (New York: Viking Press, 1974).

32. Robert Jackson argued, for example, that the UN could be likened to "some prehistoric monster, incapable of intelligently controlling itself. This is not because it lacks intelligent and capable officials, but because it is so organized that

managerial direction is impossible." Jackson is quoted in "The United Nations Agencies: A Case for Emergency Treatment," *Economist,* 2 December 1989, p. 23. See also David Pitt, "Power in the UN Superbureaucracy: A Modern Byzantium," and Johan Galtung, "A Typology of United Nations Organizations," in David Pitt and Thomas Weiss, eds., *The Nature of United Nations Bureaucracies* (Boulder, Colo.: Westview Press, 1986), pp. 23–38 and 59–83, respectively.

33. See, for example, Ismail Abdalla, "The Inadequacy and Loss of Legitimacy of the International Monetary Fund," *Development,* vol. 22, Society for International Development, Rome, 1980, pp. 46–65; Cheryl Payer, *The Debt Trap: The International Monetary Fund and the Third World* (New York: Monthly Review Press, 1974); Cheryl Payer, *The World Bank: A Critical Analysis* (New York: Monthly Review Press, 1982); Teresa Hayter, *Aid as Imperialism* (New York: Penguin, 1974); Robert Cox, "The Crisis in World Order and the Problem of International Organization in the 1980s," *International Journal* 35 (Spring 1980), pp. 370–95; Robert Cox, "Labor and Hegemony," *International Organization* 31 (Summer 1977), pp. 385–424; and Peter Cocks, "Toward a Marxist Theory of European Integration," *International Organization* 34 (Winter 1980), pp. 1–40.

34. Conybeare, "International Organization and the Theory of Property Rights."

35. Ruggie and Wijkman, however, are generally positive about the functions of IO with respect to confronting issues of publicness. See Ruggie, "Collective Goods and Future International Collaboration"; and Per Magnus Wijkman, "Managing the Global Commons," *International Organization* 36 (Summer 1982), pp. 511–36.

36. Roland Vaubel, "A Public Choice Approach to International Organization," *Public Choice,* vol. 51, 1986, pp. 39–57.

37. See the contributions to *International Organization,* vol. 36, Spring 1982, a special issue on regimes. See also Robert Keohane, *After Hegemony* (Princeton, N.J.: Princeton University Press, 1984); and Robert Keohane and Joseph Nye, *Power and Interdependence,* 2d ed. (Glenview, Ill.: Scott, Foresman, 1985). For surveys of the literature on regimes and neoliberal institutionalism, see Stephan Haggard and Beth Simmons, "Theories of International Regimes," *International Organization* 41 (Summer 1987), pp. 491–517; and Joseph Grieco, "Anarchy and the Limits of Cooperation: A Realist Critique of the Newest Liberal Institutionalism," *International Organization* 42 (Summer 1988), pp. 485–507. For other works that are concerned with less managed relations, see Conybeare, "International Organization and the Theory of Property Rights"; Wijkman, "Managing the Global Commons"; W. Max Corden, "The Logic of the International Monetary Non-System," in Fritz Machlup, Gerhard Fels, and Hubertus Muller-Groeling, eds., *Reflections on a Troubled World Economy: Essays in Honor of Herbert Giersch* (New York: St. Martin's Press, 1983), pp. 59–74; W. Max Corden, "Fiscal Policies, Current Accounts and Real Exchange Rates: In Search of a Logic of International Policy Coordination," *Weltwirtschaftliches,* vol. 122, 1986, pp. 423–38; Roland Vaubel, "Coordination or Competition Among National Macro-Economic Policies?" in Machlup, Fels, and Muller-Groeling, *Reflections on a Troubled World Economy,* pp. 3–28; and Martin Feldstein, "Let the Market Decide," *Economist,* 3 December 1988, pp. 21–24.

38. See Cox, "The Crisis in World Order and the Problem of International Organization in the 1980s"; Cox, "Labor and Hegemony"; and Hayter, *Aid as Imperialism.*

39. This dual categorization of managerial failure is somewhat problematic because what some consider to be random mistakes of bureaucrats may be seen by

others as problems endemic to the bureaucratic structure of IO. Similarly, depending on the manner in which malfunction is defined, IO can be said to malfunction systematically or unsystematically. Further research may improve upon the present typology by suggesting a better differentiation both between and within categories. Nevertheless, the dual categorization is useful as a first-cut approach to the general failures in the process of international management. The alternative presentation of undifferentiated failure does little service to the normative and theoretical importance of distinguishing endemic failures from failures that are more stochastic.

A point that deserves emphasis here is that while IO is by nature prone to several types of failure, it does not follow that IO will invariably fail. A simple analogy is that the inherent or genetic predisposition to diabetes does not always manifest itself as disease.

40. The mainstream IO literature has tended to offer a "complexity" rationale for supranational government: as interdependence becomes more complex and issue-spaces increase in density, the need for IO to orchestrate relations also increases.

41. The subject of complex, tightly coupled systems is formally explored by Perrow in the context of accidents which involve nuclear power, chemicals, and other high-risk technology and which have adverse effects on the various ecosystems. See Charles Perrow, *Normal Accidents: Living with High-Risk Technologies* (New York: Basic Books, 1984).

42. Ibid.

43. Economists of the Austrian school have underscored this point with respect to attempts at managing complex systems such as markets and prices. Centrally planned economies, contrived price systems, and other forms of control, they argue, produce outcomes that are Pareto-inferior and significantly worse than those effected by a market approach. See, for example, the following works of Friedrich Hayek: *Individualism and Economic Order* (Chicago: University of Chicago Press, 1948), p. 187; *Law, Legislation and Liberty,* vol. 1 (Chicago: University of Chicago Press, 1973), pp. 48–50; and *The Fatal Conceit: The Errors of Socialism* (Chicago: University of Chicago Press, 1988), pp. 85–88.

44. See Keohane and Nye, *Power and Interdependence;* Richard Cooper, *The Economics of Interdependence* (New York: Council on Foreign Relations, 1968); and James Rosenau, *Turbulence in World Politics* (Princeton, N.J.: Princeton University Press, 1990).

45. For a discussion of systems in international politics, see Robert Jervis, "Systems Theories and International Politics," in Paul Gordon Lauren, ed., *Diplomacy* (New York: Free Press, 1979), pp. 212–43. On the subject of chaos, see James Gleick, *Chaos: Making a New Science* (New York: Penguin, 1988).

46. Gottfried Haberler, "The International Monetary System: Recent Developments in Perspective," *Aussenwirtschaft,* vol. 41, 1987, p. 379.

47. William Branson, "The Coordination of Exchange Rate Policy," *Brookings Papers on Economic Activity,* no. 1, 1986, p. 176.

48. See "Passing the Buck," *Economist,* 11 February 1989.

49. For discussions of the Louvre Accord and its results, see "The Show Can't Go On," *Economist,* 21 November 1987, pp. 13–14; Haberler, "The International Monetary System"; and Yoichi Funabashi, *Managing the Dollar: From the Plaza to the Louvre* (Washington, D.C.: Institute for International Economics, 1988), pp. 187–92. It is not clear that defenders of the Louvre Accord are correct in attributing positive externalities to it. The argument that even misaligned rates stabilize trade flows assumes that volatility following the imposition of the exchange rate was less than it would have been if the rate had been allowed to converge by market

forces. There is more evidence to suggest that, on the contrary, the imposition and market reaction to it created more volatility than would have otherwise occurred.

50. Harberler, "The International Monetary System," p. 383.

51. Ibid., p. 381.

52. The direction of swings in response to changes or developments in financial markets, currency markets, and other complex systems is difficult to predict, as are the perceptions of investors and other actors. This brings up the question of whether these systems would be more manageable if actors knew more about the manifold effects of different policies. In some situations, even supposedly prudent policies may have adverse effects if actors in systems are adapting to rather than passively accepting policy. (Such adaptive microbehavior typifies complex, tightly coupled systems.) But his could also be the case when actors are cognitively rigid. For example, given a particular nervous state in currency markets, investors may interpret any kind of interest rate policy (even the most prudent one based on knowledge of how currency markets work) as signaling trouble for a currency. An interest rate hike to prop up the dollar, for instance, may be perceived as a signal that the dollar is weak. A rate decrease may be perceived as a signal that U.S. policymakers will let the dollar slip. And finally, no change in the interest rate may be taken as indecision on the part of U.S. policymakers and perceived as a sign of trouble.

53. See "Almighty Fallen," *Economist,* 14 November 1987, p. 11.

54. James Vick, quoted by Funabashi in *Managing the Dollar,* pp. 189–90.

55. Funabashi, *Managing the Dollar.*

56. See "Brady Avoiding Critics as Group of 7 Gathers," *The New York Times,* 2 February 1989, p. D-1.

57. Ibid.

58. Rates were imposed much more frequently under the Bretton Woods regime in the 1950s and 1960s than they have been recently. But the size and the sensitivity of exchange markets were considerably smaller than they are now. And, in fact, the destabilizing money flows of the 1960s attest to the difficulty of sustaining rates misaligned with respect to the market rate.

59. See Funabashi, *Managing the Dollar,* p. 190.

60. See ibid., pp. 28, 29, 34, 205–7, 214, and 228.

61. Especially distasteful were the U.S. threats; the U.S. insistence on a high yen rate; the constant changes in negotiating forums, including at various times the G-2, G-3, G-5, and G-7; and the attempts at unilateral management of the dollar rate, characterized by "talking the dollar down" when others refused to accommodate the downward trend of the dollar. See ibid., pp. 53, 182, 217, and 235–37.

62. An alternative interpretation of the Louvre and Plaza episodes might be that large and responsive capital markets, in combination with high mobility in the flow of goods and capital, have made it necessary for advanced industrial nations to coordinate their economic policies and that failures are a small price to pay for the necessary long-term management. No one would argue that coordination is not valuable or that the market can resolve all economic problems. But the Louvre and Plaza agreements generated significant instabilities that most likely would not have occurred in the absence of intervention. Even the necessity of long-term coordination is no excuse for generating market instability that has short-run effects and might in turn generate lasting effects. Given the adverse outcomes of linear managerial approaches taken in the past, it seems all the more inexcusable to turn to them again and again in the present.

63. For reasons relating to the unpredictability of international reactions to the construction of international managerial schemes in the area of the debt problem,

Kindleberger appears cautious about the desirability of even attempting to develop collaborative multilateral solutions. If such attempts were made and fail, he argues, and if this generated pessimistic forecasts about developments in the issue-area, the problem is likely to be exacerbated. See Kindleberger, *The International Economic Order*, p. 12.

64. See Jeffrey Frankel and Katherine Rockett, "International Macroeconomic Policy Coordination when Policymakers Do Not Agree on the Model," *American Economic Review* 78 (June 1988), pp. 318–40.

65. Paul Streeten, "The United Nations: Unhappy Family," in Pitt and Weiss, *The Nature of United Nations Bureaucracies*, p. 187.

66. Ibid.

67. Ibid.

68. It has, in fact, been a long-standing characteristic of international economic summitry for leaders to use international agreements to reduce some of their domestic economic and political costs. See Robert Putnam and Nicholas Bayne, *Hanging Together: Cooperation and Conflict in the Seven-Power Summits* (Cambridge, Mass.: Harvard University Press, 1987); and Vaubel, "A Public Choice Approach to International Organization."

69. Pérez de Cuéllar, *Report of the Secretary-General on the Work of the Organization*, p. 3.

70. James Stegenga, *The United Nations Force in Cyprus* (Columbus: Ohio State University Press, 1968), p. 186.

71. See Yeselson and Gaglione, *A Dangerous Place*.

72. See Patrick Garrity, "The United Nations and Peacekeeping," in Pines, *A World Without a U.N.*, p. 155. See also Ruggie's response to Garrity, "The United States and the United Nations," p. 348.

73. Yeselson and Gaglione, *A Dangerous Place*, p. 178.

74. The literature on collective action suggests that sometimes it is to the benefit of a community as a whole for people not to have private substitutes for poor public services. The fact that they have such substitutes encourages them to exit (vote with their feet) rather than use their voice to contribute to the improvement of those services. For example, communities will be less likely to have poor public schools if private schools do not exist. This will encourage the wealthiest and most educated to contribute to collective action schemes designed to improve the school system. Collective action is enchanced to the extent that private substitutes for public goods are unavailable. One could make an interesting argument about the destabilizing nature of the "Star Wars" program on these grounds. The program's technology would increase the risk of war among the superpowers because if developed (even by both) it would represent a substitute for further cooperation. For a discussion about the adverse effects of private substitutes, see Russell Hardin, *Collective Action* (Baltimore, Md.: Johns Hopkins University Press, 1982), p. 73.

75. Robert Rothstein, *Global Bargaining: UNCTAD and the Quest for a New International Economic Order* (Princeton, N.J.: Princeton University Press, 1979), p. 20.

76. Data show that development is positively correlated with the growth of the private sector. See Edward Erickson and Daniel Sumner, "The U.N. and Economic Development," in Pines, *A World Without a U.N.*, pp. 1–22. See also Pilon, "The Center on Transnational Corporations."

77. See Brooks, "Africa Is Starving and the United Nations Shares the Blame."

78. Hopkins identifies these problems as central targets for multilateral food aid reform in the 1970s and 1980s. See Hopkins, "Reform in the International Food Aid Regime."

79. See Claude, *Swords into Plowshares,* pp. 417–19.

80. Ibid.

81. Adam Roberts and Benedict Kingsbury, "The UN's Roles in a Divided World," in Adam Roberts and Benedict Kingsbury, eds., *United Nations, Divided World* (Oxford: Oxford University Press, 1988), p. 11. The problem is not a matter of nations believing that the UN is a real and significant instrument of world peace and that they therefore avoid other means of addressing global security issues. Rather, the problem is that any positive perceptions of the security-enhancing potential of the UN many alter their incentives to apply their full resources to other strategies. This suggests an element of moral hazard, a subject discussed in a later section of my article.

82. See Funabashi, *Managing the Dollar,* p. 41.

83. It is impossible to definitively state that in the absence of IO, nations would act more responsibly or make the necessary hard choices required for long-run stability in their economies. Certainly, nations might seek other ways to avoid making hard choices. However, to the extent that IO provides additional "outs" or, alternatively, fails to close off less responsible avenues, it augments or maintains the possibilities for destabilizing policy choices in the long run.

84. Some might argue that this tendency toward substitution was not as apparent to the founders of the Bretton Woods system, since their principal goal was to provide nations with liquidity as a way to avoid market intervention (prompted by balance-of-payments disequilibria) in the short run and thus give them the opportunity to develop more incremental adjustment policies in the long run. Furthermore, the fixed exchange rates and the circumscription of internal adjustment were a reaction to the problems that prevailed during the interwar period. The point to be made here is that the opportunities for adverse substitution which IO provides can as likely be unintended as intended. For a discussion of the early objectives of the Bretton Woods system, see Richard Gardner, *Sterling-Dollar Diplomacy: Anglo-American Collaboration in the Reconstruction of Multilateral Trade* (Oxford: Clarendon Press, 1956), chap. 5.

85. In "A Public Choice Approach to International Organization," pp. 47–49, Vaubel cites evidence that inflation tends to be higher among nations that exhibit more convergent inflation rates.

86. See Jan Tumlir, *Protectionism: Trade Policy in Democratic Societies* (Washington, D.C.: American Enterprise Institute, 1985), p. 12. On a related note, critics of super-301 and strategic American trade policy argue that these initiatives represent a destabilizing substitute for a long-term resolution to the trade deficit, which would require the elimination of the underlying microeconomic and macroeconomic causes. See "The Snit List," *Economist,* 3 June 1989, pp. 30–31.

87. *Economist,* 26 September 1987, p. 56.

88. See W. Max Corden, "The Coordination of Stabilization Policies Among Countries," in Albert Ando, Richard Herring, and Richard Marston, eds., *International Aspects of Stabilization Policies* (Boston: Federal Reserve Bank of Boston, 1977), pp. 139–40.

89. See Giulio M. Gallarotti, "Toward a Business-Cycle Model of Tariffs," *International Organization* 39 (Winter 1985), pp. 155–87. The success of GATT in lowering tariffs may be counterproductive, given the fact that nations often substitute nontariff barriers. These barriers are more protectionist and more distorting of trade flows, since producers cannot compensate for them by managing prices and costs. This illustrates the fact that IO can channel policy into less stabilizing instruments.

90. Claude, *Swords into Plowshares,* p. 446.

91. Yeselson and Gaglione, "The Use of the United Nations in World Politics," p. 396.

92. See Maurice Tugwell, "The UN as the World's Safety Valve," in Pines, *A World Without a U.N.*, pp. 157–74. The Churchill quote is from his speech on 26 June 1954 in Washington, D.C.

93. Tugwell, "The UN as the World's Safety Valve," p. 157.

94. Jeane Kirkpatrick, speech before the Anti-Defamation League on 11 February 1982 in Palm Beach, Fla., pp. 11–12.

95. Kirkpatrick, quoted by the Associated Press, 29 October 1982.

96. See Claude, *Swords into Plowshares,* pp. 89–94; and Ruggie, "The United States and the United Nations," p. 354.

97. Yeselson and Gaglione, *A Dangerous Place,* pp. 31–43.

98. Tugwell, "The U.N. as the World's Safety Valve," p. 158.

99. The ultimate outcome in this intervention was markedly different from the original intention "not to take any action which would make [the UN] a party to internal conflicts in the country." See UN Security Council, *Official Records,* meeting no. 872, 7 July 1960, p. 5.

100. See Yeselson and Gaglione, *A Dangerous Place,* p. 203. With respect to the indirect effects of IOs on African politics, Jackson and Roseberg see a quite different deleterious effect. By accepting African nations as members regardless of their political regimes, IOs serve to legitimize oppressive political systems. See Robert Jackson and Carl Roseberg, "Why Africa's Weak States Persist: The Empirical and Juridical in Statehood," *World Politics* 35 (October 1982), pp. 1–24.

101. See Claude, *Swords into Plowshares,* p. 130. Some analysts might interpret the 1990 involvement of the UN in the Iraq-Kuwait crisis as a breakdown in the deleterious Cold War use of the organization and argue that with superpower agreement the UN can be a positive force in abating and preventing crises in global security. There are several problems with this interpretation. The first and most obvious is that it is premature to draw conclusions, given that the crisis is still in progress at the time of the writing of this article. The second is that we have to question whether the UN initiated or followed the U.S. lead in attempting to resolve the crisis. The United States, defending its geopolitical and resource-security interests in the Middle East, played the major role with regard to constructing a unified response to the invasion of Kuwait. Insofar as the 1990 UN resolutions called for actions that the United States and its allies had already committed themselves to, the organization merely served as a stamp of approval or vehicle for legitimating the actions. The European Community has, in fact, at the time of the writing of this article made a collective request to the Security Council to pursue air blockade in addition to naval and ground coverage. Critics of the confrontational style within the UN forum might argue that since nations are committed to a confrontational response to the invasion outside this forum, it would behoove the UN to expend its energies toward engineering a diplomatic resolution. This would reduce the possibilities of pan-Arab antagonism (especially from Iraq, Iran, Yemen, and Jordan) toward the UN and would place the organization in a better position to fulfill its role with respect to resolving other disputes in the Middle East. Given the fact that Hussein has threatened war in response to the UN resolutions, we have to question whether confrontational resolutions are counterproductive and whether the UN has served as a positive force.

102. See Yeselson and Gaglione, "The Use of the United Nations in World Politics," p. 396.

103. Keohane, *After Hegemony,* p. 91. See also Robert Keohane, "The Demand for International Regimes," *International Organization* 36 (Spring 1982), pp.

325–56; and Robert Tollison and Thomas Willett, "An Economic Theory of Mutually Advantageous Linkages in International Negotiations," *International Organization* 33 (Autumn 19779), pp. 425–50.

104. See Yeselson and Gaglione, "The Use of the United Nations in World Politics," p. 397.

105. Ibid., p. 395.

106. See Roberts and Kingsbury, "The UN's Roles in a Divided World," p. 19.

107. See Gulick, "How the U.N. Aids Marxist Guerrilla Groups." It appears that this support has been uneven in a most destabilizing way, given the recent UN decision to allow South Africa to break Resolution 435 and confront SWAPO rebels in Namibia.

108. Massur, quoted in ibid., p. 4. The argument that IO is supposed to promote change and that the PLO and ANC are therefore justified in their use of the UN to promote conflict in the Middle East and Africa presents some problems. First, it assumes that people think it worth the costs of conflict intensification, including death and destruction, to promote change. Many would not think so. Second, it assumes that any parties advocating changes to some status quo are justified in using IOs to promote conflict. In fact, nations have historically been encouraged to bring their disputes to IOs as a way of avoiding conflict. Finally, there are both peaceful and conflictual avenues to change. Some think it a bad precedent for IOs to expend resources in anything but peaceful solutions. Certainly the traditional spirit of IO suggests diplomatic approaches to resolving conflicts of interests.

109. Operation Condor in 1966 and the immediate reception of this terrorist operation on the part of the Argentine masses suggest a sharp turning point in Argentine policy toward the Falklands in the mid-1960s. See W. Michael Reisman and Andrew Willard, eds., *International Incidents* (Princeton, N.J.: Princeton University Press, 1988), pp. 121–22.

110. In 1974, the newspaper *Cronica* began a campaign for the invasion of the Falklands. In January 1976, the Argentine foreign minister predicted a head-on collision with Great Britain. Just one month later, an Argentine destroyer fired on the British research ship *Shakleton*. See ibid., pp. 122–27. UN involvement may have contributed to the Falklands episode by exacerbating the domestic antagonism toward Great Britain and driving policy toward a more militant response. While this is somewhat speculative, one thing is certain: in its resolutions and other involvement in this matter, the UN provided sources of legitimacy that could be used by Argentina as justification for confrontational approaches to the problem. This in itself violated the traditional spirit of the UN objective to encourage peaceful diplomatic resolution of international disputes.

111. Historical limitations in the demands and enforcement of conditionality have given nations more leeway than is good for their own long-run economic stability.

112. See Kindleberger, *The International Economic Order*, p. 39. See also Charles Kindleberger, "The International Monetary System," in *International Money: A Collection of Essays* (London: Allen & Unwin, 1981), pp. 297–30.

113. Keohane and Nye, *Power and Interdependence*, p. 274.

114. Interestingly, Puchala has argued that during the first half of the European Community's existence, much of its success was actually attributable to weaknesses in getting nations to follow rules. The Community has, however, shown itself to be much stronger in the second half of its existence in both generating legislation and encouraging adherence. See Donald Puchala, "Domestic Politics and Regional Harmonization in the European Communities," *World Politics* 27 (July 1975), pp. 496–520.

115. In "Fiscal Policies, Current Accounts and Real Exchange Rates," p. 426, Corden sees the post–Bretton Woods period as a period of decentralized monetary relations, "an international laissez faire system."

116. Robert Solomon, "Issues at the IMF Meeting," *Journal of Commerce,* October 1979, p. 4.

117. Keohane and Nye, *Power and Interdependence,* p. 274.

118. Ibid., p. 273. For other contributions to this literature, see John Conybeare, "Public Goods, Prisoners' Dilemmas and the International Political Economy," *International Studies Quarterly* 28 (March 1984), pp. 5–22; Conybeare, "International Organization and the Theory of Property Rights"; Arthur Stein, "Coordination and Collaboration: Regimes in an Anarchic World," *International Organization* 36 (Spring 1982), pp. 299–324; Duncan Snidal, "Coordination Versus Prisoners' Dilemma: Implications for International Cooperation and Regimes," *American Political Science Review* 79 (December 1985), pp. 923–42; Duncan Snidal, "Relative Gains Don't Prevent International Cooperation," paper presented at the annual meeting of the American Political Science Association, Atlanta, Ga., 31 August 1989; Timothy McKeown, "Hegemonic Stability Theory and 19th Century Tariff Levels in Europe," *International Organization* 37 (Winter 1983), pp. 73–92; R. Harrison Wagner, "The Theory of Games and the Problem of International Cooperation," *American Political Science Review* 77 (June 1983), pp. 330–46; and Robert Axelrod, *The Evolution of Cooperation* (New York: Basic Books, 1984).

119. The conventional argument about the advantages of optimal tariffs assumes that other nations will not retaliate.

120. In "The Logic of the International Monetary Non-System," p. 65, Corden implies that these predatory costs increase on the margin, thus suggesting that the restraints against predation will rise as predation increases.

121. See Corden, "Fiscal Policies, Current Accounts and Real Exchange Rates," p. 436. This is not to say that the imbalance cannot be politically destabilizing.

122. Even those contributors to the literature on cooperation who are quite sympathetic to the role of IO in world politics note that limited forms of multilateral management can be desirable and effective given the proper underlying conditions in relations among nations. See especially Keohane and Nye, *Power and Interdependence,* pp. 274–76; and Ruggie, "Collective Goods and Future International Collaboration," p. 888.

123. Keohane and Nye, *Power and Interdependence,* p. 274.

124. Ibid., p. 35.

125. Ibid., pp. 35 and 274. See also Keohane, *After Hegemony;* and Keohane, "The Demand for International Regimes."

126. See the special issue of *International Organization,* vol. 36, Spring 1982.

127. See Stein, "Coordination and Collaboration"; and Oran Young, "Regime Dynamics: The Rise and Fall of International Regimes," *International Organization* 36 (Spring 1982), pp. 277–98. See also Wagner, "The Theory of Games and the Problem of International Cooperation"; and Snidal, "Coordination Versus Prisoners' Dilemma."

128. Snidal, "Coordination Versus Prisoners' Dilemma," p. 932. Even with more conflictual payoff structures, such as that of prisoners' dilemma, notes Wagner, functions relating to the dissemination of information about preferences and potential choices can play an essential role in bringing about cooperative outcomes. Furthermore, in cases in which conflictual games generate horizontal proliferation (interissue linkage in games), modest managerial assistance is required to arrive at mutually beneficial equilibria. Snidal argues that to the extent that

horizontal properties emerge, the game "becomes embedded in a broader social context, and cooperation is increasingly possible with less centralized enforcement." See Snidal, ibid., p. 939; and Wagner, "The Theory of Games and the Problem of International Cooperation."

129. For a discussion of the role of focal points in generating mutually beneficial outcomes in games, see Thomas Schelling, *The Strategy of Conflict* (Cambridge, Mass.: Harvard University Press, 1980).

130. Ruggie, "International Responses to Technology."

131. See Keohane and Nye, *Power and Interdependence,* p. 274; Conybeare, "International Organization and the Theory of Property Rights"; Vaubel, "A Public Choice Approach to International Organization"; and Wijkman, "Managing the Global Commons."

132. Conybeare, "International Organization and the Theory of Property Rights," p. 314.

133. Wijkman, "Managing the Global Commons," p. 527.

134. See Mitrany, *A Working Peace System,* pp. 28 and 73.

135. See, for example, Haas, *Beyond the Nation-State,* p. 126.

136. In *Power and Interdependence,* p. 276, Keohane and Nye make a similar point with respect to viable moderated management of crisis versus nonviable control management.

137. See Morse, *Modernization and the Transformation of International Relations,* p. 85.

138. See Hardin, *Collective Action,* pp. 62–65.

139. See Mancur Olson, *The Logic of Collective Action* (Cambridge, Mass.: Harvard University Press, 1965).

140. Ruggie, "Collective Goods and Future International Collaboration," p. 888.

141. See ibid.; Conybeare, "International Organization and the Theory of Property Rights"; and Wijkman, "Managing the Global Commons."

142. Jervis argues that cooperation is more likely to occur in economic relations than in security relations because the underlying strategic structure of the former is positive-sum, while that of the latter is closer to zero-sum. See Robert Jervis, "Security Regimes," *International Organization* 36 (Spring 1982), pp. 357–78. Of course, a disaggregation of economic relations would show a significant variation in the complexity of the various forms, ranging from commodity agreements, which are relatively simple, to macroeconomic coordination, which is highly complex.

143. See Brian Urquhart, "International Peace and Security," *Foreign Affairs* 60 (Fall 1981), pp. 1–16.

144. These schemes require neither extensive scope nor extensive level. Their effect depends on their ability to address the right issues in the right ways. Depending on underlying strategic structures in specific relational contexts, institutions that assist cooperation may be more substantive means of generating positive outcomes than institutions that manage cooperation. Often, as has been suggested in this article, big and broad functions make it more difficult to substantively address issues.

145. See Putnam and Bayne, *Hanging Together.*

146. Critics of super-301 would identify a similar motive behind the U.S. trade policy toward Asia.

147. Nowhere is this more evident than in alliance relations. See Paul Diesing and Glenn Snyder, *Conflict Among Nations* (Princeton, N.J.: Princeton University Press, 1977), chap. 6.

148. Jervis, for one, has differentiated between security and international economic regimes in terms of viability and stability. See Jervis, "Security Regimes."

149. Discussions of moral hazard in international politics have generally focused on monetary relations, but the possibilities for moral hazard appear to be more far-reaching. Jervis and Nye, for example, make interesting albeit brief allusions to possibilities for moral hazard in security relations. See Jervis, "Security Regimes," p. 368; and Joseph Nye, "Nuclear Learning," *International Organization* 41 (Summer 1987), p. 390.

Index

About the Book

The Politics of Global Governance presents both classic and contemporary readings about the organizations that are critically important in mediating global politics. Highlighting the major changes and challenges in the international system since the end of the Cold War, the book is unique in its consideration of a diverse range of international organizations, including institutions that influence the global political economy, for example, the World Bank and the European Union. It is also distinctive in its detailed coverage of contemporary policy areas, such as peacekeeping, trade, and social and humanitarian issues.

The essays in *The Politics of Global Governance* have been selected and edited for their accessibility and their ability to emphasize the major themes, theories, and approaches involved in the study of international organizations. The book features a general introduction by the editor, part introductions that provide essential background to the readings, and an appendix containing the Covenant of the League of Nations and the Charter of the United Nations.

Paul F. Diehl is professor of political science at the University of Illinois at Urbana-Champaign. His previous publications include *International Peacekeeping* and *Territorial Changes and International Conflict.*